Seductive Journey

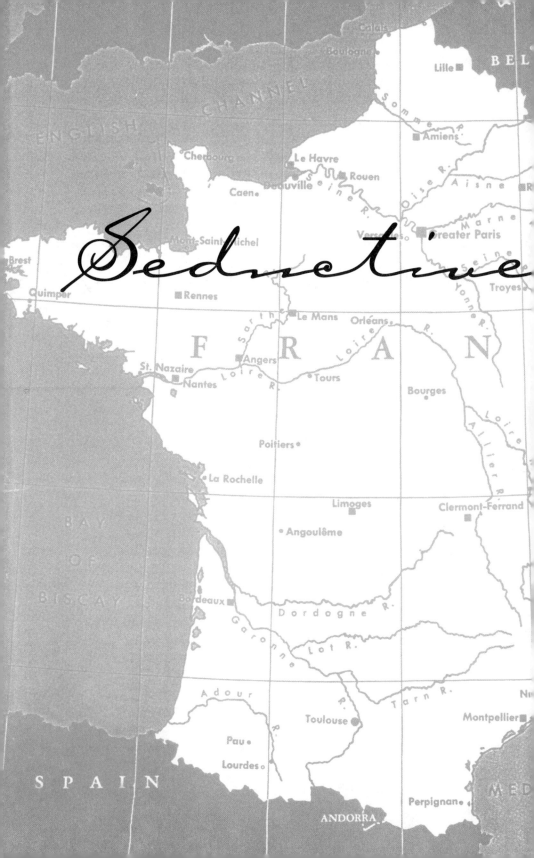

Seductive

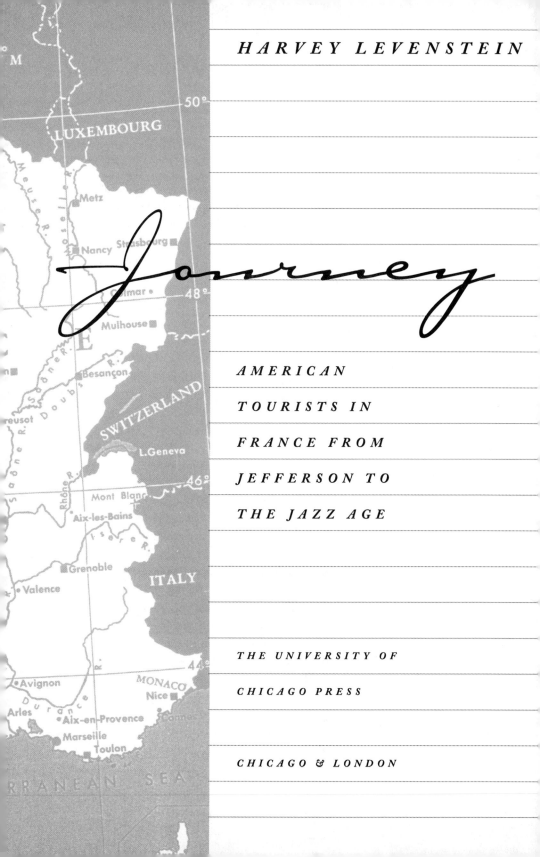

HARVEY LEVENSTEIN

Journey

AMERICAN

TOURISTS IN

FRANCE FROM

JEFFERSON TO

THE JAZZ AGE

THE UNIVERSITY OF

CHICAGO PRESS

CHICAGO & LONDON

HARVEY LEVENSTEIN is professor emeritus of
history at McMaster University in Hamilton, Ontario,
Canada. He has written a number of books on American
history, including two on the social history of American food,
Revolution at the Table (1988) and *Paradox of Plenty* (1993).

The University of Chicago Press, Chicago 60637
The University of Chicago Press, Ltd., London
© 1998 by The University of Chicago
All rights reserved. Published 1998
Printed in the United States of America
07 06 05 04 03 02 01 00 99 98   1 2 3 4 5

ISBN: 0-226-47376-7

Library of Congress Cataloging-in-Publication Data

Levenstein, Harvey A., 1938–
    Seductive journey : American tourists in France from
Jefferson to the Jazz Age / Harvey Levenstein.
        p.   cm.
    Includes bibliographical references and index.
    ISBN 0-226-47376-7
    1. Americans—France—Attitudes.   2. Americans—
Travel—France—History.   3. Tourist trade—France—
History.   4. France—Social life and customs.   I. Title.
DC34.5.A44L48   1998
306′.0944—dc21   97-49389
                                                              CIP

For Larry and Mona

Contents

PART FOUR

The Invasion of the Lower Orders, 1917–1930

Photographs follow pages 64 and 224

Preface

> Traveling is one of the saddest pleasures in life. Crossing unknown countries, hearing people speak a language you scarcely understand, and seeing human faces without any relation to your past or with your future, means solitude without repose and isolation without dignity.
>
> MADAME DE STAËL

Much of my previous work, on the history of food, was inspired by my love of cooking and eating. The present project owes much to my fondness for foreign touring. Yet my interest in both subjects stems from more than just the pleasure I derive from them. It also originates in an interest in why other people enjoy or do not enjoy these things. Our attitudes towards food are shaped very much by our culture and its history. Similarly, our expectations and experiences as tourists depend very much on who we are and where we come from.

It may seem awkward that I use the word "touring" and "tourist" here; "traveling" and "traveler" would probably read better. I do so for two reasons: In the first place, tourism is the particular kind of travel that interests me. It is normally defined as travel for pleasure, or culture, or both. Yet, despite this rather benign definition, since the 1840s, when the term became current in England, travelers have cringed at being labeled what Henry Adams called "the despised word tourist." And with good reason: it usually connotes those whose experience in new places is mediated, diluted, and impaired by such things as inflexible itineraries, omniscient guide books, stentorian tour guides, relentlessly moving vehicles, and blurry camera viewfinders, not to mention the prejudices that cloud their minds. Meaningful contact with the host culture and the chance of learning anything about it, let alone from it, is usually deemed impossible.

The put-downs of tourists have multiplied of late. The sociologist Dean McCannell sees tourism as analogous to theater, with tourists as an audience content with "inauthentic" experiences. The social historian

Daniel Boorstin thinks modern tourism embodies the tendency of consumer society to deal in safe, sanitized, and egregiously false images—to sell the masses "pseudo-events" rather than reality. People such as he and the literary historian Paul Fussell make an invidious distinction between these cosseted tourists and "travelers," who venture alone into new situations, hoping to find the unexpected. Unlike tourists, who are disgustingly passive, the travelers are an admirable lot who actively confront new environments one-on-one and learn from the unplanned experiences that follow.[1]

Anthropologists have turned their guns on tourists from a different angle. They condemn the cultural imperialism inherent in what used to be called First World tourism to the Third World, and are horrified by such things as luxury tours to New Guinea for tourists who want to videotape cannibals at war with each other.[2] Economists, who used to be optimistic about the beneficial effects of tourism to poor countries, now bemoan tourists' impact on these countries' economies. They charge that most tourist spending ends up back in the rich countries, and that the funds that stay enrich small ruling elites at the expense of the masses, who have to cope with tourism-induced price rises.[3]

The critics tend to accept the tourist/traveler dichotomy in the past as well as the present. Boorstin says travel began to decline and tourism to rise in the mid–nineteenth century, with the beginning of mass transportation.[4] Fussell's view of travel in the past is so idealized that he thinks it is impossible for anyone to really "travel" today, and has been since 1939.[5] However, I think that it is the dichotomy itself, with its idealized view of the old-time "traveler," that is the false image. Inevitably, the experience of foreign travel has always been filtered through the lenses of our expectations, stereotypes, and past experiences—in short, our own culture-boundedness. People in foreign places have always had to rely on various crutches to manage the cultural distance they encounter—to "get away to something unfamiliar [yet] make sure that it's not *too* unfamiliar."[6] It seems to me that to create a golden age in the past when none existed is to indulge in a kind of nostalgic fantasizing rivaling that of some of today's hokey, ultra-sanitized historical theme parks.[7]

When we travel to foreign places we usually expect our trips to bring some sort of pleasure, yet the very foreignness that we find exciting—the language barriers, the new topography, and the different ways people are treated (especially us)—inevitably constitutes a two-edged sword that can slash away at the enjoyment of the trip. Indeed, one often wonders, as did

Madame de Staël, quoted above, why tourists willingly subject themselves to the inevitable discomforts and humiliation of foreign travel. Powerful people, who command immense respect at home, are herded from place to place like sheep and reduced to wimps by imperious guides and snarling waiters. Yet each year millions of people throughout the world pay for such self-abasement, willingly facing the difficulties invariably involved in being "temporary strangers" in foreign lands.[8]

A raft of statistics testify to a tremendous explosion of tourism on a worldwide scale. Tourism now surpasses petroleum as the world's largest international industry, and the reason for this cannot just be that people have always wanted to see what lies over the next hill—that they travel, as a nineteenth-century definition of tourism had it, "out of curiosity"—and that now millions of them have the wherewithal to do so.[9] This begs the question of what people expect to see on the other side of the hill and what they do when get there.

There are almost as many motives for traveling as there are people. However, as a historian, I tend to think that one can explain the remarkable rise of mass tourism by categorizing these motives and examining how they, and the people, changed over time. A distinction I find particularly useful is one often made in today's tourist industries. It rests on the two main components of the old definition of tourism: travel for culture and for pleasure. "Cultural tourism" is visiting museums, scrutinizing cathedrals, studying pyramids, and making other such attempts at personal up-lift through self-education. "Recreational tourism," on the other hand, is aimed at pleasure. Nowadays, we think of it as "sun, sea, and sand" tourism, skiing holidays, pleasure cruises, even sex-tourism. It is almost certainly the dominant form of tourism today, at least in dollar terms. One of the things this book examines is the interplay between these two, and how the basis was laid for the latter's rise. We shall also see that while cultural tourism persisted, it was often as something quite different from the immersion in high culture that was its original ideal.

By examining Americans, we will be looking at people who were in the forefront of the rise of mass tourism in the modern world. We shall see how, over the course of their country's first 150 years, the trip to France moved down the class ladder, changing from something reserved primarily for the upper class to an experience increasingly open to the middle class. We shall also see it crossing the gender line, until at one stage it becomes very much identified with women. Finally we shall see it cross the racial divide to involve African Americans. These changes inevitably enmeshed it in larger tensions in American society: the resistance of established elites to newly rich parvenus, opposition by males to the emergence of the "New Woman," and by whites to African Americans' strivings for equal treatment. These conflicts were acted out among the tourists who flocked to France. They also contributed, in the mid-1920s, to an extraordinary eruption of French hostility to American tourists.

Of course all of this meant that there was never really such a thing as the "typical American tourist," yet by the 1920s observers were saying that mass tourism had brought forth just such a thing. The stereotypes, said to be found wandering all over Europe, were white, middle-class businessmen and their wives from "Main Street, U.S.A." They were provincial people, ignorant of foreign lands and languages, marked by a surfeit of naiveté, and woefully ill-equipped to function independently in a strange environment. Like all stereotypes, this hardly applied to many of the decade's tourists, but there was still enough truth in it that it stuck. This stereotype reemerged again after World War II and soon gained currency throughout the world, including among Americans themselves. By the end of the century, travel agencies would be organizing tours that promised tourists that they would not be tourists.[10]

I have been asked, often with a wink, "Why France?" Well, the answer is not quite what the winkers imply (indeed, to the extent that they reflect the old idea of France as center of "naughtiness," that is also the subject of this book). Originally, I wanted to examine the rise of American mass tourism to Europe as a whole. However, since there was little tourism to Eastern Europe, it was quickly eliminated. Then, Germany and Austria were disqualified because wars with them had naturally colored the attitudes of American tourists. Britain and Italy were popular destinations for American tourists, but it is difficult to distinguish the "pure" tourists from the Americans of British and Italian origin who went to visit family or see their ancestors' homeland. The millions of travelers from all of these countries who were immigrants going back and forth (about one third of the Italian immigrants who arrived in America before 1914, for example, returned home) complicate matters further. France, with which there were no wars and from which there have been few immigrants, thus seemed to offer the best opportunity for studying the "pure" tourist experience. That it also became the favorite European destination for American tourists was an added bonus.

Why stop at 1930? Aside from sheer exhaustion, the answer lies in the fact that the Great Depression provides a natural break to the historian studying voluntary leisure activities. Traumatic as it was to many who experienced it, the economic cataclysm provides a welcome place at which one can pause, look back, and examine the long-term forces that it temporarily halted. In this case, it allows us to look back on the effects of the rise of the middle class as the dominant force in American culture. It helps give us some perspective on the consumer culture which rose with them, and seemed to reach its peak in the 1920s, when European tourism became yet another consumer item. In due course, the middle class ascent would be resumed, providing a fitting focus for the book taking the story from 1930 to the present that I hope will follow this one.

Much of the research for this book was funded by the Social Sciences and Humanities Research Council of Canada. Aside from helping me travel to various libraries and archives, it provided for something I have never had before, a research assistant. Never was government money better spent than it was on Rocco Valeri, who, after graduating with an Honours B.A. at McMaster University, spent a full summer in libraries here and in Toronto tracking down and photocopying articles for me. Indeed, he collected so much material that I decided that writing up a full-scale bibliography would be ridiculous—I would never finish. McMaster's Arts Research Board also helped with funding, including the cost of reproducing the book's photos and prints.

My wife, Mona, acted as both staunch supporter and constructive critic. She was full of suggestions for possible sources, helped with some of the archival research, and read the manuscript thoroughly, providing excellent advice. My daughter Lisa also read part of the manuscript and made some helpful comments. Claude Fischler, of the Centre Nationale de Recherche Scientifique in Paris, spanned the spectrum in his reading of the manuscript, catching everything from errors in the spelling of French *and English* names to (as a French sociologist should) theoretical fuzziness. James Gilbert of the University of Maryland was an enthusiastic supporter from the outset, and he made some very useful suggestions when he read it for the publisher. Cynthia Aron, of the University of Virginia, gave the manuscript an excellent reading for the University of Chicago Press and also made some very valuable suggestions. Doug Mitchell has proven himself to be both a fine editor and a fine fellow.

A glance through the notes will indicate that I am indebted to many librarians on both sides of the ocean, yet space allows me to mention only a few. The staff at the Massachusetts Historical Society in Boston, where I did much of my archival work, were particularly helpful. Also, this was the first time I had done much serious research in France, and my experience with the friendly, solicitous staff at the Bibliothèque Nationale in Paris single-handedly shattered all of my preconceptions about the perils of dealing with French civil servants. At the other end of the spectrum in terms of size, the two librarians in the small archive of Thomas Cook and Co. in London were a joy to deal with, helping to make my short trip there a memorable one. Finally, I must again pay tribute to the staff of McMaster University's Library's Inter-Library Lending department, who were able to lay their hands on practically every single item I requested, no matter how old or obscure.

Part

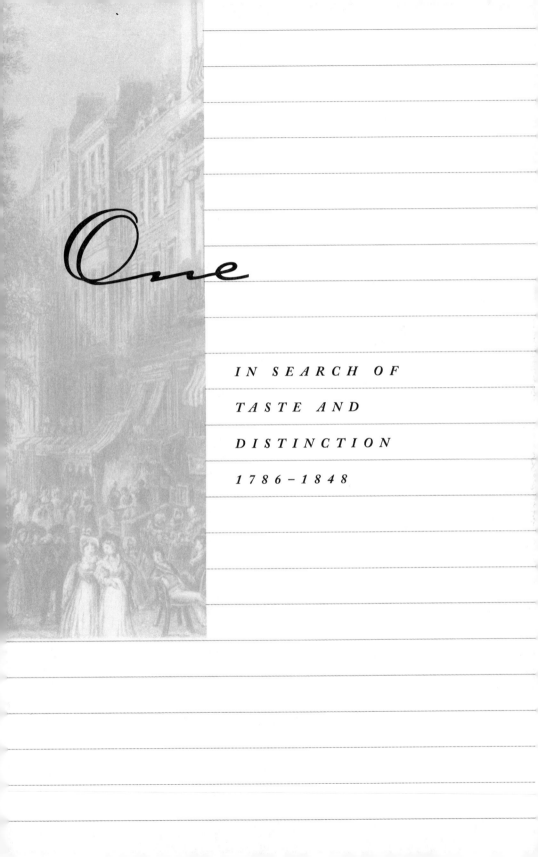

One

IN SEARCH OF TASTE AND DISTINCTION

1786–1848

One

JEFFERSON VERSUS ADAMS

The letter could not have arrived at Thomas Jefferson's mansion on the Champs-Élysées at a better time. It was June 1788. The two wealthy young Americans who sent it were in London, planning to set out on a tour of the Continent.[1] They had been told, quite rightly, that Jefferson had useful advice for American travelers on the Continent. Since 1784, when Congress appointed the tall, thoughtful, forty-one-year-old widower as one of the two American commissioners to the royal court of France, he had taken advantage of the plentiful amount of free time on his hands to do some touring. In late February 1787, he had embarked on a very long trip to the south of France and northern Italy. He had just returned from eastern France, western Germany, and the Low Countries when he sat down to reply to the young men.

Jefferson's long response began conventionally enough, with a proposed route through Germany, Italy, and France. He suggested some inns to stay in, mentioned one (run by "a most unconscionable rascal") to avoid, and noted the finest wines in each area. He told of how enjoyable it was to meander down the Languedoc Canal in the south of France with one's carriage on a canal boat, alternating walking on the tow path with sitting and reading in the carriage.[2] But then the letter took on a more severe tone, as Jefferson produced a list of "Objects of Attention for an American." The young men should study European agriculture, mechanical arts, manufacturing, and the condition of the laboring classes. Gardens were worthy of attention, not for their beauty, but for the useful plants that might be imported to America. They should take note of the architecture, but only because America's expanding population would need more housing. Painting and sculpture were "worth seeing, but not studying." They were, he said, "too expensive for the state of wealth among us. It would be useless therefore and preposterous for us to endeavor to make ourselves connoisseurs in those arts." As for the scenic countryside, when Jefferson recommended specific views it was to direct attention to such crops as olives, figs, raisins, and capers, which might be introduced into the American South.[3]

Although Jefferson was indeed a very practical man, he was also much more moved by artistic and scenic beauty than this letter lets on. In one letter to a friend he said, "Were I to tell you how much I enjoy [French] architecture, sculpture, painting, music, I should want words."[4] In another, he told of seeing a painting that transfixed him "like a statue," until he "lost all ideas of time, even the consciousness of my existence."[5]

Why, then, did Jefferson send such a hard-nosed response to the two young Americans? On the one hand, it reflects the eighteenth-century American idea that travel should not be undertaken merely for pleasure. In 1757, Josiah Tucker, the author of America's first traveler's handbook, warned that those who traveled merely to alleviate boredom "are sure of returning Home as Wise as they went out, but much more Impertinent, less Wealthy, and Less Innocent." Travel, he said, must "rub off local Prejudices" and provide "an enlarged and impartial View of Men and Things."[6] To a man of the Enlightenment such as Jefferson, privileged men such as he and the two young travelers could lead the virtuous life only through public service, and foreign travel must contribute to this.

But there was much more to Jefferson's response: there was also the example of what had happened to an earlier ideal for training the British American elite, the fabled Grand Tour—the veritable Mother of All Cultural Tourism. It had originated in the late sixteenth and early seventeenth centuries as the culmination of a young English aristocrat's education. It was to be a rigorously intellectual experience that would imbue the young milord with a mastery of foreign languages, ancient texts, philosophy, and an appreciation for the fine arts.[7] Personal tutors, who were sometimes great intellects in their own right (the brilliant philosopher John Locke, whom Jefferson revered, had been one), were to give daily lessons and arrange interviews with the major thinkers of the day. Greece being in the hands of the Turkish infidel, the Tour culminated in Italy, among the remnants of ancient Roman civilization and the heritage of the Renaissance that had brought it back to light. Latin texts in hand, the young men would traverse the scenes described by ancient writers such as Virgil and Horace.[8] They would make the rounds of art dealers and purchase reputed masterpieces as evidence of the culture they had acquired. They would visit artists' studios and select pictures of the sights they had seen as mementos of the trip and proof that they had been there. "A man who has not been in Italy is always conscious of his inferiority," said Dr. Johnson, "from his not having seen what is expected a man should see."[9]

By the mid-eighteenth century, however, the Grand Tour was being transformed by a new breed of spoiled, headstrong young men. They broke their tutors' flimsy shackles as soon as they reached the Continent and turned the trip into an occasion for sowing wild oats in the debauched courts and capitals of Europe. The tutors, who were now often almost as ignorant as their charges, were derided as "bear-leaders."[10] The Italians called the invaders the "Golden Asses" rather than the "Golden Hordes." The English writer Tobias Smollett lamented that Britain seemed to send her callow youth abroad solely "on purpose to bring her national character into disrepute."[11]

Paris, which had been originally seen as mainly a way station to Italy, now became a major destination. The dissipated young Tourists flocked to its brothels and gambling houses and made liaisons with its most notorious courtesans. By the time Jefferson arrived there in 1784 their numbers had grown exponentially, and so had their reputation for boorishness, drunkenness, and profligacy.[12] Typically, the class-conscious English blamed the scandalous behavior on the offspring of nouveaux-riches bankers and merchants—young men with "short pedigrees and long purses."[13] Jefferson thought youth itself was the problem: Few young men could resist Paris's immoral temptations. "No American should come to Europe under 30 years of age," he wrote a friend. A young man would end up "losing in his knowledge, in his morals, in his health, in his habits, and in his happiness."[14]

The fleshpots of Paris were not all that concerned Jefferson. It was also the example that French marriage set for young Americans. He wrote his friend Carlos Bellini, a teacher at William and Mary College,

> Conjugal love having no existence among them, domestic happiness, of which that is the basis, is utterly unknown. . . . Much, very much inferior is this to the tranquil permanent felicity with which domestic society in America blesses most of its inhabitants.[15]

Although he had genuine affection for a number of French women, he saw the difference between French and American women as that between "Amazons and Angels." The latter, of course, were to be preferred, particularly when it came to how he wanted his two young daughters to grow up.[16]

In this regard, Jefferson was not much different from Tobias Smollett, the English businessman-author who in 1766 published a popular book on his travels across France to Nice. Smollett wrote:

> If a Frenchman is admitted to your family, the first return he makes for your civilities is to make love to your wife, if she is handsome; if not, to your sister, or daughters, or niece. If he suffers a repulse from your wife, or attempts in vain to debauch your sister, or your daughter, or your niece, he will . . . make his addresses to your grandmother.[17]

However, Jefferson did not agree with Smollett's view of traveling in France. To Smollett, it meant enduring a Calvary of bone-breaking coaches, cheating drivers, rapacious innkeepers ("You are served with the appearance of the most mortifying indifference, at the very time they are laying plans to fleece you"), slovenly servants, and disgusting table manners.[18]

Smollett's portrayal of the French as vain, immoral, conniving, dishonest, and lazy fit in very well with the Francophobic stereotypes that had reigned practically unchallenged in England and America for centuries. The English, it will be recalled, had been at war or near-war with Francophones for much of the time since the eleventh century. The spectre of invasion by the fanatical French "Papists" in Canada, determined to eradicate Protestantism, had haunted its colonists in America until Quebec was conquered in 1759. France's intervention on the revolutionaries' side during the American Revolution had weakened this Francophobia, but suspicion of the French, particularly their moral character, still ran deep. John Adams, who helped negotiate the French alliance, noted that he agreed with fellow negotiator John Jay when Jay said, "they are not a moral people . . . he doesn't like any Frenchman."[19]

Yet despite (or perhaps because of) their low opinion of French morals, the British, and the Americans who followed, seemed to love visiting France.[20] They may have chuckled with Smollett, but they were more inspired by Laurence Sterne, whose novel, *A Sentimental Journey through France and Italy* (1767), satirized Smollett's ethnocentric travel writing. In it, Smollett is thinly disguised as "the learned SMELFUNGUS" (originally "SMELDUNGUS"), the "Splenetic Traveler," to whom the narrator contrasted himself, the sensitive "Sentimental Traveler."

Sterne's attitude toward France is exemplified by the book's famous first line about finding a comfortable inn in Calais after the Channel crossing: "They order, said I, this matter better in France."[21] Sterne's hero appreciates the French capacity for enjoying life and pointedly ignores the standard sights. Instead he savors the unplanned and the unexpected: meandering through the picturesque countryside on foot or in comfortable, lumbering diligences; enjoying chance encounters with interesting people, pleasant country inns, and yes, some sexual titillation.[22] His sensual tale helped create the kind of romantic ideal of the individual traveler—open to new experiences, unencumbered by luggage, itineraries, guides, guidebooks, or the need to see the standard tourist sights—that is still very much with us today.

Jefferson, who almost certainly never read either Sterne or Smollett (he read only serious nonfiction), did not quite fall into either camp. As we have seen, he tended toward Smollett's view of French marital arrangements. He also agreed with Smollett that touring involved tracking down the "lions," or renowned sights of a place (hence the verb "lionize.") Also, unlike Sterne's hero, he used guidebooks, tourist maps, and *valets de place*—local guides.

On the other hand, like Sterne, Jefferson was a true Francophile, who thought of France as his second homeland (Sterne, at one stage, made it his first.) He delighted in wandering the streets of Paris and its environs aimlessly, sight-seeing and people-watching. He doted on French food and became a true *amateur* of the wine.[23] He had no use for the Bourbon political system, which he thought was based on injustice and profound inequality, but declared that he loved "the *people*" of France, who were "polite, self-denying, feeling, hospitable," with all his heart, and thought they deserved a better system.[24]

Like Sterne's hero, Jefferson also prided himself on traveling light, seeking out encounters with people of all stations, and soaking up views of the picturesque countryside.[25] He also liked to travel alone, and thought that hiring a local *valet de place* in each new town, rather than the more common courier, who accompanied a traveler everywhere, was a step in this direction.[26] But the Virginian was also a cultivated man with a boundless curiosity who, unlike either Smollett (who was a mine of misinformation) or Sterne's hero (who did not care), boned up on France's history and geography and sought out the latest advances of French science and technology. His admiration for French political and economic theorists predated his arrival in France. He was particularly impressed by their achievements in the arts, lining up to see the latest exhibitions of cutting-edge painting and sculpture and going to plays, concerts, and the opera. He became enamored with modern French architecture, and spent hours sitting on a parapet watching the construction of the Hôtel de Salm, a neoclassical mansion on the Left Bank of the Seine with which he was "violently smitten."[27] In sum, he was the quintessential "good tourist," a paragon of "cultural tourism" even before the word "tourist" had come into use.

All of this was exemplified on his 1787 trip through France. Although ostensibly undertaken to bathe a broken wrist in the waters of Aix-en-Provence, his major destination was really the Roman temple at Nîmes, further to the south. (The vineyards of Burgundy and Bordeaux were also important destinations for the budding oenophile, who ordered many cases of their wines for his cellar.) Along the way he immersed himself in sights, sounds, and information. "Architecture, painting, sculpture, antiquities, agriculture, the conditions of the laboring poor fill all my moments," he wrote from Lyon.[28] Although he liked the *valet de place* he hired there so much that he kept him on for the rest of the journey, he wrote to his friends as if he were alone, extolling the advantages of touristic solitude.[29]

Like the modern cultural tourist, Jefferson was horrified by the desecration of ancient sights, particularly since he was immersed in the history of Rome, to which he often turned for guidance.[30] When he reached the Roman arena in Orange, he was shocked, he wrote, to discover "that in this 18th century, in France, under the reign of Louis XVI, they are at this moment pulling down the circular wall of this superb remains to pave a road."[31] A modern-sounding search for the sun may also have played a role in the Virginian's decision to head south during the gloomy Paris winter. Arriving in the brilliant sunshine of Aix-en-Provence in mid-March set him to wondering why "any free being" who lived north of the Loire did not pull up stakes and move to the south of France.[32]

The climax of Jefferson's trip, however, came further south, in Nîmes, where he was finally able to gaze upon its amazingly well-preserved Roman temple, the Maison Carrée. Even before seeing it, he had declared it to be "one of the most beautiful, if not the most beautiful and precious morsel of architecture left us by antiquity," and had used drawings of it in designing the new state capitol in Richmond, Virginia.[33] In Nîmes, he found that the old temple, with its superb portico of three rows of fluted Corinthian columns, more than lived up to its billing. "Here I am, Madame," he wrote a French friend, "gazing whole hours at the Maison Carrée, like a lover at his mistress."[34]

— —

Jefferson's friend Abigail Adams, wife of his fellow commissioner John Adams, was not at all as impressed by France as he. She was an intelligent, curious person who enjoyed Jefferson's company and visited many of Paris's attractions with him, yet his enthusiasm failed to infect her. She stubbornly insisted that both London and Boston were more attractive cities and harbored deep misgivings about many aspects of French life.

Admittedly, like most European cities of the time, Paris was a city of stark contrasts. Much of it was still a warren of narrow streets lined with buildings dating from the Late Middle Ages and the Renaissance. The roughly paved streets had no sidewalks, and gutters carrying raw sewage ran down the middle. Even in those days, when people were used to strong odors, the smells were sometimes so overpowering that visitors staggered about with handkerchiefs over their mouths and noses.[35] Nevertheless, there were impressive sights such as the palaces of Luxembourg, the Louvre, and the Tuileries, which were regarded as among the finest in the world. The churches of Saint-Sulpice, Sainte-Geneviève (later the Pan-théon), and the Madeleine, still under construction, were regarded as masterpieces of Baroque and contemporary architecture.[36] The Tuileries gardens, designed by the famed landscape gardener Le Nôtre, and the new enclosure and gardens of the Palais-Royal were unsurpassed in their elegance. Just outside of town lay Versailles, where Louis XIV had moved his court in the seventeenth century, with a dazzling complex of buildings, terraces, gardens, fountains, and lakes that visitors could wander through at will. One Boston couple touring there in 1776 were able to stroll through the royal apartments, peer into the monarchs' luxurious bedchambers, watch dinner being served to the Queen, and see enough nobles in their court finery to provide a lifetime of dazzling memories.[37]

Adams was not impressed. Instead, she concentrated on the aspects of Paris that bothered her. She was shocked by French disregard for the Sabbath, and was disgusted to see the Bois de Boulogne and other parks full of Sunday pleasure-seekers munching on cakes, drinking wine, and crowding various entertainments. A good Congregationalist, she did not like their ornate Catholic churches and found their ritual depressing; the mere sight of confessionals put her in a black mood.[38] She was most put-off, however, by how the French seemed to flaunt their sexuality. One of France's great contributions to the performing arts was to have women dance during the entr'actes of Italian opera—the birth of classical ballet. After seeing this for the first time, Adams wrote a friend,

> I found my delicacy wounded, and I was ashamed to look at them. Girls, clothed in the thinnest silk and gauze, with their petticoats short, springing two feet from the floor, poising themselves in the air, with their feet flying, as perfectly showing their garters and drawers as though no petticoat had been worn, was a sight altogether new to me.

Adams eventually came to appreciate the beauty of the dancing, but the knowledge that the dancers were excommunicated from the Church and practically condemned to live as courtesans continued to hinder her enjoyment of the spectacle.[39]

Adams was particularly repelled, though, by how supposedly respectable women behaved. She was disgusted at seeing a Madame Helvétius, a woman in her late fifties with whom the septuagenarian Benjamin Franklin was trying to physically consummate an affair, kiss Franklin on both cheeks and the forehead upon greeting him. She was shocked to see her hold Franklin's hand during dinner and then drape her arm around his neck. After dinner, Adams reported, "she threw herself on a settee, where she showed more than her feet," and, when her dog peed on the floor, wiped it up with her chemise.[40]

Adams was not really a repressed prude. What disconcerted her most about the French was not their sexuality per se, but how their sexual infidelities seemed to make a mockery of marriage. Like most Americans of the time, she thought marriage and the family to be the bedrock of civilized life: the sine qua non of social stability and the prerequisite of good government. Her discovery that in higher French social circles adultery was accepted as normal—that husbands and wives often did not share the same *appartement* and that both commonly and openly had lovers— seemed to her evidence of a general moral and societal disintegration. Their propensity to limit their families to three or four children, rather than the eight or nine common in America, was further evidence, to her, of this feeble commitment to family life.[41]

As we have seen, even the Francophile Jefferson was put off by French disregard for the importance of marital fidelity. However, unlike both Adamses and Smollett, he did not generalize from it to the entire French character. Gouverneur Morris, a wealthy New Yorker who visited Paris in late 1788, sided with the Adamses on this question (as he would later, on politics, when he and John Adams became bitter opponents of Jefferson). Soon after he arrived, the one-legged bachelor found himself fielding propositions for sexual liaisons from a number of married upper-class women, including two who approached him together in the Palais-Royal and made it clear "that their nuptial bonds do not at all straiten their conduct." There was little to hope for from any revolution in France, he wrote to George Washington, only months before one erupted, because there was no substratum upon which to construct the edifice of freedom. "There is a fatal principle which pervades all ranks. It is a perfect indifference to the violation of all engagements. Inconstancy is mingled in the blood, marrow, and every essence of this people."[42] Morris soon had personal evidence of this: over the next few years he shared a mistress with the then-bishop of Autun, the master diplomat Prince Talleyrand.[43]

Morris, Jefferson, the Adamses, and the two young tourists whom Jefferson advised were all members of what could be called America's governing class. In an era when the political elite was drawn very much from the social elite, they were top drawer in every sense—on the very top rung of the ladder. From then on, there would be a steady march down that ladder. As overseas tourism opened up to those on progressively lower rungs, Jefferson's Americanized version of the Grand Tour would be challenged, modified, and eventually discarded.

Two

GETTING THERE WAS NOT

HALF THE FUN

> I cannot wonder at the delightful descriptions I have
> sometimes seen of "an excursion over the waters." Gentle
> zephyrs swelling the sails. . . . Old Neptune calming the
> waters, and the gallant vessel gaily bounding o'er the waters
> of the dark blue sea as if the whole were a fairy pageant. I can
> only give it as my opinion that those who give these glowing
> representations of a voyage by sea have never tried one.
>
> ROBERT SAUNDERS, JULY 1828 DIARY ENTRY

> It seems strange that the first man who came to sea did not
> turn round and go straight back again.
>
> RALPH WALDO EMERSON

For a brief time in the 1960s, one of the transatlantic airlines used "Getting There Is Half the Fun" as its slogan. However, it soon became a term of derision among sullen crowds waiting for delayed flights in smoky airport waiting rooms, or passengers whose planes had just taken sickening plunges down "air pockets." But if the slogan was dubious then, it would have seemed downright ridiculous for those who crossed the Atlantic before the 1870s. For most late-eighteenth- and early-nineteenth-century passengers, the crossing involved more fear than fun. In August 1785, Jefferson wrote those caring for his seven-year-old daughter, Polly, in Virginia that although he missed her very much, they should wait eight months before sending her to join him in France. A winter sailing, when the storms were particularly brutal, was out of the question. It was safe to sail only from April to July, he said, "no sooner or later."[1] Also, he ordered, "the vessel should have performed one voyage at least, but be no more than four or five years old. I think . . . that all the vessels which are lost are either on their first voyage or after they are five years old. I would rather live a year longer without her than to have her trusted to any but a good ship and a summer passage."[2]

Jefferson was not being overprotective; his fears were shared by most passengers of the time. The North Atlantic is the earth's most dangerous ocean, often storm-tossed and bitterly cold. No one who has ever felt its terrible power has any affection for it; at best it commands grudging respect. Until the mid-nineteenth century, at least, the anticipation of crossing it evoked well-justified fears of drowning. When twenty-four-year-old William Lee left his wife of one year and newborn child in Boston and boarded the *Mary,* bound for Bordeaux, on January 1, 1796, they must have recalled that some fifteen years earlier his wife's father had perished at sea making the same trip. Sure enough, as Jefferson (his future mentor) would have warned him, the winter crossing turned into a nightmare. Brutal storms lashed the ship; spars broke, equipment and men were washed over the side, and the inexperienced American crew, who Lee thought "would do better to plough the earth than the seas," were as terrified as he was. Finally, after more than six weeks at sea, the weather moderated and they sighted the coast of France. However, before a pilot could board to take them into Bordeaux, another fierce storm appeared on the horizon. The desperate captain, fearing that the bedraggled ship could not survive another beating, tried to race the storm into port on his own. He failed. The ship struck a sandbank, which tore off its rudder and put a large hole in its bottom. Huge waves then drove the now-helpless vessel toward certain destruction on the shore, but the crew managed to launch two boats before it crashed there and rolled over. Soaked to the skin and exhausted, they rowed for some miles to a town, where the captain, Lee, and the two other passengers were welcomed into a comfortable house with a warm fire. The captain then returned to the ship, to watch helplessly as the villagers, using stilts to walk in the waters around wrecks, pillaged its contents. Finally, it dawned on Lee that his genial French hosts were masterminding the scavengers.[3]

Some years later, in 1817, after waiting in vain for three days for a pilot to show up to take his ship through the same dangerous channel, the frustrated captain of the Reverend William Berrian's ship also decided to take her in himself. As the ship veered through banks of shoals, it came close to being smashed to bits any number of times. The terror-stricken passengers and crew, said Berrian, either stared certain doom in the face or "rejoiced with trembling" when it was averted. At one stage, Berrian, certain that the boat was going to sink, rushed below to his bunk to retrieve his two sacks of gold, even though he knew their weight would increase his risk of drowning when he was thrown into the water.[4]

Until the 1820s, finding a boat to take one to Europe involved, literally, a catch or catch-can situation. One had to inquire months or weeks in advance about which ships might be going where and when, and see if they could accommodate passengers. They usually had room for only a few. The port records for Bordeaux, La Rochelle, and Nantes, three major ports serving the Americas, show most of the passenger ships to or from the United States carried only one to four passengers.[5] On 5 January 1818, the *James Monroe* began to change all that. The three-masted, 424-ton boat was fitted out to take about thirty passengers in a specially built passengers' cabin on deck. Most important, it was the first ship that sailed from New York to England on a guaranteed day of departure. Within five years, there were a good number of such "packet ships" on the run to Britain.[6] Although some also ran from New York to Le Havre, the packets to England became the most popular ways to cross, even for the French.[7]

Still, although the day of departure could now be guaranteed, the date of arrival could not. The vagaries of the weather meant that the run across the ocean could take anywhere from three to six weeks. Nor could arrival itself be assured, for packet ships brought no improvements in safety. Pressed to their limits by owners and captains anxious to carry the maximum amount of cargo as quickly as possible, they sank at an alarming rate. One in six went down during their average five-year life.[8] Since they involved more passengers, these disasters provided even more ghoulish tales for passengers who had already been raised on a diet of gruesome shipwreck stories. Few had not heard of the forty-one passengers who died frozen to the rigging of the packet *John Minturn* as it was smashed to pieces by a snowstorm within sight of shore.[9] Some of these stories must have flashed into the mind of Abigail Mayo, wife of a Virginia planter, in 1829, as the packet carrying her and her family to Barfleur, on the northern coast of France, suddenly crunched into a shoal. The captain turned on the mate, reducing him to tears by blaming him for the fiasco. Two French lifeboat crews on shore sprang into action, but luckily the wind changed, and the vessel lurched free and made it to port.[10] The feminist author Margaret Fuller was not so lucky. In 1850, the ship bearing her with her new Italian husband and infant child sank within sight of Fire Island, New York, taking the whole family down with it.[11]

Wooden ships and sails exacerbated fears, for when battered by sea and winds they made the most alarming noises. To many terror-stricken passengers the ships sounded eerily human—screaming, moaning, and groaning—while the furies beating at them sounded like monsters. "The sea roared and the wind howled," wrote one fearful passenger. "The belabored ship creaked and moaned, and shrieked and sighed like a living thing." The hollering and shouting of the crew added to the anxiety.[12] One optimist noted that the one advantage of being seasick was that he was oblivious to the frightening noises that caused such apprehension among those who were well.[13]

Icebergs, whose sharp splinters easily pierced wooden hulls, added another terrifying dimension. The shortest route between North America and Northern Europe takes ships up past Newfoundland and just south of Greenland, where dangerous ice fields sheer off and drift southward into the shipping lanes, particularly in May and June, favorite months for passengers. "Our principal apprehension has been from the ice," John Gardner wrote in his diary in May 1823, as his ship passed the area off Newfoundland where the *Titanic* would later go down. They had hoped that they would not "encounter any of these objects of terror," but soon two monstrous ones loomed. They spent the day staring at them in awe and "passed the night in considerable apprehension," listening to the captain pace the deck until daybreak.[14] Thomas Appleton wrote of the apprehension that consumed him as his packet began to traverse a vast sea of ice islands in April 1839. "The night was utterly dark," he wrote in his diary. "This all frightened us pretty considerably, and I could not go to sleep for hearing, in fancy, the crushing of our ship on an iceberg, and for seeing the pale and terrible splinters of an iceland."[15] The story of the packet *William Brown*, which sank soon after hitting an iceberg, could not have been far from his mind. On that horrifying occasion sixteen of the survivors, young girls and men, were shoved off the overcrowded lifeboats to drown.[16]

———

Next to shipwrecks, the transatlantic passenger's greatest fear was seasickness, and justifiably so. While no one has ever died from seasickness, countless sufferers have wished that they had.[17] Folk wisdom had it that 80 percent of transatlantic passengers would suffer from it. First-time voyagers would often delude themselves that they were among the lucky 20 percent because ships would initially sail through protected waters. Before long, though, the swell of the open sea would be felt. On America's East Coast this tends to meet ships broadside, causing them to roll in a particularly nauseating fashion. Most illusions of imperviousness would soon dissolve.

It is no surprise, then, that it is a rare diary of the crossing which doesn't have some reference to seasickness. John Gardner, sailing from New York in May 1823, wrote that, even though the weather was fine, as soon as the ship encountered the open sea's swell passengers became sick. He himself was one of the first to succumb and immediately took to his berth. Before nightfall, most of the other passengers had followed suit. Gardner remained in his bunk, he wrote, for the next four days, "with as little change of position as possible, for the slightest motion brought on the most disagreeable of sensations. During the whole passage there were not more than 5 or 6 days in which I felt able to be up the whole time. In fact, for 19 days I was sick all the time."[18]

Two years later, Zacharia Allen, a retired businessman from Providence, Rhode Island, spent two weeks seasick in his bunk (which he likened to a wooden trough) watching the water dripping through the small convex lens stuck in the ceiling that provided the cabin's only light, profoundly regretting that he had ever wanted to see Europe. Each time he went on deck for fresh air the sight of waves made him sick again.[19] Twenty-odd years later, L. J. Frazee, a Cincinnati physician, tried to record his symptoms clinically:

> First, a feeling of dizziness, then a prickly sensation extending over the whole body, succeeded by an indescribable nausea so severe as to cause me to seek my berth. Now followed the most disagreeable heavings and vomitings . . . [and] the most intense suffering that can well be imagined.[20]

Ralph Waldo Emerson's description of his eight days of suffering was more succinct: "nausea, darkness, unrest, uncleanness, harpy appetite and harpy feeding, the ugly sound of water in mine ears, anticipations of going to the bottom . . ."[21]

Perhaps the only consolation of seasickness is that no matter how sick one feels, there is usually someone else who is worse off. In 1839, the young Bostonian Amos Adams Lawrence and his brother-in-law, the Reverend Charles Mason, boarded in New York City the much heralded *Great Western*, the second ship to cross the Atlantic with its steam engines running most of the time. The brainchild of the Englishman Ishmael Brunel, one of history's greatest engineers, the 1,600-ton, 234-foot ship was huge for the time—about twice the size of most packets. Its side-mounted paddle wheels had helped propel it across in record time (fourteen and a half days), and passengers had hailed its "steadiness." Its large saloon, where passengers ate, read, and lounged, featured a profusion of deep leather sofas, mahogany tables, and abundant greenery, all promising luxury and comfort for the passage.[22]

The voyage began well enough, with a lavish meal. Lawrence's brother-in-law wolfed much of it down, went for a walk on the deck, and returned for more. As the ocean swell made itself felt, though, seasick diners began to desert the saloon. Lawrence himself went up for a two-hour walk on the deck to combat nausea with bracing sea air. The next day, the sea grew rough, and at dinner Charles became sick and rushed from the table. The storm worsened, and the next morning's entry reads: "Many missing from breakfast. Charles sick. Cannot get up." After dinner Lawrence went down to Charles's cabin and found the gloomy Charles homesick as well as seasick. The morning after brought a glimmer of hope, for the day dawned bright and the sea calmed down. Charles came into Lawrence's cabin, said his stomach had turned for the better, and joined him at breakfast. Alas, Charles "got rid of his breakfast very soon" and remained sick into the next day, when the weather again worsened. "Rains and blows," Lawrence wrote. "C puts himself under my doctorship and I give him port wine and crackers. No other drink. Which keeps him well." Not for long, though, for the next day Charles, not feeling up to it, stubbornly fended off the captain's attempts to have him lead the Sunday service. The next evening, the heavy winds returned, this time accompanied by a hailstorm. "Do not sleep till near morning," wrote Lawrence. That morning: "Dip my head into water bowl. Water leaves my nose on dry ground and runs over on the floor. Get knocked about in dressing. Charles comes in and vomits as usual."[23]

Very often, the first casualty of the heaving ships was the idea of the romance of the sea. As he lay moaning in his bunk, Frazee thought back ruefully to "the romantic notions I had formed of a voyage at sea, especially after listening to such songs as 'A life on the ocean wave' and 'I'm afloat.'"[24] The Reverend James Clarke had hoped that the crossing on the beautiful clipper ship *Plymouth Rock* in 1849 would provide him with poetic inspiration. Alas, he wrote his wife, "one feels too sick at sea to indulge in verse making."[25] "What horrid noise is that?" the Virginian John Doyle wrote in his diary. "Some of the passengers sea sick. Farewell Romance."[26]

The other side of the seasickness coin was fear of being becalmed. When Robert Saunders's packet left New York bound for Le Havre in June 1828, the passengers, huddled below to escape a pounding rainstorm, were concerned only about seasickness. However, the rain soon stopped, the wind died down, and the ship slowed to a halt. There it remained, within sight of shore, with the pilot still aboard, for eight days, awaiting a favorable wind. "Day after day rolled by," he wrote in his diary, "and found us resting quietly in the bosom of the waters, each morning hoping that the breeze would freshen when the day was done. . . ."[27]

Aside from the inconvenience of delayed arrivals, being becalmed could also evoke one of the ocean traveler's greatest terrors: tiresome or annoying fellow passengers. John Doyle noted how, as he and the fourteen other passengers on his packet sat down for their first meal together, "each person was no doubt occupied as I was, scanning the countenance and general appearance of those who were to be my companions for some weeks and of course contribute much to our mutual pleasure or displeasure."[28]

The small number of cabin passengers exacerbated this problem. When John Gardner boarded the new packet *Amethyst* in Boston in May 1823, he was heartened to see a large crowd on the jetty. However, he soon discovered that they were there only to look at the sharp new ship. There were only eight other passengers in the cabin.[29] When Ralph Waldo Emerson crossed in the winter of 1832, there were only four other passengers on the ship—two hack writers and the wife and daughter of one of the writers. Emerson found them all tedious in the extreme, yet could not escape them. "The inconvenience of living in a cabin," he complained to his journal, "is that people become all eye."[30] Later, in the 1840s, larger clippers began carrying many more passengers, but often only about thirty would be in the cabins. Up to a thousand immigrants would be squeezed into the stuffy holds in steerage, particularly on the westbound voyage, where they served as a kind of ballast.[31] The better-off passengers could hear those in steerage—they would often start out the voyage singing and soon turn to moaning—and could sometimes smell them as well, but there was no intercourse between the two classes.

Even if cabin-class tourists did find one another congenial, the days at sea would still grow tedious. One could read or play cards or watch the sails, sea, and clouds just so much before a kind of stir-craziness set in. As he began his third week at sea, John Doyle wrote that on 8 and 9 December 1840:

> The only thing of interest was to watch the various changes of wind. Even trifles light as air have their importance when shut out from communion with the breathing and living world by the confinement of a ship. I can well imagine the instinct of nature that prompts the dungeon prisoner to hold, commune and make a friend of spiders that visited his lonely cell.[32]

In 1828, Robert Saunders wrote that it was wondrous to behold the white sails billowing against the blue of sea, the castles of clouds in the sky, and the sky aflame at sunset—up to a point. Soon boredom took hold and the passengers longed for the sight of land.

> Everything which could divert for a while was eagerly caught at, as a child would pursue a butterfly. "A sail in sight" served as the event of the day, and a porpoise or flying fish excited as much interest as would be produced on land by the apparition of a gryphon, or winged dragon, or any other fabulous monster of Romance.[33]

Saunders was not exaggerating the desperation of passengers for the sight of other human beings. Until the 1830s, ships sailing in opposite directions would often pull alongside each other to exchange news, ask that the folks back home be informed that they were still alive, and give passengers and crew some new faces to stare at.[34] Later, when the practice was abandoned, the mere sight of another ship would send passengers rushing to the rails to stare wistfully at them, and then carefully note their names and appearance in the journals. "The sight of a sister ship," Francis Parkman wrote his son, "makes everybody feel not quite alone on the vast deep."[35] Saunders, after arriving safely in France, was less sanguine. A ship, he wrote, is "a dirty prison with a good chance of being drowned."[36]

Late-eighteenth- and early-nineteenth-century ships were built to carry cargo, and passengers were often treated as such. They were usually housed in one large cabin, with a heavy curtain separating the sexes at night if females were aboard.[37] Thomas Jefferson was fortunate to have a tiny cabin to share with his older daughter when he crossed in 1784, but the porthole leading to it from the open deck was so low that they had to crawl into it on all fours. Inside the tiny space, separated by an infinitesimal patch of floor, were two coffin-like bunks with no mattresses.[38] The lumpy straw mattresses provided on other boats would hardly have improved matters, and the wise brought their own.[39] Passengers' food was better than that given the crew, but that was not saying much, for there was little in the way of preservation techniques for the long voyages except the inevitable salted beef or pork. Steerage passengers were given no food at all. They brought their own.

In 1818, the new packet *James Monroe* took a great leap forward by providing passengers with two-person cabins, a well-appointed common saloon with stuffed settees and card tables, an enclosed closet on deck for washing one's body in sea water, and gold-rimmed individual chamber pots. Part of the upper deck was given over to farm animals, who provided passengers with milk, eggs, and meat for four substantial meals a day. Whereas since the days of the *Mayflower* passengers had shared the sailors' plain, dry, and often moldy hard-tack biscuits, they were now served fresh bread.[40] Competitors soon fell into line, and food improved so much that by the time the *Great Western* came along in 1838, the transatlantic packets were already renowned for their munificent meals. When Amos Lawrence went for his first walk round the deck of the *Great Western* he eagerly anticipated the ingredients of future meals: "The cattle are pent up in a small place," he wrote. "Long boat filled with turkeys and ducks. Turtles on their backs." The next two days' menus also included rabbit and mutton.[41] Five years later, Francis Parkman, aboard the Cunard steamship *Caledonia,* noted that, "Much time . . . is consumed in meals. The breakfast bountiful at half-past-eight; Lunch liberally at 12; dine sumptuously at Four; drink Tea at Six; and take what we please (at each one's discretion) at Ten."[42] In the 1890s, when people marveled at that era's luxurious new "floating palaces," old-timers who had crossed on the packets and clippers still recalled that "the table was as good then as now."[43]

Yet getting there was still not half the fun. No matter how large the ship, North Atlantic storms still tossed them about like corks. The steam engines powering the new sail-and-paddle-wheelers spewed heavy black smoke, reeked from engine oil, and made an incredible racket. Emerson, returning from Europe on one in 1848, wrote in his journal: "One long disgust is the sea. . . . Who am I to be treated in this ignominious manner, tipped up, shoved against the side of the house, rolled over, suffocated with bilge, mephitis [foul stench], and stewing oil."[44] Nor were their accommodations much improved over the early packets. Passengers still slept on two-foot-wide bunks, one bunk on top of the other, in cabins for two lighted by a smoky little lamp with the opaque glass lens that tormented Zacharia Allen. There was so little space between the bunks and the wall that getting dressed seemed to require the skills of a professional contortionist. Indeed, well into the 1860s, some Americans preferred to travel on the sailing packets and clippers, which at least were cleaner, quieter, and sometimes faster.[45]

Until the 1820s, politics probably inhibited tourism to France at least as much as the length, danger, and inconveniences of the crossing. The outbreak of the French Revolution in 1789 and the radical turn it took in 1792 certainly put a damper on its tourist trade. (Robert Johnson, a young Connecticut lawyer who toured France in 1792 and 1793, was surprised to encounter no major problems. He even left to posterity what must be the only tourist diary with an entry that reads: "On the 21st of January, the second day of my arrival, I mixed with the citizens and *saw Louis the Sixteenth beheaded.*"[46]) The Napoleonic Wars, from 1796 to 1813, and the naval blockades that ensued also had a chilling effect on travel to Europe. A surprising number of Americans did manage to get to France, but many of them were probably involved in blockade-running of some sort.[47] In the spring and summer of 1812, as war between the United States and Britain loomed and Napoléon plunged deeper into a military maelstrom on the Continent, Americans in Paris began to leave, either for home or Italy.[48]

Napoléon's final defeat at Waterloo in 1814 precipitated a stampede of British tourists—more than ten thousand in the twelve months following it—but not Americans, whose war with Britain did not end until January 1815.[49] Even the next year, only a trickle of Americans passed through the French Atlantic ports. Calais, the main port of entry for tourists coming via England, recorded only five American arrivals in May 1816, a month when tourist travel normally picked up, and only about one hundred in all of 1817.[50]

Meanwhile, other upper-class foreigners flocked to Paris, spurred by the tales of Parisian delights told by aristocratic officers in the post-Waterloo occupying armies. They rented luxurious mansions, partied with the restored French aristocracy, and crowded its restaurants and cafés, inaugurating what has been called a "golden age" of tourism to France. Americans, however, still held back. By 1819, the number of American visitors to Paris was increasing, but they still numbered only one-third of those arriving in the early months of 1812. In the winter of 1819, the

United States plunged into the worst depression in its short history, further inhibiting a revival.[51] It is no wonder that in 1823, when the young Providence, Rhode Island, patrician, John Carter Brown, having survived a shipwreck, made his way to Paris to see the sights, he found "few Americans travelling for pleasure."[52]

Had he returned a few years later, Brown would have found many more. In 1825, 678 Americans registered in the hotels and pensions of Paris, and 847 arrived in 1826.[53] That summer, about six or seven Americans arrived each day. Although the English still comprised the vast majority of visitors, Americans were consistently among the top five visiting nationalities.[54] More than half of them were the kind of propertied people of independent means who made up most of the era's tourists.[55]

The Revolution of 1830 brought an end to the "golden age" for aristocratic foreigners, as the Paris of the bourgeois July Monarchy became much less congenial to them than that of the high-living Bourbons.[56] However, it did make Paris a more comfortable place for Americans. Over the next fourteen years, while the number of visiting foreigners more or less held steady at about thirty thousand a year, the number of Americans among them increased from two thousand to more than three thousand a year.[57] "All the world (our world) is going to Europe," the well-connected New Yorker Philip Hone write in his diary on 1 June 1835.[58] By May and June 1848, Americans were arriving at the rate of three hundred a month.[59] The Revolution that broke out the next month led to a falloff in tourism, but this was short lived. In 1850 and 1851, when Napoléon Bonaparte's nephew, Louis-Napoléon, seized power and established the kind of firm authoritarian rule that well-off tourists normally find congenial, they began returning in larger numbers, helping to inaugurate what has been called the "second golden age" of tourism to France.[60] But the Americans who were part of that would be much different from those who had come before.

Three

A MAN'S WORLD

Given the terrors and discomforts of the crossing, one might ask why *any* Americans took European tours. Part of the answer would seem to be that, at a time when few could admit that they were going just to enjoy themselves, the very trials of the crossing helped legitimize the trip. No one ready to brave the North Atlantic could be accused of doing so merely, as we would say today, "to have a good time."

Curiously, in view of the physical battering it often involved, the voyage could also be legitimized on the grounds of health. In the 1760s and 1770s, spas—places where one could drink or bathe in health-giving waters—became America's major destinations for people traveling for other than business or family reasons. The presumed health benefits allowed the well-off to enjoy a refreshing change of scenery and an opportunity for socializing that could not be condemned as frivolous.[1] As the century drew to a close, medical experts began extolling the medicinal qualities of sea air and prescribed long sea voyages as cures for wealthy patients, particularly those suffering from respiratory problems. The writer Washington Irving took his first trip to Europe, in 1804, as a health measure. He was so weak from a lung ailment that he had to be helped aboard the Bordeaux-bound ship. The captain later recalled saying to himself, "There's a chap who will go overboard before we get across." Yet, after an initial bout of seasickness and some feverish nights, Irving emerged from the thirty-day voyage as fit as a fiddle.[2]

The years following the War of 1812 saw a rise in more questionable prescriptions for transatlantic voyages. Clergymen from well-off Protestant congregations seemed particularly prone to illnesses that could only be cured by a trip to the Continent. A typical memoir on one such trip begins, "The author's great errand in his excursion to Europe was the recovery of his health."[3] The Reverend Berrian, who was assistant minister of New York City's posh Trinity Church, began his account:

25

A state of great debility, and a slight tendency to consumption . . . increased by the exercise of my ministerial duties, made it necessary to take some prompt and decided measures for the recovery of my health. A sea voyage, and the mild climate of the south of Europe, it was thought would be most effectual.

The Maryland friend who accompanied him seemed in worse shape: "His journey was indeed a flight from the grave, which appeared already opening to receive him."[4]

The grave did await some on the other side. On 1 January 1818, the Reverend Samuel C. Thacher of Boston's New South Church died in the small French town of Moulins, en route from Paris to the healthful south.[5] More often than not, however, the afflicted improved and survived. In 1828, the president of Harvard College suffered some minor paralysis and was prescribed a trip to Europe. From the moment he and his wife arrived they immersed themselves in such a grueling social whirl that one must conclude that the voyage over had been a restorative one indeed.[6] The doctor who in 1830 ordered Emma Willard, suffering from some sort of debilitating ailment, to leave her women's academy in Troy, New York, in charge of her sister, board a ship to France, and have her "life's wish consummated in seeing Europe," probably did so at her suggestion. In any event, the voyage seemed to cure her too, although she was not sure whether to credit the salubrious sea air or the exercise she got in clutching to fixed objects on the pitching ship.[7]

But by then most tourists did not need health to justify the voyage. American commerce and industry were expanding rapidly, enlarging the class of people with the money and leisure for travel. In practically all of the major cities, newly rich businessmen nipped at the heels of the established landed and mercantile elites, striving for social status.[8] Despite the market values that were coming to dominate the country's culture, the mere acquisition of wealth was still not enough to legitimize their claims. In the highest circles of the still-puritanical country, merely living a pleasurable life was not enough to gain respect and distinction. Indeed, the democratic culture of the new republic frowned on the man of leisure as a throwback to pre-Revolutionary aristocratic times.[9]

Yet, democratic as the political culture may have been, the social structure was by no means a classless one. In most cities, the older upper class tried to fend off the newly rich by claiming to constitute some kind of aristocracy of taste and talents. As the nouveaux riches gained control of the economic reins, this emphasis on culture assumed increasing importance in justifying their political and social hegemony. In the words of one historian, it "purified the privileged, fitting them to rule."[10] By the 1830s, the upper classes had constructed networks radiating from exclusive cultural institutions such as the Boston Athenaeum and the Philadelphia Academy of Fine Arts to demonstrate their cultural superiority. Rich parvenus could shoulder their way into the social elite only by proving that they too were people of culture and distinction. In New York City, where the old Knickerbocker elite still held out against all newcomers, the arrivistes formed a rival oligarchy, the Bourbons, with its own cultural institutions.[11]

Since it was universally acknowledged that culture was in greater supply in Europe than in the New World, a trip there to imbibe it could thus either reinforce an upper-class claim to cultural attainment or, for the nouveaux riches, represent an important step in staking one out. So, there emerged one of life's little ironies: no sooner had the aristocratic Grand Tour of the Continent dissolved into a dissolute parody of itself than republicans from across the sea embraced its original purpose: to soak up the best of Old World culture.

As might be expected, most American tourists to France were well-off young white Protestant males who could afford both the expense of the trip and the long break from normal pursuits that it demanded. Of the more than one thousand Americans who entered Paris from 1806 to 1811, the large majority were unaccompanied males in their twenties and thirties. More of them were from Boston than any other American city, followed by New York City. Many of the names—Amory, Appleton, Lowell, Parkman—denoted well-established wealth, and would crop up later as their children and grandchildren followed their path to France.[12]

Until the 1830s, they often traveled alone. Washington Irving traveled alone for weeks in southwest France in 1804 and was not at all surprised to meet a Philadelphia doctor who had been traveling alone through Europe for years. Neither Irving nor his brother Peter, who toured Europe alone for nine months, even mentioned this solitude in their diaries and correspondence, taking it as a matter of course.[13] By the late 1820s, though, as tourism to Europe picked up and it became easier to find traveling companions, solitary travel declined. Often, those who did not set off with friends or relatives from America would meet touring Americans in one city in Europe and travel with them to the next one on their itinerary.

Twenty-seven-year-old John Georteur linked up with another young fellow in England, parted from him, and then met him again in Paris in 1827. When they finally parted, "probably never to see each other again," he wrote: "This is one of the unpleasant consequences of traveling, viz. forming fellowships then bidding farewell to friends with the certainty of never meeting them again on earth."[14]

Many of these young men were recent college graduates; an inordinate number of whom were from that "upper class boarding school," Harvard College.[15] Ralph Waldo Emerson ran into them practically everywhere on his 1832 tour of Italy and France.[16] In Paris, he became part of a group of them gravitating around the magnetic Thomas Gold Appleton, the wealthy, twenty-one-year-old son of one of Massachusetts's oldest families who, a year after graduating from Harvard, had embarked on a one-year European tour. One of Appleton's companions on the crossing had been another Harvard man, Oliver Wendell Holmes, who proceeded on to Paris, where he was to study medicine, while Appleton visited England.[17] Holmes had just begun to feel lonely in his new rooms when Emerson arrived, followed by Appleton, and then a host of other touring young Bostonians. Before he knew it, he was surrounded by so many Harvard men that he had a hard time breaking away from English-speakers to practice his French.[18] "Paris is the strangest place for meeting acquaintances," one young Harvard man noted in his diary. "I seldom go out without seeing somebody I know at home, certainly more of my friends and acquaintances than I should see in Cambridge."[19]

A tour of Europe also conferred distinction on the young Southern elite. The ambitious twenty-nine-year-old South Carolina planter-politician James Hammond, determined to acquire the polish and culture of a European tour, helped establish himself as a leading spokesmen for the slave-owning elite by touring the Continent for over a year. Accompanied by the rich wife whose money made it possible (the trip cost close to sixteen thousand dollars, an enormous amount in those days) he inevitably found confirmation of what was becoming an important part of the Southern defense of slavery: that American slaves had better living conditions than European workers and "surfs" [*sic*].[20]

Some tourists were businessmen who had made a bundle, cashed in their chips, and wanted to elevate their social status by raising their cultural level. James Colles, a fifty-three-year-old New Yorker who had made a fortune in New Orleans, retired in 1841 with the intention of moving back to New York and elbowing his way into that city's social elite. In preparation for this, he took his wife and three children on a three-year tour of Europe. Using Paris as their base, they spent most of their time relentlessly jacking up their cultural level.[21] When Philip Hone turned forty in 1821, he sold the New York auction house that had enriched him and embarked on a long tour of Europe. There, the ambitious but poorly educated future mayor of New York City began the determined effort to learn about European art, music, and literature that would help him become one of the stalwarts of the city's upper class.[22] Some of these retired businessmen were quite young. In 1839 Henry B. Humphrey, a thirty-year-old Bostonian, sold his investments and went on a two-and-a-half-year tour of Europe and the Middle East with a Joseph Langdon, of Smyrna, Turkey.[23]

Most of the married men left their wives behind.[24] Alpheus Hardy, a merchant in Chatham, on Cape Cod, was also only thirty in 1845, when, he said, he decided to "fulfill a life-long dream" and take an overseas trip before he was too old to do so. Luckily, he was married to a wealthy woman, whose income allowed him to set off with a male friend. Their main objective, he assured her, was to walk the streets of the Holy Land that the Savior had walked. Of course, this meant a number of pleasant stops along the way, including Marseille, Genoa, and the Nile. He repaid her with a four-hundred-page diary, written with exquisite penmanship, in the form of flowery letters to her.[25] When fifty-six-year-old Theodore Lyman, an ex-mayor of Boston, departed on a tour of England and a three-month visit to Paris in 1848, he left his wife behind to manage his investments and forward him money, flattering her as "Chancellor of the Exchequer."[26] Had America's wealthiest man, John Jacob Astor, not been one never to admit he made a mistake, he might have regretted sailing for Europe without his wife in 1834. When the packet bringing him back from France docked in New York City he was greeted with the news that she had just died.[27]

Although it was still the heyday of the "Cult of True Womanhood," which apotheosized the dutiful, submissive, wife, some of these wives must have resented this treatment, particularly since by the 1840s it was no longer unusual for wives and even children to accompany husbands.[28] But men still outnumbered women by far. Of the 231 adult American-born passengers who disembarked at Le Havre that year only 42 were women, most of them wives accompanying their husbands.[29] Until 1850, unaccompanied young men in their twenties continued to constitute by far the largest cohort of arriving passengers. The passengers' most common attribute, however, was wealth. Most were described as "rentiers," that is, people living off fixed investments, or "*gentilhommes*," men wealthy enough not to have an occupation.[30]

— —

Whatever their age or situation, most men undertook the tour of Europe in the manner prescribed by the masculine codes of the day. Women could express fears of shipwreck, seasickness, and loneliness, but males had to repress them. The forty-year-old Boston businessman Samuel Topliff was mortified when, as he hastily scrawled some notes to his family for the pilot of his departing ship to take ashore, "tears gushed down my cheeks, and made me feel womanish."[31] Nor, in a competitive culture that urged men on to ever-greater feats of self-improvement, could they admit to frivolous motives for the venture. Topliff told his relatives that his tour was part of his lifelong struggle to remedy the deficiencies left by an education that stopped at the end of grade school.[32] Protestants from the North struggled with consciences that told them that the pursuit of leisure, amusement, and recreation were damaging to the soul. Clergymen were determined to prove that their summer trips were undertaken for uplifting purposes—rather like research trips for future sermonizing. On their return they would write long accounts of the uplifting venture, while expressing appropriate disapproval of French religion, morals, and, especially, Sabbath-breaking.[33] Men who left wives behind felt particular pressure to demonstrate that the trip was not for pleasure.

The masculine rites of travel began aboard ship, when men would often begin a journal. Later, travel diaries would become associated more with women than with men, but in the early nineteenth century the keeping of a travel journal was still a masculine proposition. This was particularly so among New Englanders and other heirs to the Puritan tradition, for diary-writing there had begun as a deadly serious way of examining the state of one's soul. Travel journals were not quite so weighty a matter, for they also functioned much like cameras would later—to help recall the trip in the years to come. Yet, like the Puritan diaries, men's journals would concentrate on the practical details of the trip, implicitly assuming that a larger meaning would somehow emerge from this accumulation of detail. They would therefore dutifully record such things as the modes of transportation, distances covered each day, the measurements of structures, and the cost of fares, accommodations, and meals.[34] In his 1817–1818 journal of his trip to France, William Raser, a planter from Mobile, Alabama, recorded every expense and calculated the precise distance covered each day by his coach down to the quarter-mile. He dutifully recorded the exact dimensions of practically every notable building he saw, the year in which construction began, the number of volumes in every library. He went into considerable detail about such things as the defense of Orléans against an English attack in the fifteenth century and how the catacombs of Paris were run, yet nowhere did he record his emotional reaction to anything. Indeed, although he spent five days on a nonstop trip from Paris to Bordeaux cooped up in a diligence with a number of other passengers, he said nothing about them—only that one was a French admiral who had spent five years as a prisoner-of-war in England.[35]

Diaries such as this, which resemble naval or military logs, helped reinforce the quasi-military aura with which men liked to surround the planning and carrying out of the tour. During the crossing, they would pore over maps, scour guidebooks, and discuss projected routes with fellow passengers. James Clarke evoked a Napoleonic image in describing the shipboard routine to the wife he had left back in Boston with the children. "Each morning," he wrote, "we study out our routes in the guidebooks and on the maps, which are spread abroad on the cabin table."[36] The Reverend Berrian wrote that he had laid on an impressive pile of uplifting books to read on his long voyage to Bordeaux in 1817, but found that instead he spent most of his time poring over maps of his projected itinerary and reading travelers' accounts of where he was headed.[37] The guidebooks themselves were resolutely masculine in tone, written solely with the male tourist in mind, outlining the things "he" should do.[38]

Twentieth-century writers would later idealize such people as "travelers," whose experience of foreign places was unmediated by other people and things. Because many traveled alone, they were said to relish experiencing new places one-on-one, free from intrusive guides or imperious guidebooks.[39] There is certainly something to be said for this. Solitary travel does encourage interaction with locals in ways that group travel practically precludes. Moreover, since cultural uplift was usually the main justification for their trips, they often felt constrained to learn as much as possible about the places they visited. The lengthy tours gave them many weeks to explore individual cities. Whole days could be spent admiring and studying a single place, undistracted by countrymen's chit-chat, enabling them to acquire a depth of familiarity with them that was practically unattainable for later tourists, whose visits were usually more fleeting.

On the other hand, most of the solitary travelers traveled alone out of necessity, not choice. They did not relish being alone in a sea of foreigners.

Like the Harvard men discussed above, tourists sought out their countrymen wherever they could. The young patrician John Carter Brown, traveling alone in 1823, wished he had "someone of [his] own standing ... with the same views and objects," with whom he could tour Paris. Instead, he was forced to use some of his "introductory letters" to older diplomats and businessmen there, even though he found it "a disagreeable office to perform."[40] Samuel Topliff said that one day in Paris he spied another Bostonian walking down the street: Russell Sturgis, "a proud, haughty, young man" whom he had disliked intensely in Boston. Normally, Topliff would have ducked around a corner, but, facing the prospect of traveling alone through the south of France to Italy, he stood his ground and approached Sturgis. He asked if Sturgis wished to join him, for the sake of economy (sharing a courier) and "for company's sake." This he did, and they ended up getting along very well.[41]

As for guidebooks acting as intermediaries by telling travelers what to do and how to react: travelers to new places have always used reports from those who have been there before. The original Grand Tourists visited only places on a well-described route and looked seriously at only those things mentioned in the ancient texts.[42] William Gilpin's travel guides to Britain, which in the 1780s popularized the concept of "the picturesque," not only instructed tourists on how to get to the beauty spots that best embodied this ideal, they also told them which vantage points provided the best views and, like the "Kodak Picture Points" of our day, told from where to draw or paint pictures of the views to take home as souvenirs.[43] One of the first things that Jefferson, who would seem to have been a quintessential "traveler," advised the two young prospective tourists who wrote him in 1787 was, "Buy Dutens," a detailed guidebook to Western Europe written by a Frenchman living in England. Then, "on arriving at a town, the first thing to buy is a plan of the town, and the book noting its curiosities."[44]

Of course, turn-of-the-century guidebooks were not as intrusive as later ones. They were usually autobiographical, discursive, and anecdotal, proffering little in the way of practical advice. However, English-language works with more useful information, written in the third person, were beginning to appear.[45] In the early 1800s, A. and W. Galignani, the English-language bookstore in Paris, began selling a slim guide with suggested tours of France and Italy by a woman, Mariana Starke, who had previously written books on politics and military campaigns. In 1819 it began turning out its own guide to France, followed by one to Paris alone. Regularly revised, the Paris guide became an American favorite and continued publication until 1894.[46] In 1838, George Putnam wrote the first guidebook to Europe specifically directed at Americans, part of which provided suggested itineraries, brief descriptions of sights to be seen, and recommendations for lodging, as well as detailed tables of the expenses he incurred on his 1836 trip there.[47]

In the 1840s, the Englishman John Murray III's *Handbooks* came to dominate the market for guidebooks to the Continent, spawning a host of imitators. The most famous of these were the German Baedeker guides, English editions of which began appearing in the 1850s. Both Murray and Baedeker were organized on the basis of suggested itineraries through countries or regions. They had succinct descriptions of the tourist sights in each place and marked the outstanding ones with asterisks or other indications. Their information on transportation and lodging facilities was updated regularly. "Take Murray wherever you go," an experienced American traveler advised a friend about to embark on a tour of France and the Continent, "and the latest edition, as hôtels change, and with them his recommendations."[48] Mrs. Bullard's account of her 1850 trip had a cautionary tale of how, because she and her husband ignored Murray's recommendations in Lyon, touts were able to misdirect them to an inferior hotel.[49]

Nor was there a shortage of the more traditional travel accounts, which in effect told tourists what they should look for. In the early 1830s, new printing techniques led to a boom in magazine publishing, opening the floodgates for travel articles. By 1837, when the celebrated writer James Fenimore Cooper published his *Gleanings from Europe: France,* there was such a glut of travel literature on the market that the publishers lost money on the book.[50] The vast bulk of this outpouring more than justified the conclusion reached by Thomas Appleton who, after looking through Mrs. Cushing's *France and Italy* during his crossing in 1833, wrote that "there is no book that may be made so dull as a book of travels."[51] However, they did find a huge middle-class market, and continued to do so until well after World War I.[52] From the 1830s on, then, few Americans strolling the streets of Paris had not been primed about what to see there by what they had read before they left home.

Written works were by no means the only intermediaries. The practice of hiring a courier to arrange for transportation and accommodation, see to passports (more like visas today), and act as interpreter continued well into the 1870s.[53] Even those who thought them too intrusive would, like

Jefferson, still hire local *valets de place*. In her 1849 book on traveling in Europe Mrs. C. M. Kirkland decried couriers as intrusive and domineering, but her main argument was that the courier did not obviate the need for a *valet de place*. Indeed, he continued to accompany the party everywhere, "in order that when they make any purchase, however small, he may receive his commission."[54] The Virginia planter Ambrose Carlton also despised his courier, who fabricated excuses for not taking him to hotels friends had recommended. "I had no doubt as well," he wrote a friend, "that he has cheated me at least 15 per cent on our expenses."[55]

Others, however, grew fond of their couriers. At the end of her family's tour of France in 1851, Catherine Jones wrote, "We have become quite attached to old Arnaud, our [courier], and were really grieved . . . at the unavoidable separation."[56] Twenty-seven-year-old Margaret Quincy Greene described the courier her husband hired to accompany them from Dover to Paris in 1838 as, "Gante, by name. The handsomest man, ace and figure, I ever saw." She hastily added "wanting in refinement," but from the subsequent entries regarding him, each of which referred to how handsome he was, one suspects that this added a certain frisson.[57] Women were not the only ones attracted to their couriers for reasons other than their helpfulness. When Henry Humphrey, a single man, departed from France, leaving behind Gilbert, his courier, in Marseille, he confided to his diary: "I have experienced much pain this evening in parting with Gilbert, to whom I have become very attached."[58]

The final intermediary was the visual image which, seen before the actual sight, told the visitor what to expect. Indeed, few people see famous sights for the first time without some kind of representation of them in mind. Until the 1840s, Americans were limited to paintings, which few of them saw, and engravings, which though somewhat more plentiful were often distorted or sketchy. Then new printing techniques opened the door to the reproduction of engravings in magazines. The illustrated magazines that now proliferated helped make detailed pictures of the world's major tourist commonplace. The first photographs, the daguerreotypes of the 1840s, were restricted to indoor shots of people sitting stiffly still, but in the 1850s new techniques allowed photographs to be taken outdoors. Because they were still restricted to immobile subjects, photographers produced many superb images of cathedrals, castles, and other famous tourist sights, which were turned into engravings for the illustrated magazines. In 1860, the new French travel magazine, *Tour du Monde*, likened its own role to that of the fairy who, according to an old tale, visited a young prince in captivity and, at his command, had "all that was rare, curious, and beautiful in the world" appear before him. "The illustrated press is the good fairy," it said, "the public is the prince."[59]

The age-old tourist reaction to new sights—to comment on whether it did or did not match its representations—was thus reinforced a thousandfold. Who has not reacted to a new sight by saying that it looks larger or smaller, more or less beautiful, than its pictures? (In 1867, Mark Twain reported that Leonardo da Vinci's "Last Supper" was dark, dirty, and damaged by Napoléon's horses and, like most of the masterpieces he saw in Europe, came nowhere near matching the beauty of its reproductions.[60]) Indeed, for many tourists, seeing things with whose images they were familiar could be more interesting than seeing things that were completely unfamiliar. Whether experiences such as this really qualify as "cultural" tourism might be debated. (After all, how much does seeing something with which one is already familiar actually add to one's knowledge?) However, since most tourists think it does, and come away from these experiences thinking that they are somehow improved, it probably should. The real doubts over whether the trip to France qualified as culturally uplifting arose from other aspects of the experience. Indeed, as we shall see in chapter 6, side by side with these foreshadowings of twentieth-century-style cultural tourism we can also discern the seedlings of modern leisure tourism, which revolves around travel for pleasure. Yet until at least the 1850s, cultural tourism, and the hard work it often entailed, continued to reign supreme.

Four

EAT, DRINK, BUT BE WARY

Caroline Kirkland said that tourists hired couriers because of "a want of knowledge of the language of the countries through which we travel." Her solution, which was "to learn the language most needed—French—before we set out," reflected more than just practical exigencies.[1] After all, French was not the language "most needed" for haggling with Italian coachmen or finding one's way around German castles. It was the international tongue of those Europeans who were worth talking to.[2]

American academies and colleges had begun teaching it in the late eighteenth century. It rose further in status over the next few decades as Harvard and eventually Yale allowed French and German to be studied along with Latin and Greek. By the 1820s, then, American tourists who knew little or no French felt distinctly inadequate, and their travel journals, which are riddled with regrets and mea culpas, show it.

Many put in a tremendous effort to learn it before they left home. James Fenimore Cooper and his family took French lessons for a full three years before they embarked.[3] James Colles and his wife began studying it in New Orleans several years before they departed. The daily lessons eventually consumed more than half of his time, while she spent six hours a day just on the homework.[4] (Still, the highest praise his teacher, a Frenchman, gave was a grudging "not *bad*" for his pronunciation when reading.) When they reached Paris they again plunged into French lessons, and finally took some satisfaction from at least being able to make themselves understood.[5]

Others, who had some French in college, worked hard at improving it in France. John Lowell hired a tutor to come at breakfast each morning to "give [him] the words and idioms [he] needed the day before."[6] Charles Sumner, disgusted at the inadequacy of his Harvard training, engaged two tutors to help him.[7] George S. Emerson paid a French man to converse with him for two hours a day and in the evenings attended raucous popular entertainments to help him with the vernacular.[8] Margaret Fuller, who struggled through a three-hour French lesson each morning, warned a friend, "When you come, be sure you can speak French fluently first; else you must lose a great deal."[9]

During the next century, the French would become notorious for being rude to tourists struggling with their language. Quite the opposite was the case in the early nineteenth century. *Galignani's* guide said in 1831 that "the French, seldom knowing much of English, are quick in comprehending a broken phrase, and never disposed to ridicule a foreigner."[10] This seems to have been on the mark. Washington Irving could barely understand the patois of the villagers he tried to speak to in southwest France, but, he reported, "my bad French seemed to give them much fond amusement."[11] After a polite French stranger helped them clear up a major misunderstanding over train tickets in the Rouen train station, James Clarke and a friend tried to buy a "crush"—a fruit juice drink—from a young lady in a shop there. "What with the tons of centimes we could not make out at all what she meant," Clarke wrote his wife, "and finally all three of us— the saleswoman and all, were ready to fall down with laughter."[12] Even Parisians seemed tolerant of mangled French. When Clarke got involved in another misunderstanding, this time over the price of a cup of coffee, in a Paris café-concert hall, the people around him were exceedingly helpful and friendly. Ironically, a comedian on the stage had just begun to imitate an Englishman speaking broken French. They all laughed, said Clarke, "not rudely, as Englishmen would have done, but good naturedly and pleasantly, and I laughed too. The civility of the people has never been exaggerated."[13]

The civility is all the more striking because many of the stories have the French looking just as foolish as the Americans. When Elizabeth Cady Stanton's coach made a short stop at an inn one night in 1840, she asked a waiter for some cake or a cracker—or at least so she thought. Just as the diligence was leaving, he appeared at its door with a whole plate of sizzling sweetbreads.[14] Some years earlier, William Lee's traveling companion ordered turbot in a Paris restaurant. When the waiter, thinking this meant he wanted his boots polished while he dined, came back with a *tire-botte*—a boot jack to pull them off—the American exclaimed, "Why man, de ye think I can eat that?"[15]

The first place most tourists got to use their French was in one of the Channel ports. The introduction of regular packet service made England the most convenient first stop on a continental tour, and France, a short hop across the Channel on one of the little steamers that were introduced in 1819, was usually the next stop. Alas, the customs sheds at Havre, Calais, Dieppe, and Boulogne often provided a kind of "good cop/bad cop" experience that was not conducive to contemplating the mysteries of the subjunctive. The bad cops were, of course, French officialdom, whose apparent thickheadedness has always baffled Americans. Passengers would arrive pale and shaky from seasickness (there are almost as many accounts of seasickness on the Channel ferries as on the transatlantic crossing) and first confront the disconcerting French police, who would take their passports, mutter something about retrieving them later in Paris, and demand payment for the process. Then came the gantlet of grim customs officials who, after warning them that the penalties for smuggling contraband were extremely severe, would search their luggage for illegal imports—mainly tobacco and cigars. Sometimes men and women would be separated for body searches by agents of their own sex.[16]

When they extricated themselves from customs, travelers would then find themselves surrounded by a disreputable-looking mob importuning them to go to certain inns, hire them as couriers, or just begging. However, once they selected one of the inns, their baggage would be whisked over there and, as with Sterne, the more attractive side of travel in France would soon emerge. Although they often looked tumble-down from the outside, the accommodations in the Channel ports were usually clean and comfortable, with attractive amenities such as fresh flowers. The major revelation, though, would be the food. Most Americans were accustomed to meals built around great slabs of fried meat and large mounds of potatoes, grains, beans, cabbage, squash, and pies. They used condiments but had a deep suspicion of sauces, which they had heard the French used to camouflage frog, horse, tainted meat, and other disgusting things. They were therefore pleasantly surprised at the lightness and delicacy of much of French food, particularly in comparison with theirs. The Georgian Ann Gordon seemed surprised that "the viands" in her family's first dinner in France were so "delicious. . . . There is no smell of *garlic* or *taint* as we generally have supposed."[17] Even those not enthralled by their accommodations would be impressed by the food. The Philadelphian John Sanderson reported in 1835 that the hotels in Le Havre "are shabby compared to ours; the one I lodge in has not been washed since 1656; but the cookery and service are altogether in favor of the French."[18]

In America, many men swilled whiskey all through the day, washed down meals with hard cider, and, if they were high class, fell into a post-prandial stupor over flagons of port. Tourists were therefore amazed at how, as L. J. Frazee wrote, the French drank wine "as regularly at dinner as milk with our Kentucky farmers [who in fact were notorious whiskey-drinkers], yet show no signs of inebriation."[19] Jefferson had been impressed by how formal dinners did not end up as drunken brawls, as they often did in America. He wrote,

> In the pleasures of the table, they are far before us, because with good taste they unite temperance. They do not terminate the most sociable meals by transforming themselves into brutes. . . . I have never yet seen a man drunk in France, even among the lowest of the people.[20]

James Fenimore Cooper made a similar observation. "A dinner here does not oppress one," he wrote. "The wine neither intoxicates nor heats, and the frame of mind and body in which one is left is precisely that best suited to intellectual and social pleasures."[21] Light French wine and cookery, said Samuel Topliff, "always keeps Frenchmen's heads clear, and they are light of heels and merry of heart—they drink no grog [rum] to stupefy and benumb the senses."[22]

Prim and proper Emma Willard, on the other hand, was rather put off by the loquacious sociability that wine encouraged at mealtime. Accustomed as she was to the silent religiosity with which genteel Americans consumed their meals, she wrote her sister of her disgust at the Frenchmen at her Le Havre inn's table d'hôte in 1830. "Oh! the deafening racket made by these Frenchmen," she wrote, "as they went on with their meal and became animated in their conversation. Such jabbering."[23]

The leisurely pace at which the French ate also contrasted with Americans' penchant for bolting their food and rushing from the table. (The American motto, said one European observer, should be "Gobble, Gulp, and Go."[24]) Tourists discovered that unlike American inns, where all of the dishes would be placed on the table at once and everyone plunged in at will, the dishes were served in at least three orderly courses. Generally, a first course of soups and other entrées was followed by one of roasts, and then dessert. "We were compelled to eat slowly or wait for some time upon others," L. J. Frazee wrote upon first encountering this in Le Havre. "While this would not suit one of our western men who is for doing everything in a minute," he noted, it did help digestion by giving one time to chew the food. It also allowed foods to be served fresh from the oven, something which was "of no small moment to the epicure."[25] After eating "a great quantity" at a "very good" table d'hôte at his Marseille hotel, Amos Lawrence noted another advantage. "Eating one thing at a time enables one to consume an immense quantity if it be done in good order of meats first, without feeling oppressed."[26]

— —

Until the railroad pushed through to Le Havre in 1847, arriving in the Channel ports also provided the first taste of France's unique contribution to comfortable overland travel—the *diligence*. Two stories high, with three separate compartments, these lumbering wagons had been the workhorses of the French interurban transportation system since the mid-eighteenth century. Until the 1820s, most diligences carried eight paying passengers, six in the two lower compartments and two in the upper compartment, or *cabriolet*, which was the one preferred by Sterne and other tourists who wanted a good view.[27] As roads improved, diligences grew more enormous—fifteen to eighteen passengers in four compartments became the norm—and more comfortable. Smaller, faster, and more expensive stagecoaches would clatter past them, but their occupants were cramped together, shaken to the bone, and often choked on dust. Amos Lawrence's stagecoach never stopped for more than twenty minutes in the day and two nights it took to go from Paris to Lyon. Its lurching caused him to knock over a fellow passenger's wine bottle, spilling the contents on the floor. He developed a stomachache but, he wrote, "we have no time to get out to relieve ourselves."[28] Meanwhile, the ungainly diligences would lumber along at three or four miles-per-hour, allowing passengers to munch on some food, sip some wine, walk alongside, admire the scenery, and relieve themselves at will in the surrounding fields. At night, as the wagon swayed gently, they stretched out and slept peacefully on soft cushions.[29] "I would rather travel in a commodious French diligence than be cramped up—and at peril—in the swiftest English coach," said the artist Thomas Cole.[30]

So pleasant and comfortable was this mode of transport that it lasted well into the railroad age, which began in 1837 in France. The fledgling railroad companies allowed travelers arriving in Dieppe, for example, to take the diligence to Rouen and then be transferred to the waiting railroad train for the four-hour trip to Paris.[31] It also worked the other way. In 1849, an excited James Clarke purchased a ticket on the diligence from Paris to Strasbourg. "When I mounted by a ladder to the top of the diligence," he wrote, "it seemed as if I were carried back to the days of Sterne and his Sentimental Journey." To his consternation, though, the vehicle then headed for the railroad station, where its wheels were removed and it was hoisted onto a flat-bed car. Then, with the crew and passengers still inside, it traveled the first forty miles, to Épernay, by rail. There the wheels were put back on, six horses were harnessed to it and, rather than progressing at Sterne's stately pace, it sped off down the newly macadamized road, with driver and conductor hollering, "going very fast, about 10 miles an hour."[32]

Over the course of the late eighteenth and early nineteenth centuries, there had been a profound transformation in what travelers saw, or rather, noticed, as they ambled along these roads. Despite their differences, Smollett, Sterne, and Jefferson were people whose ideas of what was beautiful were shaped by the heritage of the Renaissance and its reverence for the aesthetic ideals of Antiquity.[33] The seventeenth-century Grand Tourists had little appreciation for landscape of any kind. Travel through the countryside allowed them to switch off their visual faculties and bone up on the next civilized site on the itinerary. Eighteenth-century men such as Jefferson and Sterne had a heightened appreciation of landscapes, but their concepts of rural beauty still derived from the Classics, particularly the Roman poet Virgil. His emphasis on order and harmony was reflected in the works of the late-seventeenth-century French painters Nicolas Poussin and Claude Lorrain, which portrayed an ancient Golden Age of pastoral serenity. To Poussin, and particularly Claude, as he was called in England (where his work was greatly admired), beautiful scenery was composed of classical temples nestled amidst gentle hills of fertile farmland and pastures, interspersed perhaps with peaceful streams, ponds, and some gentle trees.[34]

By the later eighteenth century a newer view of what was "Picturesque" was coming to the fore. Untamed elements—patches of raw nature—began to intrude into the strictly proportioned ideal. Placid pastures and farmland were now partially obscured by trees, rocky outcroppings, or other natural features; hills and mountains became more prominent.[35] By the turn of the century the ruins of old castles and churches were finding their way into the scenery. Soon, tumble-down mills and decrepit peasants' cottages were adding a disheveled, untamed note.[36] In 1804, the young New Yorker Washington Irving took much the same route through the cultivated countryside of the southwest that Jefferson had so admired from his carriage-cum-canal boat some twenty-odd years earlier. Although he also enjoyed the journey, Irving's diary records his disappointment that "there is nothing of the wild and sublime to be seen."[37] By 1836, when George Putnam transversed the rolling Burgundian countryside whose neat hillside vineyards and ordered grain fields had so charmed Jefferson, something like a complete reversal had taken place. Nearly two-thirds of the journey from Paris to Lyon, wrote Putnam, was through wheat fields and vineyards, "affording no fine scenery."[38] Later, traveling from Paris to Dijon in 1850, young Katherine Lawrence noted one of the practical problems of the Picturesque: "We saw several picturesque and consequently tumble-down and dirty villages," she wrote in her diary.[39]

By 1800 the aesthetic ideal of the Sublime was supplanting the Picturesque. It was not really an ideal of beauty, but instead spoke of the emotions that sights should evoke. To experience the Sublime was to be put in touch with the mystery and power of the Deity. It was a spiritual experience evoked by encountering the immense force of uncontrollable Nature. To Edmund Burke, one of its chief theoreticians, confronting the Sublime should arouse "astonishment . . . with some degree of horror."[40]

One consequence of this was a wholesale reevaluation of the French and Swiss Alps, for few things impressed one more with Man's powerlessness in the face of God than viewing towering mountains and thundering waterfalls. Hitherto they had been regarded as a massively inconvenient barrier to the Arcadian valleys, clipped formal gardens, and Palladian mansions in Italy beyond. Now they became a major destination of their own, inspiring what Burke called the "inferior effects" of astonishment: "admiration, reverence, and respect."[41] Katherine Lawrence wrote of the Alps "looking frightfully large through the grey light. There is something terrific to me in mountains, something awful; they seem like supernatural creatures."[42] The first sight of them would set the spirits soaring. "After a journey of nearly three whole days and nights [from Paris to Geneva]," Francis Parkman wrote in his journal, "I was fatigued till I was within view of the Jura mountains, the sight of which refreshed me."[43] George Putnam's heart beat faster as his diligence finally began climbing out of the cultivated Rhône Valley into the French Alps. The view of the towering mountains, he wrote, was "unique in its wild sublimity."[44]

Putnam did note that, aside from the Alps, Europe could not compete with America when it came to "the beauties of nature." Even the Rhine could not hold a candle to the broad sweep of the Hudson or Connecticut rivers; when it came to the Sublime, nothing could match Niagara Falls.[45] Indeed, Americans in search of the Sublime at home were already gazing upon any number of mountains and waterfalls of the Appalachians.[46] But

America could not compete when it came to another Sublime experience: contemplating the ruins of previous eras. The remnants of medieval Europe—the crumbling castles, the overgrown remains of hulking Romanesque monasteries and decomposing High Gothic churches—had hardly interested Jefferson's generation at all. They regarded them as sad reminders of the barbaric times that followed the fall of Rome. By the early nineteenth century, though, as people began to admire the unruly, the irregular, and the unmanageable, the ruins of the past became reminders of the eternal forces of nature and of how transient human life was. Romanesque ruins now embodied the delicious forces of natural decay; Gothic architecture began to satisfy a thirst for "agreeable horror."[47] Governments responded by halting the wholesale destruction of old structures, such as the gigantic monastery at Cluny, whose stone was being sold to builders for new buildings. By the 1830s, professional restorers such as France's Viollet Le Duc and Prosper Mallarmé were systematically restoring Romanesque and Gothic sites to what they reckoned to be their former grandeur.[48]

The rise of these romantic notions undercut the idea that culture came from contemplating the rational, orderly remnants of the ancient and Renaissance worlds. When he first landed in Bordeaux, Washington Irving encountered two young New Yorkers returning from one of the last of the classic Grand Tours. Irving wrote his brother that one of them,

> a good hearted clever fellow but not "deep as a well," says he finds himself somewhat older than when he set out, but very little wiser, two thousand dollars out of pocket and not two thousand cents worth of wisdom in. . . . In Italy he got "completely sick of Antiquities and would not go a hundred yards to see the best of them."[49]

The fact that a young gentleman could so easily dismiss the bedrock of the previous generation's culture is indicative of how the old classical ideal was fading. However, it did not mean a loss of faith in the edifying value of continental touring itself. Irving embarked on a quite different tour, in which the search for the Picturesque in the French countryside and the Sublime among medieval ruins played a major role, but the ends remained those of original Grand Tour: to become a cultured person by exposing oneself to the best that Europe had to offer.

Despite the new view of the countryside, for most tourists the France that lay outside of Paris was merely something to be transversed on the way to more rewarding places—mainly Italy, the Alps, and Germany. After taking in the sights of Paris, tourists would hasten practically nonstop through Burgundy, and from there would either go up into the Alps or down the Rhône River valley, where they might stop for a night in Lyon before pushing on to Marseille and a boat to Italy. On the way to Marseille they might pause to look at the huge medieval Palace of the Popes in Avignon, but few would bother to take a detour to Nîmes, Orange, and Arles, whose Roman ruins had enthralled Jefferson. In the 1830s and 1840s, the overland route from Marseille to Italy through the independent County of Nice became popular, particularly with travelers who had their fill of seasickness on transatlantic and cross-Channel trips. On the way back from Italy, they would cross the Alps to Geneva and either head directly back to Paris or work their way down to the Rhine, returning to Paris via Strasbourg.[50] After another stay in Paris and perhaps a look at Brussels, it was back to America, usually via Le Havre or Liverpool.

Along the way, travelers would have only the most superficial contact with the people who lived in the French countryside. Even if they were among the very few who, like Jefferson, were interested in the living conditions of the poor, the rural villages through which they passed were hardly inviting. The trip from Paris to Lyon took one through "a score of petty villages, made up of the most uncouth and wretched huts imaginable," wrote Putnam.[51] "Pass many villages," Lawrence wrote during his 1839 coach trip from Paris to Lyon, "people dirty, villages dirty. All have wooden shoes. High walls and gates. No sidewalks." When high water briefly stopped the steamer taking him down the Rhône from Lyon to Marseille, he got off and walked around Serriers, a small town. "Dirty outskirts," he noted. "We cross bridge. Dirty town. Dirty, lousy people." That night they slept in Valence, a larger town, with "filthy streets."[52] Henry Humphrey, who traveled down the Rhône Valley the same year by diligence, recorded similar impressions. "The houses of the French peasants are mean, dirty, and look poor enough," he wrote in his diary. Later, the coach taking him from Marseille to Nice passed through "some dirty poor looking villages" in an area noted for "plunder and robbery" and stopped for refreshments in one of them. "The inhabitants looked capable of doing almost anything," he wrote, "and never shall I forget the group of those old hags among the beggars who gathered around the door of the inn as we alighted to ask alms."[53] Samuel Topliff thought of getting off the diligence from Strasbourg to Paris and staying over in Metz for a night, "but such was the filthy and disgusting appearance of the inn at which we stopped that I concluded to keep on," he wrote in his journal.[54]

However, there were some pleasant surprises. Rouen was a popular stopover on the way to Paris from the agreeable Channel ports. For many, it was their first encounter with a sizable French city and the great buildings of the glorious past. Local guides would take them into the narrow streets of the still-largely-medieval town, to the city hall, and thence to the enormous Gothic cathedral, whose huge towers, soaring nave, intricately carved front porch, and acres of stained glass, would evoke sighs of "sublime," and then to the beautiful Gothic church of Saint-Ouen.[55] The tour would end with a visit to the chapel in which Joan of Arc was condemned as a heretic in 1431, and the market square in which she was burned.[56] Charles Sumner was so impressed by his two days in Rouen that as soon as he arrived in Paris he wrote a friend: "My voyage has already been compensated for—sea-sickness, time, money, and all—many times over. It was fully paid for in Rouen."[57]

Contemplating Joan of Arc's fate in the market square could evoke some contradictory emotions. On the one hand, Americans not far removed from their own war of independence could sympathize with Joan's crusade to throw the English out of her country. The tale of the brave and presumably blonde young virgin whose religious faith inspired in her such devotion to justice also played well with the American belief in the moral purity of fair-skinned virginal women.[58] "It seemed a place both cursed and blessed—cursed by the brutality of man, blessed by the angelic purity of the maiden," James Clarke wrote to his wife back in Boston.[59] The fly in the ointment, for Protestant Americans, was the French explanation of the events, which accepted the maiden's claim to have conversed with God and other miraculous events.[60]

These difficulties were part of much larger problems American tourists had with politics in pre-1848 France. Napoléon Bonaparte's assumption of dictatorial powers in 1796, followed by his crowning himself emperor, snuffed out what little sympathy remained for the Revolution after the Reign of Terror in 1793. France was thought to be living in a kind of post-Revolutionary miasma. When Washington Irving arrived in Montpellier in 1804 he was surprised at the "vivacity and gaiety of heart that distinguished the French," for he had been told that it had been "much impaired by the revolution."[61] Napoléon's military successes helped revive ancient denunciations of France as a morally decadent despotism, particularly by Federalists trying to tar the Jeffersonians as traitors in its service. America's declaration of war on Britain in 1812 did little for Napoléon's popularity in America, as warnings against allying with the decadent French and their dictator were sounded from all sides. The President of Yale College delivered a series of sermons denouncing the French as (both) atheists and "Romish." They welcomed military despotism and were hopelessly mired in immorality, he said. He concluded by shouting, "Touch not the unclean thing!"[62] The restoration of the Bourbons to the monarchy in 1814 did nothing to improve France's political image in America; American newspapers labeled them dimwitted British puppets. (The Baltimore postmaster delivered a July 4 oration in which he called the Bourbon king "an imbecile tyrant.")[63]

The liberal Marquis de Lafayette adroitly cultivated this disgust. As a dashing young officer, he had led the first French troops to come to General Washington's side and had established himself as the most attractive symbol of French support for American independence. The wily aristocrat now played the American connection for all it was worth. Practically every American visitor to Paris was invited to Tuesday soirées at his Paris mansion and to La Grange, his country estate. He would show them his collection of American memorabilia—portraits and busts of American political leaders, Benjamin Franklin's cane, George Washington's umbrella, a chair cushion woven by Martha Washington. His own beautiful cane, he would point out, was carved out of wood from the apple tree under which he and General Washington breakfasted on the morning of one of the great battles of the Revolutionary War. He was a regular speaker at American residents' Fourth of July and Washington's Birthday dinners, where their hearts would go out to the man who helped bring liberty to their country but could not do so in his own.[64] In 1824 he undertook a triumphal tour of the United States, where he was hailed as representing the spirit of Liberty, the Rights of Man, and constitutional government, all of which were sadly missing in Bourbon France.[65]

Because Lafayette was one of its leaders, the July 1830 revolution overthrowing the Bourbons evoked considerable enthusiasm in America. American orators hailed a "redeemed, regenerated France," the tricolor was again unfurled, and in some places crowds even sang the Marseillaise, in French and English.[66] New Yorkers organized a tremendous celebration, including a two-and-half-mile-long parade, surpassing almost anything the city had ever seen.[67] But Lafayette fell out with the new regime, and Louis-Philippe, the Duc d'Orléans, who became constitutional monarch, gained few admirers in America, even though he had spent some years in exile in Boston (living, it is said, in the building that now houses the Union Oyster House).

The republican uprising that forced his regime out in 1848 was initially greeted favorably in America, but this reaction was soon tempered by fears that the revolt was kindling the fires of socialism. After so many upheavals, the French were thought of as a morally spineless people doomed to political instability, something visiting Americans explained by citing everything from extreme weather conditions to Catholicism.[68] Emerson, who had been in Paris during the insurrection, wrote in his journal that he thought as "old Adams and Jay" did about the French, "that they have no morale."[69] The election of Napoléon Bonaparte's nephew Louis-Napoléon as president in 1849 seemed to bear out the prediction of the American newspaper the *National Intelligencer* that the French would turn to any man who promised them military glory. Sure enough, Louis-Napoléon met little opposition when he staged a coup d'état in December 1851 and arranged a referendum that paved the way for his assuming the title of "emperor" the next year. In America, the collapse of the republic was widely regarded as proof that the French were indeed incapable of self-government.[70]

Understandably, then, few Americans touring France thought that, when it came to politics, France offered anything but negative examples. Post-Revolutionary visits to Versailles would evoke astonishment at the scale of inequality under the Old Regime. In 1796, the young Jeffersonian William Lee wrote that its luxuries "would make even a man accustomed to a luxurious life style sigh at the depravity of human nature, and weep for the misery millions of his fellow creatures must endure to support the vices of a set of robbers, generally called nobles."[71] For the next fifty-odd years, American visitors would continue to see the class-ridden Old World as an object-lesson in the negative effects of inequality. Most thought it might do well to imitate their own brave new experiment in human governance. Liberal French people reinforced this feeling. "You are the advance guard of the human race," Madame de Staël said to Charles Ticknor in 1817.[72] In the preface to his 1838 guidebook, George Putnam warned touring American not to let their knowledge of their country's superiority turn them into braggarts.[73]

It was not that France had no redeeming socio-political qualities. Even under the restored Bourbons, the French seemed remarkably democratic in the way they related to each other, particularly when compared to the class-obsessed English. The Bostonian Samuel Topliff thought they were more like Americans—that is, affable and sociable—than were the English.[74] George Bancroft contrasted the French readiness to allow "every stranger" into their art collections and libraries with English restrictions in this regard.[75] The Revolution of 1830, which at least put equality back on the French political agenda, helped make French society even more acceptable in many Americans' eyes. Theodore Sedgwick III noted in his diary in 1836 that England's "Social Condition" was "only fit for the feudal ages," whereas in France "the spirit of social equality reigns over the land."[76]

Some even thought that Americans could learn a thing or two in this regard from the French. John Doyle noted "the apparent uniformity of condition that seemed to pervade this community" when he arrived in Calais in 1840. "I thought," he wrote in his diary, "that here I saw for the first time a specimen of that to *us* ideal thing called Republicanism."[77] Americans often remarked on how in Paris people of different classes mingled together in public places in a manner that was rare in America. "The French are by nature . . . more democratic than us," George Emerson wrote in his diary. "The different ranks in society associate together on much more easy terms."[78]

Also surprising was France's apparent color-blindness. After the French Revolution, which abolished slavery in France, and the 1848 revolution, which extended freedom to the slaves in its West Indian colonies, it was not uncommon for blacks and mulattos, such as the writers Alexandre Dumas and son, to gain acceptance in virtually all levels of society. L. J. Frazee was surprised to find that, "It is not uncommon here to see white ladies hanging to a negro's arm in the streets, to see negroes attending lectures at schools; in fact no distinction is made here in regard to color."[79] Charles Sumner was profoundly affected when he attended a lecture on legal history at the Sorbonne in 1838. "I noted," he wrote in his diary,

> two or three blacks or rather mulattoes—two-thirds black perhaps—dressed quite à la mode, and having the easy, jaunty air of young men of fashion, who were well received by their fellow-students. They were standing within a knot of students and their color seemed to be no objection to them. I was glad to see this; though, with American impressions, it seemed very strange. It must be, then, that the distance between free blacks and whites among us is derived from education, and does not exist in the nature of things.[80]

Later, arguing against racially segregated schools before the Massachusetts Supreme Court, he said, "At the School of Law in Paris I have sat for weeks on the same benches with colored pupils, listening, like myself, to the learned lectures . . . ; nor do I remember in the throng of sensitive young men, feeling anything toward them but companionship and respect."[81]

Americans were also surprised to discover that many less-educated French people had come to believe that all Americans were black.[82] In 1854, Andrew White befriended an *"ouvrier"* in Normandy who, he noted in his diary, thought "we could hardly be Americans for we were white."[83] What was most extraordinary, though, was discovering that, as L. J. Frazee noted in 1844, Americans were "not the less thought of by them, from being considered black, as they have no objection to color."[84]

White Southerners naturally tended to deal with race more elliptically. The same year that Sumner sat beside blacks for the first time at the Sorbonne, the South Carolina planter James Hammond wrote home complaining that French egalitarianism discouraged the lower orders from acting deferentially toward their superiors.[85] In 1851, during the short-lived Second Republic, the Georgian Catherine Jones complained in her diary that "there seems to be little exclusiveness, all classes mixed. Perhaps the French regard this as a feature of their *republicanism, bah!*" There were far too many "idlers" about "for a republic to prosper." Moreover, "the *drudgery* is all done by women," making it "a most complete burlesque of a republic."[86]

— —

The more they found to admire in France, the more tourists felt constrained to remind themselves that it was still part of the manifestly unequal aristocratic Old World. It was a sign of the immaturity of both the new nation and its tourists that they would repeatedly admonish themselves to resist its superficial temptations and return to their homeland with a heightened appreciation for the blessings of their own system. George Putnam's travel guide ends with the typical observation that although he saw much to admire and imitate in Europe, he saw more that convinced him that "we are, or ought to be, the happiest people in the world."[87] Emma Willard assured her students back in Troy, New York, that visiting France inevitably made one feel prouder to be an American.[88]

It is ironic, perhaps, that in 1837, both Charles Sumner and James Hammond, two future leaders of opposite sides in the conflict over slavery in America, found that visiting France and Europe heightened their

American patriotism. Twenty-six-year-old Sumner, the future antislavery Senator from Massachusetts, wrote a Harvard law professor at the outset of his three-month stay in Paris that he intended "to return *an American. . . .* I shall return with an increased love for my country, and added admiration for its institutions." After his first month in Paris, he wrote a friend extolling its attractions, but added, "Although I have seen much to interest and instruct me I have seen nothing which has weakened my attraction to my country." Three months later, he wrote the professor, "I have never loved my country so ardently as since I left it." He contrasted America's "universality of happiness, the absence of beggary, reasonable equality of men," and "high moral tone" with France, "where wealth flaunts side by the side of the most squalid poverty, where your eyes are constantly annoyed by the most disgusting want and wretchedness, and where American purity is inconceivable."[89]

For Hammond, the young Southern slave-owner who, as Senator from South Carolina, would later confront Sumner on the Senate floor in the final clashes before Secession, returning to America after fifteen months in Europe brought a surprising surge of American patriotism. As his ship entered New York's magnificent harbor he thought that, even after Europe's marvels, "I had never seen anything so fine." Tears welled up in his eyes at the sight of the Stars and Stripes and, he wrote in his diary, "I felt I never loved my country so much. I wondered that I had ever felt otherwise and was conscience stricken for the sin of having at times heretofore wavered in my affection for her."[90]

Admittedly, the twin scourges of long-distance travel—homesickness and hemorrhoids—had limited Hammond's appreciation of Europe. Others, like Sumner, had to struggle harder to benefit from France's "refinements" without becoming ensnared in its decadent class system. In January 1842, James Colles wrote his teenage son back in New York of how impressed he was to be presented at court to the King, whom he found a sympathetic person. He then hastened to add that "there is no country yet in my opinion like our own dear native land. We have not as much of refinement, but more of *everything* that is good."[91] After midcentury, as we shall see, it would become quite unfashionable for Americans in France to express opinions such as this.

Five

"THE ATHENS OF MODERN EUROPE"

Central to the "refinement" that Colles thought America lacked was what we now think of as "high culture." There was no question that pre-1850 Paris offered tourists a cultural feast that was simply unavailable in the United States.[1] The French theater was regarded as the best in the world.[2] Even those who could barely understand the language were delighted by the light touch of the ageless Mademoiselle Mars—the favorite of both Napoléon and King Louis XVIII—performing Molière at the Théâtre Français (later Comédie Française). Seeing her was "a treat I shall never forget," Charles Sumner wrote a friend in 1838. "Her voice was like a silver fruit, her eye like a gem."[3] The tragic depths plumbed by her successor, Rachel, in Racine's plays made her the most acclaimed dramatic actress of the nineteenth century. "She surpasses my hopes," Margaret Fuller wrote a friend in 1848. "There is nothing like her voice; she speaks the language of the Gods."[4]

The Opéra de l'Académie Royale continued to stage ponderous old French five-act operas that were famed for their spectacular scenery and, increasingly, their ballets. Samuel Topliff wrote his family in Boston in 1829 that the dancing was undoubtedly the finest in the world. "I have seen upwards of two hundred in a ballet on the stage at one time," he said, "moving simultaneously together . . . , any one of whom would be considered in Boston a first rate dancer."[5] In the 1830s, the famed ballerina Taglioni turned the ballet into its major attraction. On his last evening in Paris in 1836 Philip Hone was bored by the opera, *The Siege of Corinth,* but was bowled over by her "genius" when she then danced *Les Sylphides.* "The perfection of grace and beauty," he wrote in his diary, was "something *between earth and heaven.*"[6] The next year, George Putnam wrote of her: "What a bound was that! Surely she is not of flesh and blood! Such airy lightness—such exquisite grace—the very 'poetry of motion.'"[7]

The Opéra des Italiens featured exciting newer works by composers such as Rossini, while the Opéra-Comique put on lighter operettas.[8] On the very light side, there were diversions such as the Cirque Olympique, Hippodrome, and the Vaudeville. The diaries of John Gardner and Theodore Sedgwick, Jr., both rich young men from Boston, bear witness to their attraction to Americans. In 1823, the nineteen-year-old Gardner went to the Théâtre Français, the Opéra Royal, Théâtre du Café de la Paix, and vaudeville-type shows almost every night of his first ten nights in Paris.[9] "The evening need never hang heavy on the stranger's hands," Ralph Waldo Emerson wrote in his journal ten years later. "More than twenty theaters are blazing with light and echoing with fine music every night, . . . not to mention concerts, gardens, and shows innumerable."[10]

It was, however, the most visible things—France's architecture and urban amenities—that made the greatest impression on Americans. It is difficult to imagine how impoverished early-nineteenth-century America was on this score. One of Jefferson's arguments for using the Maison Carrée as the model for the Virginia state house was that there was hardly a public building in America worth looking at. The next fifty years brought little improvement on that score. The new state capitols were generally unimpressive structures in one-horse towns. There were some beautiful churches, but by European standards they were rather modest efforts. In 1828, after his first European tour, James Fenimore Cooper wrote his brother,

> I do not know of a single edifice in the Union that can be considered more than third rate, by its size and ornaments; not more than one or two that ought to be ranked even so high. . . . There is no city in our republic that does not decidedly have the air and habits of a provincial town.[11]

As for streetscapes, the art critic Robert Hughes has observed that the general aesthetic atmosphere of the early republic was a lot like "Dogpatch," the mythical hillbilly shanty-town in the comic strip "L'il Abner." Average Americans lived in "makeshift wooden structures that were the ancestors of today's trailer home, only far worse built."[12]

Nor was there much that was old and historic in America. When Charles Sumner stepped off the boat in Le Havre, the first thing that struck him was that "everything was old; and yet to me everything was new. Every building I passed seemed to have its history." In the United States, there was "none of the prestige of age about anything." It had "no history."[13] Even the graveyards in America did not seem very old. Cooper remarked that the monuments to the dead in Rouen cathedral "possessed great interest to those who had never stood over a grave of more than two centuries and rarely even over one of half that age."[14] Nor could anything in America approach the great cathedral itself, which an awed George Sumner noted was "said to be the finest specimen of Gothic architecture on the continent."[15] Emma Willard said, "I had heard of fifty or a hundred years being spent in the erection of a building and I had often wondered how it could be; but when I saw the outside of this majestic and venerable temple, the doubt ceased."[16] Not only was the soaring architecture astounding, but the skilled stonework was utterly new to Americans. In America, no building bore any stone carving at all; the only substantial carved stones Willard had seen back home were gravestones.[17] It was only when Henry Ward Beecher visited Europe in 1850 and saw real carved stone on buildings that he realized that all the building embellishments he had seen in America were made of wood, carved and painted to look like stone.[18]

In America, cities had swelled haphazardly, their shape governed by commercial considerations. The newer city streets tended to be laid out in straight lines, lined with commercial buildings pressing onto narrow, crowded sidewalks, with no space for trees such as those that graced Paris's boulevards. Parks and gardens for leisurely walking were few and far between. Until the 1850s, the only public place in New York City where one could stroll amidst some greenery was in the small park around the Battery, at the tip of the island. The rest of the city's waterfront, like that of the other major ports, was for commerce, not strolling.[19] After seeing Europe, James Fenimore Cooper condemned "the miserable and minute subdivisions" of American cities, where property developers had prevented the establishment of parks and gardens.[20] The young Cincinnatian Louis Cazenove, whose home town's riverfront was the usual jumble of commercial establishments and shipping, wrote his mother how impressed he was that Rouen, also a river port, had "a beautiful avenue of lofty trees which runs along the river and serves for a delightful promenade."[21]

But it was Paris, which the Alabama plantation owner William Raser called "this Metropolis of the World, this Wonder of the Universe," that harbored France's most impressive urban sights.[22] This was often not immediately apparent. After all, Paris's beauty owes hardly anything to its site—a turgid river meandering through some mudflats. Everything that makes it attractive is man-made, and until midcentury much of the city was not particularly beguiling. Aside from some new streets constructed under Napoléon, much of Paris in 1830 did not look all that different than it did in 1682, when Louis XIV decamped to Versailles.[23] Most of its eight hundred thousand inhabitants lived in old four- or five-story buildings crowded around dank interior courtyards. The homes of the wealthy were concealed behind high walls and stables. Passers-by on the narrow streets, most of which were only about fifteen to twenty feet wide, saw only large wooden doors and dirty stone walls. No wonder travelers were often disappointed by their first impressions. George Putnam wrote that "the narrow, filthy streets, with gutters in the center, and without side-walks, and the antique and irregular buildings, do not realize my notions of gay, elegant Paris."[24] As Emma Willard's diligence creaked past its northern gate, she "looked in vain in this quarter for the imposing objects I had fancied." The streets "seemed anything but the elegant Paris of my imagination."[25] To Caroline Cushing it seemed "dingy and somber . . . very far from elegant and pleasing to the eye."[26] The primitive sewage system, which did not suffer major improvements until the 1830s, continued to cause disgusting problems, and the carriages would spray the sewage in the central gutters onto pedestrians.[27]

However, once they reached their hotels, the prospect would improve, for they were usually situated on the Right Bank, near the Palais-Royal, rue de Rivoli, the Tuileries gardens, and the famed boulevards.[28] There, in what one of them called "the very Center of Fashion," a new world of ultra-civilized living opened up before their provincial eyes.[29] "The extent and magnificence of the *public* buildings, palaces, gardens, parks, boulevards, etc., are enough to atone for the dirty streets," said Putnam in his 1836 guidebook for Americans. "The general view of the city is imposing in the extreme. The luxurious and superb architecture . . . and the *immense extent,* as well as the great beauty and elegance, of the gardens and parks . . . must astonish even the most sanguine."[30]

The Palais-Royal was the usual starting point for seeing the city. Indeed, to its more hyperbolic enthusiasts, it was "the capital of Paris," its "heart, soul, and brain."[31] The king's brother, the Duke of Orléans, had acquired the palace from the king in the eighteenth century and turned the tract of land behind it into a real estate development. A large rectangular park was enclosed by fine four-story neoclassical buildings that overhung a walkway lined with colonnades.[32] By 1789, five years after its completion, it had become *the* center of tourists' Paris. They would stay in nearby hotels, lounge in its cafés, read the journals on its lawn, buy presents in its luxurious little shops, dine in its restaurants and patronize its gambling houses and bordellos.[33] By the 1820s these services had been so rearranged that each of its levels seemed to service a different human need. The ground floor was occupied by shops, cafés, and journal-vendors, the second floor by gambling houses and restaurants, and the third and fourth floors, originally planned as high-class apartments, lodged bordellos.[34] As visitors such as George Putnam rarely failed to mention, "a specimen of everything, good and bad" was on offer.[35] Although the complex went into a decline after the 1830s, when gambling was suppressed, legalized prostitution spread elsewhere, and new cafés and shops on the boulevards outshone its old war-horses, it continued impressing American visitors for many years to come.[36]

The boulevards had originated in the late seventeenth century, when Louis XIV ordered a vast new wall built around the expanded perimeter of the city. The older inner fortifications were turned into wide avenues lines with double rows of trees. In the later eighteenth century, Louis XVI ordered a new outer wall built, and large stretches of Louis XIV's wall was turned into boulevards. The older boulevards in the northern and western parts of the city were paved in cobblestone and large mansions were constructed along them, making them popular places for upper-class carriage rides.[37] In the early nineteenth century they were embellished with wide sidewalks and gas lighting. Attractive shops, cafés, restaurants, and other entertainments replaced most of the mansions, attracting crowds of shoppers, vendors, jugglers, revelers, demimondaines, and prostitutes. The boulevard "is certainly the best place in the world to amuse oneself in," the Reverend James Clarke wrote his wife. "You have only to put on your hat and walk into the street to find entertainment."[38] According to Putnam's rather pusillanimous guidebook for Americans, the boulevards, along with the rue de Rivoli and three or four other avenues, were "the only streets which do credit to the city."[39]

Still, for promenading, the crown jewel of post-Revolutionary Paris was the vast stretch of gardens and parkland that ran from the Tuileries palace up the Champs-Élysées toward the Bois de Boulogne, the well-tended woods on the edge of town. The Tuileries palace, which was destroyed in 1871, ran perpendicular to the Seine between what are now the two long east-west wings of the Louvre. Tourists usually began their promenades through the city in the large, sculpture-filled garden on its western side, which had been a popular place for strolling even before the

Revolution.[40] "Here," Thomas Appleton wrote in his journal, "gold-fishes leap from their circular oceans to the sun; there Apollo strains the monster python. A hundred statues appear through the trees."[41] They could then walk to the stone embankment that Napoléon had constructed along the Seine and, as James Clarke did (and countless other still love to do), walk over the iron Pont des Arts to the Left Bank of the Seine. There, Clarke wrote, "you loiter and look as much as you choose" among the stalls of the *bouquinistes,* the second-hand booksellers, that still line the embankment.[42] Most tourists, however, would walk westward from the gardens to the splendid place de la Révolution (or "place Louis XV" or "place de la Concorde"—the name changed with the regime, but it was always fixed in tourists' minds as the place where the Revolutionary guillotine stood). They then headed up the wide Champs-Élysées, where elegant restaurants, dance halls, puppeteers, and other amusements were nestled in the greenery, toward the Étoile, the grand plaza a mile and a half away. There the Arc de Triomphe rose intermittently until it was finally completed in 1836, providing the standard tourist's bird's-eye view until the completion of Gustave Eiffel's tower in 1889. Beyond the Étoile, the horses and carriages of the tonier set prevailed on the roads that crisscrossed the Bois de Boulogne, the former royal hunting park.

By the mid-1830s, few visiting Americans would have disputed the notation that young Francis Parkman made in his diary soon after arriving in Paris. An uncle had just taken him to the Tuileries gardens, the Palais-Royal, the Boulevard des Italiens, and the elegant place Vendôme, where lovely, classical-style mansions were grouped around a towering column celebrating Napoléon's victories. "Let envious Englishmen sneer as they will," he wrote, "this is the Athens of Modern Europe."[43] The artist Thomas Cole agreed. He contrasted the "very light appearance" of Paris's buildings with the smoke-blackened ones of London, calling the Parisian ones "magnificent, and far superior in number and beauty than those of London."[44] John Sanderson saw a much starker contrast. "The Frenchman seeks his recreation in the dance, the theatre, in the pure air of his gardens," he wrote, "whilst the Englishman skulks into his gin-shop."[45]

The great complex at Versailles, meanwhile, suffered some ups and downs. The Revolution opened its gates even further than had Louis XVI, turning its park into a beautiful public pleasure ground. In 1796, the American artists John Vanderlyn wrote his brother that the park was of a "beauty and grandeur I cannot describe. The imagination cannot conceive anything so enchanting."[46] However, Napoléon shunned Versailles in favor of the palace at Fontainebleau, to the south of Paris. The park became overgrown, the statues crumbled, the fountains fell into disrepair, and the buildings, emptied of treasures, decayed. The restored Bourbon, Louis XVIII, realizing that Versailles still symbolized the waste and remoteness from the people that had contributed to his family's overthrow, installed his court in Paris, in the Tuileries palace. However, he decorated Versailles's buildings with some paintings and sculpture from the royal collection, restored parts of the garden, and re-established the expensive custom of pumping up the great old fountains for special occasions. When Lucey Bakewell Audubon, wife of the famed bird-illustrator, visited Versailles in June 1831, shortly after the Bourbons were ousted, she found the extent and beauty of the gardens "beyond conception."[47] Louis-Philippe continued to improve it, transforming part of the main building into a museum of French history. Paintings and sculptures from the royal collection were now supplemented by huge canvasses that were commissioned from the nation's top painters, depicting great moments in the history of the nation. When Frazee saw it in 1844 he thought that it must be the largest single collection of paintings in the world.[48]

Ultimately, though, the great post-Revolutionary artistic shrine was the museum in the Louvre, the old palace in the historic center of Paris. Like other princely collections, the original royal collection was meant to impress visitors with the owner's wealth and taste, so it had been moved from there to Versailles with Louis XIV. In 1750, Louis XV was persuaded to make the collection accessible to *amateurs* and art students, who needed masterpieces to copy. He had one hundred and ten paintings shipped to the Luxembourg Palace, on Paris's Left Bank. Young King Louis XIII's mother, Marie de Médicis, had built that beautiful Renaissance-style palace, and the bombastic series of twenty-four paintings of her life she commissioned from Peter Paul Rubens was already on public display there.[49] The addition of the royal collection made the gallery a standard sight for foreign visitors.[50]

In 1779, however, the new king, Louis XVI, gave the Luxembourg Palace to his younger brother, and plans were made to refurbish the now-run-down Louvre and move the royal collection back there.[51] The royal authorities were still dithering over the project thirteen years later, when the Revolutionary government appropriated the royal collection. It rushed the Louvre project to completion, with a twofold aim: to preserve the collection as an example of greatness of the French nation and to provide a vehicle for "public instruction." The two cornerstones of the modern museum—conservation and education—were thus laid, and the Louvre became the model for all public art museums to follow.

The immense sixteenth-century Grand Gallery, which stretched for almost 450 yards (twice its present length) along the Seine, became the museum's spectacular centerpiece.[52] In 1796, when John Vanderlyn first visited it, the finest works from the ex-royal collection were already installed there, supplemented by masterpieces confiscated from the Church and nobility. He wrote his brother that it was longer than the entire main street in their home town of Kingston, New York. "One is in raptures," he wrote, "gazing upon the works of . . . Titian, Rubens, Poussin, etc."[53]

Napoléon took a particular interest in the museum, characteristically changing its name to the Musée Napoléon and filling it with booty stripped from the places he conquered. In 1798, Vanderlyn wrote of the excitement that accompanied the exhibition of the first batch of masterpieces from Italy. "It is a superb collection," he wrote. "To acquire knowledge of the arts, there is but one Paris."[54] Napoléon's subsequent victories over the Prussians and Hapsburgs provided hundreds of additional Old Masters. The suppression of the monasteries in French-controlled Italy provided an infusion of medieval works, which the Louvre's director welcomed as "primitive" pictures to give it "that historical dimension which a true museum must have."[55] The restored Bourbons returned some of this loot to monarchs who had supported them, but made up for this by purchasing antiquities and encouraging their aristocratic supporters to donate art works to what was again the royal museum.

By 1830, then, the Louvre undoubtedly contained the most impressive assemblage of great painting and sculpture in the Western world. The Grand Gallery alone, now lit by glass sky lights, housed over fourteen hundred paintings, with larger ones above and the smaller below. These were organized, pedagogically, into schools—French, German, Flemish and Italian—with the works in each school arranged chronologically, so that viewers could study their historical development.[56] The fabulous collection of antiquities was concentrated in vast galleries below the Grand Gallery. Their high vaulted ceilings alone, adorned with new frescoes, took the breath away from Americans, who were unaccustomed to such lofty ceilings.[57] Now, no trip to Paris was complete without a visit to the Louvre and no visit to the Louvre was complete without remarking on the enormity of the collection and the impossibility of taking it all in.

— —

The Louvre was particularly impressive for Americans because, as the Philadelphian John Sanderson wrote from Paris in 1835, "in our country, we have nothing yet to show in the way of great works of art."[58] Until the 1830s, practically the only older paintings Americans saw were the solemn portraits that adorned seats of government and the homes of the wealthy.[59] This kind of portraiture was regarded as the least demanding form of painting, hardly requiring the genius required by great history, religious or landscape pictures. Americans studying great artists therefore had to rely on black-and-white engravings. As for sculpture, there were some plaster casts of ancient works, but these were no match for the originals carved in marble. "How unlike the plaster copies!" Thomas Appleton exclaimed in his diary after seeing two familiar sculptures in the Louvre.[60] Charles Sumner wrote a friend after visiting the Louvre, "You can imagine my feelings ... when you think that Mr. Sears's house was my [idea] of a palace, the Athenaeum Gallery, of a collection of paintings, and the plaster casts in the Athenaeum reading-room and Felton's study, of a collection of antiques."[61]

Later in the century, as we shall see, the bored American husband being dragged through the Louvre by his culture-vulture wife became an object of derision. However, in the early years of the century the old aristocratic notion persisted that an appreciation of fine art was man's rightful domain. Young upper-class men in the new republic were told that developing good taste would elevate them above the barbarism of their materialistic society and enable them to lead their uncivilized countrymen out of darkness. This meant mastering the canons of Enlightenment "taste" in painting and sculpture—that is, to prize works that displayed proportion, perspective, balance, and restraint.[62]

Acquiring and displaying one's "taste" was therefore serious business. The 1792 journal of Robert Johnson, one of the last of the classic Grand Tourists, refers repeatedly to taste and proportion in art and architecture: Versailles "could only have been affected by genius and taste assisted by absolute power." Les Invalides, the military pensioners' home, "does honor to the taste and humanity of Lewis [sic] the Fourteenth." The paintings galleries at the palace of Saint-Cloud are "admirably proportioned. Those at Chantilly and Versailles [are] too long for the breadth," and so on.[63]

When Philip Hone retired from business in 1821 to devote himself to breaching New York's highest social circles, he worked assiduously at cultivating his taste in art. He read up on it and traveled to Europe to expose himself to it. Upon his return, he gained invitations to view private collections and became a fixture at every major art exhibition. He was soon delivering confident assessments of how well various American painters had mastered "the principles of art."[64] On his second trip to Europe, in 1836, he prided himself on "having more taste for pictures" than he had on his first trip, at the beginning of his quest for status.[65]

The older upper class tended to collect Old Masters, while some of the newer entrants into that class, notably Hone, supplemented these with works by American artists such as Thomas Cole. However, all the collectors shared one characteristic: they were male.[66] Since patriarchal marriage laws mean that it was a rare woman who had much property at her sole disposal, this is not at all surprising. But there was more to it than that. Post–American Revolution education for women, where it existed, concentrated on preparing them for their future domestic responsibilities, particularly as moral guardians of the home. The thought of training women to appreciate the art of Europe in the rigorously intellectual manner prescribed at the time was practically out of the question. Although the first female academies (high schools) occasionally taught drawing and painting with watercolors, it was as a useful art, like embroidery.[67] Thus few women tourists could match upper-class males when it came to art appreciation. Agnes Mayo played a leading role in founding the first female academy in Virginia, yet the long journal she kept of her trip to France in 1829 with her two married daughters, both graduates of the academy, has virtually nothing in it about art. The only opinion she ventures is a second-hand one.[68]

Prudery also kept early-nineteenth-century American women from appreciating much of France's fine art. In America, women rarely saw nudity in art. On the rare occasions when plaster casts of European nudes were exhibited in public, American moralists demanded that the galleries bar them or admit them only at special women-only times.[69] It comes as no surprise, then, that although she loved the Tuileries gardens, Emma Willard was shocked by the nude statues (mainly of females) which adorned it. She wrote to the students back in her women's academy,

> If your mother and father were here, I would leave you sitting on these
> shaded benches and conduct them through the walks, and they would

return and bid you depart for our own America, where the eye of modesty is not publicly affronted, and where virgin delicacy can walk abroad without a blush.[70]

James Fenimore Cooper, on the other hand, was disgusted to see an American man and two women pass one of the nude statues "and their bursts of laughter, running and hiding their faces, and loud giggling, left no one in ignorance of the cause of their extreme bashfulness. Thousands of both sexes pass daily beneath the same statue, without a thought of its nudity, and it is looked upon as a noble piece of sculpture."[71]

Modern French painting, which in the 1830s and 1840s was full of curvaceous nude or semi-nude women reclining, gamboling, or dying flesh-exposing deaths, also offended many American women. They would usually encounter it in the gallery of the Luxembourg Palace, which was by then devoted to the work of living artists. It "certainly affords ground for the popular idea that the *nude* is necessarily the indecent," wrote Mrs. Caroline Kirkland after visiting there in 1848. "If all art were like modern French art, I should be willing to see it swept from the earth for ever."[72]

French interior decoration provided no respite, for it too seemed to present naked bosoms, buttocks, thighs, and legs at every turn. When Emma Willard attended a big party in a rich businessman's new mansion on the place Vendôme she noted that as one entered or left "this elegant abode of pleasure" one had to pass a statue of a nude Venus crouching at the foot of the splendid staircase. "But things of this kind are so frequent in France there is no avoiding them," she sighed. "One of M. Schickler's rooms is ornamented with a Venus, or some other naked beauty, painted in fresco, a thousand times repeated, in various attitudes."[73]

Dead painters, whose works could be hung in the Louvre, fared little better. After all, the pictures of French eighteenth-century artists such as Fragonard, Watteau, and Bouchard of the semi-naked Ancients or the high-born frolicking in the fields were, in a sense, the soft-core porn of the time. Emma Willard would likely have agreed with the American man who ascribed Paris's high rate of illegitimacy to the paintings in the Louvre.[74] Many of them were "fit only for the abodes of pollution," she wrote, and were "enough to demoralize a city." As for the sculpture galleries, she was not ashamed to admit she had not set foot in them, she said. "I should rather be ashamed to say that I had."[75]

Male visitors were not immune to prudery, but the importance that they placed in engaging the art on an aesthetic level helped overcome it.[76]

Charles Sumner remarked in his diary that the paintings at the Luxembourg "seem to be of an extremely sensuous character; the forms of women are displayed with great freedom, and the most careful tints invest them with more than flesh-like attractiveness" but he was "unwilling . . . to fall in with the current which sets itself against the present school."[77] The young, recently widowed ex-preacher Ralph Waldo Emerson was extremely prudish with regard to sex, yet so keen was he to develop his aesthetic sense during his first trip to Europe in 1833 that there is no mention at all of nudity in his journal entries about the art in Paris. Instead, there is evidence of growing confidence in his artistic judgment.[78]

The young Boston patrician Thomas Appleton, who dabbled in oil painting himself, was even more self-confident. He toured the Louvre alone, for hours on end, catalogue in hand, giving the works there "a cool and thorough examination." He wrote homages to the various geniuses in his diary—"O Salvatore Rosa, thou king of the terrible; O Rubens, emperor of glowing flesh and vermeil lips; Rembrandt, sullen lord of brown shades and lightening lights," and so on—concluding with "when shall I repay you for all the high happiness of this day?" He also arranged to see a private art collection in a villa near the outskirts of town. When the owner showed up to discuss the paintings, it was Appleton who judged the collector's knowledge rather than vice versa. "He proved himself a man of taste by his comments on his own pictures," Appleton noted in his diary.[79] Oliver Wendell Holmes said he had no "taste" in art when he arrived in Paris. However, after Appleton showed him around the Louvre, the enchanted Holmes emerged more confident, proclaiming himself a particular devotee of Titian.[80]

The two young men's experience at the Louvre was by no means uncommon. Young L. J. Frazee returned to the Louvre again and again during his Paris stay. "I know of no place in the city I left more reluctantly than this," he wrote his mother in Cincinnati.[81] After he first visited it in 1839, Amos A. Lawrence wrote in his diary that it "surpasses all my conceptions of it." Going through it was "an excitement which I have never known before. . . . I hope to be able to examine it a hundred times more and study it all thoroughly."[82] After his first visit there, Charles Sumner wrote, "My voyage has already been compensated for—seasickness, time, money, and all—many times over."[83]

What did these young men think examining this immense collection brought them? In a word, what Thomas Appleton was so confident he

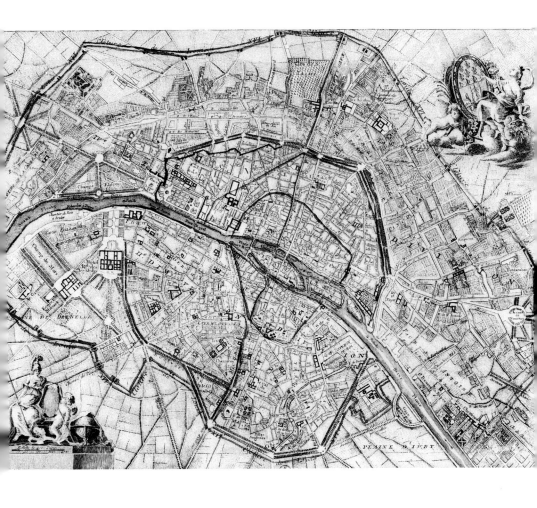

Paris in 1778. The dark lines indicate the succession of walls dating back to the Middle Ages, showing how some of them were turned into boulevards. The Seine is shown running through it, on either side of the Île de la Cité, the historic heart of the city. The area above the Seine on the map is the Right Bank; the part below the Seine is, of course, the Left Bank. Photo: Bibliothèque Nationale de France, Paris.

Top, Early-nineteenth-century tourists viewing the *Maison Carrée* in Nîmes, which Jefferson used as a model for the State House in Richmond, Virginia. Seeing it was one of the major objectives of his trip South in 1787.

Bottom, Local people on stilts in the Landes, where John Carter Brown's ship was wrecked. Although they were commonly used to negotiate the area's mud flats, they were particularly handy for looting the many shipwrecks on the silted banks of the Gironde estuary, leading to Bordeaux, the terminus of many late-eighteenth- and early-nineteenth-century voyages from America.

St. Ouen, one of two huge Gothic churches in Rouen, the first major town many Americans would encounter after landing in France. The size, age, and stonework of these churches was astounding for people who had seen nothing like this in their native land. Author's collection.

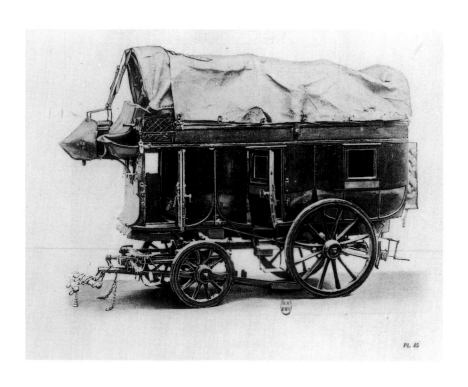

PL. 45

A medium-sized *diligence*, of the kind described by Laurence Sterne in his popular novel *A Sentimental Journey*. These slow but comfortable coaches were preferred over the faster stage coaches by many early-nineteenth-century American travelers, especially those who had read of the pleasures of traveling in them in Sterne's novel. Photo: Bibliothèque Nationale de France, Paris.

A drawing of the foothills of the Alps, from the "Picturesque Guide to France," that typifies the kind of view sought by tourists in the Romantic era. An abandoned house lurks in the middle ground, between the untamed waterfall and the disheveled bridge.

Opposite top, The garden of the Palais-Royal in its early-nineteenth-century heyday, looking north toward the palace itself. The gallery to the rear, cutting off the palace grounds just past the fountain, was a favorite place for arranging sexual encounters. The buildings on the sides, and the one from which the drawing was made, housed fine shops on the bottom floors, restaurants and gambling houses on the upper ones, and bordellos on the top floors. Photo: Bibliothèque Nationale de France, Paris.

Opposite bottom, The boulevards, whose ceaseless activity enthralled American visitors, around 1840. By then, the finest shops, restaurants, and prostitutes were deserting the Palais-Royal for them.

Above, The section of the aptly named Grande Galerie of the Louvre museum, where the paintings were arranged in historical "schools." The serious copyists include a woman, lower right, something practically unheard of in the United States before the 1850s.

Top, The Luxembourg Palace and gardens, whose art gallery became the showplace for modern French artists in the nineteenth century. The gardens were famous as the haunts of artists, students from the nearby Sorbonne, and their girlfriends, often called *grisettes*.

Bottom, The Bal Mabille, the most famous of the open-air dance halls along the Champs-Elysées, in 1846, with women for hire in the foreground. It became so famous as a place to meet part-time prostitutes, also called *grisettes*, that a New York nightspot whose dancers and waitresses doubled as prostitutes adopted its name.
Photo: Bibliothèque Nationale de France, Paris.

Top, The Café Procope, a restaurant famed for having been patronized by Voltaire and other *philosophes* in the 1830s, when restaurants were still rare in America. It was a particular favorite of the young American college graduates who flocked to Paris. Photo: Bibliothèque Nationale de France, Paris.

Bottom, Carrying out Baron Haussman's plan for slashing new boulevards—in this case, the avenue de l'Opéra—through the old quarters of Paris. New building codes encouraged the kind of street life tourists enjoyed by mandating the construction of buildings such as those in the picture, with shops on the ground floor and apartments above.

The graceful new reading room of the Bibliothèque Nationale was squeezed in among the library's older structures. Many Americans were impressed by how Louis-Napoléon fostered new construction for the arts and sciences whilst preserving and restoring France's historic heritage.

Top, The central hall of the ten long iron-and-glass sheds of Les Halles, the wholesale food market, one of the improvements to Paris's infrastructure carried out under Louis-Napoléon. It would later be fashionable for tourists to visit the working-class bars and cafés around it in the wee hours of the morning, after a night out on the town.

Bottom, The Universal Exposition of 1867, which helped solidify Paris's position as Europe's top tourist destination. Wags likened the main building, with its green garden at the center, to a plate of sausage with spinach in the middle. The buildings, all temporary, were on the Champs de Mars, the old parade ground on the Left Bank that would be the center of most future Expositions, including the one in 1889 that left the Eiffel Tower there. Photo: Bibliothèque Nationale de France, Paris.

Top, An 1867 depiction of the boulevard des Capucines and the new Hôtel de la Paix, a favorite of wealthy American visitors to the Exposition. Its ground-floor Café de la Paix later became the crossroads of American tourism to France—a place where, it was said, if one sat long enough one was certain to meet friends from back home.

Bottom, On the right stands the world's first department store, the Grands Magasins du Louvre, on the left, the Grand Hôtel du Louvre. The picture exaggerates the length of the store, but it was certainly large enough to impress many American visitors in the late 1860s, when it was drawn. Photo: Bibliothèque Nationale de France, Paris.

had: "taste." After a number of visits to the Louvre with Appleton, Holmes recorded how he further cultivated his taste by buying engravings from the *bouquinistes* and visiting other galleries. "I am grown passionately fond of paintings," he later wrote home, "and am astounded to find how my taste has improved with regard to them."[84] James Colles, the wealthy self-made businessman from New York and New Orleans, tried to make up for his educational deficiencies by spending the first year of retirement in Europe, systematically boning up on antiques, books, and art. Upon returning to New York, he turned his new mansion into a veritable monument to his newly acquired taste. He furnished it with antique furniture, rugs, and china he had collected in Paris, Amsterdam, and London and hung its walls with copies of Renaissance masterpieces he had commissioned in Italy.[85]

Since the upper class believed that good taste and refinement was reflected in good manners, some even thought that French good manners derived from their exposure to fine art. George Putnam, impressed that the "common people" strolled politely amidst the sculptures in the Tuileries gardens without mutilating or defacing them, thought that this exposure to fine art "creates and promotes among them such instinctive politeness, as well as taste and refinement."[86] John Sanderson had a similar reaction in 1835. "There is not a milliner or shop girl whose head is not a museum of pictures," he wrote. "No one can walk into these galleries on the public days and not see that there is in man a natural attraction for the arts which exalt and refine his nature." He ended his description of the Louvre: "To seem to know something about paintings is so genteel!" [87]

When young men such as this returned home, the refinement acquired on their European trip was thought to be written all over them. "They enjoy a reputation for being 'very clever' and 'very talented young fellows,' 'smart chaps.' etc.," George Curtis wrote of this group of young New York socialites. "They are often men of a certain cultivation. They have travelled . . . spending a year or two in Paris and a month or two in the rest of Europe. Consequently they endure society at home with a smile, and a shrug, and a graceful superciliousness, which is rather engaging."[88]

Ironically, by the 1830s, the kind of Enlightenment taste these men cultivated was going out of fashion in Paris. Artists such as Delacroix and Géricault, whose canvasses dripped with emotion, were taking the city by storm. Yet the genteel early-nineteenth-century American tourists who admired Poussin, Claude Lorrain, and the other seventeenth- and eighteenth-century French painters had little use for "modern" nineteenth-century French art. Even Thomas Cole, the thirty-year-old originator of the so-called Hudson River School of landscape painting, found little of value in the modern art he encountered when he visited France in 1831. He was "painfully disappointed," he wrote in his journal, to find the Old Masters in the Louvre were covered by an exhibition of modern French painters (one of the annual Salons.) "I had not expected to see so many vile productions with so few good ones—I was disgusted. . . . [T]he subjects which French artists seem to delight in are either Bloody or Voluptuous. Death, murder, battle—Venus, Psyches—are portrayed in a cold, hard, and often tawdry style . . . the whole artificial and theatrical."[89] Yet within a few years Cole himself was painting imaginary utopian scenes which were every bit as bombastic as much of the French work he condemned. The rationalist eighteenth-century norms were being supplanted by the Romantic notion that art should arouse the sentiments—that it should first speak to the emotions and only then, perhaps, to the mind.

Six

P L E A S U R E S   O F   T H E   F L E S H

> If a man has a mind to amuse himself there is no place like
> it on earth. . . . But if you want to make an absolute beast
> of yourself, without varnish or gilding, it can be done to
> the utmost perfection.
>
> FRANCIS PARKMAN

No one thought that European tourism should be all work and no play. Even the most puritanical of the republican Grand Tourists admitted that the tour's seriousness of purpose did not preclude some pleasure. "You are, I trust, about to enjoy much and to learn much in Europe," the Reverend Andrews Norton wrote the twenty-six-year-old Harvard law graduate Charles Sumner, "to lay up for life a treasure of intellectual improvement and agreeable recollections."[1] The pleasure, though, would supplement, never displace, the uplift. Peter Irving assured his brother-in-law: "I anticipate both pleasure and improvement from this excursion and flatter myself that the time it occupies will be usefully as well as agreeably employed."[2] What is striking is the extent to which the young tourists were able to live up to such vows of self-improvement in the face of abundant temptation.

Even before male tourists arrived, they had been primed by French women's alluring reputation. Washington Irving, responding to his brother's request that he report on this, confirmed that they were "admirably calculated to 'set fire to the head and set fire to the tail.'"[3] They were immensely skilled in making themselves attractive, he thought. "If the ladies of France have not handsome faces given them by nature," he wrote another brother, "they have the art of improving them vastly, and setting nature at defiance. Besides, they never grow old; you stare perhaps, but I assure you it is a fact."[4]

The fact that Paris was abroad, and far away from the snooping of hometown guardians of morality, made it all the more dangerous to morals. After witnessing some of the antics of his young, fellow Harvard graduates in Paris in 1833, the ex-pastor Ralph Waldo Emerson, now a budding writer and philosopher, wrote in his journal: "Young men are very fond of Paris partly, no doubt, because of the perfect freedom—freedom from observation as well as interference—in which each one walks after the sight of his own eyes."[5] "They say they come to Paris to see the world," said George William Curtis of young American men, but "they come that the world (that is, *their* world at home) may not see them."[6]

The puritanism of the social circles from which these tourists came made them extremely reticent about their sexual feelings. Proper gentlemen would rarely allude to them in their private journals and never even hint at them in public. In the early 1830s, when a clever French woman chided James Fenimore Cooper that there could be no such thing as love in America because Americans "were without strong feelings," he ascribed this impression to "the cold formal exterior which the puritans have entailed on so large a portion of the republic."[7]

But this puritanism was more than just an exterior posture. The revealing costumes that shocked Abigail Adams at the opera continued to embarrass succeeding generations of visitors. William Lee returned from a theater performance in Bordeaux one night in 1796 and wrote in his diary that the actresses' flesh-colored silk costumes were "wrapped so tight that you could discover every muscle," leaving their arms and one of their breasts bare. The lonely young man, who had left his wife and small child back in New York, added: "Such indecent representations can never lead the mind to virtue. All the exhibitions I have been at appeared to me to be calculated only to inspire libidinous thoughts."[8] Washington Irving was fancied as quite a ladies' man in New York, yet when, soon after landing in Bordeaux in 1804, he first saw the lightly clad women dance on the same stage, he reacted much the same as had Lee and Abigail Adams before him.[9] Over the next thirty years, American men's shock did tend to give way to titillation, but some could still be upset. John Sanderson wrote of a New England professor who was "scandalized" by "the scantiness of the wardrobe" of Taglioni, the ballet dancer. "I was born further south," the Philadelphian added, "and could bear with it."[10]

Americans were also taken aback by the amount of flesh that fashionable French women's clothes revealed. In 1796, John Vanderlyn wrote his brother that the fact that the dancers at the Opéra danced "almost naked . . . is not noticed here for the dress here is very licentious."[11] Samuel Topliff listed a number of things that French women did that were "revolting to modesty and every delicate feeling of mind," most of which involved exposing their bodies. On the street, they held their skirts up to avoid being splashed by the water running down the gutters, thereby exposing their calves. A woman would nurse her infant in public "as coolly as if alone in her nursery." Women received gentlemen in the mornings while still in bed. "A lady in *circumstances*" (pregnant) would make no effort to conceal her condition. "Women walking out with children in the most frequent and fashionable streets [would] suffer them to attend to every call of nature, while thousands of both sexes are passing by." Ladies in crowded coaches would ask the gentlemen opposite them "to arrange legs, and dovetail [alternate the placement of their legs] and this too without blushing."[12]

Americans remained just as shocked at marital infidelity as they were when Jefferson was in Paris, perhaps even more so. Washington Irving was surprised by how accepted adultery was among Bordeaux's social elite in 1804.[13] Forty-two years later, the feminist Margaret Fuller—a Transcendentalist attracted to ideas about new kinds of community—wrote a friend that she was dismayed to discover that, in the brilliant actress Rachel, "the noblest genius is joined to the severest culture. She has a really bad reputation as [a] woman." It was said that her private life "has nothing in common with the apparition of the artist."[14] The next year, her fellow Transcendentalist Ralph Waldo Emerson bragged to the British writers Thomas Carlyle and Charles Dickens that in America male chastity was not a thing of the past: "that, for the most part, young men of good standing and good education with us go virgins to their nuptial beds, as truly as their brides."[15] To Emerson, the French attitude toward sex, "this supposed freedom," was "libertinism."[16]

Fashionable French women's looks and comportment made a particular mark on upper-class American men because of the sharp contrast with the ideal American women of their own class. In the 1820s and 1830s the American woman strove for an ethereal look: slim, pale, and otherworldly. They slipped about silently in floor-length dresses with long sleeves, tight bonnets covering their knotted hair, with eyes demurely downcast.[17] French women, on the other hand, not only had few compunctions about revealing immense amounts of their skin, they covered it with make-up and fragrant powder, doused themselves with alluring perfume, and carried themselves in ways that gave every indication of wanting to partake fully in life's sensual pleasures. The Alabama planter William Raser particularly enjoyed visiting the Louvre in 1817 because, he wrote in his journal, when one's eye tired of looking at the "splendid works of art . . . he has a resource to those of nature, which are here to viewed in their greater magnificence in the Females of Paris. . . . In short, everything that could render a place enchanting and beautiful are here."[18]

A major topic of upper-class American women's conversation was the "moral character" of those around them. Their French counterparts seemed immune to this. Emma Willard advised American women not let their daughters travel to France, because "we never hear characters scanned in Paris, as with us, as to the moral tendency of their actions." It was therefore "impossible for a young woman to form any kind of judgement as to the real character of those she may meet." She learned, for example, that "a single lady, of great personal elegance, whom I often met, . . . was the *chère amie* of a married man." Another time, "in a room where a few were present, I saw, by a sudden turn, a lady of whom I had never heard ill, touch her lips to the neck of a gentleman, as he stooped for some object beside her." She also told of the French lady "whose correctness I never heard impeached" who said she was "no friend of marriage." "How absurd," the woman said to the shocked Willard, "to make one promise to love the same person forever! Why, it is impossible. Give me nothing to eat but a leg of mutton all my days, and I should starve to death."[19]

This kind of naughty talk might well have piqued the interest of upper-class American men, many of whom were comfortable with a sexual double standard at home. However, women in France's social elite were generally not interested in them. Although some Americans ascribed their stand-offishness to the language problem, in fact there was little incentive for French society women, immersed in the intricate social intrigues of their class, to bother with transient Americans.[20] American men looking for sexual encounters generally had to rely on those French women who did so for a price.

Although prostitution was common everywhere in Europe, and certainly not unknown in America, Paris had developed a reputation as a thriving center of the higher-class versions of this trade. Much of this was connected with the carryings-on of the hyperactive Duke of Orléans, a man for whom the term *libertine* seems to have been invented. Before the Revolution in which he was to perish, he sponsored enormous debauches in his Palais-Royal residence, giving fairly regular employment to hundreds of such women. The Palais-Royal and the streets around it were soon crowded with bordellos of the higher class, which became practically obligatory stops for visiting foreign men.[21]

Meanwhile, a system evolved whereby prostitution, though illegal in certain respects, was tolerated and eventually regulated in "*maisons de tolérance.*"[22] As it happened, the most popular hotels and pensions for American men visiting Paris were clustered on the very streets near the Palais-Royal that were home to a number of these places.[23] Male homosexual prostitution became more open as well, particularly during Napoléon's rule, when homosexuals occupied a number of high government posts and groups of young male prostitutes plied the boulevards and places of amusement.[24]

In the 1820s, officials began regularly checking the prostitutes in the *maisons* for venereal diseases. They also attempted to limit soliciting to these places and the immediate areas around them. Samuel Topliff, although a self-described man of great modesty, thought this system much better than the futile American one of trying to suppress and punish the trade.[25] Some years later, in 1844, Augustus Gardner, a New Jerseyite studying medicine in Paris, wrote back to a Newark newspaper that this system had led to much lower rates of venereal disease than in London, New York, and even in moral Boston, where prostitution was supposedly suppressed.[26]

The knowledge that the prostitutes there were closely supervised by the authorities encouraged visits to the Palais-Royal. After visiting there one night in 1823, nineteen-year-old John L. Gardner, obviously still under the influence of some wine, scrawled in his diary: "Res de Chaussée [ground floor]—shops. Premier—Cafés, Gambling Houses. Second and above filles. I believe no filles walk in Palais R who do not live there— Police is the order of the day."[27] Paying a visit there was the last thing he and two other American friends did on two other nights during his week in Paris, but he did not record what they did.[28]

After 1830, many thousands of unemployed men and women poured into Paris from the provinces, while the bourgeoisie expanded in numbers and wealth. One result was a great upsurge in prostitution. Although the lowest-status prostitutes (down-and-out streetwalkers in working-class areas) had little to do with tourists, those who filled the "bals," the dance halls that lined the Champs-Élysées and proliferated in the outskirts of town, kept a sharp eye out for free-spending foreigners.[29] Women also circulated in gambling houses, on the boulevards, and in the new covered shopping arcades; some passed out business cards, while whispering allusions to their talents to foreigners.

It was likely at one of the latter places that Samuel Ward, twenty-year-old son of a wealthy New York City banker, who spent three months in Paris in 1834, encountered the series of women mentioned in his diary for August of that year. He awoke late one morning, had a glass of Madeira, lit up a cigar, and set off for one of the arcades. There he met "Florentine," a woman who had been his lover on a visit earlier that year, and went to her apartment. The next morning, he withdrew three hundred francs from the bank and returned to her place, where he found another one of her lovers. Although he wrote in his diary that encountering this man, as well as her continuing liaison with a third man, "will make no difference in my regard," there is no mention of her for two weeks. Instead, the only entries are: "Lundi. Jeannette, petite brunette, frivole, artiste, small but beautiful *externally.* Mercredi. Ste Brigitte, Ste Ida, Beautiful madonna face, presence beautiful, chalereuse." The next entry in the diary, though, is in a feminine hand. It reads:

> *Florentine bien indulgente, pardonnant les desfauts d'autres afin que l'on lui pardonne les siens.* [Florentine, very indulgent, pardoning others' failings in order that they might pardon hers.]
> —*Florentine, chez Samuel, a 11 1/2 du matin, le dimanche, 31 août, 1834.*[30]

It may well have been with a woman such as Florentine that Oliver Wendell Holmes lost his virginity, and perhaps Thomas Appleton too. Practically the first thing Appleton did upon arriving in Paris was to engage a *valet de place* to show him the nightlife. It was Appleton who Holmes quoted, some years later, as having uttered the famous words, "Good Americans, when they die, go to Paris."[31]

Brothels welcoming the tourist trade also multiplied after 1830. By 1839, when twenty-five-year-old Amos Lawrence visited Paris, police controls had loosened considerably. At the Palais-Royal, a lamp vendor took him around the back and showed him "an entrance to the house filled with public girls to be had for 5 fr; at the licensed houses they have 20 fr."[32] It is likely that Lawrence patronized one of these kinds of establishment, if not in Paris, then at his next stop, Lyon. There the good Protestant wrote of going to a crowded Catholic church, kneeling, and praying. The entry continues: "Hope I have not taken the itch in this villainous town."[33] Some days later, having reached sunny Arles, his fear of disease seems to have subsided. He records meeting a young French army officer and, after dinner: "I go with him and 2 more to the café. To another house where they have music, punch, etc., etc." By then, it was legal for *maisons de tolérance* to have music, serve punch, and provide other entertainments, so it is not unlikely that the "etc. etc." included sex.[34]

Lawrence also had an encounter with one of the highest level of women who proffered sexual favors for money, the so-called *femmes galantes*, or courtesans (the most successful of whom were called "*les grandes horizontales.*") These independent entrepreneurs were usually more attractive and well-spoken than the women who worked in the *maisons* or walked the streets. They would set themselves up in luxurious apartments to which they would invite wealthy men. Often claiming aristocratic lineage or royal connections, their remuneration would come in the form of "loans," stipends, cash, or gifts.[35] Lawrence's diary for 18 December 1839, has six lines that are carefully obliterated with black ink. Then, "Pay a visit to Mme. Morlay." The next day's entry reads:

> Send in to Mad. Morlay. She shows me letters of introduction to Prince Esterhazy. Letter for the ministers, and some with the king's seal on them. They call her countess of something. She says she has come to Paris for business with her lawyers. That she is unexpectedly in want of funds (1000 fr). I offer her my purse, which has 30 or 40 in it, which she rejects and goes into her boudoir and I retire. She calls me to come back, but I pretend to be angry and so get rid of her. She is very handsome.[36]

Somewhere between Madame Morlay and the prostitutes whom Amos Lawrence feared had infected him were the women in the so-called "demimonde": well-dressed women who sought out profitable longer-term liaisons with well-off men in the cafés, theaters, parks, or (a favorite spot) the foyer of the Opéra. They were particularly partial to foreign tourists, whom they regarded as rich, prodigal, and naive or ignorant.[37] George William Curtis devoted a particularly nasty section of an 1850 satirical piece on American nouveaux riches abroad to young men who came to Paris to "see the world." By "see the world," he said, they meant to accompany courtesans to the opera and "then to return to beautifully furnished apartments to sup and prolong the entertainment until early morning." They "spend a good deal of money for nothing," he wrote, and are "quietly laughed at" by the women and their male friends, "who enjoy the benefit of the lavish bounty of our young Croesuses."[38]

Finally, there were the famed grisettes of the Left Bank. Most American visitors stayed and spent most of their time on the Right Bank. They would visit the Left Bank to see the Mint, the Jardin des Plantes, the Gobelins tapestry factory, and a few other sights, but gave the area around the Sorbonne, called the Quartier Latin (after the language of instruction in the medieval universities) a rather wide berth, particularly at night. There, among the university students, aspiring writers, and art students, a kind of counterculture—soon labeled "Bohemian"—was developing. It was also there, in the 1830s, that there arose a romantic notion of the poor young woman who shared her favors with young students and artists, or the occasional good-natured bourgeois chap, in return for small gifts and other considerations. Called "grisettes," after the grey cloaks that young working women wore, they were often garment workers and shop assistants forced into part-time prostitution by meager wages.[39]

The beguiling myth of the good-hearted grisette spread like wildfire through French short stories, novels, plays, and operas such as Puccini's *La Vie de Bohême,* which was derived from Mürger's popular story of the same name. In his popular 1838 travel book, *Sketches of Paris,* John Sanderson led Americans to believe that practically every student on the Left Bank had a grisette to minister to his needs. In the Luxembourg Gardens, he said, "you will see multitudes everywhere of bouncing demoiselles, with nymph-looking faces, traversing the garden from all quarters. . . . These are the *grisettes.* They are very pretty, and have the laudable little custom of falling deeply in love with one for five or six francs a piece."[40] By 1850, the grisette was familiar enough in the United States that in his (relatively) risqué memoir, *Wild Oats,* Theodore Witmer could digress into explaining the fine distinction between grisettes and "lorettes." (The latter, named after the Church of Notre Dame de Lorette, near where many of the Right Bank prostitutes resided, were older and demanded direct remuneration for their favors.)[41]

We will never know, of course, how many American men had encounters with women in these situations, particularly since Americans often used "grisette" to mean part-time prostitute. However, the existence of these apparently decent women in a netherworld between the angelic purity Americans demanded of their true loves and prostitutes did pose a conundrum for some. In 1848, George Emerson, a self-described "innocent" when it came to sex, wrote in his diary of a fellow American, "a man of gay life," who met "a well-mannered nice girl" from a large shop. She came to his rooms frequently for two weeks, Emerson says, "perfectly innocently, allowing him no liberties." She sent back a little present he gave her, saying she "feared that he had mistaken her": that she liked him, but "only wished some companionship" in the lonely city. They continued to meet, "but not till a fortnight would she yield to be his mistress." Since then, she would spend three nights a week in his room, "but seems to regard him as a sort of husband, never takes a cent of money and has for him a sincere affection."

To Emerson, the revelation that the cult of female virginity was not an international one was an eye-opener: "How different it is with us," he wrote, "whence if a girl falls once it is perdition. Here evidently it is not lust but a craving for affection that leads her to take such a course. She herself does not regard it as wrong and is true to the single love which she feels. Her conscience probably condemns her little and . . . who with the sternest virtue for his own guide would judge her hardly."[42]

The grisette became an enduring attraction for American men traveling to Paris. There are only two sections of the New York Public Library's copy of *Paris after Dark* (1868) that are marked with heavy lines in pencil. One is on a café-concert in the Champs-Élysées that is called "a favorite resort for domestic servants and grisettes," with "grisettes" also heavily underlined. The other, on a dance hall on the Left Bank, calls it a place where "the medical students and grisettes come out in great force."[43]

Still, for transient tourists, there was as little chance of a relationship with a "real" grisette as with a sexy French socialite. The same guidebook's chapter on "Parisian gay women" was probably more useful. It helpfully pointed out that the city offered about five thousand licensed prostitutes, of whom fifteen hundred were in *maisons de tolérance*, plus more than thirty thousand licensed streetwalkers. It "warned" that the neighborhood of the tourist hotels "swarm[s] with adventurers" who "speak English to a nicety, and overcome you with their plausible manner. . . . They are often paid large commissions by certain ladies (need we say more?) to recommend and conduct you to their dwellings." Lest the tourist use an outdated term to describe what he was looking for, it also informed him that "Lorette" had been superseded by "cocotte."[44]

— — —

Paris was also the first place many Americans encountered gambling houses run by professionals. In eighteenth- and early-nineteenth-century America, gambling was regarded, along with dueling, as an aristocratic pursuit, which made it doubly reprehensible among good republicans.[45] However, as with dueling, this aristocratic connotation added to its appeal among other Americans. In Paris, gambling was also associated with prostitution. Like the houses that sheltered that trade, early-nineteenth-century gambling houses were concentrated in or near the Palais-Royal, where they had originated. They gained considerable fame in America through the stories of the vast sums of money the aristocratic officers of the victorious armies lost there after they defeated Napoléon at Waterloo in 1815. John L. Gardner and his two American friends visited a number of them in 1823, with Gardner making notes about each:

> Francanti's [Francati's], rue Richelieu, requires introduction—elegant saloons—crowds of servants. In a superb hotel [mansion]. Bets to a great amount. Wheel of fortune and rouge et noir. Some women admitted to this house and no gens d'armes visible. No. 154 Palais-Royal: quite like Francanti's. Where [the Prussian general] Blucher lost great sums—for strangers principally. Managed with perfect order and beauty—no fear of being cheated. 113 Palais-Royal: a Blackguard place. Gens d'armes at all the games.[46]

Like the *maisons de tolérance,* these gambling houses were regulated by the police. However, a new law suppressing them came into effect at midnight on 31 December 1837, the day that Charles Sumner arrived in Paris.[47] After dinner, he headed with some friends to Francati's, where the denizens were taking their last legal chances. The next morning, he wrote in his diary, "I came to understand how people can be drawn . . . within its terrible maelstrom . . . absorbed in the whirling vortex." He felt tempted to join his friends in venturing a few francs, but the proper Bostonian enjoyed the greater pleasure that came from exercising self-restraint.[48] By midcentury, such republican and puritanical restraints were crumbling. Curtis's 1850 piece has the young Americans out to "see the world" in Paris being "plucked at gaming-houses," which continued to flourish illegally.[49]

— — —

Paris's reputation as a sex capital owed little to the written testimony of American visitors. As we noted, few Americans would mention sexual activity in letters home. Instead, they wrote of the "gaiety" of the streets and parks, giving the impression that light-hearted Parisians were engaged only in the most innocent delights. The Unitarian minister James Clarke wrote his wife about how he enjoyed walking through the Champs-Élysées at night, visiting "coffee houses such as the 'Bals Mabilles'" [*sic*] where "elegantly dressed male and female singers sang very well indeed" and people danced "with more frolic than grace."[50] What he failed to mention was that these dance halls were also full of prostitutes—that the Bal Mabille was already famous as a meeting place for, in the words of a French guidebook, "rich foreigners and beautiful mendicants, money-eaters and heart-eaters."[51]

Nor did published American travelers' accounts give more than oblique hints of this kind of activity. George Putnam's description of the Palais-Royal says only that the upper stories were occupied "by characters of all sorts, male and female."[52] In the book about his tour of France and Italy in 1817 and 1818, the Reverend William Berrian of Trinity Church in New York City wrote of the "gay and sprightly manners of the Parisians" and praised the French as gayer and more vivacious than Italians.[53] Only years later, in 1857, did it emerge that he had likely done some fieldwork on this topic. He caused a notable stir among his high-class congregants by announcing that "during a ministry of more than fifty years" he had "not been in a house of ill-fame more than ten times."[54]

Even private diaries were circumspect in this regard. Some young men used them to buttress their determination to resist temptation. Soon after arriving in Paris in 1832, Henry McLellan, a young theology student, wrote in his journal: "Of vice and dissoluteness . . . there is a fearful amount. . . . But . . . if one has a Christian heart . . . he will retire for prayer, and angelic spirits will then guard his steps."[55] Thirty-year-old Henry B. Humphrey could not even spell out words that aroused desire in him. A diary entry from Marseille in 1839 reads: "Went into glove store and saw a most b——l w——n, formerly mistress of [J. D. Doer?] of Boston."[56] Angela Mayo's succinct entry about the Palais-Royal reads: "I shall only observe that it is a little world of itself, comprising every scene that can be imagined, everything to *inform* the mind, and to *corrupt* the heart! It may be said to contain the *Infernal Region* of Paris."[57] Diarists also used the terms *gay* and *gaiety* as code words for carnal pleasure. In 1845, the forty-year-old Cape Cod merchant Alpheus Hardy noted that he had met a couple of "good New Yorkers" living in Marseille but that their daughter had been "spoiled by the facenating [*sic*] gaieties of a Paris life."[58]

George S. Emerson, Ralph Waldo's cousin, used "spoiled" in the same sexual sense of the word in 1847, when he wrote his twenty-two-year-old son of fears that the young man would be "spoilt" by the two-year tour of France and Italy upon which he was about to embark. The deeply religious son, a recent Harvard grad, doubted this. "I cannot think that temptation can have much power over me," he confided to his diary. "I thank God too frequently for having kept me innocent so far."[59]

Alas, the Harvard men young Emerson met in Paris were not quite the straight arrow he was. One of the first places to which they took him was the Bal Mabille, in which he stayed long enough to feel the stirring of temptation. Another night, after dining with a group of them, he let them go on to the Palais-Royal while he primly went alone to a magic show and a magic lantern display.[60] However, as the date of his departure for Italy approached, they cajoled him into more risqué adventures. First, they took him to another "bal," where they spent much of the evening. "I was prepared," the sensitive young man wrote, "for the women by the Mabille last summer. I thought at once there might be some temptation in such a place, but I came away feeling either sad or disgusted." The women's deportment was "perfectly decorous,"

> but what a sad world is hidden under that exterior. . . . To live from day to day from the sale of what they must have begun by considering sacred, to . . . be driven by the mere want of daily bread to pursue a course which must surely often be disgusting even in their days of success and how terrible must be its end.[61]

Two nights later, the night before his departure, his friends took him to one of the famed masked balls at the Opéra. These were Mardi-Gras-like entertainments, organized by private entrepreneurs, that began at midnight on Saturday nights. Those with more expensive tickets mingled and danced on the main floor while the demimondaines and others cavorted in the loges, engaging in increasingly open sexual activity. At first, Emerson was swept up by the devil-may-care atmosphere, noting how the women made themselves look alluring by only allowing their most attractive features to appear from behind their masks. But then, particularly as he noticed the increasingly raunchy behavior in the loges and was accosted by women trying to kiss him, he became "disgusted." Not so his Boston friends. Shortly before 2 A.M., one of them, named Gillespie, brought two attractive young women over and suggested that they all go out to dinner. However, Gillespie promptly disappeared, leaving Emerson alone with the women. After waiting for half an hour, Emerson panicked and slipped away.[62] Less than a year later, some months after returning to Boston, the sensitive young man went into a deep depression and killed himself.[63]

Unlike today, dining out provided a more guilt-free form of sharing in French sensuality. Most tourists stayed in hotels or pensions where all the guests would eat at the table d'hôte. However, as Amos Lawrence and his brother-in-law discovered, unlike in America, where the so-called "American Plan" prevailed, they were by no means restricted to dining where they lodged. Although their Paris pension served excellent meals in a mirrored dining room, they could not resist indulging in the elegance and excitement of that city's great new contribution to the art of eating, the restaurant.[64]

The modern restaurant had been born in Paris toward the end of the previous century, when a few of them opened near the Palais-Royal. It was the Revolution, however, that really set them going, by destroying the food preparers' guilds and throwing a host of aristocrats' cooks and servants out of work. Many of them now opened new restaurants near there, catering to the expanding bourgeoisie. In the 1840s, when the Palais-Royal went into a decline, they spread out along the nearby boulevards.[65]

Until the 1840s, restaurants such as these, where one could order from an extensive à la carte menu, were virtually unknown in America. When one traveled, one ate where one lodged or at taverns with limited menus. When city people dined in public it was usually at male-only celebratory dinners in large halls, where the cooking was done by caterers, often African American men who specialized in roasting large quantities of game and other meats.[66] New York City did have Delmonico's, a fine French restaurant that opened in 1827, but for some time it remained more of a curiosity than an elite destination, drawing mainly an adventurous younger crowd.[67] When the Alabaman William Raser first encountered restaurants in Paris in 1817, he wrote about them as if they were startling new sights: "The bill of fare at a good restaurateur consists of nearly 200 items," he wrote in his diary, "with the prices annexed to them."[68] Samuel Topliff had supplied Boston merchants with overseas shipping news for years, yet his reaction was not much different when he first encountered one in 1829. Like many other Americans he was particularly struck that women presided over the dining rooms, keeping track of the bills and handling the money.[69]

It was not just the concept that impressed, though; it was also the quality of the food. Abigail Mayo and her family rented an apartment for their six-week stay in 1828, but, rather than have their own servants cook for them, arranged to have their meals delivered from a nearby restaurant, using the servants only for serving and dishwashing.[70] Nor was the elegant ambiance unappreciated. The fact that after the 1820s most Americans arrived in France via England made the overall impression all the more striking. Francis Parkman thought the difference between London and Paris was epitomized in the contrast between the London "dining room," where one went to "swill porter [dark beer] and devour roast beef," and the Paris restaurant, where one truly "dined." The former was

> a quiet dingy establishment where each guest is put into a box, and sup-
> plied with porter, beef, potatoes, and plum-pudding. . . . In Paris the ta-
> bles are set in elegant galleries and saloons, and among the trees and
> flowers of a garden . . . whose occupants regale their delicate tastes on
> the lightest and most delicious viands. The waiters spring from table to
> table as wordlessly as shadows.[71]

For many Americans, it all amounted to an epiphany that changed their attitudes toward food. When Oliver Wendell Holmes first arrived in Paris his friends took him to a café for breakfast. Delighted, he pro- nounced the café au lait, brioche, and thin baguette *"magnifique."* That evening they began a whirlwind tour of the city's most renowned restau- rants that, for the young man, proved to be as transforming an experience as his encounter with the Titians at the Louvre.[72]

That Holmes was guided to these places by his friend Thomas Apple- ton, who epitomized cultivated upper-class tourism, was a sign of French haute cuisine's rising status in America.[73] When the elite Union Club opened its new clubhouse in New York in 1837, it hired a Monsieur Julien, whom Philip Hone called "a most *recherché chef de cuisine*" to produce "*bons dîners à la Paris*."[74] In 1840, Martin Van Buren failed in his bid for re- election as President in part because he hired a French chef for the White House. His opponents, in Hone's Whig party, called this evidence of his crypto-aristocratic/monarchist ambitions. Perhaps this is why three years later, when his fellow–New Yorker and bitter opponent, the Whig politi- cian Thurlow Weed, visited Paris, Weed was rather sheepish about admit- ting that he too had become converted. "I came here with a determination to eschew the refinements of French cooking," he wrote home, "but my resolutions and prejudices have yielded day by day, and dish by dish." On a subsequent trip, he wrote of his "unqualified admiration" for "French culinary science" and said that "we should profit largely by establishing Culinary Schools in America with French Professors."[75]

By 1850, expensive American hotels were hiring French chefs and reorganizing their dining rooms along French lines, but this merely whetted appetites for the real thing. The American hotel dining rooms were all superficial glitter, said George William Curtis in 1853. "No where in New York can the stranger procure a dinner, at once so neat and elegant, and economical, as in the Cafés of Paris."[76] After her first Paris restaurant meal, in 1851, the Georgian Catherine Jones wrote in her diary, "If our dinner is a fair specimen of French culinary art, I'm sure I have often ignorantly abused it. Its base imitations we only have with us."[77] Seeking out Paris's finest restaurants thus became an integral part of upper-class American touring, especially for men, for whom having a large appetite was not regarded as unseemly. First stay in a hotel, an experienced tourist advised John Lowell that year, and then take an apartment. "You breakfast in your room, dine where you please, visiting the following restaurants." There followed a list of Paris's most famous, and expensive, places, topped by Le Rocher de Cancale: "Don't omit frogs at Rocher!"[78]

Ironically, while Americans were discovering these delights, French *becs fins* were indulging in one of *their* favorite pastimes—blaming a supposed decline of French restaurants on tourists. In this case, it was the English who were the main target. In 1830, the writer Honoré de Balzac charged that their gastronomic boorishness and ridiculous demands had ruined many fine restaurants. Lord Vincent, a respected English *gourmet,* agreed. After watching a crowd of his food-ignorant countrymen descend on *Véry,* a veritable shrine of fine cuisine in the Palais-Royal, he said, "Whenever I'm away from our happy little isle, I never encounter an Englishman without blushing for my country."[79] By the mid-1840s, however, the restaurants were said to be much improved.[80] In the 1850s, when they reached another apogee of sorts, so did tourism from America.

Part

Two

PARIS AND

TOURISM

TRANSFORMED

1848 – 1870

Seven

PARIS TRANSFORMED

Good American republicans were disgusted by Louis-Napoléon's coup d'etat in December 1851, particularly when the short, beady-eyed adventurer with the long, pointed mustache went on to abolish the Republic and have himself crowned Emperor Napoléon III. In her widely read book on her trip to Europe, Harriet Beecher Stowe, an arch-priestess of middle-class morality, was particularly contemptuous of the many Americans in France who "indifferent to their own national principles of liberty," fawned over this rake, who was known to have consorted with loose women while in exile in New York:

> They come to Paris merely to be hangers on and applauders in the train
> of that tyrant who has overthrown the hopes of France. . . . They are
> the parasites of parasites—delighted if they can get to an imperial ball
> and beside themselves if they can get an introduction to the man who
> figures as a *roué* in the streets of New York.[1]

One of the ways the satirist George Curtis established that the Potiphars, his fictional nouveaux-riches tourists, were ignorant social climbers was by having them kowtow to the new dictator. Mrs. Potiphar, received by him at a ball, "sank almost to the ground in her reverence" and "actually trembled in delight when the Emperor said: 'Madame, I remember with delight the beautiful city of New York.'"[2]

Why then, despite these strictures, did Americans maneuver for introductions to this dubious monarch and toady up to the ersatz aristocrats who surrounded him? Part of the answer is that, despite their republicanism, Americans have generally had a weak spot for royals and aristocrats. (Some years after condemning Napoléon III's American sycophants, Harriet Beecher Stowe herself was accused of fawning over aristocrats, albeit British ones.[3]) Moreover, in the 1850s, their own republican experiment was lurching, seemingly rudderless, from crisis to crisis, as its democratic institutions buckled under the twin pressures of slavery and westward expansion. Authoritarianism, particularly in the new modernizing form represented by Bonapartism, could not be so easily dismissed as degenerate, at least for foreigners. Perhaps the most important reason, though, was that Paris was beginning a remarkable transformation that would make the French strongman the darling of the traveling world.

The mastermind of the transformation was Baron Georges Eugène Haussmann, who was made prefect of Paris by Louis-Napoléon in June 1853. He oversaw the construction of a network of new boulevards—seventy-one miles of new road—and the creation of beautiful new public spaces. Strict zoning laws dictated that buildings along the new boulevards be no more than six stories high and conform to certain design elements. Some of the new boulevards, such as the avenue de l'Opéra, were *percées,* created by demolishing thousands of old buildings in the congested old quarters of the center-city. These brought light, air, (and, critics charged, easy access to Louis-Napoléon's cavalry and artillery) to these often-rebellious working-class areas. The others were broad avenues that pushed into the semi-developed areas to the north and west. New, elegant, classical-style apartment buildings built of white limestone turned these districts into magnificent quarters for the well-off.[4] Over fifty thousand trees were planted and lovely little public gardens were created at the interesting intersections where the boulevards angled across other streets. The Bois de Boulogne was turned into a graceful park, with lakes, a waterfall, and gardens, inspired by the English parks Napoléon III had admired during his exile. The Parc Monceau was also remodeled on the English pattern, and luxury mansions and apartment buildings were built around it.

The Napoleonic overhaul included such things as large new railroad stations; a series of vast glass-and-iron pavilions at Les Halles, the whole-sale food market; a massive commercial and residential complex in the Opéra district, to be anchored by Garnier's magnificent new Opéra building; markets; parks; and a new sewer system that helped cleanse the Seine. New libraries were built, including the delightful reading room of the Bibliothèque Nationale, with its slim, cast-iron pillars and glass domes (where some of this book was researched); the Louvre was expanded and modernized, as was the École des Beaux-Arts, the official art and architecture school. Paris was now not only the most beautiful large city in the world, it was also the most advanced. For years thereafter, people would come from around the world—from Buenos Aires to Cairo to the Bronx (its Grand Concourse, like the Paseo de la Reforma in Mexico City, is patterned on the Champs-Élysées)—and return home intent on copying its urban amenities.[5]

The building boom was particularly impressive to the many Americans who worshipped at the twin altars of Progress and free enterprise. Despite the government's leading role in the process, the enormous costs of demolition and construction were financed by the sale of frontages along and behind the boulevards to private developers, who were the ones who actually built the new "Haussmannian" apartments.[6] John Munn, a sixty-year-old retired banker-businessman from Utica, New York, whose son was a Chicago real estate developer, particularly admired the extent to which Haussmann's projects leveled the old and replaced it with the new. "At every step is visible the march of improvement," he wrote in his diary in 1866. "The work of demolition and the creation of noble blocks of new building go hand in hand. . . . The old has become the new and broad avenues are found in which beauty and luxury prevail where naught but crooked and filthy lanes once were."[7]

Yet businessmen such as Munn invariably missed the real genius of Haussmann's plan: that, unlike American-style modernization, it did not destroy or displace the historic core of the city. Whereas downtown New York City, for example, had been marching relentlessly northward for almost two hundred years, leaving each area it deserted as a decaying backwater, Haussmann resisted developers' pleas to construct a monumental civic center in the new quarters west of the Opéra. Instead, he insisted that the old Île de la Cité, the original heart of Paris, remain the city's focal point.[8] He demolished two thirds of its squalid tenements, including those obscuring the magnificent front of Notre Dame cathedral. The *percées* that radiated out from there were lined with modern buildings, but behind them, the narrow streets and historic old quarters remained virtually untouched. Old churches and other historic buildings were restored, and small plazas were opened in front of them to improve their prospect. As a result, modernized Paris still retained much of its Old World character. In fact, what emerged was an American tourist's dream: a city that was both historic and progressive at the same time—one that presented quaint visions of the past and dynamic ones of the future. As Andrew Longacre, a Philadelphia clergymen whose lodgings overlooked a maelstrom of new boulevard construction, wrote his father in 1861, "the contrast of this newly built street with the narrow crooked lanes . . . gives an enigmatic interest to one's walks in the city."[9]

Most American tourists had no doubt that it was Napoléon III himself who should receive the credit for this marvel. "It is wonderful how much this Napoléon has done for Paris," twenty-five-year-old Eliza Gardner wrote in her diary in 1858.[10] John Munn wrote in his diary, "The city is improved as no other ever was and perhaps could be by any other than the present Napoléon and he will thus, whatever his fate, leave the grandest monument to his genius and power the world has seen or ever will see."[11] In 1867, the popular American guidebook *Harper's Handbook for Travellers in Europe,* extolled "the universal homage now paid by all Europe, nay, the whole world, to Louis Napoléon Bonaparte, who has so rapidly risen to the very highest pinnacle of fame and glory."[12] In *The Innocents Abroad,* his satirical chronicle of a American group's 1867 tour of Europe and the Holy Land, Mark Twain has a serious passage in which he credits Louis-Napoléon with bringing incalculable prosperity to France.

> He has rebuilt Paris and has partly rebuilt every city in the State. He condemns a whole street at a time . . . and rebuilds superbly. . . . He has taken sole control of the Empire of France and made it into a tolerably free land—for people who will not attempt to go too far in meddling in government affairs. . . . one has all the freedom he wants.[13]

In her travel book of the same year, Sara Lippincott was a bit more cautious. She called him "a bold, powerful, ambitious man—cold, close, and far-seeing. He is an usurper and a despot, but he has some great, and, let us hope, good things about him." (She was more effusive about the Empress Eugénie: "a beautiful, graceful, accomplished woman, . . . said to be very good and benevolent," whose love for her only son was so powerful that "though ever so much republicans, we need not hesitate to pray, God Save the Empress and the imperial boy!")[14]

Some Americans interested in the arts saw in the regime's expansion of the Louvre and École des Beaux-Arts proof that authoritarian governments were better-equipped to foster the arts and architecture than ones based on popular sovereignty.[15] Annie Fields's letters to her friends in Boston's intellectual circles are full of such praise. "The great Napoléon," she wrote in 1859, "made [Paris] the earthly Paradise of student-artists (and what artist is not a student?) collecting from all parts of the world treasures for his capital. Napoléon III is a fulfiller of his vast designs."[16] Others saw benefits accruing to those at the bottom of the social scale. After watching "working people in whole families enjoy the evening air in the wide, airy, well-paved streets," the South Carolinian William Brawley concluded Napoléon had "done nothing which adds more to the happiness of the people here than in the opening of these boulevards." The emperor understood, Brawley thought, "that to disarm them from the hatred with which socialism has inspired them, all that was necessary was to provide for their legitimate interests and to gratify their natural tastes."[17]

Yet Brawley was also one of the few visitors to bother looking at what lay behind the facade of beautiful buildings lining the boulevards. He could not help noticing that late every night platoons of miserable scavengers emerged, "creeping along with large baskets on their backs and dim little lamps by their sides—dark looking figures, stopping now and then at the little piles of rubbish. . . . Poor squalid things—it is sickening to contemplate their life. . . . Everything is gay on the Boulevards. It is only on the narrow streets which lead from them that you are brought into contact with misery—there it is superabundant."[18]

Tourists who ventured out of Paris saw little evidence of renewal. Sara Lippincott noted in 1852 how Lyon, which looked "magnificent" from a distance, was "disappointing and disagreeable" when she penetrated it. Its thirty thousand silk looms were crowded into the workers' small, dark, and unhealthful apartments. "The silk workers of Lyons are a weak and sickly race of men, and no wonder," she later wrote. She found Avignon, the next stopping point on the route down to Marseille and Italy, to be "a quiet, sad place, with an air of discouragement" and "very dirty streets." Its population had declined from eighty thousand during the reign of Louis XIV to thirty thousand, and its main industry seemed to be bilking travelers who had to stop over there.[19] Nor did Bonapartism seem to do much for the large majority of French people, who lived off the land. During his stay in Normandy, in 1864, Brawley noted that "the country people are generally poor and ill-looking."[20]

However, the existence of millions of poor and downtrodden people in Europe was not startling news to Americans. Moreover, until the emancipation of the slaves began in 1863, there was no shortage of people in a worse category in the United States. Aside from Southerners like Brawley looking for evidence that slaves lived better than the toiling masses of Europe, our happy visitors paid little attention to that aspect of French society: Americans felt they had little to learn from provincial France. The symbols of French glory were concentrated in Paris.

— —

The great Universal Exposition of 1867 was intended to show the world how France had been transformed under Louis-Napoléon's progressive regime. There had been a number of expositions in Paris in previous years— the first had been in 1798 and a large one had been staged in 1855—but although the latter had paid some lip service to the arts and culture, they had concentrated on industrial progress. The 1867 Exposition showcased progress in the arts as well. The annual Salon of paintings was staged there, rather than in the Louvre. The greater part of the exposition grounds on the Champs-de-Mars, the huge parade ground on the Left Bank of the Seine, was taken up by a gigantic Coliseum of Labor, an elliptical structure of iron, glass, and concrete where over fifty-two thousand exhibits were arranged in seven concentric galleries surrounding a palm court filled with sculpture. (Wags called it a plate of sausage with spinach in the middle.)[21] Although most of its exhibits celebrated technical advances, and many of the cultural exhibits reflected Europe's fascination with the arts of the Orient, the fair's central purpose was to symbolize France's position as cultural capital of the world.[22] It seemed to work. American and other foreign visitors wrote reams of articles extolling French achievements in the arts and sciences for the press back home. Henceforth, France was unquestionably the Western world's foremost arbiter of taste and culture.[23]

In his introduction to a guidebook for visitors to the Exposition the great writer Victor Hugo agreed that France was culturally supreme, but said this was because of the Revolution of 1789, which Napoléon III and his ministers had betrayed. Paris was the "*hôtel de ville*" [city hall] of the ideas of democracy, equality, the rights of men and women, and the movement for free universal education. Foreigners were coming to the Exposition "to incorporate themselves into civilization," to enter into "mysterious communion with the French conscience. Do they read Montaigne, Pascal, Molière, Diderot? No. But they breathe them in."[24] Yet, for most foreign visitors, particularly Americans, Paris and its Exposition meant nothing of the kind. What they came away with was the idea that Paris had emerged as the most beautiful city in the world and was now Europe's greatest tourist destination. Between April and October 1867, Paris hosted over eleven million visitors, ranging from the Czar of Russia and the Sultan of the Ottoman Empire to many thousands of less exalted excursionists from England and America. Seventy years later, Sara Delano Roosevelt, mother of President Franklin Roosevelt, would recall how thrilled she was, as a girl of thirteen, to see the Czar and the King of Prussia there, and to dine at the Vienna Bakery restaurant "while hearing Johann Strauss conducting his beautiful waltzes."[25]

The infrastructure for this had been laid in the previous fifteen years, as an increasing stream of tourists, including many Americans, came to witness the city's amazing transformation. Large new hotels such as the Grand Hôtel du Louvre, on the rue de Rivoli, across from the Palais-Royal, and the Grand Hôtel de la Paix, on the place de l'Opéra, found particular favor among Americans. The latter boasted seven hundred rooms, a gilded dining room which could seat six hundred, and seventy salons for such things as reading, music, conversation, and billiards. In 1867 Thomas Cook warned that these two luxury hotels would be "monopolized" by Americans, and blamed a 50 percent rise in their rates on their free-spending ways. "Should John Bull and his family 'put up' at either of those great caravansaries," he warned, "they will have to rub elbows with their transatlantic cousins, whilst their comparative liberality will be rather severely tested."[26]

Furnished apartments, rented by the month, opened by the dozen, as did modest pensions catering to English-speakers. The number of hotels with names such as "New York," "London," and "États-Unis" swelled.[27] *Paris-Promeneur,* an 1863 tourist publication, carried many English-language hotel advertisements, some of which would indicate that translation services had not quite kept pace with the rise in foreign tourism. The Hotel Rivoli said, verbatim, that its guests would "find there all desirable covenienties, cumfort, consent and good service. Great and small apartments opulently garnished. Servie in the apartment, at the map and fixed price. Moderoted price." The Hotel d'Yorck called itself "an excellent house, of the second class, frequented by first class Travellers, newly furnished tronghont [*sic*]."[28]

Another sign of the growing presence of American tourists were restaurants claiming to serve American food.[29] When John Munn heard of a restaurant that served buckwheat pancakes (likely Madame Busgne's, whose pancakes and New England-style fish balls set many visiting Americans to dreaming of home[30]), he and an American friend immediately investigated. To their delight, they found a tidy little place where they were greeted in English by a Welsh servant. The pancakes with butter and syrup were the equal of the best back home, Munn noted in his diary. "On the first taste they were so palatable, so home like, as to make us forget our locality." They then tried another "Yankee luxury," pumpkin and mince pie, which was a good approximation of the real thing. Two days later, Munn was chagrined to learn that the day before, on Thanksgiving Day, he had missed an even better opportunity: "At one of the Restaurants, some energetic Frenchman has bated our countrymen with American dishes and yesterday he was overrun by them, all seeking a piece of Roast Turkey a la Americain."[31]

Even a few drinking establishments sought the American trade. Mark Twain said a number of places had signs such as "ALL MANNER OF AMERICAN DRINKS ARTISTICALLY PREPARED HERE," although requests for these drinks were met with blank incomprehension. There were also many shops with "English spoken here" signs where the English-speaking clerk was invariably out on an errand.[32] English-speaking tourists were better off when it came to reading material. Aside from the ample stocks of American and English magazines at Green's and Munroe's banks, Paris had Galignani's English bookshop on the rue de Rivoli, which also published a daily newspaper, *Galignani's Messenger.*[33]

The 1867 Exposition's extraordinary success in attracting overseas tourism left a permanent imprint on French entrepreneurs. From then on, Paris would take the lead in using world's fairs to establish itself as the world's leading urban tourist destination. The next one, in 1878, attracted sixteen million visitors. Thirty-two million people attended the one in 1889, with the Eiffel Tower as its centerpiece. Chicago's spectacular Columbian Exposition of 1893, whose major buildings popularized the French Beaux-Arts style in America, topped this, but did so by patterning itself on the French expositions. (The organizers argued that Americans looking for such excitement could now do so at home.) Nevertheless, the French reestablished their dominance of the genre with the Universal Exhibition of 1900, which left as part of its legacy the immense Grand Palais and Petit Palais, now the sites of major art exhibits.

These fairs were interspersed with other advances that kept Paris in the lead of urbanism: the first electric lights in 1877, which, when installed on the boulevards, helped earn it the sobriquet "City of Light"; the subway system, with its distinctive Art Nouveau entrances spelling out "Métropolitain"; and the Gare d'Orsay, a huge limestone, iron, and glass railroad station on the Left Bank of the Seine that included a beautiful luxury hotel. There was even an intricate system of underground vacuum tubes that allowed documents to be transmitted quickly between buildings in the center-city.[34] When one adds all of this to France's leading role in high culture, fashion, and all-round taste, one can well understand how, at least until World War I, few Americans visiting Paris doubted that they were seeing a culture that in many important ways was far more civilized, especially in the strict, urban sense of the term, than their own.

Eight

KEEPING AWAY FROM THE JONESES

By 1850, America had felt the full impact of a "Transportation Revolution" that changed it every bit as drastically as any of the much vaunted technological revolutions to follow. As new canals, steamships, and then railroads joined remote hinterlands to its seaports, American agriculture became commercialized and trade and industry expanded. Cities boomed, and along with them rose a middle and upper class whose lives were increasingly characterized by a clear demarcation between work and leisure. How they passed their leisure time rapidly became an important sign of their social status. Transportation improvements helped tourism become a high-status leisure activity. Visiting places of spectacular natural beauty such as Niagara Falls gave one a certain distinction. At upper-class spas such as Saratoga, New York, and Warm Springs, Georgia, health concerns now played second fiddle to socializing with the right people. Owning a place at new summer resorts such as Cape May, New Jersey, and Newport, Rhode Island, offered social cachet along with cool seaside breezes. But visiting Europe remained perhaps the greatest sign of distinction. As we have seen, it seemed inseparably associated with high culture and upper-class taste.

However, an unsettling trend was emerging: The transportation revolution was also opening up European tourism to a considerable number of people below the very top of the social scale. Even people hitherto moored in the country's unfashionable West could afford it. When Mrs. A. T. Bullard of Saint Louis accompanied her preacher husband to Europe in 1850, her fare to Niagara Falls and New York, with a side trip to Boston came to only $33.50—not a terrible burden for a couple like them who probably lived on over $2,000 a year. The fare on boats such as the "large and elegant packet" they took to Liverpool was about $175. In 1852, the clergyman James Clarke took an eleven-week tour of Europe for less than $600 without, he claimed, any severe cutting of corners.[1]

By then, the fleet of dependable steamships created by Samuel Cunard, of Halifax, Nova Scotia, had been plying the routes from Boston and New York to Liverpool on regular schedules for over ten years. In 1849, American competition arose, in the form of the *Atlantic* and the *Pacific*, the first two steamships of the government-subsidized Collins Line. They and their sister ships, the *Arctic* and the *Baltic*, were famed for the unprecedented luxury of their furnishings, their fine cuisine, and the breakneck speed that their captains coaxed from them. They soon became the favorites of many of the wealthy American families now taking the tour of Europe.[2] However, in 1854 the *Arctic* collided with a French steamer and sank, taking with it 220 of the 260 people aboard. Two years later, the *Pacific* left Liverpool for New York and was never heard from again. In 1858, a disillusioned Congress torpedoed the Collins Line by cutting off its subsidy.[3]

The threat of Confederate raiders during the Civil War precluded a revival of passenger travel under the Stars and Stripes, but the end of war saw the formation of a new American line, the New York and Havre Line. The *New York Daily Tribune* acknowledged that its two boats were not very fast but, it said, it was "the cheeriest and most patriotic line afloat [with] a cool-headed officership that is also companionable and kindly." However, by the end of 1867 it too was no more. The Cunard Line, with its aloof officers and record of never having lost a passenger, remained dominant. Its main rival was the "French Line," whose two steamers charged the same as Cunard ($160) and took one directly to Le Havre. (It was favored by "pleasure-seekers," said the *Tribune*, who appreciated the Bordeaux wine that was served free at breakfast and dinner.) The British Inman line charged less and its new screw-propeller ships crossed faster than the others' paddle-wheelers. However, its passengers paid a high price in terms of foul, oil-soaked air and the interminable racket of the screws.[4]

Transportation improvements also revolutionized overland travel on the Continent. Since the late eighteenth century, the French had been renowned for their well-constructed roads and bridges.[5] In 1840, they began building railroads that radiated northward from Paris to the Channel ports, southeastward to Lyon and soon, down the Rhône valley to Marseille on the Mediterranean. In 1864, the railhead reached the County of Nice, newly acquired from Italy, where wealthy sun-starved Britons had already staked out a wintering spot.[6] One could now go from Calais to

Nice, a trip which in 1763 had taken Tobias Smollett fifteen days, in less than two.

People on both sides of the Atlantic marveled at the fast pace of modern travel. In 1860, as Annie and James Fields prepared for a train trip that would take them from Geneva to Paris in one day, a friend quoted an ex-miner as saying to her: "This is a fast age. People nowadays are born with their clothes on."[7] In 1863, the French tourist broadsheet *Paris-Promeneur, Paris-Touriste* said improved transportation had led to a widespread "passion for travelling." It was not that people were any more curious than their ancestors had been, but "a truly magical quickness in covering distances" had created "a certain agitation, a pressing need for movement, which our ancestors did not know."[8] Four years later, the American magazine *Putnam's* said,

> If the social history of the world is ever written, the era in which we live will be called the nomadic period. With the advent of ocean steam navigation and the railway system, began a travelling mania which has gradually increased until half of the earth's inhabitants, or at least half of its civilized portion, are on the move.[9]

The dawn of the whirlwind European tour now glimmered. In 1800, few people thought of taking a European tour that lasted less than a year. In 1853, the preacher Henry Ward Beecher took one that lasted only four weeks. He landed in Liverpool, took the train to London, went to Paris for a week, and returned via London and Liverpool.[10] The kind of quick one-week tour of the main sights of Paris that he took soon became common. By 1863, guidebooks were even providing itineraries for breathless one-day and two-day tours of the city's highlights.[11]

However, even for these quick tours it was still common to hire *valets de place,* or, as they were coming to be called, guides.[12] They were particularly useful for the new upper-middle-class tourists, whose French was often shaky at best. After puzzling over some guidebooks to Paris in 1867, Mark Twain and his two friends gave up and hired a *valet de place,* even though he suspected that such guides were crooks—a suspicion that was soon confirmed when theirs turned out to be "an accomplished knave."[13]

Twain's conviction that "the guides deceive and defraud every American who goes to Paris for the first time," may explain the enthusiasm he later expressed for the efforts of the Englishman Thomas Cook, the originator of the prepaid conducted guided tours.[14] Indeed, at the very time that Twain was cursing his guide, Cook was leading the first such tour of Americans to the Paris Exposition of 1867.

Cook was a pioneer in lowering the class barriers to tourism in Great Britain with reduced-fare train trips to temperance rallies for the working and lower-middle classes. He expanded to other destinations, gaining fame by selling prepaid transportation and accommodation to 165,000 out-of-town visitors to London's Great Exhibition of 1851. Organized tours to the Continent followed, and in 1861 he arranged for a delegation of fifteen hundred working men to travel to a meeting in Paris. The following year, Cook arrived in Paris with another group of over a hundred distinctly unfashionable English men and women. As they gathered on a street corner and prepared to set off on a tour of the city, they were set upon and dispersed by Napoléon III's police, suspicious that they might be trying to rouse the Paris masses.[15] The tour was nevertheless a success, and the next August Cook and his guides returned with one thousand of his "enterprising Tourists," this time divided into small groups.[16]

In late 1865, Cook sent his son to America to begin organizing tours of Britain, France, and Switzerland for what he called "the middling and select classes of Americans." The first such guided tour, a trip to Rome, Naples and Venice in February and March 1866, was not a great success.[17] However, Cook managed to gain a permanent foothold in the American market the next year by selling Americans prepaid vouchers for reduced rates on steamship tickets and accommodations for the 1867 Paris Exposition. They could stay at "Cook's English and American Exhibition Visitor's Home" (a bed-and-breakfast dormitory in a defunct high school), a "British-American Spring Exhibition Boarding House" fashioned out of a vacant mansion, or regular second-class hotels.[18] We do not know how many Americans actually responded to Cook's pitch. He claimed American travel agents sabotaged his efforts with underhanded practices. Nevertheless, he said, by 1870 he had conveyed over seventy thousand British and American tourists to Paris.[19]

The growing accessibility of transatlantic tourist travel encouraged at least one of the new American super-rich to up the ante. In 1853, when the self-made shipping and railroad baron Cornelius Vanderbilt, the newest claimant to the title of American's wealthiest man, finally paused in his acquisitive frenzy and decided to visit Europe, he was not about to travel with whomsoever might happen to be aboard a packet. Instead, he spent half-a-million dollars to build his own steam yacht to take his family and a small party of businessmen friends and their wives across. Nor could he say he was undertaking the trip for self-improvement: that would call attention to his origins as a semi-literate Staten Island boatman. Instead, it would be a portrayed as a combination holiday and royal visit by a new kind of noble American merchant-prince.

To assuage lingering puritan doubts about the morality of holidays from work, the Reverend John Choules, who was invited along to minister to the passengers' spiritual needs, assured the public that his patron more than deserved the break. "After more than thirty years devotion to business, in all which period he had known no rest from Labor," he reported, "he felt that he had the right to a complete holiday."[20] And so, on 19 May 1853, the *North Star*, a 260-foot, 2500-ton wooden ship, with two masts for sails and two stacks for the steam engines driving its side-mounted paddle wheel, prepared to set off for Europe. Not only was it larger than any private yacht ever conceived, it was larger than most commercial packets. Indeed, it was the size of a large warship. "What will the wealthy noblemen of England, the proprietors of sailing yachts of fifty and a hundred tons, say to a citizen of the United States appearing in their waters with a steamship yacht of twenty-five hundred tons burthen?" asked the proud *New York Illustrated News*.[21]

The Vanderbilt guests unpacked in the ten satinwood- and rosewood-paneled staterooms. They admired the lavish dining salon, whose marble and granite walls were hung with medallion paintings of famous Americans, and settled into the green velvet sofas in the lavishly decorated saloon, with its Oriental rugs and a new kind of steam heater in the center. Then came a major setback. One hour before sailing time, the hand-picked crew of stokers, whose strength and skill was expected to keep the furnaces roaring to set a transatlantic speed record, struck for higher wages. Vanderbilt, no man to truck with labor's demands, especially with four or five hundred admirers gathered to wish the vessel off, fired them all on the spot. A new gang was immediately recruited from among the seamen hanging around the dockyard. Within an hour the boilers were fired up and the ship set sail—for all of three minutes. Its engines suddenly stopped and, as Vanderbilt and his guests watched helplessly, it drifted silently onto a shoal, where it settled quietly and ignominiously, with a sizable gash in its hull. The U.S. Navy was prevailed upon to put its dry dock at the millionaire's disposal and the boat was rapidly repaired. Vanderbilt then set off again, with his green crew of firemen slowly stoking the boilers, at a reduced speed, claiming that safety, not speed, had been his main concern all along.[22]

Despite the rather chastening departure, the patriotic New York press saw the yacht as a triumph of American mechanical skill. Their expectations, and Vanderbilt's, of the reception it would receive in Europe reflected the beginnings of a distinct shift in American attitudes toward Europe and its class system. In the old days, construction of an impressive boat such as this, and the previous year's victory of the sailing yacht *America* against the best of Britain, would have been trumpeted as triumphs of simple republicanism over effete European aristocracy. Now, they were called evidence that America was producing its own aristocrats, who could hold their own with the nabobs of the Old World. "We are sure the English nobility and gentry will give the gallant 'commodore' a reception commensurate with his rank as a merchant prince—one who goes abroad in a style not inferior to their own youthful sovereigns," said the *Illustrated News*.[23] As it turned out, when the party arrived in Europe, the crowned heads and nobles of Europe were distinctly unenthusiastic about meeting the American noble, whose low-bred origins were well-known. Indeed, in France, only businessmen proposing deals seemed eager to meet the international social climber.[24]

At least Vanderbilt, insulated on his yacht, could pick and choose the Americans he would meet in France. Other upper-class Americans in France were finding this increasingly difficult. Before about 1850, when single male upper-class visitors predominated, elite Americans visiting Paris could be rather nonchalant about chance meetings with their countrymen, who were likely to be as well-connected as they. The Paris diary of George Hillard, a forty-year-old socially prominent Bostonian who arrived in Paris after a year-long tour of Europe in April 1848, records a social life that revolved around such informal encounters. He did have a formal letter of introduction to the Count Alexis de Tocqueville, author of the famous book on American society and politics, but his encounters with Americans were generally casual. On the morning of his first full day in Paris he dropped by Greene's bank in search of company. (It functioned, somewhat as American Express would later, as a mailing address and meeting place for Americans.)[25] There he ran into a Mr. Miller from Boston, who invited him to dine with him that evening at "Meurice's hotel." At dinner, he encountered a Colonel Hamilton and his party as well as the

Samsons. The next day, Miller took him to the porcelain factory at Sèvres and to the recently departed King's palace at Saint-Cloud. Upon returning to Paris, he dropped in on George Sumner and was introduced to a "Mons. des Nourrais," an upper-class French politician. The next day, while dining again with Miller at the Hôtel Meurice, he met a Dr. Loring, from Boston. "Took leave of Miller," he records, and "proposed to Loring to go with me to see Rachel," the actress. The next day, while he was at Sumner's place, Joseph Coolidge called on him. That evening, while dining with Sumner at *Les Trois Frères,* he "saw Bancroft and Porter from New York." The next day, he "went to Meurice's and left a card on Mrs. Lambert and saw Dr. Loring and two young Goddards from Providence." Life continued like this, with other Americans turning up, until finally, after relaxing with the New York newspapers in Galignani's English bookstore, another popular meeting spot for Americans, he returned home and was "much startled . . . with the apparition of my brother J. H., who had come for a brief visit."[26]

The few pre-1850 tourists who were not upper class or very wealthy were simply isolated from these circles. When Bayard Taylor, an aspiring journalist from New York, and his cousin arrived there in 1846, practically broke, at the end of a two-year walking tour of Europe, the two socially unconnected young men lived in run-down lodgings and ate at working-class eateries. As a result, Taylor wrote, "I did not make a single acquaintance during the whole of our stay in Paris."[27]

The post-1850 influx of tourists from less stellar backgrounds severely inhibited Hillard's kind of casual upper-class bonding. Here, the American experience paralleled that of the United Kingdom, where the well-born were becoming alarmed that, once they crossed the Channel, touring British nouveaux riches could camouflage their class identities and gain entrée into upper-class preserves.[28] If anything, upper-class Americans were even more threatened, for class distinctions were much more blurred in America than in England, where people betrayed their origins the moment they opened their mouths. The banks, hotel lobbies, restaurants, Galignani's, and the other places where Hillard had run into his peers were now filled with these new tourists. Since foreign hotel keepers, restaurateurs, and other gate-keepers of public places could not be relied upon to distinguish between America's nouveaux riches and their higher-class compatriots, upper-class Americans were forced to meet in places where they could be insulated from parvenus. It became the upper-class mode, then, to rent a large apartment with cook and housemaids, hire a carriage and footmen, and spend one's time either entertaining Americans in one's own place or visiting them in theirs.

Of course the apartment and the carriage were not in themselves the keys to social acceptance; it was the connections that counted. In 1867 *Putnam's* magazine ran a cautionary tale of a social-climbing American nouvelle-riche woman who in America is "laughed at for murdering the King's English, and wearing *outré* apparel." However, she persuades her husband to come to Paris, where "her beautiful apartments, her showy landau, her opera-box, her elegant toilette, and above all, her luxuriant dinners, do attract her errant countrymen and women, even those who ignored her on the Fifth Avenue."[29]

But this warning to the upper class to keep up its guard was hardly necessary. In the 1850s, upper-class Americans had begun fleeing what they saw as the crassness of the new American arrivistes and setting up households in London and Paris. By 1867, the American colony in Paris numbered over five thousand—second to the British in numbers and first in wealth. Many of them were well-off rentiers who, either before or after the war, had exiled themselves to civilized Paris to escape what they saw as the crassness of the newly rich businessmen who had horned their way into America's top social circles. In Paris, they had created a circle into which only the most socially acceptable visitors could gain admittance, no matter how beautiful their apartments or fine their chefs.[30] Hoping to evoke airs of the famous "salons" of yesteryear, they had adopted the French system of "receiving" visitors on a given day of the week. When upper-class tourists arrived, expatriates would greet them with cards indicating the days that they "received."[31] At the initial visits, visiting cards would again be exchanged, and the tourists would then "receive." They would then be invited to rounds of dinners, balls, and other social events. During several months in their rented apartment in Paris in 1854 and 1855, Elizabeth Eppe and her mother, Virginians from Appomattox Manor, the plantation where ten years later General Lee would surrender, spent practically every day calling on other Americans, including a number of Northerners.[32] Other Southerners formed their own networks, socializing with the Northern elite mainly at the invitation of George Mason, the Virginian who was American minister to Paris in the late 1850s.[33]

A favorite place for making connections was at the Sunday services at the American Chapel, founded in the early 1850s. The preferred method was for the visitors to be picked up in a carriage by one of the resident American elite and be taken there to be introduced to their peers. They would then ride through the Bois de Boulogne to view the French elite, in their beautiful finery and opulent carriages.[34] In the 1860s, an impressive American Episcopal Church joined the Chapel as a social focal point. When the well-born young New York doctor John C. Jay, Jr., visited Paris in 1866 he spread his favors around, going to the Chapel on his first Sunday in town, the Episcopal Church on his second, and, on his third Sunday, the English Church.[35]

Amos Lawrence's return to Paris in 1870 after an absence of forty years exemplified much of the changed face of upper-class tourism. On his previous trip, as a bachelor, he stayed in a hotel. He spent many of his days walking the city and his nights at the Palais-Royal and on the boulevards, where he ran into a number of other Americans and Frenchmen. Now, arriving with his wife and children, he was instantly submerged in the expatriate community. They moved into an apartment, took delivery of the carriage they had rented from the Amory family, who were taking the waters at Vichy, and went to hear his brother-in-law, now living there, deliver a sermon at the American Church. The diary for almost every day thereafter records visits, rides, and meals taken with an array of socially prominent Americans—Low, Bemis, Gardner, Carter Brown, and so on—many of whom were there permanently or for extended periods. When the family visited Versailles, there was no need to worry about catching the last train back to Paris. Americans with apartments overlooking the Palace gardens invited them to use them. So comfortable were the accommodations that they stayed three nights.[36]

Until 1870, the expatriates were also the main source of prized chances to meet real aristocrats. In 1840, the Virginia merchant John Doyle had noted that "there are some American families who are leaders of the first society" but added, "I fear their republican sensitiveness is blunted by the contagion of Royalty and aristocracy around them."[37] Later upper-class tourists had no such republican reservations. The social high point of Francis Lowell III's visit to Paris with his wife, daughter, and small son, in March 1851, was an invitation, likely gained through an expatriate, to what the daughter called "a grand dinner" at the *hôtel* of "a Countess in the Faubourg," the aristocratic Faubourg St. Germain.[38] Three years earlier, George Emerson, having obtained an invitation to a similar party through his expatriate uncle, was dazzled by the hostess' elegant *hôtel*, which was "decorated in exquisite taste, full of beautiful flowers and sweet music and blazing candelabras and gay people." He was particularly impressed by the pedigrees of the female guests, who included the daughters of prime minister Guizot and the daughter of King William IV of England. It was, he said, "the handsomest private party I have ever seen."[39]

It was through an expatriate friend that Annie and James Fields were invited to the hunt at Compiègne, north of Paris, with no less than the Emperor and the Empress. To their profound regret, they passed it up because foul weather was forecast and they assumed, wrongly, that the royal couple would not show up. However, a Frenchman they had met in Boston did get them an invitation to the home of the famed Romantic poet and republican Alphonse de Lamartine on the day he was "receiving." Although they could not understand him, Annie pronounced the poet "loveable, true and simple." She resolved the conflict between her admiration for both Lamartine and the emperor by saying of the former: "He is as firmly a republican as ever, but speaks of 'Louis' with kindness and hope." [40] Soon after, Annie wrote her sister, "We had a beautiful dinner in a beautiful house, and all French of the 'Ancien Regime.' It was in the Quartier St. Germain too, which has a mysterious interest for us from its old aristocratic reputation which is indeed wonderfully sustained."[41]

Of course one did not have to rely on expatriates to meet other elite Americans. Itineraries would have been exchanged and meetings arranged with the friends and relatives who were also going abroad. "It is almost like returning to Boston to come to Paris," Annie Fields wrote a friend soon after arriving there in October 1859. "At every turn and on every stair we meet Boston friends."[42] Ann Gordon and her Virginia planter husband, returning to the luxurious new Grand Hôtel du Louvre in September 1857, at the end of their wedding trip tour of Europe, found it full of Southern friends and acquaintances.[43] Mary Babcock, wife of a wealthy Buffalo lawyer-businessman, spent the first part of her month-long visit to Paris in 1865 searching for other Buffalonians. As soon as she and her daughter arrived, they walked up the Champs-Élysées, not to take in the sights, but to look up the Putnams. She was disappointed that most of the Buffalonians she had hoped to see had moved on to Italy for the winter, but her diary records that she nevertheless managed to connect with a rather amazing number of Americans. Her four weeks there were a never-ending round of calls, carriage rides, walks in the park, teas, dinners, shopping expeditions—all with other Americans—and an occasional visit to a tourist sight.[44]

Eliza Endicott Peabody Gardner's 1859 diary provides a grim record of the down side of this nonstop socializing. The first two days she and her husband spent in Paris were marvelous, as they saw the sights, visited the Louvre, and walked the boulevards. On the third morning, however, they had to begin "making visits." They returned two calls that had already been made on them and went to a third home. The next day, Eliza visited two different women and, when she returned to George, they were visited by a Mr. and Mrs. Shaw, followed by another friend. The evening was taken up with obligations to the family back home, as she had to write letters to her mother, uncle, and sister in Boston. The next morning it was so hot that she "hardly had courage to move." But, she knew, "it is no use to give up to these uncomfortable feelings so I put on my bonnet with the hope of finishing off my duty visits." Off she went on another round, interspersed with visits from other people to her. It was either too hot or too wet for touring during the next few days, but on the 15th of June, nine days after the whirl began, the weather turned glorious. Eliza and George had had more than enough of visiting, but could not break away. "The day was very favorable for sightseeing," she wrote, "and we were much annoyed by being kept at home nearly all the morning by visitors." The next day's entry reads: "Another delightful day, and were both so furious at being obliged to lose it in this poky social visiting. It seems to be the bane of travellers, at least so it has seemed with us."[45]

One would think that the Civil War would have cut into overseas travel. Yet although the Northern blockade of the Confederate states impeded Southerners from crossing the Atlantic, an increase in Northern travelers more than made up for this. Indeed, more Northerners—26,600—went abroad in 1864, the last full year of the war, than the total of 24,100 from both North and South who went in 1861, the year it began.[46]

The unabated flow of tourists reflected the degree to which they were wealthy, older, and female, and therefore exempt from military service.[47] They were hardly insulated, though, from the war's terrible costs. The Boston socialite Mary Eliot Parkman took her annual extended vacation in France in the summer of 1862, but her plans to go south for the winter with a friend from Boston were disrupted, she wrote home, by the news that "she has a son wounded and taken prisoner in the fight at Culpepper Courthouse. . . . That fight was particularly fatal to the 2nd Regiment, which is full of our friends . . . formed of Boston men." The friend would probably return immediately to America, she said.[48] The abysmal survival rate in Confederate prison camps makes it unlikely that she ever saw her son again.

William H. Brawley, a South Carolina plantation-owner's son, was also wounded in Virginia in 1862, but he was probably luckier. He lost an arm in the battle and was mustered out of the Confederate army. In 1864, he managed to run the Union blockade and get to Bermuda. "I tremble to hear of the slaughter of the good and the brave of our Southern land," he wrote home from there, but he was soon on his way to Paris. There he found the Americans divided among supporters of the two sides. "I have met many Confederates here," he wrote in his diary, "and have been received very kindly. Most of my time has been spent with them."[49] The war news reaching Paris over the next year could not have made their gatherings particularly gay.

The war's end did bring a substantial increase in transatlantic tourism. When it was announced in 1866 that Paris would host a giant Universal Exposition in 1867, a major motive was said to be to attract American visitors. The huge iron steamship the *Great Eastern,* by far the largest ship ever built, was refurbished to allow it to take twenty-eight hundred passengers a trip from New York to France.[50] In May 1867, Mark Twain wrote the editors of a California newspaper to persuade them that sending him on a group tour of Europe and the Holy Land would be a newsworthy event because thousands of would-be tourists were already crowding the docks of New York. One hundred thousand Americans were expected to travel to Europe that summer, he said, "chiefly to Paris."[51] Although his estimates were inflated—around forty thousand Americans made the transatlantic crossing that year, only one thousand more than in 1866—this did represent a substantial increase from the wartime average of about twenty-five thousand.[52]

Some were young men who were by no means in the same financial league as the vast majority of tourists. Falling cabin-class rates now made a five-hundred-dollar Continental tour feasible for those willing to cut corners.[53] When governments began mandating that transatlantic lines provide food and minimally acceptable accommodations to steerage passengers, some adventurous young men even risked the voyage via those dark, airless, vermin-infested holds. (In 1867, the *New York Tribune* reminded people aspiring to travel on the cheap of Laurence Sternes's admonition that, "Those who go to the continent to save money would spare themselves and their friends much unnecessary trouble if they would save it at home."[54]) But the number of Americans traveling Europe on a shoestring was insignificant compared to the number of rich ones with money to spare. Many now came from the booming cities of the Midwest, which were producing new fortunes at a prodigious rate. "We met a good many people from Chicago, which made it very pleasant for us," wrote the sixteen-year-old Chicagoan Harriet Hanford, who was touring Europe and Palestine with her uncle, and was writing home from Paris in 1869.[55] Others were from older Eastern cities, prospering on trade with the expanding Midwest. All were greeted with disdain by the resident expatriate socialites and their upper-class tourist friends, who resolutely turned their backs on the arrivistes. When Francis White, a newly rich thirty-one-year-old Boston leather manufacturer with no pedigree, arrived in Paris in 1855 with his twenty-seven-year-old wife, a formerly impecunious failed elementary schoolteacher, they missed church services on their first Sunday because they knew no one who could give them directions to the American Protestant church.[56]

Without upper-class networks to greet them, many of these tourists of lesser social standing gravitated to the same banks, hotel lobbies, and restaurants where the upper classes had earlier encountered each other. The offices of the American banker John Munroe and Co. supplanted the British Greene's as a favorite meeting spot. Shortly after arriving in Paris with his family in August 1865, John Munn, the self-made Utica, New York, businessman went there to draw some money and check his mail. How pleasant it was, he noted in his journal, to be surrounded by one's countrymen. When he returned to Paris in 1866, after a year of touring Europe, he again went straight for Munroe's, to sign in at its register. There he noted with satisfaction, "I found the names of hundreds of my countrymen." He and they would call regularly at the bank, looking for familiar names in the register, and call on them at their hotels.[57]

Munn thought Munroe himself was a snob, who snubbed him until he noted that some of his correspondence carried the prefix "Hon." before his name. But there was never any question of Munn being invited into the upper-class expatriate social circles to which Munroe himself belonged. Nor was there much chance that Munn would meet any French people other than service workers. Certified Boston Brahmins could anticipate the occasional invitation to tea in the exclusive Faubourg Saint-Germain.[58] For someone like Munn, who was merely wealthy, this was impossible. There is no record in his extensive journals that he or anyone in his family met a French counterpart. Most of what he learned about Paris came from an English clergyman he befriended—a frequent visitor to France who, unlike Munn and his family, spoke the language.[59]

Yet Munn did not seem to notice the absence of encounters with the

French. Instead, like most of his countrymen, he enjoyed being surrounded by Americans. A contented note in his diary reads, "Our hotel
is filled almost entirely with Americans who seem to have driven out all
the others. Any hotel keeper in Paris who does not encourage our people
makes a great mistake." He was delighted that, "On the Boulevards I meet
hundreds of my own countrymen," and that so many of them congregated
at Munroe's. When he and his family moved into a pension, they sought
out one with an English-speaking landlady, where practically all the guests
were American or English.[60] Each evening, he noted with satisfaction, "we
meet at table 15 or 18 genteel people." They would then retire to the salon
for lively conversation, usually involving time-honored comparisons between Britain and America.[61]

The only Americans who lacked the company of other Americans of
their own class seem to have been the servants who accompanied the very
wealthy. Most of them, like the Lowell family's servant Lorenza Berbineau, were child-minders. Because the six-year-old boy she was charged
with was ill, she spent the first three days of their stay in Paris confined to
the hotel, gazing down at the life on the streets from the window. When
the young boy's condition improved, she was taken on rides through the
town with him and his sister, but she did not mix with anyone outside of
the family until two months later, after they returned from Switzerland
and booked into a different hotel. There, at breakfast, she met two English
maids and a courier. "It was pleasant," she wrote, "to find those you can
talk with." Unfortunately for her, the next day the Lowells, dissatisfied
with their quarters, changed hotels.[62]

The growing importance of social networking to the upper classes touring
France after 1850 naturally meant that cultural tourism tended to be
moved to their back burners. For many of them, self-improvement now
came not so much from the civilizing objects one encountered as from the
civilized people one met. Yet this was also a time when tourism was becoming less identified with males. An exponential increase in the number
of women making the trip still helped keep culture on the stovetop, as it
were, but this was alongside other things one found in Paris that, like culture, were increasingly thought to be within the purview of women.

Nine

THE FEMINIZATION OF

AMERICAN TOURISM

In the 1840s, upper- and upper-middle-class women began challenging the purely domestic image that tied them to home and hearth. Attendance at female academies rose and women became an important element of the sophisticated reading public. They built on the prevailing conception of them as more moral than men to expand their moral authority outside their families and into some of society's most important institutions. They played a more active role in Protestant church congregations and joined the social movements, such as temperance, antislavery, and women's rights, that these churches spawned.

Some of these women also chafed at the distance that the world of "separate spheres" created between husbands and wives. As business civilization conquered the cities of the early nineteenth century, men increasingly worked away from the home, spending their days and many evenings in their offices, shops, and clubs. Tourism thus represented one of the few pursuits in which husbands and wives could share experiences outside of the home, forcing them to walk, ride, dine, or even just talk with each other to an altogether unusual extent. As a result, women, aided by improvements in transatlantic shipping, rapidly brought an end to the tradition of married men touring Europe alone.

Often, it did bring couples closer together. When, after some months of traveling together, James and Annie Fields found themselves in Paris on their wedding anniversary in November 1859, he wrote her a poem that epitomized the closeness that prolonged travel together can breed:

> Comes to our Wedding Day
> Over the seas and far away—
> And no matter where we roam,

Where the heart is there is home,
Where we pitch our tents, arise
All that's best beneath the skies.[1]

Such sentiments would hardly have arisen back in Boston, where he was busy juggling his careers as an author, editor, and publisher, and usually dined at his men's club.

The diary of Eliza Gardner offers a rather poignant indication of how some wives appreciated this enforced sharing of experiences. Like Annie Fields, she was also twenty-five in 1859, when she arrived in Paris with George, her husband of five years. They spent the first full day there sightseeing and then, after dinner, walked the boulevards. "I could hardly realize that I was the same individual who had always led such a humdrum life at home," she wrote in her diary.[2] The next night, after strolling the boulevards again, they returned to their hotel room. "George took his cigar at the open window," she wrote, "and I sat with him. The pleasure of enjoying his society so incessantly is unspeakable, and I am becoming very dependent on him."[3] (Such happiness was not destined to continue. During the next ten years three of their children died, two of them in a single outbreak of cholera.)[4]

Of course not every touring young bride was thrilled with this closeness. Twenty-four-year-old Ellen Twisleton, newly married to a wealthy Englishman who was nineteen years her senior, was exhausted by his constant companionship during their visit to Paris. She wrote her sister back in the States:

> Generally, lately married ladies find themselves with plenty of time to get rid of as they settle, easily, the arrangements of their small menage and their "lords and masters" are absent the greater part of the day. But *my* monarch has nothing in life to do but wait on me, and has himself the most unceasing and unburdened activity, so that he fills up every day for me, from morning till night, with so much seeing and doing, it takes all my energies to accomplish.

If they had an evening to themselves, she said, he spent it reading aloud to her from the classics.[5]

Although the less arduous crossing encouraged an increasing number of women to sail to Europe, women were still too vulnerable to male aggression to think of traveling on the Continent alone.[6] Yet even had it been easy for women to travel alone, few would have wished to do so. For many women, much of the pleasure of the experience seemed to come in the sharing of it, if only as "Letters from Paris" for newspaper readers back home. Indeed, so great was the outpouring of women's travel accounts that travel writing itself became thoroughly feminized in the public mind.[7]

As married couples traveling together became the norm, women shared in the usual sightseeing excursions. They also enjoyed the occasional meal at a restaurant, which was a masculine activity back in the States. "As we were in France," said Catherine Jones in her diary, "we acted as the French do, that is, stepped from 'the sublime to the ridiculous' and from the Louvre to a Restaurant," apparently her first such experience.[8] Tours of the Paris sewers, which became popular after Haussmann constructed a special system to separate the more disgusting parts of the city's effluence from the overflow of water, also attracted both men and women. John Taylor Johnston, who took his wife and children, reported that it was "a most interesting and unusual trip which involved no foul air or anything disagreeable."[9]

Both men and women also made the trip out to Père Lachaise cemetery, on the outskirts of the city, where they could engage in the popular mid-Victorian pastime of judging a people by the cemeteries they keep. Seeing people praying and weeping by the flower-bedecked chapels on the tombs changed Sara Lippincott's view of the French:

> The French are usually considered light, irreligious, and heartless but visiting this cemetery, and seeing what loving care they have for their dead, is enough to convince any one that very many of them must be true-hearted, serious minded, full of good and tender feeling.[10]

Some men reacted similarly. The Virginian John Doyle wrote of how touched he was to see "numerous persons, *particularly females*" placing various trinkets and ornaments on the tombs of loved ones. "I could but think," he said, "that we dealt unjustly with the French as a Nation in considering them as deficient in the deeper and finer feelings of our Nature."[11] Most moving to Victorians, who loved tales of angelic women dying undefiled, was the tomb reputed to contain the remains of the star-crossed eleventh-century lovers Abélard and Héloïse. The sanitized version of their tale, fed to puritanical Americans, had it that, because he was a priest, they were forced to separate before the relationship was consummated. He was confined to a monastery and she to a convent, and the letters they exchanged were romantic staples of the day.[12] (Few tourists seemed aware that Abélard was in fact quite a ladies' man, and had fathered a child with Héloïse, before being castrated and sent to the monastery.)

Males and females were also about equally unimpressed by the cemetery. Eighteen-year-old Katherine Lawrence, who visited it on a grim late-November day, said it was "not so beautiful as I expected."[13] Catherine Jones called it the only thing that disappointed her in Paris. She thought it did not compare with those in her native Georgia.[14] Charles Sumner was put off by the elaborate tombs, the trinkets, and the surfeit of inscriptions. He preferred Boston's Mount Auburn cemetery, "clad in the russet dress of Nature, with its simple memorials scattered here and there," apparently unaware that, like many American cemeteries, Mount Auburn's layout was patterned on Père Lachaise.[15]

About the only sights at which males now predominated were at a state-of-the-art abattoir and the other major venue for Victorian fascination with death, the Morgue. There, unidentified bodies that had been fished out of the river or found on the streets were displayed naked, on stone slabs, with cool water dripping on them and their clothing hung on hooks over them to help in identifying them.[16] In 1858, after it had moved from its shed on the Left Bank to sparkling new quarters on the Île de la Cité, John Taylor Johnston took his two sons there, but not his wife and two older daughters. They stared at a workman who had been murdered by a blow to his head and "a fine young handsome fellow with black hair etc., a case of suicide; the other two bodies had been so long in the water and were bloated and discolored beyond recognition."[17] When Edwin Van Cise visited what he called "the Paris dead house," he was disappointed to find only one corpse on display, a young lady with only a bruise on her forehead. However, he was able to recite to himself a moving poem about seeing a young woman's dead body.[18]

Many of the women were impressed to see women working as shop assistants, restaurant supervisors, and in other such business-like roles. However, Catherine Jones, whose husband owned a slave plantation in Georgia, added a new twist to the Southern argument that their slaves were better off than European workers and peasants by concluding that the slaves were treated better than French women. She wrote in her diary that she was

> shocked to find that the *politest nation* in the world allowed their
> women to perform so much manual labor—so much—drudgery—but
> La Belle France must acknowledge to her shame, that mostly by the

sweat of women's brow is the bread of the peasantry gained. Yet they seem happy and cheerful—reminding me strongly of our negroes—which comparison they may not fancy, but I think very apropos. The only difference is in our negroes having their *comfort* better cared for.[19]

One consequence of the concept of "separate spheres" was that well-off women were able to parlay their gender's supposedly greater sensitivity to "fineness" into leadership roles in what was known as "polite culture." As a result, there was a growing sense among the American elite that an appreciation for the arts was primarily the province of females.[20]

As the wealth and number of well-off Americans had expanded exponentially in the 1830s and 1840s, so had their homes and the number of objects—furniture, paintings, prints, and sculptures—within them. By the 1850s, it was generally assumed that the woman was in charge of decorating the family home and that its objets d'art reflected her taste.[21] Officially, men still purchased most works of art, but that was mainly because of their legal control over family purse-strings. As she stood transfixed by a painting in the sales room of the Sèvres porcelain factory outside of Paris, Mrs. A. T. Bullard could think of nothing but how much she wanted to see it hanging on the wall of her own house in Saint Louis. "*I must have it*," she thought to herself. "In my imagination I transplanted it to my own home, and felt I should be satisfied if I had this one *gem* of art, if I could not afford another." The price of six thousand dollars turned out to be far too steep for the Presbyterian minister's wife, but it is significant that she thought in terms of whether *she* could afford it, even though legally all marital property was her husband's. Nor does the good preacher's opinion on the quality of the work seem to have been solicited.[22]

Women also established themselves as men's equals as patrons of art museums. Their confidence in assessing art was encouraged by a new democratic approach to art advocated by a number of influential art teachers in the 1840s and 1850s. These crusaders sought to "republicanize art" by breaking the monopoly on its patronage hitherto enjoyed by "princes and nobles" and teaching ordinary people how to create and enjoy it.[23] Caroline Kirkland exemplified this kind of cultural egalitarianism in 1849 by prefacing her description of the Louvre with the assertion that anyone with "a sincere love of Beauty and some plain common sense" should be able to make "irrepressible comments upon works of Art . . . without the slightest pretense of connoisseurship."[24]

Over the next ten or fifteen years, women achieved a kind of ascendancy over art appreciation, in the course of which the canons of "taste" came to reflect what were then regarded as feminine sensibilities. In her examination of popular fiction of the Victorian era, Ann Douglas argued that literary taste in America underwent a process of "feminization." This reflected the growing importance of women as church-goers and readers and the efforts of preachers and writers to cater to them. It was most apparent in the sentimentality that pervaded American religion and popular literature, something epitomized by the prolonged death scene of Little Eva in Harriet Beecher Stowe's *Uncle Tom's Cabin*.[25] I would suggest that this was also evident in women's taste in art. The scene which Mrs. Bullard said she was "half crazy to own" was not far removed from Stowe's famous scene of innocent purity preparing to ascend into Heaven. "It was a representation," she wrote, "of a young and lovely girl, beautiful in death, and robed for the grave; her attendants stood in such apparent anguish that my *own* heart was melted—and above was traced in delicate letters, 'like a flower I have perished and passed away.'"[26]

By the mid-1850s, a new approach to art appreciation that validated this sentimental response had emerged. The old props of eighteenth-century connoisseurship—restraint, balance, and so on—had been knocked out by a combination of the rise of romanticism and the 1840s movement for democratic art. Now, great art had to first affect the emotions. Yes, one should take note of the artist's technique, but that was after first applying the test of sentiment: to see whether the work stirred one's deepest emotions. Harriet Beecher Stowe's brother, the famous preacher Henry Ward Beecher, demonstrated this approach to readers of the *New York Independent*. Writing of his first encounter with the modern paintings in the Luxembourg Palace during his first tour of Paris in 1855, he said,

> There is but ONE *first time* to anything and he is foolish indeed that squanders it by giving himself to analysis, instead of yielding himself to sympathy and enthusiasm; and the more artless and unashamed his enjoyment, the better.[27]

Waxing autobiographical, he lamented that whereas he had "grown fond of pictures from [his] boyhood" and "felt the power of some few, . . . nothing had ever come up to a certain ideal that hovered in my mind; and I supposed that I was not fine enough to appreciate with discrimination the works of the masters." However, he discovered that he was wrong to blame his failure to appreciate fine art on his lack of expertise, for these canvasses overwhelmed him emotionally:

> To find myself intoxicated, to find my system so much affected that I could not control my nerves—to find myself trembling and laughing and weeping, and almost *hysterical,* and that in spite of my shame and resolute power to behave better,—such a power of these galleries over me I had not expected.[28]

Beecher's use of the word "hysterical," which—originating as it does in the Greek word for uterus—was closely identified with the psychology of females, exemplifies how this conception of how to look at art was becoming feminized by midcentury. It would have been inconceivable for an educated man of Jefferson's generation, or even young Thomas Appleton's, to react to pictures in this way. But Beecher was part of an important new current among upper-middle-class males that originated among the kind of evangelical Protestants who supported the reform movements of the time. These were men whose masculinity was not threatened by waxing sentimental. Indeed, they often spoke of their deep love for each other and fondly embraced in ways later generations would regard as distinctly homoerotic. Beecher, who thought nothing of kissing another man and cuddling up on his lap, was being disingenuous in implying that he felt shame at expressing his innermost feelings by trembling, laughing, and weeping.[29] Had he really felt this, he would not have held it up to thousands of readers as exemplary behavior. The only shameful aspect might have been that he carried on like this in a public place.

Letting intellect, training, and expertise take a backseat to emotion had profoundly egalitarian implications, for it made anyone's assessment as respect-worthy as anyone else's. Two years earlier, during their first visit to Paris, Harriet and her other brother, Charles, provided excellent examples of how democratizing this feminized way of looking art could be. Her popular book about this trip, *Sunny Memories of Foreign Lands,* told an exemplary story of how the two of them had told a Monsieur Belloc, the head of the Imperial School of Design, how much they admired the modern pictures they had seen at Versailles, Luxembourg, and the Louvre. Belloc, who thought that artists had produced little of value since the Old Masters, had replied that there were, perhaps, a couple of good paintings in the Luxembourg, and one or two good modern ones in the Louvre, but, "with an inimitable shrug," declared "all the rest of French modern paintings [were] poor paintings." Initially, Charles was cowed, but when Belloc went on to deride his absolute favorites—Horace Vernet's battle paintings in Versailles—he could take it no more. "Monsieur," his sister quotes him as saying firmly, "I do not know the rules of painting, nor whether the picture is according to them or not; I only know that I like it."[30]

A passage in Charles's journal, published as part of *Sunny Memories,* was also used as an example of how sensibility must take precedence over reason in art appreciation. It describes Harriet after she encountered Rubens's huge *Marie de Médicis* canvasses, full of fleshy maidens and lustful allegorical animals, which were now in the Louvre: "Her cheek was flushed, and her eye seemed to swim. 'Well, H.' said I, 'have you drank deep enough this time?' 'Yes,' said she, 'I have been *satisfied,* for the first time.'"[31]

Readers would not have known, as Charles perhaps did, that Harriet's marriage was then being wrecked by her spurning of her husband Calvin's sexual advances.[32] But the passage really demonstrates the degree to which genteel American women had changed since earlier in the century, when their prudery prevented them from engaging much of the world's art. In 1831, Emma Willard found these same Rubens canvasses immoral and disgusting. It was "bad taste," she wrote, "to trick out vice to make it alluring to the unwary."[33] Whereas Willard had refused to even venture into the undraped sculpture in the Louvre's galleries of antiquaries, Stowe, the current guardian of middle-class morality, declared the bare-breasted figure of the still-little-known *Venus de Milo* her favorite piece.[34]

Stowe continued to despise Louis-Napoléon, but there was no denying that his grandiose notions of France's civilizing mission helped turn Paris into the visual arts capital of the Western World. The expansion and renovation of the Louvre and the opening of other galleries to join the Luxembourg Palace as showcases for French modern artists made it a destination for viewing practically the entire panoply of Western art. Government support for the École des Beaux-Arts increased and private art schools flourished. Foreign artists, including many Americans, now went to Paris, rather than Rome or Düsseldorf, for the finest training. Each year, the international press covered the government-sponsored Salon of paintings in great detail, acknowledging that here was where the cutting edge lay.[35]

Serious encounters with art now became an essential part of the experience of the growing number of American women visiting France. Earlier, the rare young women who went to France for "finishing" would be instructed in language, music, comportment, and fashionable dressing. Art was not a high priority.[36] In September 1835, when Henry Wadsworth Longfellow guided twenty-five-year-old Clara Crowninshield through Paris at the end of an eighteen-month Grand Tour of Europe, he waited over a week before he took her through the Louvre. Then, she wrote in her diary, they "went through a long gallery of paintings, but so hastily that no one had time to make an impression on me."[37] In 1850, however, eighteen-year-old Katherine Lawrence, also born into the Boston elite, wrote of how she confidently "ciceroned" her mother through the Louvre, heading first for Murillo's *Assumption*, to judge whether it was worth the enormous sum the government had just paid for it. She toured churches, galleries, and museums with the Murray guidebook in hand, not to be influenced by its judgments but to compare its assessments of the art and architecture with her own.[38] When Annie Fields's teenage sister joined her on her visit to Paris in 1859, Annie's husband dropped out of the museum scene completely, as the two sisters, munching chestnuts, would "haunt the Louvre" together.[39] In 1870, another teenager, Harriet Hartford, who was touring Europe with an uncle, wrote her mother in Chicago assuring her that her tour was paying cultural dividends. In Marseille, the sixteen-year-old wrote, "we went to the picture Gallery and saw some of the best paintings I have ever seen." In Avignon: "We went first to the Museum. There we saw some very fine paintings and some ancient curiosities."[40]

Young women also took up painting and drawing with a seriousness of purpose far beyond the earlier aspirations to merely turn out decorative objects for the home. Liza Gardner was more enthralled by the Louvre than her husband in part because it had the originals of pictures that she, a serious amateur artist, had copied from engravings. Her diary entry after her second visit says: "So lost in admiration of many of the pictures that I hardly realized the fatigue, the standing and the straining of the eyes caused me." She emerged so mentally exhausted that she had to lie down for several hours.[41] In 1858, the writer Nathaniel Hawthorne was rather surprised to see some women artists copying masterpieces in the Louvre. In 1869, Adele Grafton was not surprised at all to see "women by the score" doing this.[42] By then, serious women artists such as Mary Cassatt were joining the growing number of male American artists seeking to complete their training in France.

As often happened when things became feminized, the feminization of art appreciation probably contributed to its decline as a mark of distinction among cultivated males. Andrew White, a brilliant Yale graduate who later became president of Cornell University, visited France for nine months in 1854 with the intention of immersing himself in a kind of post-graduate course in high culture. In Paris, he attended innumerable plays and concerts, visited practically every church and architectural site in town, and scoured the bookstores for handsomely bound books and rarities for his library, but his journal says nothing of art. It mentions walking in the Luxembourg Gardens, but not visiting its gallery, and does not refer to the Louvre at all.[43] The upper-class New York physician John C. Jay, Jr. toured Paris for over three weeks with his father in November 1867, taking all the major sights and a number of theaters, yet they only dropped into the Louvre once, after an afternoon of shopping, and did not bother at all with the Luxembourg.[44]

Most males now felt no need to demonstrate an appreciation for fine art. When Nathaniel Hawthorne and his wife visited Paris in 1858, he noted in his journal that he spent a day "glimpsing" some of the Louvre's galleries and was more impressed by the building than the art. Two days later, they returned to look at the museum's superb collection of Old Master drawings. "To an artist," he wrote, "the collection must be intensely interesting; to myself, it was merely curious, and soon grew wearisome. Much of the time, while my wife was looking at the drawings, I sat observing the crowd of Sunday visitors."[45] Mark Twain seemed equally uninterested in the Louvre, devoting only one paragraph to it in *The Innocents Abroad.* He ventures that Rubens and his ilk fawned too much on their princely patrons and then says, "But I will drop the subject, lest I say something about old masters that might as well be left unsaid."[46]

Feminization was also apparent in purchasing art. Earlier in the century, wealthy men, following in the Grand Tour tradition, would commission artists to copy masterworks from the Louvre and other great museums for their homes in America. James Colles commissioned a large number of works when he toured Europe in 1843 and 1844, but his wife, who accompanied him, seems to have played no role in choosing them.[47] After midcentury, however, wives seemed to play at least as important a role as husbands in deciding which art works to buy. The Fieldses, for example, toured a number of Paris artists' studios together and jointly decided what to purchase.[48] By the 1860s, touring women were ordering art on their own, even though their inferior legal status still made it difficult for them to do so.[49]

Only the highest-status, or at least most expensive, level of art collecting remained a male preserve. In France, men alone bid at the auctions at

Hôtel Druout, where eighty-two men held a monopoly on auctioning fine art in Paris. In America, all of the real "collectors" were men. Of course, collectors in this sense are much different from people who simply buy things they like. They are people with a passion for acquiring all of or the best of something and putting them in some kind of order. Historically, they were often monarchs or aristocrats who sought to manifest their power by monopolizing certain kinds of valuable objects. Later in the nineteenth century, wealthy capitalists would assume this role. However, in mid-nineteenth-century America, where art appreciation was not particularly highly regarded, serious collecting was just an outlet for a small number of wealthy men with a compulsion to own fine art. John Taylor Johnston first visited France as a twenty-three-year-old in 1843 and 1844. Five years later, his father made him head of a New Jersey railroad that prospered mightily, providing him with a fortune that he used to form a large collection of American and European art. When his New York City home could no longer hold it, he built a gallery over its stables and opened it to the public, who hardly took any notice of it. In October 1868, he returned to Paris with his wife, five children and two servants, to do some serious buying. Although his wife accompanied him on some visits to dealers, she seems to have played little role in deciding what to buy. Indeed, when he made his final rounds of artists' studios to decide what to buy, he asked two other male American collectors to accompany him, not his wife. Two years later, he became the first president of the Metropolitan Museum of Art.[50]

— —

The growing identification of tourism to France with shopping also helped feminize tourism to France in the public mind, bolstering the impact of the idea that art appreciation was a womanly thing in that regard. Until the 1840s, the purchase of things outside the house was not regarded as a particularly feminine activity. Men usually made the most important purchases for the home. Lower- and middle-class townswomen tended to produce much of what the household consumed themselves and shopped for the rest in public markets. Upper-class American women sent their servants to the market and purchased items such as material for their clothes from merchants who came to their homes. Sometimes one visited craftsmen or artisans in their shops, but these were workshops, not sales shops. In the 1840s and 1850s, however, shops devoted mainly to selling finished consumer goods began appearing in America's larger cities. "Shopping" now became a way for the wives of the rising urban-middle and upper-middle class to break out of the kind of imprisonment imposed on them by the separation of homes from workplaces.

Although Napoléon had derided the British as "a nation of shopkeepers," in fact shops had a head start in Paris, where the ground floor of the Palais-Royal had been lined with small shops selling jewelry and other luxuries since the turn of the century. These were the first shops to illuminate their windows at night, and strolling by them never failed to dazzle visiting American men and women.[51] Later, shops selling a wider variety of things opened along the new rue de Rivoli and on some of the boulevards. Yet, before about 1850, Paris shopping was not particularly identified with women tourists. Men would load up on gloves and other accessories, often claiming they were beguiled into making unnecessary purchases by the attractive young sales women, something unknown in America. "They have an irresistible way of recommending their wares, charming you by their ineffable sweetness and apparent naiveté, while they draw as liberally as possible on your purse," George Putnam wrote in 1838.[52]

In the mid-1840s, a cheaper process for producing plate glass was developed that, when combined with the use of thin cast-iron framing for storefronts, turned shop windows into tempting showplaces for artfully arranged wares. "Window-shopping" now became a popular pastime, particularly on the boulevards. Then, Haussmann's policies encouraged a spectacular proliferation of shops, for they mandated that stores occupy the ground floors of apartment buildings on the main avenues. Annie Fields wrote a friend, "No one ever told me before I came the distinguishing feature of the streets here, that is to say, *every* house has a shop on the street and that there are literally *no* houses without shops."[53] William Brawley, a bit of a yokel from the rural South, meticulously noted what "shop windows" were in his 1864 diary, remarking that they were "an education in themselves."[54]

Brawley was especially impressed by the bookstores, map-sellers, photography shops, florists, cutlery shops, and a model steam engine store.[55] By then, though, tourist shopping in Paris was already associated mainly with stores catering to women, particularly their clothing. Paris's reputation as a women's fashion capital, which predated the 1789 Revolution, flourished in the first half of the nineteenth century. The few American women fortunate enough to visit there then would return newly fitted from head to toe with all its wonders. Instead of visiting the Louvre, Clara Crowninshield spent most of her first week in Paris in 1836 being fitted out by dressmakers, corset-makers, milliners, and bootmakers. "On our feet from morning till night," she wrote in her diary, "and yet have seen nothing but the inside of shops."[56] Until the 1850s, however, most fashionable American women learned of Parisian trends through design books and ladies' magazines. Men visiting Paris would send back the latest fabrics for their wives' dressmakers to work on at home.[57] Within ten years, when almost as many women as men were coming to Paris, this was no longer necessary. Adele Grafton suggested that women coming abroad "take almost nothing" and buy all their clothes in Paris.[58]

By the time the great influx of women tourists began in the 1850s, the wealthiest patrons did not have to plod from shop to shop. The clothing craftsmen came to their hotels or apartments for fittings. The servant Lorenza Berbineau recorded the mob scene in the Lowells's hotel rooms in 1851. "We have dressmakers, milliners, and washerwomen all in a bunch," she wrote. "It is really quite laughable to see so many in all at once." The next day brought more of the same: "We have dressmakers, boot makers, and several [other] people. They all come in a bunch. Mrs. Lowell has a head ache this eve." However, there was no rest for the acquisitive. The next day's entry reads: "We have dress makers boot makers trunk makers and all sorts of people."[59] Almost twenty years later, the scene in the rooms occupied by Amos Lawrence, his wife, and two daughters was not much different. "Dress makers and milliners and such people come every morning to see my party and take their orders," he wrote in his diary.[60]

Not everyone was impressed with Paris dressmakers. Southern women, accustomed to having skilled slave women make their dresses from imported materials, sometimes had difficulty paying French women to do it. A fellow Georgian warned Catherine Jones, "They are a great set of rascals and must be watched." "So far," Jones wrote in her diary, "our experience coincides with her opinion. Their prices are exorbitant and we are not half as well *fitted* as Mary [her slave] can fit me at home." Later, when a seamstress brought her sister a dress that she thought overpriced and ill-fitting, Jones told her *valet de place* "to tell her that if my seamstress at home (*a negro too*) could only see what miserable fitting dresses her young mistress and I wore, she would be extremely mortified."[61] The nouvelle-riche Bostonian Caroline White was doubly frustrated, first because she was not yet used to dealing with service people, and then because her inability to speak French to the young dressmaker who came to her rooms meant she could not tell her what she wanted. "I feel *all wrong*," she wrote in her diary.[62]

Those a notch below the very wealthy could still shop in style. In the

1850s, dressmakers and milliners began opening elegant shops on the boulevards. When, after a year of touring, John Munn arrived in Paris in November 1866 with his wife and daughter, the first thing the women did was to head for the dressmaker's and milliner's shops to replace their wardrobes. Some weeks later, he confided to his diary that they were still at it. After an hour of window-shopping with him on the boulevards, they left him to go to "that Heaven of their sex, the dress makers."[63]

By then, another important innovation in nineteenth-century shopping, the modern department store, was taking root. These had originated in Paris in the 1840s, as *grands magasins de nouveautés* [*nouveautés* meaning "dry goods," that is, anything used to cover the body] organized into departments such as gloves, corsetry, and hosiery. These large stores used their buying power to offer factory-produced items at prices with which the older craftsmen and smaller shops could not compete. By offering money-back guarantees to assuage fears that their goods might be shoddier than hand-made ones, they managed to develop a reputation for quality that appealed to a largely female middle- and upper-middle-class clientele.[64] The most successful of these new stores, the Grands Magasins du Louvre, looked like a palace, with architectural details copied from the Louvre palace across the road. Because it was also situated across the road from the Grand Hôtel du Louvre, the most popular hotel for Americans, and employed some English-speaking salespeople, it was very popular with American tourists, who particularly enjoyed having men dressed as flunkies carry their purchases around for them in such an aristocratic-looking setting.[65]

Even some of the most resolute women could not resist Paris shopping. Annie Fields, who had serious literary and intellectual interests, spent the first month of her stay in Paris stolidly holding out against the temptation to shop in what she called "the most beautiful and dearest city in Europe." However, within a few weeks, her resolve had crumbled. One fact in Paris "to which all must yield," she wrote, was that "there is no escape for you, no admiring of well-arranged shop windows at magnificent distances. No indeed, in you must go and *buy something*, or else no matter how many oaths you take, you have never been in Paris."[66] Ten years later, when she and her husband returned to Paris, there was no thought of resisting temptation. They spent what she called "five very busy days devoted to shopping in the most determined manner" before resolving to "turn a new leaf" and do more uplifting things.[67]

Most women did not see a conflict between Paris's role as a fashion center and its role as a capital of high culture. In the years that followed, they would often be called two sides of the same coin. The French genius for the visual arts was thought to be reflected in sensitivity to beauty in all aspects of life. It seemed natural that the people who lived in the beautiful city that Haussmann had created, that harbored the Louvre, the Opéra, the Champs-Élysées, the Bois de Boulogne, and the Boulevards, would also lead the world in producing beautiful things to wear.

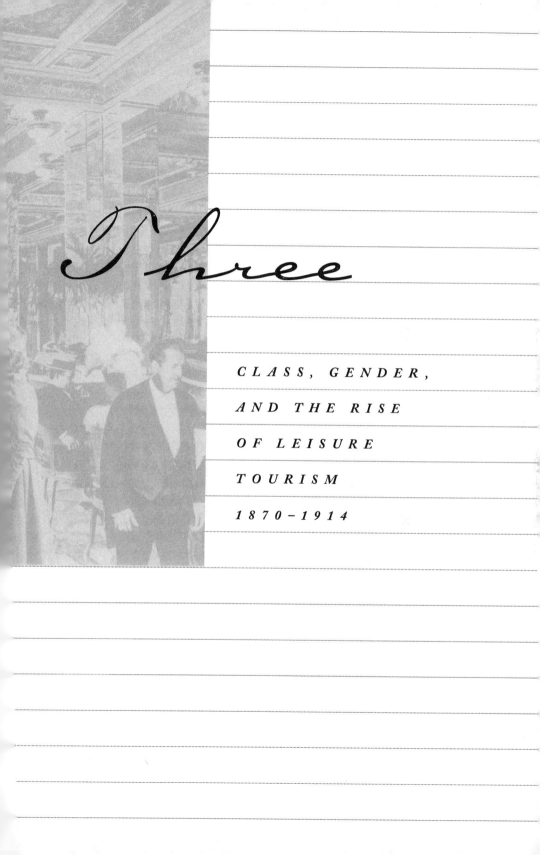

Three

CLASS, GENDER, AND THE RISE OF LEISURE TOURISM 1870–1914

" T H E   G O L D E N   A G E   O F   T R A V E L "

The launching of the White Star liner *Oceanic* in 1870 marked the beginning of a new epoch in transatlantic passenger travel. The luxurious, four-hundred-foot vessel changed the crossing from a trial to be endured into an event to be anticipated with pleasure. First-class passengers' accommodations were relocated from their historic location at the pitching stern of the ship to the more stable section amidships, where they would not be bothered by the noisy new screw propellers. They could now relax in spacious cabins with running water and gas lamps and socialize in a large salon extending the width of the upper deck. Large portholes at either side provided views of the sea while marble fireplaces at each end lent an air of cozy comfort. Passengers now ate leisurely meals on padded chairs instead of benches.[1]

The *Oceanic* still had to rely on both steam and sail for propulsion and could take up to fifteen days to cross, but over the next ten years steady improvements in engines and hulls reduced the dependence on sails and made eleven-day crossings common. By 1890, steam-only boats had reduced the fastest crossing time to six days. Reliability also improved. Ships propelled by twin screws made vessels more maneuverable, safer, better able to ride out storms, and less prone to breakdown. The old fears of meeting one's end in collisions or storms receded. "There are fewer accidents to steamships at sea now-a-days than occur to trains in any line of railroad," said an 1895 tourist guide (omitting to add that it was a time of real carnage on the American railroads). "You are probably more likely to be involved in a smash-up of your carriage in getting to the pier than not to get safely across the Atlantic."[2]

New hulls and methods of propulsion also allowed the liners to swell in size. In the 1870s, the largest ships carried a maximum of 250 first-class passengers and, like the first packets, still depended on cargo for the bulk of their profits.[3] By the 1890s, ships devoted almost wholly to passengers were coming into service. These carried upwards of one thousand in first and second class, with another thousand or so squeezed into steerage. The Germans threw their growing muscle into shipbuilding, turning out ornate monster ships that were larger, faster, and more luxurious than any others afloat. The British countered with their leviathans, and a determined race for size, speed, and luxury developed, paralleling the arms race that would climax in war. The speed record plunged to four and a half days as the British weighed in with fast liners such as the *Mauritania, Lusitania, Olympic,* and *Titanic.* Like the German ships, they boasted huge Baroque salons, marble swimming pools, glassed-in palm courts, and enormous mahogany-paneled first-class dining salons seating five or six hundred amidst a sea of white linen, sparkling crystal, and polished silver. The Germans countered with the enormous *Imperator,* noted mainly for its huge figurehead, a nasty-looking eagle with a tiny Kaiser-like crown, and its bilious, top-heavy roll.[4] The French entry in the race, the *France,* was launched in 1912. It could not compete with the British and Germans in size, but equaled them in luxury and bested them in hauteur. It offered a *grande luxe* section of "princely suites of rooms," each of which included a drawing room copied from one in a Touraine château and a dining room, which allowed a family or group of friends to make the entire crossing in "complete isolation" from the other passengers.[5]

The completely private suites were a rather extreme response to the contradictory demands of the new leisured class. On the one hand, they wanted opportunities for ostentatious displays of consumption; on the other hand, since many of the people who could afford first class were not at all acceptable in the highest social circles, they wanted exclusivity and privacy. To assuage them, the old table d'hôte dining arrangements were replaced by seating at small tables, which they could reserve months in advance.[6] Ships published lists of their first-class passengers in the newspapers and handed them out to passengers upon boarding, allowing them to plot their on-board social strategies in advance.[7] As a result, even before the ship sailed, the first class sorted themselves out by social rank. "The great personages of our boat form a party by themselves," a French woman traveling to America wrote in 1895. "They seem determined to make no acquaintances."[8] According to one observer, the first-class passengers who boarded the *Titanic* on its doomed maiden voyage from Cherbourg and Southampton in 1911 were so certain that they were in the most select company that, unusually, "No one consulted the Passenger List. They met on deck as one big party."[9]

The new comforts were also part of what Alain Corbin has called "the progressive erotization" of vacations.[10] Young men and women found that the pampered, luxurious, voyage in first class could fuel thoughts of romance. When the vivacious twenty-five-year-old Boston Brahmin Mary Lawrence noted the name of Otho Cushing on the first-cabin list of the new *Oceanic* in 1901, she recalled how attractive this artist had been four years earlier, when she saw him in the Hague. "Well! Here at last was one interesting fellow traveller," she confided to her diary. She soon sought him out, declaring him "one of the most fascinating people I ever met. . . . He is absolutely as perfectly made as one of his own Greek gods and goddesses. From top to toe he is absolute grace." Cushing subsequently looked her up in Paris, but a long-term liaison was not in the cards.[11] Nine years later, boarding the same ship with her husband of four years for a grim, unfashionable November crossing, the first-class passenger list set her heart to sinking. "There was not a soul on the passenger list that we had ever heard of before," she wrote in her diary. When the ship docked she wrote, "There was nobody on the *Oceanic* . . . that I ever care to see again."[12]

Aside from the usual nannies and child minders, the upper class often brought a maid or valet.[13] Since the servants could not be put into steerage or second class, where they would be cut off from those they served, ships added special servants' quarters, complete with a dining room, beneath the first-class quarters.[14] Pets were also were given special accommodations. The main problem with them was their propensity to wander off and get lost once they reached the unfamiliar shores of Europe.[15]

Although the luxurious accommodations were usually enough to please even the most demanding of the new moguls, there were still some for whom only their own floating palace would do. For thirty-odd years after Cornelius Vanderbilt's huge side-wheeler waddled across the Atlantic, the prospects for a safe, speedy voyage on a yacht large enough to accommodate a plutocrat, his family, friends, and servants, were still quite problematical. In 1887, Jay Gould, one of the greatest risk-takers among the Wall Street robber barons, prudently sent his yacht *Atalanta* ahead of him to Europe and awaited word of its safe arrival before following on a liner.[16] By the turn of the century, though, British shipyards were turning out large luxury yachts that could cross both safely and swiftly. In January 1897, the wealthy New Yorker Eugene Higgins, aided only by a crew of sixty-six, sailed his new 306-foot steam yacht *Varuna* to France in eight days, a record for a vessel of that sort. The *Paris Herald* reported that along with the usual paneled and gilded saloons, plush couches, mahogany furniture, silver, and two guest suites with adjoining rooms for valets, it had a paneled fencing room. The most striking feature, though, was a full-fledged armory, just aft of Higgins's immense cabin. This, it reported solemnly, was "filled with rifles, cutlasses, and revolvers enough to enable the crew, if need be, to withstand a spirited attack of pirates in a hand-to-hand conflict."[17]

For those satisfied by the relative safety of first-class luxury liners, the ritual of departing changed little over the years. One would visit the ship the day before sailing to check the accommodations and cross the right palms to ensure a deck chair in a protected spot, a civilized time on the daily list for the baths, and, if one feared seasickness, dining room seats at the end of a table that afforded quick, unimpeded passage to the rail on the leeward side of the open deck.[18] On sailing day, relatives and friends would come aboard to share bon voyage champagne, tea, coffee, sandwiches, and cakes. Sometimes, crafty thieves would join the festivities and loot the cabins.[19] Tourists would depart in state rooms filled with flowers, fruit baskets, candies, and piles of "steamer letters," to be rationed out over the course of the voyage. They would hastily write thank-you notes, to be taken ashore by the pilot when he left.[20]

Of course, as the jockeying for seats in the dining room might suggest, no amount of flowers or letters could help matters once those first Atlantic swells set the ship to rolling. The North Atlantic had not changed, and even the largest new ships were still at its mercy. About 80 percent of travelers still felt some seasickness, most for about one to four days. Guidebooks' assurances that the affliction was incurable but not fatal may have provided little solace, but were accurate enough.[21] The experience of Amy Rosenthal, a young woman from Chicago, was more or less typical. She and her aunt and uncle set off from New York in late May 1902, in perfect sunny weather, pleased that they felt no symptoms of seasickness. As soon as they reached unprotected waters, though, the swell kicked in and the weather turned. Amy, forswearing the gory details, wrote simply: "I was terrific sick for four days, after which I enjoyed myself immensely."[22]

While all eyes were fixed on the fast liners' amenities for the super-rich, the transformation of steamship travel had a greater impact on the less-than-rich. Until the 1870s, most lines followed the lead of Cunard, which offered a choice of only first class or steerage, and carried about one cabin-class passenger for every ten in steerage. Some introduced a second class, but it was not much of an improvement over steerage.[23] The larger ships that began coming down the line in the 1870s and 1880s, however, began carving inside spaces into small second-class cabins for which they charged about two-thirds the first-class rates.[24] By the turn of the century, the standard second-class cabin contained three or four upper and lower berths, one of which doubled as a sofa during the day. There was hardly any room for luggage, most of which had to be stored in the holds, and passengers often slept with the doors open to combat stuffiness and claustrophobia.[25] Nevertheless, this contributed to a steady rise in transatlantic tourism. From 1880 to 1900 the number of tourists bound for Europe more than doubled, from about 50,000 to almost 125,000. In the peak year of 1913, close to 250,000 people took first or second-class passage to Europe from America.[26]

The spiraling competition for luxury sliced into the lines' profit margins in first class, encouraging them to promote second class vigorously among the more economy-minded classes.[27] Some lines even used first class as a kind of glamorous loss-leader for the more profitable second class.[28] A French woman who sailed first class from Le Havre to New York wrote of how the second-class passengers were allowed to press up against a barrier to see the fashions worn by first-class patrons, who were playing that delightful new American game, shuffleboard.[29]

Another offshoot of the race for speed and luxury was that, rather than sending older, slower boats to the scrapheap, they were set to sailing between Boston, Philadelphia, or Baltimore and equally unfashionable ports such as Glasgow, Antwerp, and Rotterdam at lower fares than those on the main New York–Liverpool or New York–Cherbourg routes. By 1887, although the first-class return fare on most steamers sailing from New York to Liverpool was about $260, one could find first-class fares to and from less popular ports for as low as $150.[30] Cutthroat competition in the 1890s brought these fares down even further. The shipping lines, led by the master oligopolist J. P. Morgan, tried forming a cartel, but their efforts to fix prices were stymied by Cunard's refusal to join. They were only able to fix minimum fares for summer season trips leaving from the most popular port, New York.[31] Even then, whenever the economy stumbled or overcapacity loomed, the cartel would falter and fares would be shaved. In the mid-1890s, when a middle-class family's income was upwards of one thousand dollars per year, budget-conscious tourists leaving from Boston or Philadelphia, or catching the older, slower boats from New York to ports such as Glasgow, could pay as little as $55 round trip.[32] In 1898,

Henry Seaver, a young architecture student at M.I.T., and a draftsman acquaintance managed to negotiate first-class cabin fares from Boston to Liverpool and from Naples to Boston for only $60 each.[33] Fares rose somewhat over the next ten years, but not to their previous levels.[34]

Conditions on the slower, unfashionable boats were hardly Spartan. In June 1890, Alfred Roe resigned his high school teaching position in Worcester, Massachusetts, and boarded the cheapest boat he could find, the Red Star line's *Waesland*, for his long-dreamed-of trip to Europe. He did not mind sacrificing speed for price, he wrote in his diary, because speed often came at the expense of safety. A typical dinner on this cheapest of all liners consisted of oysters, consommé, chicken croquettes, filet of sole, roast quail, chicken Chasseur, filet of beef, two kind of potatoes, asparagus with poached eggs, stuffed tomatoes, and a plethora of desserts.[35] Ironically, in 1902, a lumbering British hulk rammed the *Waesland*, for which he had sacrificed speed for safety, sending it to the bottom with considerable loss of life.

By the early 1900s, some adventurous middle-class tourists were even venturing into steerage. The scandalous condition of the immigrants in the holds had led governments to mandate better food and more space there. Moving steerage to the fore and aft of ships increased levels of biliousness, but it also provided a bit of open deck for fresh air.[36] Renamed Third Class, by 1910 it was attracting more than a few penny-wise American tourists, particularly for the return voyage. The *New York Times* reported favorably on it in August of that year. An average of one thousand Americans a week were arriving in New York in steerage, it said, most of them young men who had gone over first or second class but had gone "broke" in Europe.[37] *America Abroad*, on the other hand, would not recommend it because of its inferior sanitary condition and "*régime*." It did say, though, that it was "well-worth visiting during the voyage by those interested in social science."[38]

If it was the golden age of steamship travel, it was at least the silver age for the continental railroads. The railroad network that developed between 1860 and 1914 allowed faster, more comfortable rolling stock to reach practically every town and village in France. Tiny spa towns such as Vichy and Aix-les-Bains, which had dozed through the ages since the Romans bathed in their springs, now became easily accessible. In 1863, a Paris tourist magazine reported that the spa towns had "witnessed an influx of tourists and sick people from all over." Chemists had used the latest techniques to analyze the composition of the waters, and doctors had reported on their therapeutic effects. Then "government and speculators had quickly endowed these places . . . with magnificent establishments [the buildings where one actually takes the waters.]"[39] Luxurious new hotels, casinos, promenades, race tracks, and concert halls were added, encouraging the idea that pleasurable activities aided therapy. Finally, therapy began to take a backseat to pleasure, as the spas became integrated into the fashionable social circuit.[40]

By 1870, the older spas were meeting stiff competition from new seaside resorts. Sea bathing cures had begun challenging spa water cures in late-eighteenth-century Britain, but aside from a brief period in the 1820s when restored French aristocrats flocked to Dieppe and mingled with their British counterparts, they did not become became fashionable in France until the 1850s.[41] It was only after the trend-setting Empress Eugénie immersed herself in the Channel at Boulogne-sur-mer, and pronounced it to be both healthful and fashionable, that their popularity took off. In 1863, *Paris-Promeneur, Paris-Touriste* said the new *bains de mer* were just as healthy and fashionable as the mineral baths, and had the added advantage of healthful sea air. Indeed, many people went there "less for bathing than to breathe the air of our beaches, which is so pure and invigorating." By then, not only had Boulogne been opened up to rail passengers from Paris, but so had Dieppe, Havre, Trouville, and other soon-to-be-famous resorts. An express train made the run to Calais in a little over six hours. *Paris-Promeneur* ran a cartoon of a woman representing Paris bound for the Channel resorts with a caption reading: "Doctors have ordered the city of Paris to take the Waters, and the Waters have done much good . . . for the railroad companies."[42]

Meanwhile, the British had ventured southward to the Mediterranean, where they sought refuge from winters in their green but sodden land under the blue skies of the County of Nice, which was acquired by France in 1860.[43] In 1864, the railroad from Marseille reached Nice, opening it and the other towns along the Côte d'Azur—the Riviera—to an influx of mainly British winter residents. (Its winter, it was said, was the equivalent of Britain's summer.[44]) American expatriates followed, buying or renting villas there. In February 1867, there were eight hundred of them in Nice alone.[45] In the mid-1870s, the railroads began running sleeping cars and then dining cars on what soon became a mere eighteen-hour run down from Paris. Sumptuous all-first-class express trains (such as the famous Blue Train, which left London for Nice every winter evening) followed, with fine china and silver service in the dining cars, plush, wood-paneled smoking cars and even boudoir cars. The royal families and aristocrats of Europe, following the trail blazed by the Russian court in the 1860s, arrived in private cars and private trains to occupy fanciful villas in Cimiez, in the hills overlooking Nice. Entrepreneurs constructed huge hotels catering to a leisured class who arrived, with their teams of servants, for stays of three to five months.[46] Between 1860 and 1911 Nice, the first city in the West to develop a tourist-based economy, had the highest growth rate of any city in Europe.[47]

In the 1890s, first-class rail fares in France rose, while second and third-class fares fell substantially. Yet trains carrying all classes of cars arrived at their destinations just about as quickly as the relatively few all-first-class trains. As a result, first-class travel slumped, as second class and even third class became perfectly acceptable to middle-class travelers.[48] This increase in affordability highlighted one of the railroads' problems for elite tourists. Except for the private trains that carried the truly grand and the royal, and the all-first-class luxury sleeping-car trains, they could be distressingly egalitarian. Everyone got on and off at the same time and, unlike steamships, passengers could not be segregated on the platforms. Moreover, until well into the new century all passengers arriving by rail in Paris had to claim their baggage at customs, where they jostled together while waiting to be questioned and sometimes searched. Nor were the fare differences between first and the other classes enough, particularly on shorter runs, to ensure that only the well-off and well-behaved traveled first class. The seating arrangements in French cars exacerbated the problem for, unlike American cars, the aisle ran down one side and people sat in enclosed compartments. First-class passengers lived in terror that their compartment-mates might be like those Annie and James Fields had to put up with on the overnight train from Paris to Marseille in 1860: "2 or three garlic'y workmen and one traveller so exceedingly drunk as not to know in the least when he should get out but was obliged to be put out by some fellow-sufferers."[49]

Also, since only two of the European compartment's seats were the window seats coveted by tourists, one's social inferiors could exercise unwanted power over one's touristic experience. As the train carrying John Munn and his family from Paris to Turin ascended into the mountains, they fumed as two poorly dressed local men monopolized the window seats, apparently oblivious to the scenery. Then, to his surprise, "one of them . . . saying 'cascades' pointed to one side of the car and presently one of the loveliest visions met our gaze. . . . For this little act of kindness my heart softened toward him." Meanwhile, however, a French woman maneuvered the Munns's woman friend out of her window seat with a false claim that she wished to speak to someone at the next stop.[50]

Experiences such as these were not often compensated for by pleasant encounters with French people, for the American compulsion to strike up conversations with strangers on trains was not shared by the French. "We met a courteous Frenchman on the train," wrote Henriette Frank after crisscrossing France by rail in 1908, "about the only polite Frenchman we met in trains."[51] Even renting a whole car was not a foolproof solution. The wealthy Matthews family of New York thought they had a whole car reserved for their trip from Paris to their rented villa in Dinard, in mid-June 1901. However, when they arrived at the station, they were chagrined to find that the eight of them—parents, four children, nanny, and maid—had but two compartments to share.[52]

The relatively egalitarian nature of railroad travel may be one reason that the upper-class American presence at the French seaside resorts did not become very noticeable until after the introduction of a higher-status way of getting there, the automobile. At first, when the automobile was still a novelty, trips through the countryside were by no means easy. In 1900, Sheffield Phelps, a wealthy Yale graduate, shipped his Locomobile steam automobile over from the States to Bordeaux and set off with a fellow Yaley with the improbable name of Poultney Bigelow on what was to be a long trip through southwest France. They had barely made it past their first overnight stopover when the car's twenty-five hoses and steam valves began leaking profusely and it came sighing to a halt. After an ignominious tow by a farmer's horse, the car ended up in the hands of a small-town mechanic who, in ten days of hammering and tinkering, could not repair it. Finally, the exasperated Bigelow returned to London while Phelps took the train to Menton, on the Riviera, instructing that the machine be shipped to him when it was repaired. By the time it arrived in Menton, with valves still leaking, the freight and repair bills had mounted to almost two thousand dollars. "I am sick at heart!" Phelps wrote Bigelow, at the thought that it had cost that much "for a day and a half of motoring."[53]

Bigelow, whose best-known previous contribution to journalism had been a spirited defense of the Czar's anti-Semitic laws, turned the experience into a cautionary tale for readers of the *Independent* who might harbor similar dreams of touring France by automobile.[54] But perhaps he should only have warned against doing so in American cars, for France was then the world's leader in automobile design and production. A 1907 French guidebook intended for Americans noted wryly that when it came to automobiles:

> Paris leads all other cities in the world. The finest cars are built in Paris; there are more of them on the streets of the capital; they are driven at a faster speed, more money is spent on them and, probably, more pedestrians are knocked down and run over by [them] than in any other city of the world.[55]

By then, a number of companies were offering chauffeured rental cars to tourists, both for driving in Paris and trips to the country.[56] The spread of asphalt paving also made France's already excellent system of straight, well-engineered roads even better. "We could see," began a 1905 article about an American party who rented an automobile and driver for a motor tour in France, "that it would be a long time before we have any roads in America so ideal for automobiling."[57]

Renting a car and chauffeur thus emerged as the perfect way to avoid the hoi polloi in the train stations and distinguish one's touring experience from the increasingly numerous run-of-the-mill "tourists." Those who toured in an automobile "escape opprobrium," noted the author Booth Tarkington after taking one such trip. "They are not called 'tourists,' but 'automobilists,' or 'motorists.' . . . This is the only escape."[58] Edith Wharton's 1906 book about her chauffeured trip through France begins: "The motor car has restored the romance of travel. Freeing us from the irritating compulsions *and contacts of* the railway, the bondage to fixed hours and the beaten track."[59] In all of these rang the familiar refrain: railroad travel restricts your freedom and imprisons you with undesirables. The auto enabled you to avoid the tourists. One optimistic article estimated that in 1907 forty thousand Americans had left Paris for automobile tours of the countryside.[60] (Most were probably day trips to places such as Fontainebleau and Barbizon, just outside of Paris.[61])

For many upper-class men, it was not enough to wend one's way at a leisurely clip through the countryside, taking in the sights from the back of a chauffeured car. Engineers were squeezing more speed from the enormous new automobiles, and exploiting it became a mark of an upper-class machismo. Women were thought to respond with an appropriate rush of the sexual juices. The *Paris Herald*, reporting on one of these races in Trouville, quoted an American woman as saying

> No one who did not see the race can in the least imagine the ecstasy of exquisite sensation that permeates one's being when a machine flashed by at that frightful speed. . . . You realize the awful danger to [the driver]. You sympathize in the keenness of the delight he must feel. It comes over you with a rush that he possess[es] all that goes to make a real man—courage, skill, steady nerves, well controlled muscles, and self-reliance and clear brains.[62]

The *Paris Herald*, whose publisher, Gordon Bennett, was an avid promoter of auto racing, also slavered over the fast times Americans achieved on the trips to and from various resorts, with or without a chauffeur. A typical issue, in July 1907, said that two Pittsburgh men had made the 220-mile run from Cherbourg to Paris in less than twelve hours. Above it was a story about the theatrical impresario Martin Beck's "quick run" from Lucerne to Paris. It reported that when the French chauffeur, who was driving at speeds of up to one hundred kilometers an hour, hit a bump, Beck smashed his head on the ceiling, suffering a minor wound.[63]

Thanks in part to this thirst for speed, each summer the roadside along the routes leading to the resorts would be littered with the smoking wrecks of powerful automobiles and the bodies of the social elite and their chauffeurs. One of the most infamous of the accidents occurred quite early on, in 1902, when thirty-six-year-old Charles Fair, an heir to a huge California fortune, insisted on taking the wheel of his car from his chauffeur on the drive from Paris to Trouville. The couple had arrived in Paris from New York in June and made the Hôtel Ritz their headquarters for summer touring. They bought the forty-five horsepower red Mercedes there and took automobile trips to Vichy, Aix-les-Bains, Ostend, and other spas and resorts. Like his brother-in-law, William K. Vanderbilt Jr., of New York and Newport, he was fond of traveling at high speed. Unlike his brother-in-law, he was, in the words of the *Herald*, "not very expert" at the wheel. Indeed, on the day he bought the car he collided with another auto in the Bois de Boulogne. Now, with his terrified wife sitting beside him and the chauffeur in the back, he seemed determined to break his brother-in-law's record of two and a half hours for the trip. The chauffeur sat petrified as he pushed the car up to eighty, ninety, and then one hundred kilometers an hour—frightening speeds when one considers that two months later a champion racing driver averaged only fifty-five kilometers-an-hour on the trip. When he reached one hundred and ten kilometers-an-hour—over sixty-five miles an hour—the chauffeur panicked, but before he could do anything a front tire exploded and Fair lost control. The car veered off the roadway and smashed into a large tree. The Fairs were catapulted into the tree trunk and died almost instantly, leaving the tree trunk splattered with their brains. The chauffeur, mercifully, was thrown free and emerged relatively unscathed, except that he kept repeating the phrase "one hundred and ten kilometers."[64]

Mechanical failures also caused many accidents. Aside from blowouts, one of the most common, and most dangerous, was failure of the steering gear. In July 1912, the wealthy young Washingtonian Natalie Barney, who was establishing herself as a leader in Paris's lesbian community, almost ended up like Fair. Returning from Aix-les-Bains to Paris in her chauffeur-driven car with two American friends, she insisted on taking the wheel herself. The steering failed and the car swerved off the road, overturning and throwing the occupants out. Although Barney and one of her friends were just bruised, the chauffeur was killed instantly. The third American woman suffered a severely fractured skull from which she later died.[65] A few weeks later, a chauffeured automobile carrying a Mme. Bernstein, New York heiress to a banking fortune, suffered a breakdown en route to Paris from Étretat (a posh Channel resort) and crashed into a tree. Mrs. Bernstein and her two female friends were flung out, and two of the women's legs were broken. Other motorized vehicles were no safer. The day before, a thirty-year-old Yale graduate on a motorcycle hit a bicyclist in a small town in the Jura hills. He catapulted off the motorcycle, hit his head on the cobblestoned street, and died.[66]

Despite the risks, traveling by auto became de rigueur for Americans visiting the resorts and spas. By 1910, the quality of American luxury cars equaled those of Europe. One could now ship one's own car and chauffeur to France and back for the cost of renting a chauffeured car in Paris. The transatlantic shipping companies set up special departments to handle the growing number of Americans doing this.[67] By 1912, the automobile had practically displaced the train as the preferred way to get to the spas and resorts. "Automobilists love Evian," the *Herald* announced that year. The two hundred guests in one hotel, including many Americans, had seventy automobiles among them. Vichy's luxury hotels encouraged automobilists to make it their headquarters for auto tours with a special guidebook and road map detailing trips to Paris, Nice, Trouville, and Biarritz.[68]

However, *pace* Edith Wharton, who extolled the automobile for allowing one to explore at a leisurely pace, Americans touring in cars became known for quite the opposite: what one of them called "a bad case of '*speediosis*'" that betrayed an utter lack of interest in anything they were transversing aside from the road.[69] Another American said, "[They] burn up the roads between the historic towns of Europe with the evident intention of covering as much ground as possible each day, and retaining only the vaguest impressions of the interesting places and beautiful scenery en route."[70] As the Vichy hotel owners' map indicated, the machines were used to speed the American upper class, not to France's famous cultural attractions, but to its social ones—to other spas and resorts. The new way of traveling had become yet another factor weakening cultural tourism among them.

Eleven

PRISONERS OF LEISURE:

UPPER-CLASS TOURISM

As the century drew to a close, the iconoclastic Norwegian-American economist Thorstein Veblen discerned the emergence of a new kind of ruling class in America. This "leisure class" rested its claims to superiority not on its contributions to the productive process but on ostentatious waste—what he called "conspicuous consumption." This meant, not just the consumption of material goods, but of time as well—"conspicuous leisure."[1]

There was more than enough evidence for Veblen's theories amidst the monster mansions of Chicago, where Veblen taught for while, but nowhere was there more support for his theory than in the behavior of upper-class American tourists in France. Here, in the years after the Civil War, was an excellent example of how the values of the upper class changed from ones of production to ones of consumption. The antebellum upper class had felt compelled to justify their visits there as somehow productive—in terms of health, cultural uplift, and even patriotism. As the nineteenth century drew on, however, upper-class touring increasingly involved ostentatious leisure and extravagant consumption. In the 1840s and 1850s, health and then patriotism had become negligible considerations. Now cultural uplift fell by the wayside. Pursuing it became the mark of tourists in the class below.

By 1870, a new wave of refugees was joining Paris's expatriate community. Many of the old upper class fled America in disgust, repelled by the new class of plutocrats who, enriched by the Civil War, were corrupting politics and vulgarizing "society." These genteel exiles, with steady incomes from bonds, real estate, and other fixed investments, installed themselves in imposing mansions in Paris's most fashionable neighborhoods, near the Champs-Élysées.[2] The influx was temporarily halted when Louis-Napoléon's humiliating defeat in the short war he provoked with Prussia forced him to surrender and abdicate in September 1870. A new government in Paris continued to resist the Prussians but, after a punishing six-month siege and bombardment, it surrendered in March 1871. A mixed bag of liberals and socialists then seized control of Paris, forming the government of the Commune to challenge the French conservatives who had made peace with the Prussians. Paris was again besieged and bombarded, this time by a conservative army headquartered in Versailles. Not until that July were the conservatives able to subdue the starving Communards.

The sieges, bombardments, and bloody final assault wreaked havoc upon Paris's touristic jewels. Many of the imposing mansions near the Arc de Triomphe were destroyed; the famous arch itself was pockmarked by shell fragments. During the final assault, both the Tuileries Palace and the seventeenth-century city hall were set ablaze and destroyed—exactly how and by whom remained in dispute. There was no dispute, however, about what happened to the surviving Communards. The last of the holdouts, 147 of them, were lined up against a wall in their final redoubt, Père Lachaise cemetery, and shot. During the next week, teams of conservative army execution squads summarily shot from twenty thousand to twenty-five thousand more Commune supporters. About ten thousand more were shipped off to prisons, many in France's notorious overseas prison colonies.[3]

Needless to say, the conflict disrupted tourism, but not as much as one would imagine. When the war broke out, Thomas Cook began making preparations for postwar battlefield tours. If the war was "short and sharp," he said, "thousands will rush to the scene of the recent conflict, and it will be well to stand in readiness for such an agreeable eventuality."[4] The continuing resistance in Paris dashed these hopes, but in the summer of 1871, as the noose tightened around Paris, other enterprising British tour operators organized one-week tours for groups who picnicked on the hills surrounding the city and watched the bombardment. When the conservative troops finally fought their way into the city, tourists followed hard on their heels, sniffing through the ruins.[5]

Edward Van Cise, a touring American lawyer, arrived in the smoldering city at the end of July, and damned the Communards for having upset his sightseeing plans. He set out with some other tourists for Versailles, but was chagrined to find that they were not allowed inside the palace. Instead, he wrote, "we were obliged to content ourselves with an outside view . . . and taking a peek at some of the 3,000 communists imprisoned in the orangerie."[6] Annie Bradley, a twenty-two-year-old from upstate New York, was also upset. She went to see the Jardin des Plantes, but discovered that the lofty trees of its arboretum, many of which had been planted during the reign of Louis XIV, had been cut down for firewood and that most of the exotic animals in its famous zoo had been eaten. "Was never so disappointed in a place in all my life," she wrote in her diary.[7]

Europe's most popular tourist destination bounced back remarkably quickly. Craters and shell holes were soon filled in, and the expatriates returned to reopen and patch up their mansions. By the summer of 1872, upper-class American tourists were pouring back in. "All the world were in Paris, and among them the Nortons," the Boston Brahmin Mary Parkman wrote home that September.[8] The Tuileries palace was left in ruins (as a reminder, it was said, of the Communards' barbarism) but a virtual replica of the Hôtel de Ville, the city hall, replaced the one that was destroyed.[9] One entrepreneur hired twenty destitute artists to paint a circular diorama of the Siege of Paris. In 1874, twenty-two-year-old Aimee Rotch Sargent wrote that she and her father were greatly impressed by its depiction of "bombshells bursting from point-to-point and the dead and dying scattered about." She was particularly impressed by

> a life-like [painting] of a snowy Paris street with half-starved wretches clamoring at the shut door of a boucher's and upon the other side of the scene a bomb-shell had just burst and one could almost hear the cries of the wounded men, women and children. Papa was as delighted as me and said it was all most wonderful.[10]

Another businessman opened a panorama depicting Paris's defenses against the Prussians. Others took Americans on tours of Strasbourg, to see the devastation caused by new types of shells, and the battlefield at Sedan, near Metz, to see where Louis-Napoléon's forces were surrounded and defeated.[11]

With various monarchists, Catholics, and other conservatives now safely in control, expatriates fed visiting Americans a diet of horror stories about the depredations of the Communards, who were described as homicidal maniacs whose program was the abolition of private property, religion, and the destruction of civilization.[12] Myths such as that the Communards forced hundreds of people into the city hall before they burned it became standard fare in American guidebooks to France. "It seems singular," said one intended for high school students, "that the citizens of Paris should ever so far lose their reason as to destroy a building of such interest and permit their companions to die in the flames, but when the French people are excited and angry they are always ready for a riot."[13]

The alliance between France's fading landed aristocracy and the *grande bourgeoisie* of finance and industry that had restored conservative rule soon frayed and fell apart. In the late 1870s and early 1880s, aristocratic finances took a beating from falling agricultural prices and crooked banking schemes. The Radical party, self-proclaimed heir to the republican and libertarian principles of 1789, steadily gained power. It allied with other republicans to weaken the conservative Catholic Church and strengthen the secular institutions of the new Third Republic, particularly public education. At first, industry and commerce remained in the doldrums, but toward the end of the century the boom returned. As commerce expanded, so did the number of nouveaux-riches businessmen and investors. Their lavish tastes in food, wine, clothing, housing, and entertainment underlay that veritable orgy of consumption known as the Belle Époque.[14]

The resurgence of republicanism and the political and economic decline of the aristocracy hardly dented the way expatriates and their touring American friends fawned over practically anyone with a title. Of these there was now no shortage. Louis-Napoléon had been very liberal when it came to doling them out, and Paris's reputation as the pleasure capital of Europe induced a new flow of sybaritic blue-bloods from all over Europe.[15] For Americans who turned up their noses at their homeland because it was so lacking in people with pedigrees, the dizzying milieu of exotic titles constituted a kind of Nirvana. In 1887, James Gordon Bennett, the immensely wealthy thirty-year-old owner of the *New York Herald,* fled sexual scandal in New York by exiling himself to Paris. He started a Paris edition of that newspaper, soon dubbed the *Paris Herald,* and began inundating expatriates and touring Americans with breathless accounts of the carryings-on of the princes, princesses, and the rest of titled Europe, among whom "Commodore" Bennett himself proudly cavorted.[16]

Most members of Paris's expatriate "society," who were practically all Protestant, were excluded from the highest reaches of French society, which, with its bunker mentality, was now ostentatiously Catholic. "The Faubourg St-Germain is as strange a territory to many of them as though it were situated in the heart of the Congo basin," said Richard Harding Davis in 1895.[17] Nevertheless, the breathless accounts of the international set's doings in the *Herald,* supplemented by Paris's hyperactive gossip mills, helped the expatriates become an impressive community of what David Riesman called "inside dopesters," full of titillating stories of aristocratic carryings-on.[18] Moreover, there were more than enough titled foreigners, including a generous sprinkling of down-on-their-luck fortune-hunters, to give visitors the illusion that they were mingling with high society. One social climber, a Miss Fanny Reed, made a good living by introducing visiting young American women into these circles.[19]

Prominent journals back in the States fueled this aristo-mania. One French observer said he was "stupefied" by how the American press reported that, now that "the season" was over in Paris and the last polo match had been played, everyone was off to Boulogne, and the capital was now empty. It was, he snorted, "as if a couple of dozen idlers were all of Paris." What the French regarded as the delusive declarations of obscure, ineffectual marquises, he said, were reported as serious news in America.[20]

In April 1890, the staid old *North American Review*, which numbered Henry James among its regular contributors, asked a Madame Julietta Adams to write on "Society in Paris." The result was a fourteen-page catalog of princes, duchesses, marquises, and counts of the Faubourg-Saint-Germain, lauding their fine breeding, elegance, and good taste. She even extolled their intelligence, something even their greatest sycophants normally refrained from discussing. Yes, she conceded, there was infidelity in their marriages, but this was because few of them could afford love-matches. Many had fallen on hard times by investing in a fine Catholic bank which was ruined by a jealous Jewish one. The resulting "Krach" had destroyed their fortunes and "a number of *mésalliances* were judged necessary to reestablish certain budgets." Although the aristocrats were now forced to deal with the Jewish bankers, they remained disdainful of them:

> Practiced eyes have no trouble in perceiving the shades of tone, manner, and carriage of a gentleman at the Rothschilds', or the Baron De Hirsch's, or the great Jew bankers' of Paris. The slightest detail is perceptible, and the dukes, when they consent to seat themselves at the table of the financiers, always find their cooking too spicy in flavor. You may wager one hundred to one, that they will not sip the fine wines of the Jewish bankers with the pleasure they feel in drinking . . . those whose aristocratic cellars have a wide renown.[21]

Yet, whatever the tottering aristocrats of the Faubourg may have muttered behind their backs, by 1890 the wealthy Jewish families such as the

Rothschilds and Sterns were part of Paris's society's highest circles.[22] This was more than could be said for their counterparts in America, where upper-class vacation resorts had become notoriously anti-Semitic, refusing to accommodate even extremely wealthy families with impressive Sephardic pedigrees. For upper-class American Jews, then, a vacation in France came to represent what it later represented for African Americans: a refuge from discrimination at home. After the banker Edward Seligman and his family were barred at the door of the Union Hotel in Saratoga when they arrived to take up the suite of rooms they had reserved in the summer of 1877, he henceforth alternated vacationing in predominantly Jewish enclaves in America with summering in European spas. Other wealthy Jewish families, such as the Schiffs, Strausses, Kuhns, and Loebs also became fixtures in France's spas and resorts.[23]

They felt particularly comfortable in France, the first country in Europe to legally emancipate Jews, but not because anti-Semitism was absent there. Indeed, as the Dreyfus Affair amply demonstrated, it was endemic in certain higher circles.[24] However, the social status and financial power of the Jewish financiers put a damper on it in the spas and resorts. Moreover, the fading French aristocracy might look down upon them, but no more than they did on upper-class Protestants. Indeed, by 1910 Paris's "smart set" included many Jews, but few Protestants. "The Paris Upper Ten class Protestants with Jews," said one American observer, "and tolerate their society solely on account of their money."[25] In any event, like upper-class Protestants, most touring upper-class Jews seemed content enough in their own social circles. The Paris diaries of wealthy Chicago Jews read much like those of the Lawrences and other Boston Brahmins, except that the social calls are made to Americans with names such as Wallach, Rothschild, Eisendrath, and Thalman.[26]

— —

By the 1880s, the expanding railroad network had allowed a kind of year-round international upper-class tourist circuit to evolve. Socialites would assemble in Paris for a few weeks in October and then head south for the winter, to Nice, Cannes, Menton, Pau, or Biarritz. Some would then press on to Italy before drifting back north in the late spring, via the alpine spas such as the "Anglo-American colony" Aix-les-Bains.[27] After subjecting themselves to its famed water treatment, which involved squatting on small stools and being sprayed by sulphurous water while muscular "*doucheurs*" kneaded their bodies, they would gather again in Paris in mid-May. There they would go to the horse races at Chantilly, attend a dizzying round of balls and dinners, and finally clatter through the Bois de Boulogne to the Grand Prix race at Longchamps in early June. The British would then go to London for their "season," while the others would head for resorts or spas such as Trouville, Dieppe, Boulogne, Vichy, Spa itself (in Belgium), and be rejoined by the British in mid-July. In late September or early October, they would suddenly evacuate their villas and hotels (The closing dates were never firm, for the early departure of one or two of the social lions would often lead to a stampede of those fearful of being left behind with an unfashionable crowd) and return to their homes to mull over which resorts would be graced with their presence during the coming year.[28]

Expatriate Americans joined in the resort-crawling with some enthusiasm, but socialites back in America, who had their own fashionable watering places, were relatively slow to join the European circuit.[29] In the 1890s, though, they began frequenting the spas in larger numbers, often plugging into the circuit twice a year, returning to Newport or Saratoga for their summer "seasons."[30] Soon after Isabel Shaw, a young Boston woman whose parents sent her to Paris for culture and polishing, arrived in Paris in the cold, damp December of 1899, her aunt Anna (explaining that "these two months are the dead season in Paris") whisked her, her own daughter, two servants, and thirty-eight pieces of luggage off to Pau, in the warm southwest, which was full of British and American socialites.[31]

The aunt had not overpacked. Seventeen trunks per person was considered the norm for women of that class, for social life at the resorts was a veritable orgy of conspicuous consumption of clothing and leisure. The daytime promenades, tennis matches, picnics in the country, concerts in the casino concert halls, pony rides, reading in the reading room, billiards in the billiard room, parading into dining salons while the orchestra played, and swirling across the floor at nighttime balls: each activity demanded expensive clothing. Women needed at least four daily changes of clothing—morning toilettes, tennis outfits, afternoon toilettes for visiting, and fancy evening clothes—as well an array of robes, hats, parasols, boas, fans, gloves, and shoes. At the seaside resorts, elaborate bathing costumes were also in order, including special hats, shoes, stockings, and, of course, a maid waiting at water's edge holding one's peignoir.[32] Showing the world that one had nothing productive to do could be hard work indeed.

Spas and resorts vied furiously for the fashionable trade, trembling before the whims of jaded monarchical and aristocratic trendsetters. Rumors that a monarch was buying a villa in a town would set off a real estate boom; their defection, a collapse. Queen Victoria's arrival could instantly catapult a resort and a hotel to the top of the ladder (she was the only European monarch who preferred hotels to villas). Anne Bense and her family chose the Hôtel d'Angleterre in Biarritz in April 1885 because the Queen had stayed there just two weeks before. (She was less impressed that ex-president Chester A. Arthur was still there.[33]) The Queen's next trip to the old fishing village, in 1889, solidified its new ranking at the top of the table for British and Americans, sending its southwestern rival Pau into a permanent decline.[34] In 1891, she shifted her loyalties to the Côte d'Azur, helping propel that region's rise as an Anglo-American favorite. Thenceforth, every November, when the royal railway carriage carrying her and her retinue of about one hundred arrived in Nice, crowds of grateful Niçois would turn out to welcome it, giving heartfelt thanks for the infusions of tourist money she brought in her wake.[35]

Victoria's switch to the Riviera was not un-Victorian, for the area had not yet developed its later image as a rather sexy place. Indeed, its tourist industry still owed a lot to its reputation as a healthy place for invalids, particularly those suffering from consumption/tuberculosis.[36] When Frances Haxall, a wealthy young woman from Richmond, Virginia, who herself was suffering from a serious pulmonary disorder, arrived in Nice on a European tour in 1875, she was depressed by "the sight of poor consumptives, of whom there is no end in sight in this little town." She moved down the coast to the lovely little town of Menton, where she found a pension full of "bright" young people. However, she wrote her sister, two of the Americans there "are slowly dying. It is so sad, so very sad." Although she feared she herself might not make it back to Virginia, she did, but within two years she too was dead.[37]

However, just down the road in the poor principality of Monaco (a dependency of France), the town of Monte Carlo was blazing a trail into a different future for the Côte. In the early 1860s it promoted itself primarily as a moderately priced *bains de mer* featuring "*hydrotherapie maritime*" in salt and fresh water. It did boast of a "Casino rivaling the most glittering ones in Germany," but also "Halls for conversation, reading and games. Concerts twice a day; Fetes, Balls, Soirées, Sea Excursions, etc."[38] The extension of the railroad from Nice in 1868 and new restrictions on gambling in other European spas helped turn it into a "purpose-built gambling city." The shrewd Frenchman who operated the concession assiduously cultivated an aristocratic image for the place. He hired Charles Garnier, designer of the magnificent Paris Opéra, to knock off a similar opera house for the resort, and crowned his success by luring the Prince of Wales to make a highly publicized visit in 1875. The aristocratic veneer stuck, even though most of the over 150,000 people who visited it each year were by no means pedigreed.[39]

Nice, its nearby competitor, was forced to allow casino gambling in 1884; Cannes and other seaside resorts soon followed. Although old-time upper-class *hivernants* [winter-residents] now grumbled that the casinos attracted parvenus who stayed there for a mere three months, the Riviera managed to profit on the association of aristocracy and casinos in the public mind.[40] By the early twentieth century, the convalescing invalids, discouraged by hotel owners who felt that their coughing deterred the more profitable guests, had switched to mountain retreats, and the Côte d'Azur was well on its way to establishing itself as Europe's prime playground of pleasure.[41] Every October, the society columns would begin their weekly winter listings of the "white wings"—the grand yachts—many of them American, arriving in Nice.[42]

For many upper-class tourists, the only thing that rivaled socializing as an activity was shopping. Most tourists returned home with souvenirs to remind them of a trip. The upper class wanted far more: to appropriate parts of Europe as evidence of their power and distinction.[43]

Those who were truly in the major leagues could buy old chateaux, or settle for their contents. The financial crisis of 1883 that landed many of France's old landed families in financial distress coincided with the rise of a new generation of American super-rich who were constructing monstrous new homes in locations such as New York's Fifth Avenue, San Francisco's Nob Hill, Philadelphia's Main Line, Chicago's Golden Mile, and Newport. Many of them were knock-offs of French chateaux designed by American graduates of Paris's École des Beaux-Arts such as Richard Morris Hunt. These ersatz aristocrats felt that nothing less that the furniture of real aristocrats was fit for their new palaces. Wealthy moguls such as the department store king A. T. Stewart descended on France accompanied by agents who ticked off long lists of antiques and works of art. William K. Vanderbilt, Cornelius's grandson, had Hunt design an enormous mansion at Fifth Avenue and 57th Street in New York City whose art gallery boasted 208 pictures from Europe, hung in three superimposed rows, in the style of the Paris Salon.[44] He then had Hunt design a smaller, seventy-two-room Newport "cottage" whose ornate public rooms were entirely decorated with furnishings from Paris. The two grandest rooms were built and decorated entirely in Paris, reassembled in Newport, and hung with more European art.

Descendants of the old antebellum elite such as Edith Wharton looked down on the new plutocrats, but by the 1880s they were being forced either to accept them into the uppermost social circles or, as in the case of the old New York Knickerbocker families, fade into social oblivion. Most of the new members of the elite, including almost all of Mrs. Astor's famed New York "Four Hundred," were notorious ignoramuses with little real interest in high culture. However, some of the wealthiest of them, including heavyweight power-brokers such as the bankers J. P. Morgan, August Belmont and Jacob Schiff, the steelmaker Henry Clay Frick, and the sugar baron Henry O. Havemeyer, became serious patrons of the arts.[45]

To leaders of the "robber baron" generation of the 1860s, such as Jay Gould, art was for women. However, as we shall see in the next chapter, in the late 1870s and 1880s a kind of male counterrevolution against the feminization of art appreciation took place. A number of turn-of-the-century plutocrats became serious collectors, like the monarchs and aristocrats of old, collecting masterpieces for the power and distinction conferred by their ownership.[46] J. P. Morgan, perhaps the most knowledgeable of this generation of megalomaniacs, came to Paris only to shop. He shunned expatriates and avoided other visiting magnates by staying in a distinctly unfashionable hotel. Each morning, no matter what the season, he would have a breakfast of strawberries sent to his suite and would seat himself behind a desk while a line of art and antique dealers entered, one by one, from the antechamber. He would greet them, be shown their wares, and say only "I'll take it" or "No," sometimes dispensing millions in the course of a few hours.[47]

Most other plutocrats were less serious collectors, contenting themselves with buying what dealers told them were masterpieces of Old World art. The *New York Times* reported in 1910 that there were 2,000 pictures attributed to Rembrandt in the United States. The same year a Paris paper claimed that more than 15,000 fake Old Masters had been shipped to America in the previous twelve months alone, including 1,812 Rembrandts, as well as 2,849 Corots and hundreds of Marie Antoinette's harpsichords.[48] Nevertheless, the American press proudly reported on the millions the moguls were spending to add European masterpieces to the nation's treasure trove.[49]

Of course not all collectors were male plutocrats. Upper-class females got into the act too. The artist Mary Cassatt, whose prominent Philadelphia family controlled the Pennsylvania Railroad, moved to Paris in 1874 and became a part of the Impressionist group of painters. When her blueblooded Philadelphia friend Louisine Elder married into New York's Havemeyer family, which controlled America's sugar industry, Cassatt took her under her wing when she visited Paris and helped her amass the superb works, including many by her friends Edgar Degas and Claude Monet, that later became the core of the Metropolitan Museum of Art's Impressionist collection.[50] Cassatt's advice to the doyen of Chicago society, Mrs. Potter Palmer, also led her to buy a host of Impressionist works, including thirty-two Monets, most of which were bequeathed to the Art Institute of Chicago.[51] Dr. Claribel and Etta Cone of Baltimore, two unmarried sisters whose father had made millions in textile mills, were fortunate to have the Baltimore expatriates Leo and Gertrude Stein to shepherd them around Paris. The brother-and-sister team helped them put together a fine collection of post-Impressionists, especially Matisse and Picasso, that is now the most valued part of the Baltimore Museum of Art. The Boston millionairess Isabella Gardner, relying often on the advice of the professional "connoisseur" Bernard Berenson, amassed a large enough collection of masterpieces to fill a marvelous new museum of her own. On the other hand, Mrs. Charles Hamilton Paine, a wealthy Boston widow who moved to Paris, spent her fortune collecting worthless fakes peddled to her by a dubious English-born "Comte d'Aulby," who assured her they came from the royal houses of Europe.[52] In any event, notwithstanding these women, big-time collecting remained very much an extension of the world of male power-brokers.[53]

For most upper-class Americans, though, the words "shopping" and "Paris," taken together, meant women's fashions. In the 1850s Gaston Worth, an Englishman who worked in a Paris silk store, revolutionized the industry by persuading its owners to start turning the silks into dresses and cloaks themselves. In 1858, he struck out on his own, eventually hitting the jackpot in the usual way—through the patronage of the Empress Eugénie and by coming up with a new signature style. In his case, it was the bustle, a wire construction that would protrude from fashionable ladies' rear-ends for the next thirty-odd years. By the 1870s, he and couturiers such as Paquin and Doucet who followed him were outfitting the social elite not just of Paris, but of the entire Western world.

Unlike the old female dressmakers, these famous designers did not come to hotel rooms. Instead, the wealthy women would arrive (in carriages, with their liveried footmen) at their shops, which were on or near the rue de la Paix, which runs up from the elegant place Vendôme. They would swoop in through the anterooms hung with Gobelin tapestries and be ushered upstairs, where they would sit in luxurious sofas in private, palm-lined salons, while models—selected to be of the same build as the patrons—displayed the salespeoples' suggestions.[54] At first, some Americans were dubious about the new system. In 1879, Isabella Gardner had to persuade a reluctant Marian Adams (wife of Harvard historian Henry Adams) to be fitted for a Worth's gown. Adams was so pleased with the result that when another friend told her that the great couturier was "habitually drunk," she replied with Lincoln's reaction to similar charges regarding General Grant: "Then giving a little whisky of his kind to some other dressmakers might not be amiss."[55] Soon, when elite women such as William Vanderbilt's daughter married, they would sail to Paris just to have their wedding dresses made by Worth.[56] By the turn of the century, the top French fashion houses were selling close to two-thirds of their products to foreigners, so many of whom were American that they used "American" as the generic term for foreigner.[57]

Paris's milliners were also regarded as the world's best, a not unimportant consideration at a time when an upper-class woman's choice of hats was considered about as important as her taste in dresses. In their shops customers would wander through rain-forests of hats displayed on tall mushrooms. Saleswomen would signal models to display the basic styles that interested the customer and then discuss the particular combinations of silk ribbon, dried flowers, and plumes that would look best on her.[58] When Jay Gould's daughter Anna married a French aristocrat in New York City, she let it be known that she was taking only six hats with her to Paris because she would buy all of her hats there.[59]

Since stops at Parisian jewelers, corsetières, shoemakers, and even lorgnette makers were also mandatory, fashionable upper-class women would come to Paris for four weeks of nonstop shopping twice a year.[60] By the turn of the century, serious shopping had become so specialized that at least one woman, a Miss Meyer, made a living just by taking visiting American women shopping. She was one of the first people Amy Waters of New York City contacted when she and her husband arrived on their first trip to Paris in July 1907. A quick tour of the major sights had to wait until the day after Miss Meyer took Amy to select some gowns. Then, the next day, Amy was back with Miss Meyer, to be taken for a fitting and to more shops. Two of the following days were divided between shopping and sightseeing, but the day after that it was back to full-time shopping with Miss Meyer. During their remaining week in Paris, one whole day was spent at fittings and most of the other days were spent shopping. It is no wonder that when they left it took Amy two full days to pack.[61]

Waters's devotion to shopping was by no means unusual. The first thing twenty-five-year-old Mary Lawrence did when she arrived in Paris in 1901 was to admire the lovely view from her hotel room overlooking the place Vendôme. The second thing was to get her sister and go out "to look at the shops" and order some hats and other items. Later in the week, she recorded that "Ruth, Papa and I shopped madly. . . . Parasols, stockings, little French girls and other knick knacks." Her sister Sally, meanwhile, had hooked up with Miss Meyer. "We were more successful by far than Sally with Meyer," Mary wrote in her diary, "which rather pleased us." A week later Mary went shopping with Meyer, but had what she called "a provoking morning. Bought two cheap hats and then found one that suited me absolutely, so of course I now hate the ones I have got and can't have that lovely one."[62]

Wealthy young women were initiated into this world of expensive shopping early. Sixteen-year-old Grace Matthews of New York City trolled the fashionable stores on the rue de la Paix with another young American friend one day in May 1901, inquiring about the price of pearl necklaces. However, when she returned to her hotel she was delighted to find that her mother had already bought a lovely pin for her, "with pearls on the top, a lot of diamonds, three rubies and two emeralds," for about two hundred dollars (then about eight months' wages for an American sales clerk).[63]

The pressure of getting all of this stuff delivered and packed by sailing time could be enormous. In 1878, young Jennie McGraw wrote her father that her cousin Emily, whose ship was leaving the next day, was "in such a state of mind of velvets, furs, silks, and dear only knows what."[64] Soon, professional packers—men who folded, pinned, and arranged women's clothing for damage-free shipping back to America—began offering their services.[65]

For upper-class women whose financial circumstances could not match their pedigrees, the prospect of a visit to Paris without shopping could be a dismal one indeed. A friend of Mary Lawrence's whose husband's literary avocation seems to have left them somewhat pinched (although not destitute enough to prevent them from spending over a year traveling in Europe) wrote her from Paris that "Paris does not attract or fascinate us as it used to. . . . We are too poor to amuse ourselves getting clothes at Paquin or Doucet."[66]

Not everyone found clothes shopping exhilarating. Mrs. Charles Hunt claimed not to enjoy the substantial amount of time she spent shopping for clothes and accessories in stores. Much of the rest of her time, it seemed, was spent being measured for dresses by a seamstress whose deliberateness practically drove her crazy. "She seems so slow!" she exclaimed to her diary. Then, at the end of her stay, as she was packing to leave, she blew up at another working woman: "The miserable dress maker who has been repairing clothes for us came with a bill last night that made me so angry. I shall not pay it until I get home. It is exorbitant."[67]

For the upper class, one of Paris's other great attractions was also linked to conspicuous consumption—fine dining. The late nineteenth century saw another resurgence of inventive French cooking. Talented chefs from the provinces replaced many of the elaborate formal dishes of the Second Empire with dishes that emphasized the taste of their ingredients rather than the architectural skills of the chefs. *Service à la Russe,* in which the individual diner's plate for each course was assembled in the kitchen, had come into vogue, allowing diners to concentrate on the tastes and ingredients. Twelve-course dinners of dishes prepared long in advance went out of fashion, replaced by fewer courses of dishes made to order. August Escoffier applied the principles of the American industrial engineer Frederick Winslow Taylor to restaurant kitchens. By breaking down complex tasks into simple ones he gave customers an unprecedented choice of these freshly made dishes. New life was breathed into old restaurants such as Voisin and Café Anglais and newer ones, such that the dining room at Escoffier's Hôtel Ritz, came to the fore.[68]

But although many of the dishes were new to upper-class Americans, French cuisine itself was already familiar, and highly regarded, among them. This was part of a world-wide phenomenon. From the Czar's court in Saint Petersburg to the mansions of Buenos Aires, people with pretensions to high status took pride in their taste for French haute cuisine. In 1883, New York City's top hotel, the Hoffman House, created a major splash by luring away the chef of Paris's Café Anglais, who had previously worked for the Rothschilds.[69] Three years later, the French newspaper *Le Monde* noted that at the annual charity dinner to which New York's finest chefs brought their most impressive dishes, the dishes were almost all French. "In New York," it said, with more than a soupçon of smugness, "as in the rest of the world, all the cooks worthy of the name are French."[70] Elite Americans could not have agreed more. By 1890, no upper-class kitchen was complete without a French chef at the helm. Cornelius Vanderbilt, Jr. brought five of them to his Newport "cottage" each summer to oversee the staff in its huge kitchen.[71]

So, when upper-class Americans went to France, eating haute cuisine at its source was usually high on their agendas. When Henry Adams and his wife visited Paris in 1873 and 1879, they shunned dinners in their hotels completely. Practically every evening, week after week, they dined in restaurants, usually the finest, such as Voisin, Véfour, and Foyot.[72] The diary of the two weeks that fifty-year-old Gherardi Davis, an old-family New Yorker from that city's "Silk Stocking" district, spent in Paris in 1908 reads like he was there on assignment from some turn-of-the-century version of *Gourmet* magazine. He ate at a virtual roll call of celebrated restaurants: three times at Lapérouse, twice each at "Henry's," Laurent, and Marguery (only "fair" one of those times), as well at Voisin, Bœuf à la Mode, and others.[73] By then, the super-expensive Café de Paris, which served only champagne with meals and scorned mentioning such a sordid thing as prices on its menu, was known as "an unchartered American club."[74] Young women learned to feel comfortable lunching or having tea (but not dinner) in fancy restaurants early on. Sixteen-year-old Grace Matthews and her American friend Marie took a cab to the Luxembourg Gallery, then returned to Marie's hotel, the luxurious Plaza Athénée, for lunch à deux. Then, Grace's 1901 diary says, it was off to Brentano's for some American magazines, another cab to the Salon, and finally "a most fashionable tea house. Marie had ice cream and I took tea."[75]

Still, for the social elite, even the most expensive restaurants shared the same pitfalls as railroads—they were open to anyone who could pay the tariff. Yes, they did have "Siberias" (Americans then called them the "discard" sections), but a table in the fashionable part was easily gained by crossing the maître d's palm. Henry Adams, a rather rabid anti-Semite, was disappointed that the only other patrons of his favorite Paris restaurant in 1895 were "Russians, Jews, and cocottes of the first rank."[76] In 1911, the food and travel writer Julian Street wrote of how disgusting it was to see the balding "'Mr. Feldman' kind of man," with "a well-upholstered neck" and "diamonds on the fingers . . . distributing largesse with a plump and lavish hand" to have a special table brought out for him at Café de Paris or Maxim's.[77]

Until about 1900, persisting notions of propriety also posed problems on the gender front. Victorian women who reveled in gustatory pleasures were suspected of having an unfeminine taste for other forms of carnality. Proper young women were told that sensitive poet Lord Byron had said that the very sight of a woman eating made him sick.[78] American women in "society" could have tea out, but evening dining in public places remained a mainly male-only affair. Before about 1880, this did not pose too many problems for traveling women because the American upper classes usually ate their dinner, the major meal of the day, in the mid- or late afternoon. After that, when evening dinners or suppers became the fashion, ladies could dine only at each other's homes, not in public places. Fine restaurants such as Delmonico's were patronized almost entirely by males or American demimondaines.[79] There is no record of Mrs. Astor or Mrs. Vanderbilt ever setting foot in there. Paris restaurants were even more problematic for elite American women. Not only were its finest restaurants much frequented by demimondaines, they were often the locales for sexual encounters. Even if disconcerting sounds did not drift down from their second-floor private *cabinets* (or, in the case of the Café de Paris, up from the plushly furnished catacombs beneath the dining room), few could remain ignorant of what was taking place there.

By the turn of the century, however, the restrictions were breaking down. The taboo against women enjoying food faded. Even Queen Victoria, despite her advanced age, was reported to have polished off a dinner of two soups, filets of fish, fried smelts, saddle of mutton, chicken croquettes, sweetbreads, roast capon, vegetables, and dessert when she arrived in her hotel in Hyères in January 1892. ("Now, was this not a dainty *menu* to set before the Queen?" said an American tourists' magazine.)[80] In 1898, the *New York Times* announced that the days when eating for a woman was "worse than a crime, an error in taste," were over. "Now woman, a healthy animal, may eat, say what she eats, and even play the role of the gourmet."[81] Shortly thereafter, the Prince of Wales gave his cachet to women dining out in the evening—if accompanied by males—by taking his much admired mistress, Lily Langtry, to dine at the Savoy hotel in London.[82] Paris's luxury restaurants also began concentrating more on satisfying their customers' palates, and less on their libidos, by curbing much of the obvious sexual hanky-panky. So, it seemed perfectly natural that practically the first thing the recently married Bostonians Arthur and Mildred Cox did when they arrived in Paris in 1908 was to meet up with a woman friend and head for the Café Marguery, to try its famous sole, which Mildred pronounced "most delicious." Two nights later, they dined on "delicious duck and champagne" at the famous Tour d'Argent.[83]

Nevertheless, for elite women without male company, evening dinners in Paris restaurants remained problematic. In his book on Paris restaurants, Julian Street told of receiving a letter from "a gentleman whose daughter was in Paris with another lady," asking in which restaurants they could dine "without transgressing the conventions." Street replied that American women were "constantly transgressing the conventions in such matters—in a manner altogether breezy and delightful," but always accompanied by males. He warned that they should not go anywhere for dinner without male escorts and should "patronize only the more conventional establishments for luncheon."[84]

But this kind of restriction was but a minor part of a larger problem: In the end, the ritualized behavior that this upper-class social scene demanded remained terribly constricting. Moreover, being constantly involved in displays of conspicuous consumption and flaunting one's leisure was an experience devoid of any of the sense of personal cultural development with which previous generations of elite tourists had returned from Europe. The French socialites of the time have been labeled "prisoners of pleasure."[85] In the American case, one is tempted to lean more toward Veblen and label them "prisoners of leisure." Whichever one chooses, though, both mean that, among the upper class, cultural tourism had been largely replaced by what would later be called "recreational tourism."

Twelve

HOW "THE OTHER HALF" TOURED

> The Old World offers to the student, to the man or woman of
> culture, to the pleasure seeker, and even to the health seeker,
> many things that cannot be obtained in America, and to say
> this is in no wise to disparage our own country. . . . But the
> great art collections and relics of the venerable centres and
> seats of learning and culture, the relics and remains of historic
> places and personages, of the art and skill of the past, and the
> varied life of the great centers of art, industry and pleasure
> have an inspirational and educational value entirely their own.
>
> *Cook's American Excursionist*

As the century drew to a close, falling steamship fares and the expansion
of second class opened up travel to many people for whom the trip to
Europe had hitherto only been an impossible dream. The travel diary of
thirty-year-old Laura Libbey, a New Yorker who embarked on an eight-
month European tour with her sister and a friend in 1892, begins:

> When one has longed for something from earliest childhood to middle
> age which seemed utterly out of reach, has thought of it, dreamed of it,
> built air castles about it, and then suddenly the way seems opened for a
> realization of all these hopes, it is hard to feel it is actually ones self that
> is really doing in the flesh what up to this time has only been dreams
> and imaginings.[1]

Contrast this with how Mary Peabody, an upper-class Bostonian of about
the same age, described the shipboard party marking her departure on her
fourth European tour in 1910: "Everybody seemed so thrilled about such
a deadly stupid thing to have done—leave home and friends and hap-

piness to get on a nasty uncomfortable ship, with hundreds of dreadful people, to go to the other side of the world, where everything is strange and lonely."[2]

Of course neither Libbey nor her companions were by any means poor. Most such people who could afford the expense and the time for a European trip would today be called upper-middle class. However, from the day they sailed until the moment they returned, their travel experiences were distinctly different from those of the upper class.

For one thing, socializing was more relaxed. Single people would be assigned to cabins with other singles, encouraging new relationships.[3] The space squeeze in second-class cabins ruled out the formal sartorial displays put on by the peacocks in first class.[4] It also forced people to spend most of their time mingling in the public spaces. This inevitably led to hopes of shipboard romance, such as infected Elizabeth Telling, a thirtyish Smith College graduate from Philadelphia. She was very taken with an attractive middle-aged Philadelphian who charmed her and her sister. He ultimately accepted her invitation to look them up in Paris, but when he did, she developed "doubts" about him. His faux pas? Finding her younger sister more attractive.[5]

The continental rail system also became more affordable for the middle class. Peasants and workers were shunted into third class, where they sat in rows of wooden benches. Second-class coaches, configured in compartments of six or eight, with cushioned seats, were comfortable enough for upper-middle-class travelers such as the future settlement-house-founder Jane Addams, who toured Europe in second class in 1884.[6] In 1891, a middle-class magazine recommended Americans use second-class rail in France and even suggested third class might do for short distances, although it advised avoiding the latter when they were crowded with peasants, because of their smell.[7] A 1900 handbook for American women traveling in Europe said "a woman who must be economical may assuredly travel third class," but warned that only a first-class ticket would do for an overnight journey.[8]

With no expatriates to take them in hand upon their arrival, few middle-class tourists dared arrive without an itinerary. "People who go over with no fixed plans usually come home disgusted," Thomas Cook and Son warned, "and most generally never see anything."[9] Since cultural tourism was supposed to be the chief objective of their tours, the upper-middle class would be particularly diligent about poring over guidebooks, noting the outstanding sights that Baedeker marked with asterisks and correlating them with Bradshaw's complex compendium of European rail-way timetables.[10] Many entrusted planning the itinerary to travel agents, notably Cook's. It negotiated reduced rates for transportation and accom-modation, sold coupons for them, and stationed uniformed interpreters at major sea ports and train stations to assist its customers. Most people who used the coupons were more than satisfied.[11] In 1880, Mark Twain wrote a testimonial saying that Cook's had "made travel easy and a pleasure." The prepaid tickets and coupons ensured against being overcharged and "Cook's servants at the great stations [would] attend to your baggage, get you a cab . . . procure guides for you, and horses, donkeys, camels, bicycles, or anything else you want."[12] (He likely regretted these kind words after Cook's lost all his baggage on a trip to Sweden and never recovered it.)[13]

In the public mind, the name Cook's was still associated with "person-ally conducted" group tours, even though they constituted only about 5 percent of its business.[14] In 1871, it organized its first such tour for Ameri-cans, a trip to Europe for a group of Masons from Allegheny City, Penn-sylvania. Then, in 1873, it sent over its first "Annual Vacation Party"— 148 people from twenty-seven states who took up the entire liner *Victoria*. From then on, these annual tours became fixtures on the tourist circuit. In 1878, demand for tours to that year's Paris Exposition saw Cook's shut-tling groups of fifty and one hundred across the Atlantic, including the Allegheny County Masons again, another Masons' group from Philadel-phia, and 250 people from the New England Conservatory of Music and Normal School, led by their director.[15]

Cook's success was based on its special appeal to the middle class. In promoting its 1878 tours to Paris, it contrasted the middle class's concern for economy with the profligacy of the upper class, who, it said, was as willing to pay outrageous prices for Paris hotels as they were for meals at Delmonico's.[16] The "Exhibition Boarding House" catered to a middle class fearful of, in its words, "trusting themselves in strange hotels, conducted by foreigners, of whose language the majority of visitors know nothing."[17] Upper-class tourists usually became converts to the light French breakfast of coffee and breads;[18] Cook's advertised that it did not force its patrons to face a long hard day of touring on such insubstantial fare and promised that all its breakfasts would include meat and eggs.[19] Indeed, from then on it regularly assured Americans that the meals on its tours included a "guaranteed meat breakfast."[20]

Tours were also scheduled with middle-class vacation schedules in mind. The Annual Vacation Tours of Europe left at the end of June in order to accommodate "teachers and those engaged in Educational Work, and others, who can only leave home and duties during Summer Vacations." They were also arranged with middle-class time and income constraints in mind. One such tour, in 1878, of Britain, Belgium, and France, lasted only forty-seven days (twenty-two of which were at sea) and cost but $300, including passage, accommodation, transfers, meals, and sightseeing.[21] "It is often easier and cheaper to spend a summer abroad than to stay home," Cook's said in 1883.[22] Finally, Cook's always made clear that the motive of the trip was to be uplift, not summer relaxation. The Annual Educational Vacation Parties, Cook's said in 1883, had been "of the greatest benefit to thousands of toilers in educational and other fields who might otherwise never have seen the historic and classic spots in which have been enacted so many scenes of great drama of social and political progress."[23]

By the time of the next Paris Exposition, in 1889, Cook's was sending six "Vacation Parties" to Europe each summer, as well as special tours leaving throughout the year. The most popular one remained the one tailored to teachers' summer vacations, now costing $500, and it was with teachers that Cook's would most often be associated in the public mind.[24] However, in the 1890s it also developed tours for special groups, such as pilgrimages to European shrines for Catholics, and took advantage of falling fares to lower its prices to rock-bottom levels. In 1899, an all-inclusive 43-day tour of the British Isles and Paris cost but $275.[25] In 1900, it even offered a one-month tour to England and that year's Paris Exposition for $100.[26]

Americans thinking of booking prepaid tours to Europe with other American travel agents were deterred by their propensity to go belly-up, leaving stranded clients hounded by bill-waving hoteliers.[27] American Express was no alternative. Although its freight forwarding service and new system of traveler's checks gave it international connections rivaling Cook's, its stubborn President, James Fargo, refused to have "gangs of trippers" leaving from in front of its offices "the way they do from Cook's." "There is no profit in the tourist business," he declared, "and even if there were this company would not undertake it."[28]

What Fargo probably meant was that it did not pay to court a middle-class clientele who were only going to make one quick tour of Europe in their lifetimes. Yet this was precisely the market for Cook's "Vacation Parties" to Europe. In 1891, the newspaperman William Coffut recommended them because, "for those who can go but once, it is better to travel fast and far and get intelligent glimpses of all the great historical centers than to travel slow and spend all the time in one or two countries." One would see twice as much with Cook's as with "private parties," which were "always tempted to make diversions and detours, to travel slow."[29] Yet the fast pace of the tours was also their Achilles Heel, particularly among the upper-middle-class women who were becoming an important segment of the travel market.

Cook's realized that it was having trouble cracking this market as early as 1877, when it blamed a slump in sales on Americans' perception that dealing with Cook's was "not the correct thing . . . that it is not fashionable; that to do so would give the impression abroad that they were *economizing*, and this idea, to some Americans, is simply horrible."[30] It tried listing about 150 English patrons from "the nobility and higher classes," as well as the Emperor and Empress of Brazil, whom it had served, but to no avail. It also emphasized that Cook's tours offered women traveling alone welcome protection from foreign predators. Seventy-seven of the 148 people on the first "Annual Vacation Party" were women, it said, "most of them alone," and "several marriages were the result of the trip."[31] Yet its reputation for setting a torrid pace put many women off. An Iowa woman wrote Cook's in 1877 saying that its system seemed ideal for her and a "lady friend," who had hitherto feared traveling alone in foreign countries, but she was concerned that their health would be damaged. She had heard that "the excursionists travel so fast and visit so many places in such a short time . . . they have only time for a mere glance at the places they visit and become worn out from the fatigue of constant travel."[32]

Cook's reply was reassuring about the fatigue factor, but missed the more important concern—the "mere glance at the places they visit." The upper-middle class did not avoid Cook's tours because they smacked of unfashionable economizing or endangered their health. They did so mainly because the fast-paced tours hardly allowed the studied contemplation of the High Culture objects that, for their class, was the chief desideratum of a European tour. Even Coffut, in his testimonial, admitted that "with one of Cook's parties you cannot expect to make a study of the art galleries of Europe. That would require years and years. . . . You will, however, go into the famous galleries, and pass through them, and see the famous pictures."[33] An article in the *New York Times* reflected the upper-middle-class view of this: it extolled the pleasures of visiting "old friends" among the works in the Louvre on one's third trip to Paris, while noting with condescension that "the same flock of 'personally conducted' tourists swoops through the halls, and is gone in twinkling."[34]

Upper-middle-class tourists were equally careful about distinguishing themselves from the shallow upper class, who disdained museums and sightseeing in favor of nonstop socializing. When Caroline and Frank White returned to France in 1882, they had by then prospered in Boston real estate. Yet their Paris stay involved more or less the same kind of relentless museum-going and sightseeing as their first visit in 1855, when she was a twenty-seven-year-old ex-schoolmarm and he was still an up-and-coming self-made man intent on self-improvement. They visited the Louvre again (at least four times) and examined Notre Dame, the Invalides, the Panthéon, and innumerable other buildings of architectural and artistic interest. Yet she still fretted in her diary that "it is very little I gain at so much expense as we are at." Significantly, in Paris they did not socialize with any other Americans, resident or touring. (She did note that at the Arc de Triomphe she saw "some American ladies of whom I feel ashamed. They are so loud in style.")

At the end of that cold November, in Cannes, they inadvertently encountered the upper-class style of touring. After exhausting all of the resort's sights—mainly views from the hills overlooking the town—wet weather kept them penned in with their hotel's other guests, who seemed perfectly happy to spend their days lounging in its salons with no uplifting purpose in mind. Initially, Caroline found them a "pleasant" lot to chat with in the evenings, but then had a crisis of conscience: "It seems a rather idle, useless life we are leading—as none of us are physically incapacitated for work." They soon pulled up stakes and moved down the coast, to Menton, where the sightseeing was a bit better. After a month there, much of which was spent climbing up and down the cliffs seeking out crumbling old medieval villages, they headed off to see the art treasures of Italy.[35]

The Whites's attitude toward the upper-class *farniente* approach to traveling comes as no surprise. It was typical of the White Anglo-Saxon Protestant upper-middle class with whom they now associated: people who had turned culture into a major weapon in their struggle for social status. Above them, a class of gaudy plutocrats were engaged in astounding displays of luxurious consumption—yacht racing, expensive costume balls, champagne parties on horseback in hotel ballrooms—that they could never hope to emulate. Below them, a new middle class of semi-educated businessman nipped at their heels. The upper-middle class now looked to Culture—an appreciation for life's "finer things"—as their distinguishing characteristic. For these adherents to what was called "the genteel tradition," culture meant, in the words of their English guru Matthew Arnold, "the best that has been thought and known in the world. . . . the study and pursuit of perfection." In the upper-middle-class vernacular of the time, it meant "refinement."[36]

Although the widest avenue to refinement was paved with the written and spoken word, an appreciation for the visual arts was also indispensable. Yet the latter retained many of its decidedly feminine connotations. Indeed, a love of Beauty was regarded as one of the defining characteristics of American womanhood, something infused with moral and religious significance. Now, not only were womens' homes to reflect this higher sensibility, so were their public lives, through patronage of the art museums, kindergartens, and other institutions that cultivated aesthetic appreciation.[37] Influential writers and social commentators like Henry James and Henry Adams complained that American men of their class, who were concerned only with business, had left a cultural vacuum that women, ill-equipped to do so, were filling.[38] To James, American men had "the elements of modern man with the *culture* quite left out."[39]

As a kind of male counterattack against the feminization of high culture developed, the Stowes's type of emotional sensibility came to reek of the weak feminine "sentimentality" for which her novels were being increasingly criticized. Its emphasis on giving sway to one's emotions ran completely counter to the later-Victorian middle-class ideal of manhood, which emphasized manly self-control. Even Henry James, hardly a macho figure himself, has the male hero of his novel *The Bostonians* say: "The whole generation has been womanized, it's a feminine, nervous, hysterical chattering, an age of hollow phrases and false delicacy and exaggerated solicitudes and coddled sensibilities."[40] There was no room for men snuggling in each other's laps in this clear-headed world.

As result, a new approach to art appreciation arose that, by emphasizing intellect over emotions, tended to restore male experts to primacy and relegate women to the role of appreciative acolytes. Ironically, much of its inspiration came from John Ruskin, the same English art critic whose ability to imbue the contemplation of visual perfection with a religious and moral quality had appealed so mightily to the Stowes.[41] The egalitarianism implicit in some of his doctrines had not only reinforced their democratic approach to art, it had even made him popular among British socialists.

But Ruskin was a veritable supermarket of ideas—the kind of thinker from whom one could pick and choose. His new American disciples, such as Charles Eliot Norton, the art historian who became president of Harvard, pushed their carts past the egalitarian shelves. Bemoaning America's "horrible vulgarity," Norton blamed its egalitarianism for discouraging the emergence of the sophisticated standards and deference to authority that were necessary for true art to develop.[42] He and his followers reached for the aspect of Ruskin's thought that contributed to elitist connoisseurship: It was not enough to be merely moved by perfection, the Master had said. Only through intense study of its underlying principles could one gain real insight into God's domain.[43] This, in turn, would lead to a kind of manly empowerment, a counterpart, of sorts, to the "muscular Christianity" of the day. In 1914, the progressive writer Carl Vrooman, urging men to visit Europe's art museums, recalled: "I was reared with [an] inclination to regard most art . . . as something effeminate and enervating, but when I began to see that art is power, I began to respect it."[44]

Arnold's and Ruskin's belief that contemplating perfection was morally uplifting inspired Victorians to search for the archetypical—the perfect representation of things. Yet America seemed to offer few opportunities to do so. Most people who pined for high culture agreed with Henry James's famous 1879 list of his country's deficiencies—"no cathedrals, nor abbeys, nor little Norman churches . . . no literature, no novels, no museums, no pictures."[45] Although art museums stocked with "perfect" objects from Europe were opening in American cities, they were no match for the treasure-troves of the Old World. A woman in James's *The Pension Beauregard* says:

> To care only for the best! To do the best, to know the best—to have,
> to desire, to recognize only the best. That is what I have always done,
> in my quiet little way. I have gone through Europe on my devoted little
> errand, seeking, seeing, heeding only the best. And it has not been for
> myself alone; it has been for my daughter. My daughter has had the
> best.[46]

The Louvre was regarded as particularly rich in perfect objects. Along with two pictures (da Vinci's *Mona Lisa* and Murillo's *Immaculate Conception*) that were thought to represent humanity's highest achievements in that form, it had two ancient Greek sculptures (the *Venus de Milo* and *Winged Victory*) that were said to represent the female body at its most perfect. In 1885, Anne Bense saw in the *Venus* "the type of the perfect

woman, to me the most marvelous object among all these rare treasures."[47]
Four years earlier, sixteen-year-old Emily Rotch wrote in her diary: "After
I had seen the *Venus de Milo* I cared very little for the other statues. The
Venus was so beautiful."[48] Some people bothered with little else. "Looked
in the Louvre long enough to see the *Venus de Milo*," Sanford Cutler wrote
when he arrived in Paris.[49] Thirty-one-year-old Elizabeth Telling, who
later became and artist, photographer, and travel writer, stopped at the
Louvre only once on her first trip to Paris in 1913, to make what she called
a "pilgrimage" to the *Mona Lisa* and *Winged Victory*.[50]

The new connoisseurship was also based on organizing the artistic geniuses into historical "schools" of distinctive painting styles. Although
most genteel upper-middle-class tourists were quite flummoxed by the in-
tricacies of this, they did know that they were now supposed to be looking
for more than what merely moved them. On her fourth visit to Paris, in
1888, Caroline White, now a well-established matron in suburban Brookline, again returned to the Louvre. Whereas on her previous trips she had
confidently listed the pictures she admired most in her diary, this time
there was a note of hesitancy. "We must go again and again if we really
wish to feel we know what the gallery contains," she wrote, "and it would
require months to become acquainted with each school of painting."[51] By
1910, the stakes in the connoisseurship game had been raised enormously.
Charges of wholesale fakery of Old Masters filled the air, leading to the
rise of "scientific attribution."[52] Now, professional connoisseur/consultants
such as Bernard Berenson, Isabella Gardner's adviser, debated the authen-
ticity of works in terms far above the ken of even those who had studied
art seriously. The millions of dollars at stake added a further dimension to
the cult of artistic expertise.

Although Norton and disciples such as Berenson felt a particular pro-
clivity to the art and culture of Renaissance Italy (Norton thought Paris
was almost as vulgar as New York City), they helped reinforce the idea
that travel to Europe was essential in the formation of the truly cultured
person.[53] The rise of the parallel notion that the cultured person should
also appreciate modern art helped make Paris central to this experience,
for this was a field in which it now had no peer.[54] The quality American
press treated its annual Salon as the most important art event of the year,
describing its most noteworthy pictures in detail—a not undaunting task,
since there were about twenty-five hundred pictures on display.[55] Serious
tourists, including male ones, no longer dismissed the modern works at
the Luxembourg museum as lewd or frivolous, but scrutinized them with

care. The 1890 diary of Robert Boit, a forty-year-old college-educated businessman, reflects a kind of self-confidence in his artistic taste that had almost been lost in males of Mark Twain's generation. After visiting an art gallery in London, he wrote, "I whose tastes in painting have been educated in the French schools cared very little for this display of English art." In his five days in Paris he visited the Louvre three times and then went to see the paintings of the "much admired" Claude Monet, of whom he wrote:

> He is clever. He is top of his little nave just at present and his pictures bring $800 to $1200 a piece. . . . I venture to predict that in thirty years his canvasses will be practically all worthless and relegated . . . back to attics and the spiders.

Although it is probably a good thing that Boit did not become an art dealer, one is struck by the confident judgments in this diary entry and a subsequent one on the Luxembourg museum.[56]

By 1900, Paris was also *the* place for Americans learning how to produce art. A mere listing of the American artists who studied in Paris between 1880 and 1914 would take up much of this book.[57]

Reasserting the primacy of high culture played a major role in enabling the upper-middle class to construct a touristic ideal distinct from both the social tourism of the upper class and the frenetic sightseeing of the middle-class Cook's tourists. In an 1878 article called "A Little Tour of France," Henry James gave the upper-middle-class readers of the *Atlantic Monthly* a little lesson on this kind of intellectual tourism—in how not to let their sentiments be their guides. As he initially approaches the cathedral at Reims, he examines its prospect from a distance, first with the naked eye and then through opera glasses. He then scrutinizes the architectural details of its exterior, first from the vantage point of his hotel and then close up. Finally, he subjects every nook and cranny of the interior to very close inspection, during which their significance is illuminated by literary and historical references. As if to affirm the masculinity of the process, these then lead to thoughts on politics, a subject which in fact hardly interested him.[58]

In 1898, Edward Everett Hale, one of the nation's most popular authors, produced, with his wife Susan, a kind of manual for upper-middle-class European touring. In *Young Americans Abroad: Being a Family Flight by Four Young People and Their Parents through France and Germany*, the fictional Horner family crosses, not on one of the luxury vessels of the White Star or Cunard line, but on a more modest steamer of the French line. When they arrive in Paris, Mr. Horner, the self-described "general," allows his wife, who is one of his "aides and lieutenants," to make the decision to stay there for a month. Machismo then asserts itself, however, as the general orders that maps, railway timetables, and Baedekers be spread out over the table. "We want to have some system in our sightseeing," says Mr. Horner, "and not devour Paris like a box of *bon-bons.*" Mrs. Horner's femininity is reaffirmed by reminding the reader of her frailty: While the children, "indefatigable sight-seers," joined the father in visiting the places "so wisely recommended by their beloved Baedeker's Guide, [she] saved her strength by resting at home nearly every other day."[59]

The account pointedly puts down the kind of social whirl that characterized upper-class tourism:

> Though careful not to neglect their American friends, they avoided all dinners and invitations of a simply social character. They went often to the theater, but otherwise stayed at home in the evening; the rest and quiet were most welcome after their active day; and maps and guidebooks, volumes of history and reference covered the tables of their pretty salon, and came out every night for consultation.[60]

To emphasize the point, the Horners visit "the Stuyvesants." They are "part of that large American colony, which stays on year after year, thinking of itself on the apex of earthy bliss, but in fact having but a dull time of it." Why is their life so dull? Because

> Paris is a delightful place to visit for a time, and the best place in the world to study art, or pursue any special object of intellectual culture; but to live without any such aim must be monotonous, at least, for good Americans who are better employed at home in helping the progress of their young country.[61]

The chapter of the book devoted to the cultural centerpiece of the tour, the Louvre, is particularly revealing. It begins by distinguishing their kind of in-depth touring from the frenetic pace set by lesser-middle-class tourists with only two or three months to see Europe. Because they stayed in Paris for a month, it says, they could visit the museum many times and give its masterpieces the attention they deserved. The most striking thing, though, is how it reveals the extent to which Harriet Beecher Stowe's democratic approach to art had been displaced by a cult of expertise, in which women could play an active, albeit subsidiary role. The Horners are especially pleased that Mary, their eldest, responding to the tutelage of a spinster aunt, tours the gallery with notebook in hand, learning about the different styles and techniques. She is "soon able to recognize a Fra Angelico, or a Bellini, and guess pretty nearly, if not always right, the school of painting to which a picture belonged. . . . A Raphael she could soon recognize at a first glance."[62] This ability to recognize artists' style and technique was the very thing that Bernard Berenson and other male connoisseurs were turning into a lucrative new professional field, but there is no suggestion that it will serve the children for anything other than gaining refinement.

As their stay nears its end, the Horners are happy that all of their children "had found out that a gallery is not like a shop window, where you stare, admire, and pass on . . . but a place to be approached in reverence and with an acknowledgment of ignorance." To reinforce the point, representatives of the Stowe tradition are put down:

> "That's pretty!" "that's horrid!" "I don't think much of that!" were the criticisms they heard one day in the Salon Carré of the Louvre, from two young persons with a strong American accent, one of them nibbling from a box of sugar plums. . . . It would be well, if, instead of judging at a glance these pictures . . . these women had tried to think of why they were world-reknowned, and to weigh the importance of the judgement of several centuries against their own flippant taste."

The Horners, on the other hand, wished their children "to know what is a really correct standard of taste in these matters, and to feel that if they differed from this, it was a defect in their judgement."[63]

Two years after the Hales's book appeared, the Chautauqua Assembly published *A Reading Journey through France.* The organization had originated, in 1874, at a Methodist summer retreat outside the bucolic town of that name in upstate New York. By 1896, it had spawned a network of speakers and educators who fanned out across the nation setting up discussion groups. It had also become synonymous with middle-class self-improvement and the genteel notion of culture as, in Matthew Arnold's words, "sweetness and light."[64]

The book, intended for discussion groups, demonstrates how serious an enterprise the trip to France could be for those determined that traveling there should be uplifting. The text begins with some practical facts on traveling in France and then examines its history, art, and architecture in considerable detail. At the bottom of each page are "Search Questions" such as, "What facts about himself must the foreigner register at his hotel or pension?" or "Why was the obelisk of Luxor given to France?" Each chapter is followed by bibliographies, topics for essays, reports, and discussions, and map studies. Typical of the latter is: "Map Drill: The Bastille to Place de la Concorde (Route 2 in Baedeker reversed). Three minute reports on Place Vendôme, St. Roch, Palais Royal, Théâtre-Français, St. Germain, Tour St. Jacques."[65] Readers could also buy a colored map of Paris, with phonetic pronunciations (such as, "d'Argenteuil=dar-zhaN-terl Omit r sound") for over two hundred place names, with which it said "the student should become familiar."[66]

Other advice on acquiring culture could be equally demanding—and bizarre. Grant Allen's 1899 guide for men wishing to acquire culture in Europe recommends that the first two weeks be spent in Paris, visiting churches, but without entering the Louvre. The tourist should then go to Italy, study its art, and then return to Paris. On the way back to Paris, he should stop to study the medieval art at the ruined monastery in Cluny, in Burgundy. Most of the next two weeks would then be spent in the Louvre, where he would now be able to appreciate its Italian pictures and recognize how Renaissance art was built upon the medieval. What advice did he have for the man who said he wanted to "pick out the kernel of it all in six weeks"? "None. . . . You ought to *make* time for in which to afford yourself *this valuable education*. It is not my fault you if you persist in rejecting so great salvation."[67]

Neither the Hales's nor the Chautauqua volumes advise trying French haute cuisine. Indeed, the Horners pointedly avoid fine French restaurants and eat simple little dinners in their hotel apartment. When they lunched out, "in general the Horners found it wiser to order 'un bon bifstek,' or to confine themselves to the dishes they knew to be solid and good" from their experience on the modest steamship over.[68] This more-or-less re-flected what was, at least until the 1890s, a standard middle-class tourist reaction to French food. Unlike the upper class, who doted on haute cuisine, they were accustomed to straightforward cooking, rooted in their British heritage and their servants' limitations.[69] For most of those who came in the 1870s and 1880s, then, French cooking meant, not the Café Marguery's silky filet of sole garnished with mussels and shrimp and glazed with a hollandaise-style sauce, but the simpler dishes of their hotel's table d'hôte. Dinner at the Washington lawyer Van Cise's Paris hotel in 1871 consisted of soup, then a light meat such as veal, or fish, then a heavier meat such as beef or mutton, or fowl. This was followed by a vegetable course, such as beans and salad or beans and potatoes, bread and cheese, and a dessert.[70]

Van Cise's meal was, for the time, adequate if uninspiring. What was missing was not sophistication, but the sense of abundance that made Americans of his class feel so secure at home. In *A Tramp Abroad*, his 1879 chronicle of European travel, Mark Twain said "the average American's commonest form of breakfast consists of coffee and beefsteak," and European hotels did not provide palatable versions of either. The tables d'hôte "do not satisfy" Americans, he said. "The number of dishes is sufficient but then it is such a monotonous variety of *unstriking* dishes." What was missing was a "big, generous" American roast of mutton or beef, or "a vast roast turkey . . . with his heels in the air and rich juices oozing from his fat sides."[71] The high school teacher Alfred Roe felt the same. The night before he departed from his modest Paris hotel he wrote in his diary, "Then came the horrors of the table d'hôte. I eat stacks of indigestible stuff and yet am quite hungry."[72]

When they visited Paris in the 1880s, Frank and Caroline White avoided their hotel's tables d'hôte.[73] Yet neither they, or Roe, or many other middle-class tourists seem to have ever ventured into a luxury restaurant. Although Roe was a fairly serious penny-pincher, price could not have been the only deterrent to their having a fling in one of Paris's palaces of haute cuisine, particularly after 1890, when the American dollar rode high in relation to the franc.[74] The Whites were well-enough-off to employ three full-time servants in their large Brookline home, yet seem never to have even sampled haute cuisine. Instead, in Paris they normally dined in one of the decidedly downscale "bouillons," simple restaurants serving plain food to which they had first been introduced in 1875.[75]

One reason for this hesitance was likely the persistent middle-class American suspicion of dishes with sauces, which were still thought to camouflage tainted or inferior European meat. Some, such as Van Cise, also thought the sauced dishes gave diners a false feeling of being sated.[76] There was also a feeling that spending lavishly on sophisticated food in plush surroundings was a conceit of the upper class, who cared only about fashion, rather than substance. *America Abroad*, a publication aimed at middle-class Americans touring Paris, advised avoiding "the fancy restaurant which seeks only to please patrons who do not care what their bills come to as long as they know they have dined at a very *chic* resort." It reserved its most enthusiastic recommendations for a number of modest places, patronized by businessmen, with prix fixe dinners.[77] Finally, because, unlike the upper class, middle-class tourists were unaccustomed to haute cuisine and its often perplexing rituals at home, many of them must simply have been afflicted with the kind of gastronomic conservatism that affects most tourists confronted with the food in foreign lands, whether they are British working people forking back "bangers and mash" on Spain's Costa Brava or Japanese businessmen slurping noodle soup in Manhattan.

The middle-class influx of the 1890s thus saw the emergence of a host of Parisian entrepreneurs trying to lure them with approximations of American food and drink. Hotels set up "American bars" for men who preferred bellying up to the mahogany over sitting on rickety café chairs. In 1893, Fuller's, a confectionery firm in Buffalo, opened a Paris outlet that thrived on serving ice cream sodas, popcorn, peanuts, chewing gum, and other American delicacies.[78] Two "American and English Grocery Stores" sold other down-home products.[79] The Cosmopolitan Bar and Restaurant offered thick steaks and chops, cut and cooked the American way, washed down with "English and American drinks in their native simplicity or complexity." The chef/owner of Aldegani's restaurant (who claimed to be "well acquainted with the exigencies of the American palate") advertised that "while the basis of his fare is of the Italian school so popular in the United States, it is mine host's proud boast that he can prepare American dishes like a Bostonian."[80] A 1911 advertisement for a French-run establishment sounds even more Bostonian: "Speciality of Lobster Newburg, Little Neck Clams, Blue Points, Soft Shell Crabs, Broiled Lobster, Clam Chowder, Clam Fritters, Fresh Green Corn on the Cob, etc. . . ."[81]

By then, however, middle-class reservations about French restaurants were waning. The palaces of haute cuisine had been supplemented by a host of simpler restaurants, many with cooks from the provinces, serving less elaborate food more in tune with middle-class American tastes. Brasseries, introduced into Paris by Alsatians, had become popular. They served sausages, smoked meats, sauerkraut, and beer—items which German immigrants had helped popularize in America—as well as standard French dishes. *America Abroad* assured wine-leery Americans that "Beer is almost as much of a national drink with the French as with the northern nations."[82] As soon as the twenty-three-year-old Broadway actress Jane Cowl, a Barnard College graduate, and her husband checked into their Paris hotel in 1907, they went across the street to a brasserie that had been highly recommended to them in New York. The next day, the couple tried the "famous bouillabaisse" at the Café Drouant, and so on, for more than a week. None of these delightful dining experiences involved haute cuisine, and all were a mere three courses.[83]

Middle-class Americans also discovered good modest restaurants in provincial towns. The Georgia teacher Willie Allen, extolling a simple meal in Fontainebleau in 1895, wrote her sister-in-law, "You will laugh at me speaking of delicious sausages but that modifier is too tame."[84] Elizabeth Telling's first lunch and dinner in France, at a modest restaurant in Cherbourg in February 1914, were, as they so often are to first-time visitors, a kind of epiphany. She wrote home: "Those little blue-shelled fishes with crabs in them, and such bread and butter—a dream for an epicure!—and eggs and steak (not horse!) and soufflé potatoes."[85]

In Paris, the *Bouillons Duval,* a chain of restaurants set up by a philanthropic slaughterhouse owner to provide good meals at low prices for people of limited means, drew an unanticipated tourist clientele. Caroline and Francis White, although by now very well-off, dined in one or another of them almost every day during their fourth visit to Paris in 1888.[86] *America Abroad* recommended them, as did Baedeker. The *New York Times* said that there, for twenty-five cents, one could get a meal "as good as any to be had at home, short of Delmonico's."[87] Others discovered neighborhood restaurants serving prix fixe meals at rock-bottom prices. Henry Seaver noted in his diary how "very good" the 1F.60 (thirty-two cents) set menu was at the Paris restaurant at which he dined frequently in 1898.[88]

By 1914, it was even becoming fashionable for middle-class travelers to make invidious comparisons between these simple meals and haute cuisine. The food in the great hotels and restaurants of Paris had become "hopelessly standardized and cosmopolitan," said an article in *The Nation* that year. "In out-of-the-way streets, there are provincial hotels and eating places furnishing their customers with the 'dish of the day,' where the proprietor, man or woman, puts his skilled hand to the making of home cookery." These the author contrasted with the unhealthy haute cuisine of the upper class: An American millionaire supposedly told him he was "healing his stomach" by lunching at a cheap wine shop that sat only six people.[89]

By then, French gastronomes were beginning to follow suit. The palaces of haute cuisine were on the threshold of one of yet another makeover, leading in the direction of a more simplified cuisine.[90]

— —

The Hales's and Chautauqua volumes give even shorter shrift to shopping than they do to fine French food.[91] Another middle-class "how to" book, a 1902 high school text called *A Little Journey to France,* mentions it, but gingerly, saying, "Ladies visiting Paris for the first time find the shops so fascinating that they spend *almost* as much time in visiting them as in the art galleries and viewing the public buildings."[92]

Of course there were many women who hated shopping and/or feared being cheated in a foreign country and language. Laura Comer, a fifty-four-year-old widow from North Carolina arrived in Paris in 1872 "having anticipated much that would be unpleasant," she wrote, and found it. On the first day, she suspected her *valet de place* of cheating her and fired him on the spot. After spending most of the next day shopping in the Grands Magasins du Louvre, she wrote in her diary, "I dislike shopping very much and would never go if I could help it." Although the next morning found her back in the same store, she finally made it across the street to the Louvre, but was put off by the nudity. "One week in Paris is plenty for me!" she wrote as she prepared to leave. "I shall rejoice when out of the city."[93]

For many American women, though, Paris department stores were what the *New York Times* called them in 1895: "happy hunting grounds for American women." The huge Bon Marché, labeled "the cathedral of modern commerce" by Émile Zola, opened in the early 1880s on the Left Bank, near the aristocratic Faubourg Saint-Germain, and raised the ante in size and decor. Shoppers entered through a glassed-in rotunda, passing into a lavish interior where glass domes illuminated a large central court featuring a graceful iron staircase and galleries lined with intricate wrought-iron railings.[94] Mary Mayo, a fifteen-year-old from Richmond, Virginia, being initiated into the world of serious shopping by her mother, confidently declared that they now considered the Grands Magasins du Louvre was "not comparable to the Bon Marché."[95]

The Grands Magasins du Louvre countered by renovating and expanding, emphasizing the palatial theme derived from its neighbor. ("This great shop reminds me of Wanamakers," said a Philadelphia women, referring to her home town's trail-blazing department store, unaware that it was copied from the Grands Magasins du Louvre.[96]) Bon Marché responded by training 250 employees to speak English and act as interpreters for American and British shoppers, accompanying them through each department until the final toting up of the bill.[97] Still, the Louvre's location near the major tourist hotels gave it an edge among touring middle-class American women.[98] Every afternoon, an American guidebook reported in 1887, "hundreds of American ladies, visiting and residing in Paris, make it their rendezvous for the afternoon."[99] Many touring American women would divide their time between the two great stores and then press on to some smaller shops.[100] "An American in Paris gravitates, invariably, toward the Bon Marché, the Magasins du Louvre, or the beautiful Avenue de l'Opéra," Willie Allen wrote her sister-in-law. She quickly added that she "did find time for several visits to the Louvre," but by the end of the century tourists were chuckling over stories such as that of the young woman who, when asked upon returning to America what she admired most in the Louvre, replied that she preferred its gloves to those at Bon Marché.[101]

One final contrast with upper-class tourism lay in the Protestant middle-class fascination with gambling—not in doing it, but in watching it. American books and magazines portrayed Europe's gambling casinos as places where the glamour of extreme wealth mingled with the terrors of addiction and self-destruction. Theodore Dreiser wrote of what a "gripping experience" it was to watch "the collection of nobility and gentry, of millionaires, adventurers, intellectual prostitutes and savage beauties" playing at the Nice casino.[102] A delicious myth that there were almost daily suicides at Monte Carlo's casino became popular in the 1870s and early 1880s. The blood on the casino stairs was quickly washed down and the bodies were whisked away and buried in unmarked graves, they said.[103] For decades thereafter, magazines would run drawings of overgrown, numbered headstones in the supposed "Suicide Cemetery" at the bottom of a Monte Carlo cliff, and describe how despondent losers regularly blew their brains out on the steps of the casino or threw themselves under the wheels of speeding trains.[104]

Protestant women were particularly fascinated to watch the gamblers, who they perceived as zombie-like, self-destructive addicts, much like those in contemporary descriptions of opium dens. To Ann Bense, the gambling rooms in Monte Carlo were "as still as a mausoleum. No excitement was observable. People pressed up and in quietly, but dim and bloodshot eyes, a tense restraint, and eager alertness told that excitement of the most sordid and gross variety existed."[105] Mary Lawrence's father, a Boston clergyman, waited outside while she and her mother examined them. "No one looked in the least excited," she wrote in her diary. "It was all done very quickly and quietly—just like a business."[106] To Laura Libbey it was a "sad, curious, and never to be forgotten sight. . . . The men sat immovable, winning or losing as the case may be. . . . Hardly a week passes without someone, driven to desperation by his losses taking refuge in suicide." The sight of women gambling was especially shocking: "I saw young girls playing there not out of their 'teens,' old women rouged and powdered, their wrinkled hands fairly trembling with eagerness as they clutched their winnings or ventured new sums to recoup their previous losses."[107] Caroline White was also surprised that "a good proportion" of the gamblers were, "shame to them, women." They were "hard, not to say wicked looking— though mainly dressed magnificently."[108]

One reason the magnificently dressed people at the tables aroused such disgust was that gambling was, for those who could afford it, the ultimate in recreational tourism. It therefore represented quite the opposite of what the genteel upper-middle classes thought the trip to France should be all about. They, after all, had picked up the torch of cultural tourism that the upper-class layabouts in the casinos had discarded. Yet as the century drew to a close, the high-minded upper-middle class were turning their guns not on the upper class, but on the middle-class people below them. At the same time, women tourists, who were intimately identified with cultural tourism, were coming under bitter attacks from all sides. The result was the rise of climate that seriously questioned the connection between cultural self-improvement and European tourism. At first, it cast doubt on whether, for most tourists, one existed. Later, it would fuel doubts about whether one should exist. Ultimately, it would help bring both the upper-middle and middle classes around to the upper-class view of France as primarily a venue for recreational tourism.

Thirteen

CLASS, GENDER, AND THE

RISE OF ANTITOURISM

> Half a dozen Americans stand at one end of an aisle of Notre Dame in Paris, another half dozen at the other end. The two parties exchange glances of hostility at first sight.
>
> Says a lady of the first half-dozen: "The place is spoiled. One can never come here without finding a lot of *Americans!*"
>
> Says a lady of the second half dozen: "Let us go. Here come a lot of *Americans!*"
>
> BOOTH TARKINGTON

There has never been a shortage of Americans critical of the behavior of their fellow citizens abroad. However, until the mid-nineteenth century the criticisms were usually directed at individual tourists, rather than whole genres of them. By 1850, though, there were enough of the new generation of nouveaux-riches tourists visiting Europe to provoke a strong current of what could be called class-based antitourism. The increasing feminization of tourism then added another dimension to this, so that by the end of the century it was common to deride the people who probably comprised the large majority of American tourists to Europe as being unable—because of class, gender, or both—to appreciate what Europe really had to offer.

Ironically, given the misogynist turn that antitourism would later take, one of most prominent of the early antitourists was the feminist Margaret Fuller. In an article written from France for the *New York Tribune* in 1848, she divided Americans visiting Europe into three groups: the servile, who fawned over European aristocrats; the conceited, who were ignoramuses

177

who thought everything in America was better; and the "thinking American."[1] To Fuller, the "thinking" Americans were clearly well-born, cultivated people such as she, while the first two types were the nouveaux riches. Harriet Beecher Stowe was more specific on who the "servile" Americans were: those who fawned over the parvenu court of Louis-Napoléon, she said, were themselves parvenus.[2]

Nouveaux-riches tourists became popular objects of derisive humor. In 1853, *Putnam's* magazine ran a series of satirical pieces by George William Curtis featuring a fictional family of rich but ignorant arrivistes, the Potiphars. To make his point that the "best society" ("best" because of its virtues, not its money) was being replaced by vulgar people who were merely rich, Curtis has them take a trip to Paris. This they do only because they have heard it was "the thing to do." In Paris, they are shunned by the "best society" (both American and French) but remain as blissfully ignorant of this as they are of the French language. One of their closest encounters with the French upper class comes at the opera, where they mistake two courtesans for aristocrats. They give the Louvre ridiculously short shrift, yet Mr. Potiphar is conned into buying a fake Poussin by a trio of villains, including a dark-haired one "of a slightly Hebrew cast and countenance."[3] In *The Innocents Abroad*, Mark Twain satirized two of Fuller's types: the ignorant nouveau-riche super-patriot who asserts the superiority of everything American and the parvenu snob, a "hermaphrodite" who affects French manners, speech, and dress.[4] Some years later, in his novel *The Gilded Age*, he has a family who aspired to Washington's "Aristocracy of Parvenus" visit Paris, "that Paradise for Americans of their sort.[5]

In the time-honored American way, the descendants of one generation's nouveaux riches became another generation's social arbiters, appropriately disgusted by the vulgarity of the new generation of climbers. In an 1878 article in *The Nation*, the well-bred writer Henry James, a man fixated on manners, dress, and deportment, declared that "a very large majority of the Americans who annually scatter themselves over Europe . . . are ill-made, ill-mannered, ill-dressed." Describing his compatriots congregating at a Paris bank, he wrote, "The spectacle was not gratifying. *Are* we the worst-looking people in the world?" Better-bred Americans, he said, tried to explain "the common facial types, the vulgar manners, the 'mean' voices, the want of acquaintance with the rudiments of the science of dress" to Europeans by saying that "in America, everyone travels and that the people at the bankers are much better than the corresponding class in Europe, who languish in downtrodden bondage." However, it was to no avail. The European merely saw people who were "rough."[6] Two weeks later, a well-bred reader wrote the editor that James's assurances to Europeans that there was indeed a "better class" of Americans were not true. In fact, he said,

> the better class are few in numbers, ignored in politics . . . living here but with no roots in the soil. The "low Americans," as the swells of the Paris colony call them, the shabby travelers in brown linen dusters, who gaze at the treasures of Europe with a mixture of simple wonder and contempt—sensations probably very likely those experienced by the Gauls of Brennus when they stared at the temples and statues of old Rome—are the real American people.[7]

Twenty years later, these "low Americans" were looking quite high class. As the century drew to a close, and the middle-class invasion of the most popular tourist and cultural sights gathered steam, so did class-based antitourism. In August 1895, Henry Adams, descendant of presidents and statesmen, visited the monastery at Mont-Saint-Michel in Brittany, which he adored, only to find "a mob of tourists of many kinds of repulsiveness." It was depressing, he wrote a friend, "seeing . . . the deadly twang of my dear countrypeople on the rue de la Paix, which is actually visible and tangible as well as penetrating to the ear."[8] The almost-equally-high-class writer Edith Wharton chronicled her strategies for avoiding these middle-class tourists. There were two Lourdes, she wrote: the one she went to, "undescribed and unvisited, is simply one of the most picturesque and feudal-looking hill villages in Europe." She steered clear of the other, with its Grotto, Basilica, and crowds of pilgrims and tourists. It was a "vast sea of vulgarism." When she arrived at another popular tourist destination, the restored medieval town of Carcassone in the southwest of France, she welcomed the fact that it rained all day, because "it eliminates that tout-and-tourist element which has so possessed itself of the ancient *Cité*." As for museums, she always bypassed the Baedeker-starred masterpieces that tourists sought out. Instead, she made "pious pilgrimages" to works of "obscure merit" that had not "become the picnic ground of the art-excursionist." "One trembles," she said, "lest it should cease to shine in its own twilight heaven when it has become a star in Baedeker."[9]

Magazines that catered to a genteel, upper-middle-class readership were especially partial to put-downs of the middle-class tourists on the social rung below them. In 1901, the *Century* magazine carried a series of lampoons of American tourists in Europe by the popular humorist Charles B. Loomis. Each piece represented a different type, but all shared one characteristic—being part of the undeserving middle class. The first portrays one of Fuller's "conceited" tourists, a self-made New York businessman who the author meets on the steamer over. "I hate picture-galleries," he says, "and I'm glad to say I've forgotten the little history I ever knew, so their towers and abbeys won't take my time for two minutes." When they encounter each other later in a Paris café, he asks the author to order a coffee for him, saying he's proud that he doesn't know a word of French: "I wouldn't on principle," he says, "if I lived here all my days." "No one can get away from the English language and expect to be worth anything as a man. Look at the Italians; only fit to black Americans' boots."[10] The next tourist, "Simple" Symon, from New Jersey, is a complete ignoramus who the author meets on his way home from a two-week tour of Europe. When asked which countries he visited, he responded, "Brussels and Belgium and Paris and England." He says he spent two of his four days in Paris in his hotel room, reading a joke book, and another day reading his home-town newspaper in the railroad station at Fontainebleau. He saw only one picture in Paris, in a place whose name was "somethin' about a panther" (the Panthéon): "A feller who could talk English" told him it was about "Jonah of the Ark; some of Noah's folks, I suppose."[11] There follow an empty-headed young woman of seventeen who judges each nation by how neat and clean they are and a condescending snob who pretends to have been everywhere and seen everything but is exposed as a phony when, in an encounter in Paris, it turns out that he knows no French.[12]

In 1905, a contributor to the *Atlantic Monthly* (the Talmud of the genteel class) wrote that he had originally refused to believe all the stories he had read about American tourists. However, he returned from his first trip to Europe "a convert to Charles Battell Loomis." There followed some of the usual stories of American ignorance of local geography and history, including a tale of a party of proper young Boston men and women who went every night to the Moulin Rouge, Maxim's, and the Bal Bullier, apparently oblivious to the sexual hanky-panky taking place there.[13] The next year, hard on the heels of the popular Loomis series, the *Century* ran a series that played on similar themes, called "Seeing France with Uncle John." Poorly educated middle-class tourists rush through Paris in a fog of ignorance. They dash through the Louvre in twenty minutes and are content to merely drive by the other great museums in cabs, and so on.[14]

Since genteel readers were assumed to know some French, middle-class tourists' ignorance of French was a ready target. Loomis's New Yorker had been told that in restaurants he should point at the next person's table and say, "Ooey, kelk-de-cela" (Yes, some of that), as a result of which he spent ten times what he intended.[15] The humor in a *Harper's* piece called "Boggs Visits the French Capital" revolves almost entirely around the buffoonish businessman making a fool of himself through his misplaced confidence in his ability to speak French. He asks waiters for "un petit cheval [a "pony," or shot] of cognac" and spends his first day going from the Hôtel de Ville to the Hôtel des Invalides to the Hôtel Dieu (city hall, military pensioners' home, and hospital) looking for a hotel room.[16]

Genteel journals commonly lamented that these low-class cretins gave Americans a bad name in Europe. An 1899 article in *The Outlook* said that "too frequently" there were, among American tourists to Europe,

> those of whom the well-bred tourist cannot help exclaiming to himself, "Where in the world did they come from, and what can they find in Europe to interest them?" They know nothing of art or history, nor do they wish to; they vastly prefer Long Branch and the Catskills to Interlaken and the Engadine, and are not happy unless telling people so.

It was unfortunate, he said, that foreigners judged Americans by these tourists.[17] A 1905 article in *Harper's Weekly* lamented that Paris had been invaded by loud, vulgar Americans. "It is no use assuring Parisians that they come, they must come, from Oshkosh," it said. "They have never heard of Oshkosh." It then quotes an Englishman at the author's hotel, observing two "screeching" American families, saying: "I make it a rule never to put up at a hotel frequented by Americans. American tourists . . . are spoiling European hotels just as the Jews spoil any American hotel to which they are admitted."[18] Harold and Mary Peabody, card-carrying Boston Brahmins, acted on this principle in 1910. Although they loved their suite in the hotel they checked into on the rue de Rivoli, they quickly moved to another hotel because, she said,

> The hotel is full of dreadfully cheap Americans all trying to be French, and all rigged up in the latest hideous fashions, quite regardless of their figures, their age, or how they do their hair. The funny part is that many of them see the ridiculousness of the others. Some are simply screams of merriment, but make you blush for your country by their utter vulgarity and disgusting cheapness.[19]

With so much written about American ignoramuses, cultured tourists were not surprised to encounter them. Henriette Greenebaum, a well-read woman from Chicago, wrote in her diary of encountering a Texan who, she said, only a Mark Twain could describe:

> He had not seen anything that was as fine as New York, nor any horses and cattle that could beat ours, nor anything else. . . . Someone said we have not as fine museums and works of art. He said, "We don't want them either."[20]

Booth Tarkington wrote of meeting an Iowa businessman in France who complained that he could not understand any of the signs in Europe and that "everybody hollerin' in all these *languages*" was driving him crazy.[21]

Lowest on everyone's pecking order were the Cook's group tourists. Labeled "Cook's Hordes" and "Cook's Vandals," their dependence on their guides was taken as evidence of their ignorance of foreign languages; the speed at which they toured was thought to preclude learning anything uplifting about where they were.[22] An 1890 article on Americans on the Eiffel Tower in *Harper's Weekly* has "a party of tourists from Nutmegville, New England, in charge of a sort of cattle driver from some tourist agency."[23] In Loomis's stories they are rushed from sight to sight. At one of the exhibits at the Paris Exposition of 1900 they "waited a moment and then pressed feverishly on, as is their wont." The man who supplied the dimwit from New Jersey with gobbledygook about Joan of Arc ("He said they were going to burn her because she wouldn't go into the ark") could not tell him more because, the New Jerseyan says, "'the big crowd the feller was with all tramped out of the building, and he ran after them.' 'Cook's tourists?' 'That's it. They seemed in a hurry.'"[24] Chauncey M. Depew, the Republican Senator from New York who oversaw the Vanderbilt railroad empire, was typically condescending. Writing of the benefits of European travel, he said that "'The Cookies,' as they are called, are . . . a never ending source of delight. They are so genuine."[25]

As the satires proliferated, Cook's made the mistake of resorting to legal action. It sought an injunction against a Broadway play, Clyde Fitch's *The Girl with the Green Eyes,* that featured a Cook's tour group in Europe as comic extras incapable of distinguishing the *Apollo Belvedere* from *Diana the Huntress* and indifferent to both. The suit failed, but the real humiliation came from the leading lady's comment that "the action is funnier than the tourists."[26]

So, again, one of life's little ironies: By the turn of the century, middle-class Americans traveling in Europe who did things that were routine for upper-class tourists in the first half of the century—seeking out countrymen with whom to share the journey, traveling with a guide, consulting a guidebook, ooh-ing and ahh-ing at the landscape, or even just "sightseeing"—were being labeled what Booth Tarkington called "the shameful term 'tourist.'"[27] The worst part of it, so it seemed, was the tourists' apparent obliviousness to this. "Unaware of his low estate," said Tarkington, "he knows nothing of the disdain in which he is held by his fellow-countrymen of the colonies."[28] Henry James said the vulgar tourists "neither know nor care what [the European] thinks of them."[29] To Henry Adams, the average tourist was "emotional, stupid, or ignorant."[30] When he arrived at Chenonceaux, the famous Loire chateau whose picture gallery straddles a quiet river, and discovered that its new owner, a Cuban millionaire, would not allow tourists in, he said, "I could not blame them. To be a tourist is to lose self-respect and invite insult."[31]

The feminization of art appreciation in the 1850s and 1860s added a gender dimension to antitourism. Men who sought to preserve European travel's traditionally masculine connotations would often do so by denigrating art. In James DeMille's *The Dodge Club,* an 1869 comic novel about the exploits of a group of rollicking American men touring France and Italy that was serialized in *Harper's Magazine,* the mere outline of a chapter on art is substituted for a fully written one. This is accompanied by an explanation that equates writing about European art museums to the kind of talks given to "the Kennebunkport, Maine, United Congregational Ladies' Benevolent City Missionary and Mariners' Friend Society."[32] This was followed, a few months later, by the century's most famous satire on European tourism, Mark Twain's *The Innocents Abroad,* whose masculine heroes' manifest ignorance of art is intended to affirm their manliness and make them sympathetic to the reader.[33]

Yet despite such efforts to reassert its masculine cast, tourism to Europe became increasingly identified with women. In large part this was because Culture—still its chief desideratum for the genteel class—remained feminized in the public mind. An appreciation for it was now thought to spring naturally from their passive, unexploitative, nonmaterialistic nature.[34] Even male high priests of Culture such as Charles Eliot Norton, who hoped its lofty ideals would redeem America from its vulgar materialistic morass, thought that women played an important role in transmitting its values to future generations.

By the mid-1870s, then, it was fashionable for mothers and daughters to spend a year or more in Europe, with cultural improvement high on their agendas. Some brought "traveling companions," educated but impecunious women paid to accompany single older women or their daughters. (This is how the novelist Louisa May Alcott first saw Europe in 1865.) The young women would have language and music lessons and be taken to the art museums, where they would make lists of the artists and their masterpieces, and sometimes append their own comments. "Beautiful," was fifteen-year-old Mary Mayo's one-word judgment of the Louvre.[35] Postcards and photographs cut from guidebooks would illustrate the comments.[36] Winter's approach would see them heading south, with the daughters now keeping careful diaries in schoolgirl French, for a sojourn on the French Riviera.[37] Some would then move on to Italy, for another infusion of culture. In the spring they would wend their way north again, stopping in mountain spas such as Aix-les-Bains and Saint Moritz, before returning to Paris in May. There, the husband might show up and a "mademoiselle" would be hired to take the children sightseeing and help them with French while the parents became reacquainted.[38]

Some women were so determined to master the French language and culture that they lodged alone in all-French pensions and avoided contact with English-speakers. In October 1878, Jennie McGraw, a wealthy widow from upstate New York, forsook the luxury of the Plaza Athéneè hotel to move into a cold fifth-floor room in a pokey pension in order to improve her French. Alas, she wrote, after two months of "a family life in which I have no real part," frustrated by her inability to either learn French or use her own language, she hailed the day when she finally headed south to the Côte d'Azur, where other Americans—and a good hotel— awaited her.[39]

The tourist industry responded enthusiastically to these new female customers, who moved demurely from place to place in opaque "traveling veils." The French railways introduced compartments for "dames seules" (ladies only); when they debarked on station platforms they were met by platoons of deferential porters and coachmen who smoothed their way to and from their hotels. "Women travelling alone receive far more consideration from men of all classes than under any other circumstances whatever," said one 1889 guidebook for women traveling on the Continent.[40]

American women sharing double rooms in French hotels were further delighted to find something unheard of in American (and English) hostelries: twin beds.[41] No wonder guidebooks pronounced it easier for women to travel alone in Europe than in America.[42]

By the late 1880s, it was becoming common for women to travel in small groups with other women of their own age. Groups of four or six were favored, so two women could share a hotel room. Four could fit into a carriage for the price of one, and if there were six, they could occupy a whole train compartment. However, as a handbook for touring women wisely warned, "each person added to the number of a party increases the chance of inharmoniousness in an alarming ratio."[43] Perhaps this is one reason some groups fluctuated in number, as women met and separated in different places.[44]

Women's predominance on the tourist circuit came to be quite noticeable. When John F. Tarbell, a middle-aged U.S. Navy paymaster from Rhode Island, arrived in Nice in February 1877, on a final cruise, he was delighted to find "lots of pretty American girls," most of whom were wintering there with their mothers.[45] Well over half the American tourists registering in Paris hotels in the summer of 1888 were women. Indeed, there were almost twice as many women unaccompanied by men as there were men unaccompanied by women.[46] A reporter observing passengers debarking from the liners from Europe in New York City at the end of the summer in 1907 estimated that there were one-third more women than men.[47]

Some concerns were raised over the effects of this female invasion of Europe on family life back in America. An 1899 article on the popularity of Paris's modest pensions said that "there is always a predominance of women at these pensions—a mother with a daughter or so, who are in school or taking lessons. One meets so many families living thus abroad whose husbands and fathers are at home at work, one cannot but wonder at how many American homes must be broken up while these women live on, often idly, winter after winter, with no thoughts of household responsibilities to disturb them."[48]

Putting culture at the top of the female touring agenda helped deflect criticisms such as this. A series of articles in the *Ladies' Home Journal* in 1900 called "Edith and I in Paris: The Experience of Two Bright Young American Girls at the French Capital" made a special point of saying that each morning, before embarking on their extensive sightseeing rounds, the two bright young women spent at least one or two hours examining the masterpieces in the Louvre.[49] In *European Travel for Women* (1900), Mary Jones advised that each woman in a group traveling together should specialize in architecture, painting, sculpture, or another of the arts so that she could instruct the others in it. For "Preliminary Reading" before the trip, Jones provided a list of twenty-three books on art and architecture and twelve more on history, including some in German.[50] She may have gotten this idea of specialization from *Three Vassar Girls Abroad* (1883). In it, one of the heroines specializes in art and spends practically every morning of their two weeks in Paris in the Louvre. Another specializes in music, while the third, who has no cultural speciality but has the purest soul, was master of the "beloved Baedeker," providing interesting information on the other sights.[51]

Women worked hard to live up these expectations. When Laura Libbey arrived in Paris with her sister in 1903, she wrote in her journal that "To see Paris thoroughly in the space we could allow was an impossibility." However, after two solid weeks of relentless cultural tourism, including spending their first five mornings "among the treasures of the Louvre," she wrote with puritan satisfaction: "We had no idle moments with which to reproach ourselves afterwards."[52]

Of course, such tours could turn into real grinds. In 1884, Jane Addams, the twenty-three-year-old future Chicago settlement-house founder, embarked on a two-year-long slog through the museums, cathedrals, and concert halls of Europe with her stepmother, two of her college friends, their aunt, and one of her former college teachers. By day, the women went on sightseeing excursions with groups, guides, or Baedeker, and trudged through miles of museums. In the evening, they dragged their exhausted bodies to operas and concerts. "Sometimes," Addams wrote back to her brother in the States, they got so tired of sightseeing that they wished, as one put it, "never to see another picture again as long as I live."[53] Young girls sometimes cracked under the pressure of this kind of touring. In November 1889, after five months of practically nonstop cultural touring, fourteen-year-old Henrietta Schroeder, of New York City, sat in her Paris hotel room and poured out her anguish and homesickness to her diary, culminating with: "I don't believe any human being has ever suffered as much as I have!!!!!!"[54]

For most, however, the desire to be uplifted would ultimately prevail. The day after young Henrietta's homesick outburst, she wrote over the entry in large, black-ink letters: "HOW SELFISH OF ME! HOW MEAN OF ME!"[55] Addams reconciled herself to the exhausting pace because, she said, there was still never enough time to "comprehend the extent of the Louvre" or thoroughly digest the other sights.[56] She was also driven on by the hard-working tourist's fear of being superficial. "It is easy to see how a light-headed American traveller grows conceited from a foreign tour," she wrote. "You gain a great deal of showy knowledge." She vowed not to succumb to "the temptation to play the dilettante. Many of the people we meet are disappointing on that very account."[57]

Even on the Riviera, which offered little of high-cultural interest, American women managed to turn sojourns into uplifting experiences. In the 1880s, they turned a Doctor McDonald, an Anglican lay preacher with long hair and a flowing beard who was the author of several books on the meaning of life, into a major attraction. Invitations to the combination literary soirées/religious services at his hillside villa in Menton were the hottest tickets in town. Anne Bense was particularly taken by his combination of strength and tenderness—something unusual in America, where strong men were rarely tender and tender men were rarely strong. "His eyes, when aroused, are flashing," she noted in her diary, yet "the expression of the man is benevolent and gentle. His voice is full of pleading, almost tears. . . . He speaks with force and from the strength of his conviction."[58]

By the 1890s, these determined attempts at culture-centered tourism were becoming enmeshed in the controversy surrounding the emergence of the so-called "New Woman." High-quality women's colleges and state universities were now producing an educated elite of women who were trying to establish beachheads in medicine, social work, and other professions. Thousands of middle-class women joined women's clubs, which brought them out of their homes to discuss the issues of the day and made them feel that they had a voice in current affairs. Younger women were bicycling, exercising, and participating in sports—things that seemed to express their long-repressed sexuality. The drive to gain the vote gathered steam. Of course, exactly who this "New Woman" was depended very much on who was discussing her. Moreover, although many women saw her as an omen of their bright future, many men saw her as a dangerous threat to the established order. Inevitably, women's high profile in European tourism seemed to present such men with a ready target.

Ironically, some criticism of the married New Woman sprang from the critics' notions that she was, in one of their own words, "the superior of her husband in education, and in almost every respect."[59] This was most apparent in the popular stereotype of women tourists as overbearing culture vultures, marching through the Louvre bent on improving themselves. A popular turn-of-the-century doggerel had it that:

> Mrs. Dick is very sick
> And nothing can improve 'er
> Until she sees the Tooleries,
> And gallops through the Louver.[60]

The backlash was also fostered by changes in middle-class men's concepts of manhood. A more physical, aggressive ideal of masculine behavior was coming to the fore, embodied by "take charge" men like Theodore Roosevelt.[61] So, the other half of the Mrs. Dick stereotype was the weak, submissive husband being dragged along by her. In this reversal of what was supposed to be the normal order of things, the women were clearly in charge, not only of the cultural aspects of the tour, but of the whole touring experience. Their emasculated husbands were portrayed as longing to return home to America, where the proper family power structure could perhaps be reestablished. Henry Adams's typical male tourist was:

> Bored, patient, helpless; pathetically dependent on his wife, and daughters, . . . the American was to be met at every railway station in Europe, carefully explaining to every listener that the happiest day in his life would be the day he should land on the pier in New York.[62]

In an article for *Everybody's Magazine,* Booth Tarkington wrote of meeting a desperately unhappy Iowa businessman whose wife ventured into every church they passed because she wanted to report on European architecture to her women's club. He dreamed only of the day when his disgust with touring would surpass his fear of seasickness and he could convince her to return home ahead of schedule. Tarkington concluded:

> He has hundreds of fellow-sufferers every year upon the Continent; like him in their loneliness, dazedness, and comprehensive protest . . . most of them bearing their woe in silence, and only turning the eyes of a sick dog upon the women-folk who have dragged them down to the sea in ships. The Continent holds no charm for them; they plainly hate it, seeing "nothin in it."[63]

Men such as this represented exactly the opposite qualities—physical weakness, cowardice, and passivity—of those extolled by partisans of emerging new ideal of manhood.

— —

Genteel women's freedom to engage in cultural tourism did not lead to similar freedom in other touristic spheres. As with the upper class, the Victorian restrictions on women's dining out unaccompanied by men became more onerous in the last two decades of the century, when the time of dinner shifted decisively from the afternoon to the evening, a time when they would be assumed to be on the prowl. One night, Jane Addams and a woman friend studying in Paris had an enjoyable evening meal at a modest restaurant, followed by a wonderful ride along the boulevards in the top deck of an omnibus. This was possible, she wrote her sister, only because they were accompanied by a male family friend. "We can do nothing of the kind," she added sadly, "after he leaves us."[64] In *European Travel for Women*, Mary Jones warned, "Although Paris is essentially a city of restaurants and cafés, there are none to which it is pleasant for ladies to go by themselves, and you had better avoid them." She could only suggest several tea shops in "the English and American quarter" and, for lunch, one of the *Bouillons Duval*, where "you are waited upon by young women; although the company is not exciting, it is respectable."[65] Other guidebooks said unaccompanied women could at least eat lunch at first-class restaurants, but most middle-class women bypassed them. In the 1890s, when they discovered Paris's pensions, they would breakfast there, lunch out at a modest place such as a Bouillon Duval, and return to the pension for dinner. In the evening, groups of women from the pension would go to the theater, opera, or concerts, but not to restaurants.[66] Not surprisingly, some women felt that real independence came only from traveling with a man. "I never knew what fun one could have if one had a man to trot around with all the time," a recently married friend wrote Mary Peabody from France. "One sees and does so much more and feels so independent."[67]

— —

Women tourists were also criticized for being the opposite of the New Woman: shallow creatures who went to Europe only to shop, flirt, and find titled husbands. The first charge had little impact on upper-class women, who felt thoroughly at home among the couturiers and jewelers of the rue de la Paix. However, many middle and upper-middle-class women were more ambivalent about shopping. In the 1860s, the Scotch-

Irish immigrant A. J. Stewart copied the French and opened up an immensely successful department store in New York City. In the ensuing decades, imitators providing an equally abundant selection of goods opened in New York and many other American cities. In some ways, this was a liberating process for middle-class women, for it legitimized their leaving the home for trips downtown and gave them more control over personal and household expenditures. At first, most religious leaders accommodated themselves to this rising consumer economy, but in the 1880s moral guardians such as the ex-preacher Edward Everett Hale began warning that the plethora of consumer goods being churned out by the new urban-industrial economy was encouraging an orgy of base materialism. By the turn of the century, Protestant reformers who preached the "social gospel" and advocates of "the simple life" were also condemning the materialism associated with rising consumerism and the growing quest for luxury.[68] Since shopping for clothes and luxuries was now closely associated with women, the criticism seemed directed mainly at them.

Some middle-class women took this to heart and felt particularly guilty about shopping for fashionable clothes. Jane Addams inadvertently betrayed this when she arrived in Paris at the outset of her long cultural hegira in 1884. One of the first things she did was to go to a dressmaker to be fitted for a "traveling dress," a necessity in those days when luggage had to be sent ahead to major cities and women traveling by train had to spend days living out of small handbags.[69] In a letter home, she pointedly regrets having being seduced by style at the expense of comfort. As if by divine retribution, the sleeves were too tight and, unable to move her arms freely in it, she had to take it off to write the letter. In other letters, she took pride in resisting the shops' temptations. American women usually broke their finances in the dazzling little jewelry shops of the Palais-Royal, she said in one, but she "emerged unscathed."[70]

"Willie" Allen, a Georgia schoolteacher touring Paris with five other women in 1895, tried to make their shopping seem like madcap fun, rather than anything serious. "It is amusing to see how crazy we are over the shops," she wrote home. "Not an hour passes but some one comes in with a remarkable purchase—usually of the value of 18 or 19 cents." Eleven years later, when escorting a group of high school girls in Paris, she noted how disruptive it was that one of them was allowed "to extravagantly buy anything that struck her fancy—demoralizing the others quite good deal."[71] Mrs. Warren Tufts, a New York City widow on a conducted tour of Europe in 1907, noted with disgust that "members of the touring party

[were] hopelessly weak when sightseeing; must have carriage," yet were "very strong when shopping; walk many miles."[72]

More damaging to women, though, was the idea that each summer Europe was being invaded by armies of pretty, young, empty-headed American "flirts." (This was rather ironic, since, for most young American women, European touring posed quite the opposite problem: dealing with ogling men and suggestive comments.[73]) Henry James, who was regarded as perhaps the most incisive observer of American behavior in Europe, was probably the major purveyor of this idea. His 1878 novel, *Daisy Miller,* about a very pretty and very superficial young American girl whose flirtatiousness with European men ultimately leads to her death, made her name synonymous with this stereotype. Concerns spread over the dangers courted by women such as she, who did not realize that what constituted innocent flirting in America was taken much more seriously by European men.

Perhaps worse, Daisy Millers were also said to be giving American women a bad name abroad. The author of *Under the Tricolor,* an 1880 book about Americans living in Paris, assured her readers that she always told the French that although "Daisy Millers" did exist and were to be seen in Europe, the more common kind of young American woman was to be found in Louisa May Alcott's books.[74] When one of the heroines in the didactic book *Three Vassar Girls Abroad* is approached in a museum by a strange Frenchman who asks to carry her sketching box, she rebuffs him sharply. "I suppose he thought all American girls were like Daisy Miller," says her approving friend.[75] The influx of unmarried women in the 1880s and 1890s compounded these concerns. The *New York Herald* welcomed the "New American Girl" as "better dressed, better mannered, more lovable and lovelier than any maiden in Europe," but a Mrs. J. Sherwood wrote that each year Europe was flooded with eleven thousand virgins, all of whom were beautiful, but not all of whom were well-behaved. "Beautiful, rich, vulgar. Beautiful, rich, fast. Beautiful, rich, loud," were the universal criticisms, she said. A thoroughgoing snob, she thought it was the daughters of the nouveaux riches—the flirtatious Daisy Millers—who should be "repressed."[76]

By 1910, Mrs. Sherwood's time was being called the good old days. After touring Europe for a year in 1909, Ruth Cranston, a recent women's-college graduate whose father was a Methodist minister, contrasted that day's ill-educated, uncultured young women tourists invidiously with their predecessors of fifteen to twenty years earlier. The articles extolling the "new American girl" merely fed these girls' egotism, she wrote in the *Independent*. In fact, Europeans thought the American girl was "a well groomed, assertive, totally illiterate composition of good looks and bad manners. She is an evolution of all that great wealth and self-effacing parents with no grandfathers could combine to produce." Her flirtatious behavior and insistence on being taken to the Moulin Rouge, Maxim's, and other such places "to look upon mere filth" was an embarrassment to her nation. An expatriate woman told Cranston, "From one end of the continent to the other! American girls are held as playthings, empty-headed little geese, whose mothers have no more sense than they." A Frenchwoman told her that the Continent was now "overrun with so-called 'travelling schools' made up of one or two dozen attractive, ignorant girls from newly rich families, and conducted by women whose own culture is of the near-refined type." Was it any wonder, she asked, "that Americans in general, and American girls in particular, are ticketed crude and illiterate, and shut out of the best European circles?"[77]

There was also a notion that the young women's mothers prowled Europe in search of aristocratic adventurers who would add romance to their boring lives: that, as Van Wyck Brooks said, middle-class American women were becoming "a nation of Madame Bovaries."[78] Of more concern, though, was the idea that Europe was awash in nouveaux-riches mothers looking to marry their daughters off to impoverished aristocrats. In *About Paris* (1895), Richard Harding Davis wrote that "one hesitates to speak of the girl or woman who has married a title. . . . She herself knows what her lot is; . . . it is just pathetic, sordid, and occasionally ridiculous."[79] In 1909, Ruth Cranston thought matters had deteriorated on that score. "Fifteen years ago," she wrote, "the American girl had not sold herself by the dozen to impecunious and invariably contemptuous nobility."[80]

In fact, in France, such intermarriages were not all that common—the language and cultural barriers were normally too great for all but the most determined gold diggers and social climbers to overcome.[81] When they did occur, though, there were often grounds for suspicion. The story of Count Boni de Castellane, a rascal who ran through many millions of Jay Gould's daughter's fortune before she finally divorced him, was famous.[82] The young Boston socialite Isabel Shaw wrote to her mother of a reception in Paris, given by the Colburn Perfume Syndicate, that was "packed full of dyed Americans who had married Barons." It was interesting, she wrote, to meet the "very charming" Baron de Trouville, who had proposed to the firm's heiress, Louisa Colburn, immediately after meeting her. "Miss C. is neither attractive nor particularly gifted, but finds him 'most agreeable.' So that's how these birds get hold of good American money."[83] Stories such as this hardly complimented the intelligence of the brides, who were assumed to be the only Americans who had not heard that Continental aristocrats married for money and routinely engaged in adultery.

On the other hand, women who avoided sleazy-sounding foreigners and married British aristocrats were considerably admired. Marriages such as that of the beautiful, fabulously rich Consuela Vanderbilt to the Duke of Marlborough were portrayed as storybook romances, joining blue-blooded families from both sides of the ocean. (After all, by then the Vanderbilts' wealth and power could be traced back three generations—practically to the Norman Conquest in American terms.) The Duke's tragic flaws, which made Consuela's life a misery, naturally went unreported. Mary Lawrence, whose Boston blood ran very blue, was thrilled when Consuela, whom she regarded as one of the most beautiful and fortunate women on earth, sat behind her at the American Church in Paris one Sunday in 1901.[84]

In 1900, America's favorite illustrator, Charles Dana Gibson, published a book of drawings, *The Education of Mr. Pipp,* that gained immense popularity by artfully combining most of these stereotypes of women touring Europe. Old Mr. Pipp is an appropriately tiny, frail-looking, wealthy businessman whose two beautiful daughters and enormous, domineering wife make him take them on a European tour. His status in the family is established in an early drawing, which shows them all entering an ambassador's reception with the two daughters and the mother, towering over the stooped Mr. Pipp, in the lead. It is entitled, "The order of precedence heretofore observed by the Pipps." In Paris, he is forced to sit for hours while his ugly wife and stunning daughters are fitted for dresses—"the real purpose of the trip." He is taken to the opera, where, as his wife glowers, he falls asleep. There, as in practically every other place the daughters go, they seem interested only in attracting the attention of men. The wife hires as a courier a phony Italian "count," who flatters her endlessly and connives to have two confederates steal her jewels. However, the trip ends successfully as Mr. Pipp breaks the bank at Monte Carlo, buys his daughters jewelry in Paris, and takes them to England. There, one marries a wealthy British aristocrat and the other marries the American manager of Pipp's iron works back home.[85]

An interesting aspect of the tale is that the reader is expected to sympathize with these Daisy Millers—apparent nincompoops whose main activity was flirting and whose only stimulation came from being ogled—rather than with the mother. One reason, of course, is that the mother is a culture vulture who has emasculated her husband. Another reason, though, is that the daughters are (literally) incredibly beautiful. (Indeed, these tightly corseted "Gibson Girls" became a new, impossible ideal for American women to strive for: a slim-hipped, full-bosomed figure with an eighteen-inch waist.)

The emerging French stereotype of American women tourists was not dissimilar. The bossy, social-climbing, culture-vulture American millionaire's wife became a favorite target among them too, while the idea flourished that the daughters were pretty, rather spoiled, and flirtatious .[86] Until the turn of the century, the word *flirt*, which entered the French language in the late 1860s, soon after it originated in America, was used mainly to describe American women. This reputation for flirtatiousness was particularly fascinating for the French bourgeoisie. The men would find it quite baffling that young virgins would engage men in frank exchanges with sexual undertones and yet have no intention of following up on this.[87] Young, convent-educated bourgeoise French women, on the other hand, who were trained to believe that it was the quiet, demure woman who snared the husband, were fascinated by the ease with which American women handled themselves in the company of men and their apparent refusal to defer to men. (They tended to ascribe the differences to the Americans' coeducational schooling, and contented themselves with the knowledge, said one observer, that they would ultimately find liberty in marriage, while the Americans would lose it.[88])

By 1900, some bourgeoise French women were emulating these forward young American women. Sexy American dances were popular in fashionable women's circles; there was even a cocktail boomlet. The word *flirt* was transformed from a pejorative for aggressive American women to a description of a fashionable way of behaving. In the summer of 1904, the bourgeoise women's magazine *Femina* reported that "*le flirt à outrance très américain*" (very American outrageous flirting) was now the vogue in stylish Dinard.[89] The popular writer André Tardieu derided these

Frenchwomen's attempts at American-style flirting, not because they were unseemly, but because they were pale imitations of the real thing—like greenhouse plants compared to a sturdy outdoor tree.[90] *Femina* was undeterred. It ran a story on two attractive young American "millionairesses" visiting Paris who did daring things (such as row boats and mount camels) that implied that French women would do well to imitate them. "American women are freer than French ones," it concluded, and this probably gave them more energy to do such things.[91] It was not until after World War I, however, that American women's role would become a serious issue in France.

Fourteen

MACHISMO, MORALITY,

AND MILLIONAIRES

Some men live as prudes in their own village
And make the tour abroad for their wild tillage—
I knew a tourist agent, one whose art is
To run such tours. He calls 'em . . . house parties

EZRA POUND, "L'HOMME MOYEN SENSUEL"

The conventional wisdom among better-educated Americans in the later nineteenth century was that men were terribly vulnerable to sexual urges. They were thought to be unique in this regard for, as one of the standard works on sexuality put it, "the majority of women (happily for them), are not very much troubled with sexual feelings of any kind."[1] Men's task was to restrain these passions, and self-control became the hallmark of the era's ideal of strong, self-reliant masculinity. As the twentieth century dawned, however, middle-class men were increasingly engaged in bureaucratic occupations that precluded traditional expressions of manliness. Many were frustrated by desk-bound jobs that seemed to demand traditionally feminine virtues—neatness, cooperation, consideration for others—rather than more masculine heroic and individual feats. They were thus susceptible to calls to reassert middle-class male power and authority by "masculinizing" aspects of American life, such as high school education, that seemed to have succumbed to feminization. Self-restraint now took a backseat to admiration for culture-heroes, such as President Theodore Roosevelt, who embodied male physicality and aggressiveness.[2] Sex, an obvious manifestation of this, now became a weapon in the counterattack against the feminization of tourism to France. After all, the kind of sex with which France was most closely associated—men's encounters with grisettes, courtesans, or prostitutes—clearly involved masculine domination.

As we have seen, sex was always part of France's lure for American men, but as an *underground* attraction. It was never acknowledged to be on a touring agenda. The guardians of the Victorian moral code might regularly charge that it was, but tourists would never admit it.[3] By the turn of the century, however, it was not uncommon to list sex as a reason for coming to Paris. By 1913, even the staid *Atlantic Monthly* could acknowledge that tourists thought of Paris as "the modern Babylon":

> Everybody has gone to Paris, for three hundred years, to taste the forbidden fruit. And Paris has prepared elaborately and artistically the suggestive degeneracy which most of these tourists go to Paris particularly to see. Paris gives any one a boost toward the abyss, if he seeks it . . .[4]

In 1913, on his first trip to Paris, the forty-year-old Theodore Dreiser, whose novels reflected the new masculine frankness about sexuality, was even more direct. "The tomb of Napoléon, the Panthéon, and the Louvre are the significant attractions of that important city," he wrote. "Those things have their value and constitute an historical and artistic element that is imposing, romantic, and forceful; but over and above that there is something else, and that is sex."[5]

The old idea that France was the land of loose sexual morals had been regularly cultivated in America during the second half of the nineteenth century, with a particular emphasis on women who exchanged their favors for material rewards. Moralists regularly charged that the popular French novels and plays about courtesans and grisettes condoned prostitution and concubinage. Julia Ward Howe, revered author of the words to "The Battle Hymn of the Republic," welcomed France's defeat in 1871 because, she said, "French literature has done much to corrupt American women. Unhappy France has corrupted the world."[6] In 1880, Andrew White, president of Cornell University, said it was "a thousand pities" that France was "widely known to the world . . . by novelists and dramatists widely retailing filth."[7] Realist writers such as Émile Zola, who wrote sympathetically of the prostitutes and Bohemians of Paris's Latin Quarter, added fuel to these fires. In his 1901 book on French literature, the American professor George M. Harper bemoaned the "preoccupation of French novelists with sexual relations." A Frenchman lecturing on his country's literature in the United States observed, "The American public has come to regard modern French novels as immoral productions of the worst kind."[8]

As he aged, Mark Twain changed from mild Francophilia to frenzied Francophobia, mainly because of his growing revulsion at French sexual license. The notebooks he kept during his 1879 trip are full of full of outrage about French sexual morality. Not only were French novels dirty, he thought, so were their newspapers. They were "the nation of the filthy-minded. . . . They have bestialities which are unknown in civilized lands." Twain was particularly repelled by their tolerance of adultery and courtesans. "A Frenchman's home is where another man's wife is," he wrote. "It is a country which has been governed by concubines for 1000 years." Men in every rank in society, down to "the scavenger, rat-catcher, and beggar," were "ruled by their concubines." It was "a country ruled in all its big and little details by foul and selfish and trivial-minded prostitutes."[9]

Twain's fulminations never made it into print, but even if they had, they would have been drowned out by other voices that spoke of sexual France in a much more attractive manner. Portrayals of Paris's Latin Quarter as full of artists having sex with their models were especially popular. *Trilby*, an 1894 novel about an English art student on the Left Bank who falls in love with a pretty, angelic, seventeen-year-old French model of that name, caused a sensation in America. Too respectable to marry her (she poses nude), the artist leaves her in Paris and returns to England. She falls under the mesmeric spell of Svengali, a Polish-Jewish evil-genius music teacher with a huge hooked nose. The repulsive but hypnotic man turns her into a great singer and becomes her lover and impresario. The English artist is astounded when she performs in London, but is helpless to prevent her fall as, after Svengali's death, she loses her voice, her career, and finally, her life.

When *Harper's Magazine* serialized the novel, it portrayed one of its characters, an artist who is a rake and a poseur, with a drawing that bore a marked resemblance to the American artist James McNeill Whistler. He had been a friend of the book's English author, George du Maurier, when both were struggling art students on the Left Bank, but they had subsequently fallen out. When Whistler threatened to sue, *Harper's* published an apology. The drawing was changed and du Maurier toned down the offending passages for the published volume. *Harper's*, though, claimed

that, thanks to the publicity, it gained one hundred thousand new sub-
scribers for the serialization, and gleefully called the published volume "the
best-advertised book of the year."[10] Trilby parties, Trilby shows, Trilby
tableaux, and Trilby burlesques became the rage among society hostesses.[11]
Soft "Trilby hats" became fashionable among men. The *New York Times*
reported from Paris in 1897 that the student cafés, where "long hair and
flat-brimmed hats were de rigueur," were now thronged with "American
and English tourists, their heads full of 'Trilby' and 'Little Billee' [Trilby's
pet name for her beloved artist]."[12] For the next twenty-five years, the
name Trilby was synonymous with pretty, vulnerable Paris models.

Nonfiction books and magazines added apparent verisimilitude to the
stories. Frank Smith's *The Real Latin Quarter* (1901), which purported to
portray the reality behind the fiction, still made the models seem readily
available for sexual encounters. He told of an American artist in Paris,
painting a ceiling panel for a millionaire's mansion on the Hudson,
awaiting his model's arrival at the studio. The painting will be unappreciated by the millionaire, he said, "but the painter does not care, for he has
locked up his studio, and has taken his twenty thousand francs and the
model with him to Trouville."[13] His book also gave a lurid, detailed description of the annual Bal des Quat'z Arts, which began with a costume
ball at the Moulin Rouge dance hall in Montmartre and was followed by
parade of costumed art students and nude models through the city to the
Latin Quarter for a night of drinking, dancing, and disrobing.[14]

By 1897, the middle class was so avid for stories of sexual Paris that,
in an effort to increase the middle-class readership of his New York newspaper, the publisher William Randolph Hearst sent the creators of the
"Yellow Kid," an immensely popular comic strip (America's first) featuring
the antics of a gang of irreverent slum kids, on a European tour. In the
first cartoon, the gang flies over Paris in a balloon saying "TOUS LES SOIRS
AU FOLIES BERGER DE YELLOW KID AVEC DE GANG." A copy of *Trilby* is
falling from the balloon and one of the signs down below says "*poor trilby.*"
Another sign says "TO THE LATIN QUARTER," while the pet black cat says
it is not going to the "Chat Noir," the risqué Montmartre café. The next
week's cartoon, on their trip to the Louvre, is full of references to nudity.
Its focal point is the *Venus de Milo;* a sign reads: DIS GALLERY IS FULL OF
NUDES BUT DERE AIN'T NO NAKED WALLS; the accompanying text says,
"d'clodes wot dem statchoos didn't have on wud start a hole dry guds
store"; and so on.[15] The budding young movie industry was quick off the
mark. One of America's earliest movies, made in the early 1900s, features

an older American businessman on a European tour who unknowingly drinks and dances with two prostitutes in a Paris café-concert and is saved from them only at the last minute.[16]

Smith's book also perpetuated the hoary notion of the faithful grisette. The students and artists of the Quarter all had devoted little girlfriends, he said, who worked in shops and factories to support them.[17] So did *Harper's Weekly*, which assured readers in 1902 that the grisette and the "irregular *ménage*" continued to thrive in the Latin Quarter, just as they had in the days of Mürger's *Mimi* and when du Maurier and Whistler were art students there.[18] Others engaged in the equally hoary exercise of declaring the grisette to be no more. However, they would reassure tourists that she had been replaced by women who were even more accessible to those with some ready cash. An 1875 guidebook called *Paris at Night* said that the grisette, who "loved her penniless student [and] made his *mansarde* ring with her merry laugh," had been replaced by the *lorette*. It warned that such women were interested only in money, yet gave exact directions for finding them. Both the *New York Times* and Julian Street also pronounced the grisette "extinct," but Street added that she had evolved into the "model or the *cocotte*" (hooker).[19] French guidebooks did not go quite that far. They said the grisette had been replaced by the stylish and alluring *coquette* (tease).[20]

By the turn of the century, tourists were also being told that the Left Bank Bohemian scene had had its day—that it had been replaced by Montmartre, a place where women were even more available.[21] Montmartre would never have achieved this renown had it been just another seedy redlight zone. Until recently, it had been a village on a hill overlooking the Right Bank where artists and poets had found cheap lodging. However, in the 1880s, some of the more entrepreneurial of them began attracting the bourgeoisie to cafés and cabarets where poets and singers would denounce their stuffiness and materialism and extol the life devoted to pleasure. Hard on the heels of the Paris bourgeoisie came foreign tourists. They may not have understood the songs and poetry, but they did grasp what the unaccompanied women who also gathered there were all about. By the mid-1890s, just as the number of American tourists was growing, Montmartre was in decline as an entertainment center but on the rise as a center of prostitution.[22]

The interesting thing is that much of Montmartre's business came from tourists who came to observe, not hire, prostitutes. Indeed, much of its success rested on being accessible to respectable people who could patronize places frequented by low-lifes in a titillating yet entirely safe fashion. The district's most famous turn-of-the-century attraction, the Moulin Rouge, was ablaze in suggestive red light, and patrons entered through what seemed like the doorway to Hell, but particularly after 1903, when it changed from a dance hall to a music hall, what they saw was not terribly risqué, even by American standards. Until 10 P.M. it offered standard music hall entertainment. Then, from 10:30 to 12:30, its famous can-can dancers performed, kicking their legs high in the air or doing "splits," in a style that had been identified with the Paris working class since Revolutionary times and had become popular in café-concerts in the 1860s. These revealed much of their legs and thighs, but by then this was relatively tame stuff. An American observer called it "at its best, dreadfully boring."[23] A French guidebook recommended it to husbands and their wives.[24] Richard Harding Davis wrote that the audience was "composed mainly of young women and Frenchmen well advanced in years and English and American tourists."[25] For most tourists, the real attraction lay in its lobbies, where prostitutes in eye-catching outfits strolled about slowly or sat at little tables subtly beckoning to men. They were not allowed to solicit aggressively, however, and gave men accompanied by women a wide berth. At the most famous music hall on the tourist circuit, the Folies Bergère, which was located between Montmartre and the Right Bank tourist zone, the segregation was equally explicit. Prostitutes were confined to its *promenoir* [gallery-lounge], whose bar Manet's painting immortalized, leaving patrons free to observe or associate with them as they chose.[26]

Montmartre cafés were also popular for prostitute-watching. Down the street from the Moulin Rouge, in places such as the Rat Mort (so named after a rat that was supposedly killed for interrupting two customers during a tryst in one of its private rooms), the music took a backseat to the main business: prostitutes who lured tourists into buying overpriced champagne and perhaps other favors. Yet, these too were standard tourist sights, perfectly safe for gawkers, as long as they purchased something to drink, even a cup of coffee.[27] "It was strange," said Theodore Dreiser, "to see American innocence—the products of Petoskey, Michigan, and Hannibal, Missouri, cheek by jowl with the most vicious women which the great metropolis could produce."[28]

True, there also were some rock-bottom dives, but the absinthe-drinkers there were generally a somnolent group, staring quietly into space or dozing away peacefully, like those in the paintings by Cézanne and

Toulouse-Lautrec. In fact, one reason tourists felt safe in Montmartre was that there was little obvious drunkenness there. According to Julian Street, it was "to the discredit of Americans that they supply such [offensive drunkenness] as there is." "Montmartre is dissipated," he said, "but not in the oppressive, ugly manner of the New York Tenderloin," the redlight district on Manhattan's West Side.[29]

Tourists who found Montmartre a bit tame could head off to the narrow streets around Les Halles, the all-night wholesale food market. According to one guidebook, an expedition to its sleazy "dives" would take one down to the true "hells" of Paris. However, it was quick to add, the district was perfectly safe, even for women, as long as one did not go alone. One agency even offered tours, conducted by "specially recruited" guides, of the warren of flea-bag hotels, seedy cafés, brothels, and down-and-out bars.[30] Of course male tourists could turn to the other guides who sidled up to them on the boulevards, offering to take them to places where they could participate in or watch a variety of sexual practices. Theodore Dreiser, who regarded Paris's demimondaines so benignly, was disgusted by "a small Jew" who approached him with these suggestions of "filth arranged for the stranger."[31]

We know practically nothing about what was on offer for those tourists who preferred same-sex encounters. In both France and America, the tendency in the later nineteenth century was to condemn same-sex sexual practices as aberrations that must be cured or punished. However, in France, unlike America, homosexual practices were not criminalized. Nor was homosexuality as closeted. Gay males were prominent style leaders in Belle Époque society and much in demand in its cleverest salons. Male homosexual prostitution was almost as flagrant in Montmartre as female prostitution.[32] But aside from the fact that it offered the anonymity of a foreign place, there is no indication that pre-1914 Paris was any more attractive for visiting gay males than any other city, including New York, which then offered a gay subculture that was easily accessible to touring men.[33]

We know even less about female homosexuality in America, where its very possibility was hardly recognized. On the other hand, by the turn of the century, Paris had an international reputation as "the capital of same-sex love among women." It was often labeled "Paris-Lesbos." Prominent personalities such as the actress Sarah Bernhardt and the writer Colette did not hide their homosexuality—at least from French associates. Works of art depicting lesbian sexual encounters that in America would have been greeted with stunned incomprehension and then destroyed were accepted with a shrug. There was a well-known lesbian subculture and some openly lesbian cafés. We also know that some American women, such as Gertrude Stein and Natalie Barney, were open about their lesbian relationships, and that the lesbian salon in Barney's house on rue Jacob was a magnet for British and American lesbians well before World War I.[34] However, we know nothing of any American women who were encouraged by this to visit there as tourists. There is certainly no mention of any of this in the diaries of those New Women who might have been drawn in that direction."[35]

One manifestation of the new machismo was that genteel young American Protestants turned away from their religion's previous emphasis on finding moral guidance in one's inner self and instead looked for it by experiencing "real life."[36] This helped fuel a new cult of the outdoors and the cowboy. Some urbanites, like Theodore Roosevelt, even joined them on the range to expose themselves to real life. Many well-off women also felt impelled to break out of their protected environments and explore what life was really all about. Sexual Paris seemed to present to them ample opportunities to find "real life" in watching, or imagining, others arranging sexual encounters.

The sanitized version of sexual Paris fed to the readers of genteel middle-class magazines portrayed a place where women could experience "real life" with a minimum of danger to one's physical or moral health. Their Paris was one where stunningly dressed demimondaines swirled down the boulevards and through the Bois de Boulogne, attracting admirers eager to arrange discreet assignations. The real action in the theater, said an 1892 article in *Harper's Magazine,* took place in the intermissions, which revealed "the latest arrangements between wealthy seigneurs and distinguished Cythereans" (temple prostitutes).[37] A French woman thoughtfully provided *Scribner's* readers with the address of a stylish café where "ladies of easy morals" gathered to "wait for Fortune to appear to them in the shape of a wealthy foreigner."[38]

Perhaps the most influential person fueling this acceptably risqué view of Paris was the popular writer Richard Harding Davis. His mid-1890s *Harper's* articles from Paris were illustrated by Charles Gibson, of "Gibson

Girls" fame. "Americans go to Paris to enjoy themselves," began an article on a young man's fun-filled three-night foray into the city's music halls, café chantants, and dance halls. At the Moulin Rouge, it said, young women "parade quietly" before the patrons, "and are much better behaved and infinitely more self-respecting and attractive in appearance than women of their class in London and New York." The illustrations by Gibson make most of the women in the night spots, even those who are supposed to be down-and-out, look equally attractive.[39]

Some genteel women tourists were tempted to try life on the Left Bank first hand. In 1895, "Willie" Allen, a well-off forty-two-year-old unmarried schoolteacher from Georgia, convinced her traveling companion, a Mrs. Smith, that they should try staying in "the student quarter." One night in a Left Bank pension proved enough; they moved back to the tourists' Right Bank the next day. "The streets are so narrow, the people so dirty, and Paris so hot!" she wrote home, "that I declined Bohemian life at once."[40] Other women went to see demimondaines in action. Francis Shaw, an American studying music in Paris, wrote his mother of how, after he and two male friends took a touring Californian mother, her daughter, and a woman friend from Denver to dinner, the women insisted on visiting a "gilded hell." Luckily, he wrote, they were "so taken up with the dresses and hats of the push [the audience] that they had hardly noticed what was going on on the stage." A few nights later, he reported, he took a young friend of the family and her aunt, from Rednor, Pennsylvania, "to a quiet, respectable place for supper, and they loaded me with abuse. They said they wanted to mix with demimondaines."[41]

In the 1840s and 1850s, wealthy Americans had worried about the impact of immoral France on their sons. By the turn of the century, they were worried about their daughters. The growing number of women who went to Paris to study art threatened to establish a beachhead of immorality onto which other young women might venture. The art course at the government École des Beaux-Arts, which was in the words of one young American woman, "famous in the world for its fine work and its bad behavior," was more-or-less off-limits for American women. (This was mainly because the admission tests involved drawing from nudes, something that was still rarely taught to them in American art schools.)[42] However, by the end of the century, many women were studying at private art schools or with individual art teachers. Young women also came to Paris for music lessons and to attend the Sorbonne, which in 1896 finally acknowledged that an American B.A. might be equivalent to the "*bac*," the French college entrance exam.[43] Since most students lived near these places, which were in or near the Latin Quarter, American parents became concerned that their daughters would be sucked into its Bohemian vortex.

There were reassuring voices. In his otherwise lurid *The Real Latin Quarter*, Frank Smith said that the young women were isolated from the depraved life of the dissipates of the Quarter by language and "their view of life." They were shocked by such French practices as kissing in public, and anyway, the French ignored them. "They are as safe, I assure you, within these walls of Bohemia as they would be at home rocking on their Aunt Mary's porch."[44] There were also assurances that young men were in little danger. A 1902 article in *Harper's Weekly* said that the American student "stands a little aside" from the life of the Quarter, "watching it and never dipping into it. . . . Most of our Yankee boys come into the Latin Quarter not to live the life but to study it aloofly, through rather dazed eyeglasses."[45] That same year, in *The Independent*, the Reverend Sylvester Beach, who ministered to the spiritual needs of young Americans in Paris, lamented that Americans knew no other Latin Quarter than the one in "flamboyant literature" such as *Trilby, The Real Latin Quarter*, and the "lurid reports of newspaper correspondents." He would "attempt no apology for French students, whose unsavory reputation has perhaps given character to the Quarter," but was outraged that the over three thousand American students there had been so "caricatured and slandered."[46]

Wealthy American philanthropists helped build a network of institutions to act as a wall of morality around these young students and those merely there for a visit. In 1894, New York City socialites met to found what became the American Girl's Club, which provided lodgings and a dining hall for students and tourists.[47] A Men's Club followed, and regular religious services were organized by the above-mentioned Reverend Beach. Then came a British-American Student Hostel, the British-American Young Women's Christian Association, Reid Hall, a residence for American college women, and an English-speaking Students Union that in 1912 claimed a membership numbering one thousand.[48]

The existence of these institutions helped make it easier for well-off young women to persuade their parents to fund three-month or six-month study trips to Paris. Often, upon arriving, they would primly register at one of the clubs or hostels, but would soon find the stuffy, moralistic atmosphere the opposite of what they wanted from Paris. They would then declare that the food was inadequate, the reception too cold, or the restrictions too onerous, and find other women with whom to share artists' studios, small apartments, or furnished rooms. The more adventurous would move into a room alone. "The efforts made by good Christian Americans to preserve the Puritan and moral atmosphere of the American home here in wicked Paris are the most amazing things I have ever seen," the recent Columbia graduate Randolph Bourne wrote home in 1913. "Of course the effect is to drive any person with any gumption out of the students' hostels and students' clubs."[49]

By 1905, enough of these young Americans had moved into the cheaper area south of the Latin Quarter, near the Boulevard Montparnasse, to turn that area into a center of American Bohemianism. Concerns that a stay in Paris would erode young women's morals grew in proportion to this new American student quarter. An article in the April 1906 *Ladies' Home Journal,* entitled "Is Paris Wise for the Average American Girl?" answered the question decidedly in the negative. Its woman author said that most of them used studying music, art, or French "as a pretext" to plunge into a Bohemian life. To save money, they lived in "appalling" places and ate in restaurants that served "garbage." They had men up to their rooms and sometimes even allowed them to stay until after midnight. They also associated with "a large number of foreigners—French, Italians, Russians, Roumanians, Greeks—everything—men whose attitude toward her sex is as unlike an American's (in his own country) as one could possibly imagine." American parents should understand, she said, "that there is something in the atmosphere of Paris, or rather of the American Quarter of Paris, that assails even the well-balanced and fairly sophisticated."[50]

In early 1914, a controversy broke out in the American press over the charge that girls who went to Europe to study music returned home "stripped of their health, their jewels, their innocence, even their belief in God."[51] Mrs. Oscar Seagle, an American living in Paris, provided a rather ingenious defense against this in a letter to the *New York Times.* She argued that young girls were "a thousand times more likely to meet attractive, sometimes wealthy men" in America than in Paris. This would distract them from their work and "create a longing for luxury and pretty clothes, which is very dangerous." In Paris, on the other hand, the few American students she would meet were hard-working and "invariably poor." As for French men, since "they neither understand the gentle art of flirtation nor platonic friendship between the sexes, they draw a very decided line between nice girls and the other sort."[52] The editors of the *Springfield Republican,* on the other hand, warned:

> Daisy Miller was a model of discretion compared with some American girls who, with no home training and no standard of decorum, plunge into the bohemianism of student life. . . . There is a giddy, egotistic, reckless type of American girl that ought to be kept out of that environment.[53]

Moralistic strictures notwithstanding, American visitors still tended to find in France a people who excelled at the "art" of enjoying life's pleasures. In 1895, Henry Adams, who purchased sexually explicit sculptures in France that he hid when he returned to the United States, wrote a friend that, over the past twenty years, "The people [of Paris] have lost their old taste, of course, and never had much morals to lose; but as far as I can see, they are still a long way at the head of the world in all matters connected with the art of living."[54] A young Columbia professor, George Carpenter, was impressed by how "balanced" were the pleasures of the French middle class, whose insistence on enjoying eating, drinking, and other things in moderation reminded him of the ancient Greeks.[55]

Sex was thought to be right up there among these pleasures. In 1893, Henry James took the middle-aged literary critic William Dean Howells, who was visiting his art-student son, to visit James Whistler's charming little house on the Left Bank. As he sat in the lovely garden, admiring Whistler's latest beautiful paramour, Howells seems to have suffered a full-blown midlife crisis. He turned to another young American there and blurted: "Live all you can. It's a mistake not to. . . . This place makes it all come over me. I see it now. I haven't done so—and now I'm old. It's too late." After returning to America earlier than planned, he wrote his son: "Perhaps it was as well I was called home. The poison of Europe was getting into my soul. They live more fully than we do."[56]

Of course most of the sexualization was less than explicit. Indeed, staid middle-class magazines continued to churn out articles such as "French Cathedrals," "The Seine," "Unfrequented Chateaux near Fontainebleau," and "The Pleasant Land of France: Vagabond Glimpses of Two Old Provinces." However, they also turned up the crank on the historic code word for sex ("gaiety") in an outpouring of articles on light-hearted, gay Paris. "The Playground of Paris," a 1903 piece in *Harper's*, began with the simple sentence, "Music, laughter, and light." Paris, it said, was a "temple [to] the twin goddesses of Gayety and Beauty. . . . a city that has laughed, sung, and fiddled her way through all the shifting hours of her history."[57]

— —

The growing acceptance of sexual titillation as a goal of tourism helped undermine the dominant role of high culture, already weakened by its feminine connotations, in middle-class tourism. It was part of a larger process whereby pleasure was finally accepted as a proper goal in life among genteel Protestants. Already, by the turn of the century, "having a good time" had become a respectable term in their lexicon.[58] In September 1907, after watching throngs of happy returning tourists debarking from the liners on a New York pier, *Harper's* editor wrote approvingly that Europe had become "our national playground beyond-seas."[59] For a good many of these people, having partaken of France's gaiety, not its culture, had made the trip worthwhile.

The relative decline of high-culture tourism was abetted by the greater availability in America of the kind of high-culture experiences that had bowled over earlier generations of American tourists. About the only European artistic superstars who appeared on American stages for much of the nineteenth century were some British actors and singers such as Jenny Lind, the Swedish sensation who toured the Continent in the 1850s. In the 1880s and 1890s, however, operas and symphony societies in major cities regularly imported European conductors and soloists, some of who stayed permanently. Early-nineteenth-century American theater-goers could only see Mademoiselle Mars or Rachel by going to Paris. By the turn of the century, they were making fun of how many "farewell tours" their successor, Sarah Bernhardt, had made in America. In art appreciation, Americans had done some remarkable catching-up. As Grand Acquisitors such as Morgan, Havemeyer, and Frick began donating masterpieces to impressive new art museums, one could see almost as many Old Masters in New York as in Paris.

So, as the Great War approached, middle-class tourism was perceptibly changing. Many still sought a kind of uplift that could be characterized as "cultural tourism." Like the pre-Civil War upper class, they still hoped that sightseeing, museum-going, and admiring Paris's beauty would somehow improve who they were. However, although a visit to the Louvre was still de rigueur, it was becoming acceptable to give it a quick once-over and label it too immense to really appreciate. The Opéra might still be on the must-see list, but more likely to admire Garnier's spectacular building than for the performances. Self-improvement was by no means forgotten, but the idea that it could somehow come from "having a good time" was beginning to germinate.

The French, meanwhile, were practically oblivious to the changing nature of American tourism. Indeed, until 1917, the conception of America, and Americans, to which most of them subscribed remained remarkably un-complicated by the kind of Cartesian fine distinctions for which they were known in the Anglo-Saxon world.

Ever since Benjamin Franklin's extraordinary success in courting royal support for America's antimonarchist revolution, American travelers had benefited from a generally benign view of them among the small propor-tion of the French who were more than vaguely aware of their existence.[60] As we saw, early-nineteenth-century French liberals generally admired their political and economic system. Any problems American tourists en-countered in France generally resulted from their being mistaken for En-glishmen. Although the post-Napoleonic French upper class got along well with their English counterparts, the rest of the French generally despised them, both as historic enemies—"perfidious Albion"—and for their reputation as supercilious, arrogant snobs.[61] Early-nineteenth-century American travelers often told of being greeted initially with hostil-ity and then, once their nationality was made known, being inundated with apologies. When the Reverend Berrian and his American companion sat down to eat at the table d'hôte in their hotel in Montpellier in 1819, the French guests subjected them to "incivility . . . raillery and insult," cul-minating in an imitation, in broken French, of "the travels of a *Milord Anglais* in France." However, when the mimic discovered that the objects of his fun were not English, he was acutely embarrassed and apologized profusely.[62] Abigail Mayo and her family had a frigid reception at the gates of the ancient Palace of Justice in Rouen from the old director, who an-nounced it was closing time and ordered the gateman to shut the doors in their faces. However, when she made it clear that they were not English, but American, he brightened up, ordered the doors opened, and gave them a personal tour.[63] On arriving in France from England in 1832, Oliver Wendell Holmes noticed the customs officers going through Englishmen's luggage with fine-toothed combs, but once he and his companion identified themselves as Americans they were given a friendly greeting and passed through without inspection.[64]

Of course, until the publication of *Uncle Tom's Cabin* in 1852, what little most French actually knew of the United States had derived mainly from such romantic sources as James Fenimore Cooper's novels about the frontier and George Catlin's traveling Indian troupe. Charles Sumner said he was nonplused when one of France's top businessmen "asked me, with the greatest simplicity, if our noblest and most respected families were not the descendants of Montezuma!"[65] The arrival in France, in 1889, of William Cody's ("Buffalo Bill's") popular Wild West show put a somewhat different spin on this, but reinforced a popular tendency to identify America with the wild frontier.

As for the more politically savvy among the French, liberals had begun doubting America's commitment to its libertarian ideals in the 1830s, amidst outraged reports of American maltreatment of Indians and slaves.[66] Conservatives were put off by the bullying of the rising industrial giant when, after the Civil War, the triumphant Union government threatened to crush the French army supporting Louis-Napoléon's client, the Austrian Emperor Maximilian of Mexico, unless it withdrew and left him at the mercy of his Liberal opponents, who ultimately shot him.

Still, the defeat of slavery allowed French republicans to revive their earlier associations, when America had been a beacon of republicanism in the dark, post-1815 night. In 1865, Edouard de Laboulaye, a republican legal theorist, rallied several thousand French donors to send a strong signal disassociating themselves from Louis-Napoléon by building a huge monument to commemorate the centennial of American independence. It would invoke Lafayette's aid to America and emphasize that America's greatness rested on the twin foundations of religion and republican-liberal ideals. In 1871 the prominent sculptor Auguste Bartholdi was enlisted into the project. He reworked a design for an unbuilt torch-carrying monument for the entrance of the new Suez Canal called "Egypt Bringing Light to Asia," changing its Asiatic features into a Northern-European-looking "Liberty" holding the Declaration of Independence. While Gustave Eiffel supervised the crew building the statue's skeleton in Paris, Richard Morris Hunt, the first American architect to graduate from Paris's École des Beaux-Arts, was hired to design its massive pedestal, to be paid for by American donations.[67] Fundraising problems on the American side caused delays and scaling back, but the impressive monument finally opened, with great fanfare, in New York harbor on 28 October 1886. By then, however, its original symbolism was fading. Americans, never too sure of what it was about in the first place, soon turned it into a symbol of immigration from Europe.

French liberals, well aware of the generally dismal state of American government, by now looked upon America not as a guiding light of political liberty but of *economic* freedom. To people such as the French novelist Jules Verne, who might nowadays be called "modernizers," Americans were an energetic, dynamic people whose impressive material progress owed much to a system devoid of the ancient barriers of entrenched privilege that impeded invention and entrepreneurship in Europe. By the turn of the century, this new American economic order was epitomized by the new business enterprises, called "trusts" or corporations, and the far-seeing millionaires, such as Andrew Carnegie, who organized them.[68] In the general public mind, the "millionaire" became the quintessential American. "L'Oncle d'Amérique," a deus ex machina stepping in to save the hero or heroine with a large infusion of cash, became a popular figure on the French stage.[69]

The French modernizers thought America excelled in the practical arts and efficiency. What it lacked, of course, was the culture of the Old World, and this was something that France could provide.[70] In 1904, an enthusiastic French ex–minister of public works gained the support of one of the French modernizers' idols, President Theodore Roosevelt, for an audacious scheme to turn the venerable Palais-Royal into "an American commercial center."[71] But by then there was no need to forcefeed American business into Paris. It was already noticeable in such areas as its newspapers, printed on fast new American typesetting machines, and in the place de l'Opéra, where most of the buildings were already occupied by American businesses and advertisements for American companies hung everywhere.[72]

At the same time, the growing manifestations of American business power provoked a deep suspicion of American industrial capitalism and those who dominated it. French conservatives regarded American millionaires as avaricious, ill-bred men who rose to the top in a society that respected nothing but wealth. Leftists saw them as representing an inhumane new industrial system whose relentless pursuit of efficiency and profits ground millions of workers into dust. The middle classes, devoted to an economy of thrift, were particularly disgusted by stories of the millionaires' wasteful ways. "It would take many columns to enumerate the sumptuous stupidities of the rich North Americans," said an 1899 article in the newspaper, *Le Temps*. "One orders a fake Malmaison as a home. Another sees the palace of the Doges and tells his architects to construct a 'Little Venice.' Another proudly shows off his horde of phony Chinese porcelain and hangs kilometers of fake Gobelin tapestries on his walls."[73] An American wrote from Paris in 1910:

> Time was when the average Parisian of neglected education . . . was under the vague impression that all Americans were black. . . . Today he is convinced that all Americans are millionaires, and in this sweeping generalization he is encouraged by the obstinate refusal of the Paris newspapers to refer to an American, visiting or residing in Paris, otherwise than as the "richissime" (enormously rich) Mr. or Mrs. So-and-so. This possession of enormous wealth is widely supposed to be coincident with enormous gullibility in all that concerns the acquisition of works of art.[74]

In its 1904 report on the two liberated American tobacconist heiresses visiting Paris, *Femina* said they were annoyed at how the French press called all American women rich, extravagant "daughters of the king of something." It nevertheless labeled them "two young American billionaires . . . the daughters of M. Gehl, the king of the tobacconists."[75] The American automobilists roaring through the French countryside did little to dispel this illusion of a nation of millionaires. "While you are *en automobile* you will get accustomed to being overcharged," one wrote in 1908, "for they seem to argue that 'these Americans who bring cars over here must all be millionaires with gasoline to burn.'"[76] In all of this, the French were as yet only vaguely aware of the rest of the American tourists in France, the vast majority of whom were not extraordinarily rich. The Great War and its aftermath would soon change that.

Part

Four

THE INVASION

OF THE LOWER

ORDERS

1917-1930

Fifteen

DOUGHBOYS AND DOLLARS

The "Guns of August" that rang out in 1914, inaugurating World War I, did so at the height of the tourist season. As Austria-Hungary, Russia, Germany, France, and Britain methodically mobilized for war, dumbfounded tourists congregated in their hotels, wondering what to do next. Among them were thousands of perplexed Americans in France, who watched in amazement as the streets filled with marching men who just moments before, it seemed, had been at their beck and call.

The tourists scrambled to make their way to the seaports and liners to take them home, but soldiers heading for assembly points clogged the stations and railroad schedules were scrapped. The French government froze foreign currency transactions, so banks could not honor Americans' letters of credit and travelers' checks.[1] Americans short of cash to pay their hotel bills and purchase tickets for home besieged their consulates. J. P. Morgan and Company, the bank whose special relationship with the French government would later cause it to be accused of drawing America into the war, came to the rescue. It persuaded the French to allow it to transfer enough gold to cover its own letters of credit and advance money to Americans with other banks' letters of credit and American Express travelers' checks. It even loaned money to those who would merely sign a receipt. (Later, it said, only one such tourist failed to pay it back.)[2]

The mob at Morgan's Paris offices soon subsided. By the fall, most tourists were home, leaving the French tourist industry as one of the war's first casualties. One tourist agency is said to have taken some Americans and British on tours of the trenches in the spring of 1915, but, like many of the generals, its mindset was mired in the last war.[3] Unlike Paris in 1871, this war's slaughter offered no safe vantage points for morbid tourism. The French tourist industry could do little but wait for war's end, when, said a French tourist bureau, the Americans and British would surely favor the spas and resorts of France over those of Germany and

Switzerland, "in order to avoid encountering the detestable German there."[4] Meanwhile, the next Americans arriving in large numbers would be in uniform.

Of course, one cannot count as tourists the many hundreds of Americans who, before their country declared war on Germany in April 1917, came to France as ambulance drivers, relief workers, and nurses, or as volunteers for the French Foreign Legion and the Lafayette Escadrille of pilots. Yet they did reflect France's enduring reputation as a magnet for cultural tourism. Many were upper-middle-class young college graduates who were the products of a distinct Francophilic turn in American higher education at the turn of the century. They had been steeped in French literature and had been taught that, unlike Britain and America, France valued artistic creativity and individuality. Wartime propaganda portraying France as fighting to save civilized culture and democracy found an enthusiastic audience among them. Some, such as the poet Alan Seeger, died for this ideal.[5]

The men of the American Expeditionary Force (AEF), who began arriving in France in July 1917, cannot be thought of as traveling for pleasure and uplift either, even though actual warfare occupied so little of the majority's time there that one historian called them "as much tourists as soldiers."[6] Nevertheless, their perceptions of France could not fail to affect the future of American tourism to that country. This was particularly so since France was both the main staging point for the AEF and the site of most of its military engagements. By war's end, more than two million American soldiers had been stationed there, mainly in large cantonments in the northern and western parts of the country.

Most of them were enlisted men ("doughboys," named after the dough-like shape of the old infantrymen's buttons), who were generally from the lower classes. The large majority had less than seven years of schooling; one-quarter were illiterate. (The first—deeply flawed—I.Q. tests put more than half of them in the "moron" category![7]) They tended to regard the French as "backward" and lacking in American "push," failings that seemed exemplified—particularly for those who were billeted in rural French homes—in appalling standards of sanitation and personal hygiene. However, there was also considerable admiration for the French peasantry's stoicism and the townspeoples' resolve in the face of the war's awful toll.[8]

Not surprisingly, the troops thought sex was more freely available in

France than in America, even though the army strove mightily to prevent them from taking advantage of it. While the doughboys were training in the States, Secretary of War Newton D. Baker repeatedly assured America's mothers that the army would protect their sons from predatory women. The authorities subjected trainees to intense antiprostitution campaigns, festooning the camps with slogans such as "A German Bullet is Cleaner than a Whore."[9] When the troops arrived in France, their commanding officer, General John Pershing, declared all brothels off-limits to them. Enlisted men on leave were virtually banned from Paris; officers were limited to twenty-four hours there.

Pershing, who read the reports of venereal disease rates first thing each morning, was motivated by more than just his high moral code. These afflictions sometimes had a more devastating effect on units' manpower levels than enemy fire. But the antiprostitution campaign was undermined by the troops' belief that, thanks to government inspection, the rate of venereal disease among French prostitutes was a mere 7 percent, as compared to about 50 percent among their American counterparts.[10]

To make matters worse, not only did the French government continue to abide *maisons de tolérance,* it encouraged them to operate near leave centers as more-or-less official whorehouses for their army. (When French Premier Georges Clemenceau sent the Presbyterian President Woodrow Wilson a letter offering to have some set up for the Americans, Newton Baker intercepted it, exclaiming to an aide, "For God's sake, Raymond, don't show the President this or he'll stop the war!"[11]) Soon after the Americans began to arrive, word spread in the prostitute subculture that the "Sammies" were much better paid than the "*poilus,*" the French enlisted men. The three *maisons de tolérance* already in the port of Saint-Nazaire, a town of eighteen thousand that was one of the two main disembarkation points, gleefully ran up the Stars and Stripes, while hordes of out-of-town streetwalkers invaded its sidewalks and cafés.[12] In the rest of the country as well, migrating prostitutes would follow hard on the heels of arriving Americans.[13]

Not all the encounters between young enlisted men and French women involved prostitutes. Some associations were in the grey area where the relative wealth of the Americans attracted French women who might not otherwise have been appreciative of their charms. There were even some marriages.[14] (It was later charged that the doughboys abandoned five thousand of these wives when they returned to America.[15]) Nevertheless, most doughboys almost certainly left France with the stereotype they arrived with—that the French had loose sexual morals—more than amply confirmed.

— —

The thousands of American officers and civilian volunteers from the middle and upper classes who spent most of the war in Paris tended to reinforce the growing preconception among those classes that Paris was the pleasure capital of the world.[16] After an initial bout of asceticism, the French authorities had decided that it was best for morale to allow as much business-as-usual as possible in the pleasure industries. Sporadic air raids and occasional shelling from the monstrous German cannon "Big Bertha" meant streets were blacked out at night and dance halls remained closed, but theaters, restaurants and other attractions stayed open.[17] Champagne still flowed, and the dollar went far toward buying a luxurious lifestyle. Indeed, American officers and volunteers were cautioned against alienating the French by lavish overspending.[18] The *Stars and Stripes* warned arriving troops not to treat France like a tourist playground. Too many of them, it said, came over expecting to find "a universal pleasure resort."[19]

Yet temptation lurked everywhere. The diary of Howard O'Brien, a married intelligence officer stationed in Paris in 1918, says that on his first night there he was "all but raped." "From the Opéra to the Étoile a million girls all whispering: 'Will you sleep wiz me?'" Only through a supreme effort, he wrote, did he manage to resist. Most of his officer friends readily succumbed, reassuring themselves with the same stories about safe sex as the enlisted men. Later, after watching prostitutes being subjected to their physical exams and checking their medical histories, O'Brien concluded that his chances of emerging unscathed would be more like "one in a million." Nevertheless, he continued to function as a kind of procurer for the American politicians, businessmen, labor leaders, and journalists who descended on Paris. For them, he noted, it was the "usual *cherchez la femme.*" He himself was content to swill prodigious amounts of champagne and dine sumptuously at fine restaurants with American friends.[20]

A few days after the Armistice, Frank Smith, an Arizona county judge who had resigned his position to work for the Red Cross in Paris, wrote in his diary that the Folies Bergère was, "as usual," crowded with Americans and English. "The other sex was in evidence," he added, "but less pressing than formerly. The demand is exhausting the supply." A few days later, Smith and friends dined at Maxim's, and then "Jack and Joe took a few turns with the girls upstairs, and Harry and I, having caught nothing, remained to watch. Thence to the Folies . . . and from there to the Place de l'Opéra." Some days later, Smith wrote that an officer friend thought that the Americans who had become acquainted with "the more accomplished and alluring of the opposite sex here," who were "chic and feminine, packing the necessary wallop on all occasions," would not be satisfied with "Mamie and Gerty back at home with their passion for gum and ice cream sodas."[21]

— —

Some of the restrictions on American enlisted men visiting Paris were lifted at war's end, making the wartime policy seem wise. *Le Matin* reported that during the month of December 1918, American soldiers in the Department of the Seine, which included Paris, were charged with committing 34 murders, 220 assaults, and being involved in nearly 500 bloody brawls. It complained that although the U.S. Army set up a special unit of tough military police to control the Sammies, they were of little use in investigating serious crimes. In mid-January 1919, they were reassigned to raiding Montmartre night spots in search of deserters.[22] Even there, the results were unimpressive. Paris was soon plagued by an estimated fifteen hundred deserters, many of whom made their livings as pimps, cocaine peddlers, or robbers.[23]

But misbehavior was by no means an enlisted man's monopoly. As O'Brien strolled through place de l'Opéra on New Year's Eve 1918, he noticed, his diary says, "American officers, drunk and disgusting, furnishing spectacle for American privates, sober and disapproving." At 2:30 A.M., he heard a girl crying out and discovered a drunken officer beating her with a broken umbrella. He spent the rest of the night trying to get the young man, who kept claiming to be "from a fine old Southern family," to remember where his hotel was. On the other hand, the same day a YMCA man had told him of taking a group of polite enlisted men on a sightseeing tour and, to save them money, to a Bouillon Duval for lunch. After thanking him profusely, one them then pulled out a pocketful of francs and asked: "Say, mister, now where's this here Maxim's?"[24]

The hundreds of thousands of men who waited in camps in the north and west of France through the winter, spring, and summer of 1918–1919 for transport back to the States were bored, restive, and testy. As soon as the war had ended relations between the enlisted men and the French had taken a decided turn for the worse. For the French, victory had brought with it, not bucolic peace and prosperity, but economic turmoil. Prices soared and inflation threatened to wipe out carefully hoarded savings. To the American soldiers, few of whom were well-versed in economics, the reason prices rose was clear: now that their usefulness was over, the greedy French were gouging them. "Lafayette had been repaid," a veteran wrote, "but the thanks of the French were expressed in increased prices to the soldiers. The mass of the soldiery never understood and never forgave."[25]

From the French perspective, the doughboys' public drunkenness was disgusting and their violent behavior—especially their propensity to brandish guns to settle arguments—was particularly alarming. From January through September 1919, reports from all over France of a populace terrified by drunken, gun-wielding Americans poured into the Ministry of the Interior in Paris. Armed doughboys held up people on the streets and in railroad stations; they robbed stores, looted wineshops, and shot at each other and the French. Drunken soldiers stole cars and ran down pedestrians, in one case killing a fifteen-year-old boy. In one egregious incident that occurred late one evening in September 1919, two drunken doughboys in a stolen car drove up to a gas pump in a village in Brittany and demanded a free fill-up. Upon being refused, they proceeded to terrorize the village, careening around firing shots everywhere. Eventually, they passed out in their car, but the next day they went to a neighboring village where they forced a woman who ran a wine shop to serve them beer. After an hour and a half of drinking, one soldier pulled out a revolver, aimed it at her, and said "pour vous." When the panic-stricken woman fled, the soldier turned the gun on her nineteen-year-old son, shooting him in the stomach and arm.[26]

The situation was exacerbated by the fact that the French authorities could not interrogate and try the Americans they apprehended, but had to turn them over to the American military police. The clumsy M.P.'s made matters worse. The French police complained that they ransacked French homes at all hours of the day in illegal searches for deserters. In May 1919, near Tours, M.P.'s shot two French railroad employees whom they suspected of pilfering wine from a railroad car, killing one of them. Yet two weeks earlier, the French authorities said, the M.P.'s had done nothing when a French army officer who had come across thirty Americans pillaging wine-laden railroad cars in the same place was threatened with an axe and driven from the scene.[27]

Sometimes the frustrations boiled over into overt demonstrations of anti-Americanism. In September 1919, two drunken doughboys wrecked the train station at Corsept, near Saint-Nazaire, shot at a peasant who refused them a ride in his wagon, and then, lying in wait on a country road, robbed, shot, and killed two passing cyclists. A large crowd of locals then gathered in town, vowing to arm themselves and, according to police, "drive every American they encountered out of the country."[28]

The French and the AEF tried to distract some of the better-educated soldiers with four-month courses in "French Civilization" in French universities. The U.S. Army tried to keep the rest of the men occupied with training exercises and games. When it did set them free, it attempted to keep them away from Paris by expanding a wartime program of paying for one-week stays in "Leave Zones," where soldiers were put up in hotels and entertained by chaste female YMCA workers.[29] "Nice is full of Americans," a Virginia nurse wrote home in December 1918, from a hotel in which every room was taken by Americans. She even ran into her "first beau," whom she had not seen in ten years.[30] The hoteliers and restaurateurs of the "Riviera Leave Zone" were so grateful for this infusion of cash-rich Americans that the Nice authorities reserved its famed seaside promenade for their exclusive use. By the time the program was terminated in May 1919, almost 150,000 doughboys had spent over fifty million francs while basking in the Riviera sun.[31]

That month saw the largest number of troops (one-third of a million) repatriated to the States. It was not a moment too soon, for them or the French. This is reflected in two little volumes, entitled "My Impressions of France and the Army," to which an American YMCA volunteer asked enlisted men to contribute while waiting to be shipped back from Saint-Nazaire in the summer of 1919. A large proportion of the contributors were men who had attended the "French Civilization" courses in Bordeaux, Toulouse, Montpelier, and Grenoble and had lived with French families there. They were almost universal in their admiration for the French, extolling their hospitality and close family life. However, they regretted that the vast majority of soldiers, who had no such positive experiences, were returning home with a very negative view. Most, they said, had met only the "3rd class" French people: the prostitutes and "venal peasants" of the small "soldier-ridden" towns near the front, rather than the "upper class," who were friendly and upright. One soldier said that, like the other doughboys, he had looked upon

> the ignorant peasant class of Frenchman who inhabited the region we occupied . . . as a wine-imbibing, immoral person with low ideals, an aversion to taking a bath and whose chief aim seemed to be the garnering of the Americans' francs. Had I returned to the U.S. at the end of

that period I would have doubtless joined the million and a half who are already engaged in discussing the "frog" around the fireside.

When finally granted a pass to visit a French city, he continued,

> we're besieged by a bevy of pretty girls—many of whom (regretfully we have learned) were refugees from devastated sections and who entered a shameful life solely because they had to find a means of livelihood and Americans had lots of money! Then we go home and discuss the morals of France![32]

He was correct about the kind of stories the doughboys would be telling. During 1919 and 1920 the French ambassador to Washington frantically tried to quell the rumor, spread by the returning troops, that the avaricious French had actually *rented* the trenches to the Americans who had come to die for them.[33]

Even before the American soldiers began returning home, many Frenchmen were banking on a new invasion of American tourists to help salvage their devastated economy. The most obvious lure, they thought, would be the devastation itself. In January 1919, the head of the Touring Club de France hailed this "friendly invasion." The Americans would first visit the battlefields, he said, as "pilgrimages of mourning or out of curiosity." However, they would then want to see "the mountains, pastures, rivers and streams which produced this heroic race." (An American journalist had assured him of this.) They would thus spend billions of francs "to help dress our wounds."[34]

By the summer of 1919, the Michelin tire company had already produced a three-volume English-language guidebook, *Americans in the Great War,* for American battlefield tourists.[35] Groups of Cook's tourists were leaving London, Paris, and Brussels almost daily for battlefield tours. American Express in Paris began renting cars that, like Cook's, were chauffeured by veterans, for more personalized tours.

Other veterans began complaining that the curiosity seekers were defiling the sacred ground upon which their comrades had bled and died, but the pounds and dollars over the horizon glittered too brightly, and rationalizations abounded.[36] "It is not curiosity" that prompted the tours, said Cook's, but a "desire to enter more fully into a sympathetic idea of the heroic sufferings and endurance of these brave fellows." The tourists

Top, The White Star line's *Olympic* and the North German Lloyd line's *Krönprinzessin-Cecilie,* two of the behemoths in the competition for speed, size, and luxury on the transatlantic run, crossing paths in Cherbourg, 1911.

Bottom, The ruins of the Paris Hôtel de Ville (city hall) after the suppression of the Commune in 1871 destroyed much of the center of Paris. American tourists were fed the false tale that fanatical revolutionaries had herded hundreds of innocents into the building before burning it. Photo: Bibliothèque Nationale de France, Paris.

Top, The carriages of the upper class heading for and returning from the Sunday display of finery in the Bois de Boulogne, a ritual in which wealthy visiting Americans often joined. Photo: Bibliothèque Nationale de France, Paris.

Bottom, Charles Garnier's magnificent Opéra building in 1875, shortly after its completion. The grand Hôtel de la Paix and its Café de la Paix are on the left. The rue de la Paix, lined with luxury shops patronized by wealthy Americans, and the avenue de l'Opéra join the place de l'Opéra from the south, at the bottom of the picture.

Top, The Casino at Monte Carlo, also designed by Garnier, which helped rid the Riviera of its stodgy image as a health resort. Upper-class Americans enjoyed gambling there, while more puritanical middle-class tourists relished stories of how losers who blew their brains out on its steps had their bodies whisked away for burial in unmarked graves.

Bottom, The famed Promenade des Anglais in Monte Carlo's competitor, Nice. After failing to discourage visitors to Monte Carlo's casino by spreading the rumors of waves of suicides, Nice built its own casino, now destroyed, on the left. For a time, at the end of World War I, it was reserved for American soldiers patronizing the "Riviera Leave Zone."

Top, Beach time at Trouville, a Normandy resort that, along with its neighbor, Deauville, became part of the upper-class tourist circuit in the 1880s. The adults are fully dressed, in afternoon wear. The women, in long dresses, are mainly sitting under umbrellas, for until the 1920s tans were the mark of low-class people who worked outdoors. Only a few adults venture to the water's edge, where children, also fully clothed, play. Luxury hotels and fanciful villas line the shore.

Bottom, The Café Américain, a luxury Paris restaurant, in 1899. By then it was becoming acceptable for American women accompanied by men to frequent such cafés and restaurants in the evening.

Top, Dining at a Bouillon Duval at the 1878 Exposition. These clean, simple, and reasonably priced restaurants were favorites among turn-of-the-century middle-class American women, who particularly appreciated the polite waitresses in domestics' white aprons and bonnets. Photo: Bibliothèque Nationale de France, Paris.

Bottom, The Petit Palais during the 1900 Exposition. By then, visitors were so impressed with that architectural style, originating in the French École des Beaux-Arts, that it was imported to the far corners of the globe. It was introduced on an impressive scale to the United States in Chicago's Colombian Exposition of 1893, which was intended to outdo Paris's famous expositions.

Top, Les Grands Magasins au Printemps, a department store that opened in 1889, with the kind of glass domes and iron galleries that were necessary before electric illumination. Although its rivals, the Grands Magasins du Louvre and Bon Marché, remained popular among American tourists, it ultimately benefited from its location near the place de l'Opéra when tourism gravitated in that direction.

Bottom, "Mr. Pipp" and family, Charles Dana Gibson's contribution to the popular stereotype of brow-beaten businessmen being dragged through Europe by social-climbing wives and pretty daughters looking for husbands who used culture as a pretext for the tour. The caption read, "In Paris. He has the opportunity of enlarging his horizon and of developing an interest in the real purpose of the trip."

Above, The summer garden of the Moulin Rouge in 1890. A belly dancer would perform on a small stage between the elephant's legs. Americans were usually more interested in watching the prostitutes than the show. Photo: Bibliothèque Nationale de France, Paris.

Left, George DuMaurier's illustration of the evil Svengali and the hypnotized Trilby in one of her triumphant concerts. The author/artist tried, with mixed success, to make her look like one of the beauties in the works of the pre-Raphaelite painter Edward Coley Burne-Jones.

Top, The Yellow Kid, America's first popular newspaper cartoon character,
visiting Paris with his gang, helping to reinforce Paris's titillating image.
On arriving, they headed for the Folies Bergère and the night spots of Montmartre.
Here, in the Louvre, they make wisecracks about the nudity in the works.

Bottom, Charles Dana Gibson's seductive portrayal of a Latin Quarter student out for a
drink with his grisette. The illustration, for one of Richard Harding Davis's mid-1890s
Harper's articles, implies that she might also take an interest in passing men, perhaps
American tourists. Within ten years, idealized portrayals such as this and Mr. Pipp's
daughters would, in less restrictive clothing, become the renowned "Gibson Girls."

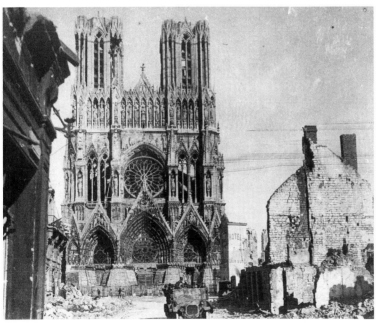

Top, More than one hundred soldiers waiting for their turn to dance with six YMCA volunteers in the posh spa town of Aix-les-Bains, in one of the "Leave Zones" the U.S. Army created to keep the troops away from the legalized brothels and other temptations of Paris.

Bottom, The shell of the devastated cathedral at Reims, which became a major destination of American postwar battlefield tours. Photo: Bibliothèque Nationale de France, Paris.

Top, Florence Jones (left) at "Chez Florence," the Montmartre nightclub she and her husband opened in 1924. White American tourists often demanded that black men be ejected from Paris bars and clubs. Clearly, this was not the case here. Photo: Bibliothèque Nationale de France, Paris.

Bottom, Young American women on one of Dorothy Marsh's popular guided tours, posing with their guides in an open charabanc overlooking the French Riviera. Photo: Sophia Smith Collection, Smith College.

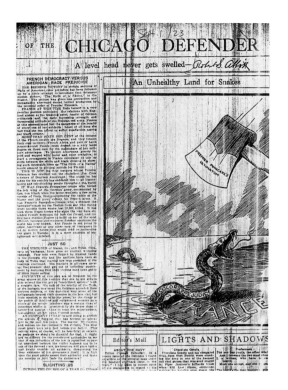

Top, An editorial cartoon in the African American paper the *Chicago Defender*, lauding the French government for condemning American tourists' racist behavior in France.

Bottom, American tourists in charabancs on a guided tour of Paris. In 1926, French mobs attacked similar vehicles carrying them on "Paris by Night" tours.

A common French view of why American tourists came to France.
The 1927 magazine cover is entitled "Gout Américain" (American taste).
Photo: Bibliothèque Nationale de France, Paris.

would regard the "consecrated fields . . . not as show but as a shrine."[37] "The world must see what the German did," said an article on why American visits should be encouraged.[38] "It is a natural curiosity" to want to see the devastation, said another. French people who found this irritating should remind themselves of the dollars and pounds that the many thousands of tourists would be spending.[39]

Shipping and Continental transportation were still too disrupted for much American tourism to develop in 1919, but hopes ran high for 1920. The French government, expecting "an enormous influx of Americans" that year, opened tourist offices at major ports of entry to distribute information on touring the battlefields. A government agency encouraged companies to build nearby hotels and organize automobile trips to them. It even suggested airplane tours over them. It commissioned tasteful souvenirs—sketches and descriptions of the sites—from the Ministry of Fine Arts and assured the public that the tourists would act with appropriate decorum. In early June, as it braced for an expected two hundred thousand American visitors and licked its chops at the minimum seven thousand dollars it calculated each would spend in France, it panicked over the lack of accommodations at the battlefields. Several former American ambulance trains were quickly acquired, to be shunted onto sidings and used as hotels.[40] The trains were not needed, for the American invasion of the battlefields turned out to be one of the great nonevents of 1920. Financial instability in America and stories of overcrowded trains, inadequate accommodations, and price-gouging in France discouraged tourism.[41] Fewer than one hundred thousand Americans visited all of Europe that year.[42]

At first, promoters of battlefield tourism tended to use the terms *pilgrimage* and *tourism* interchangeably.[43] However, efforts were soon made to distinguish between pilgrims—that is, people paying homage at sacred places—and those who visited "out of curiosity." The latter kind of tourism inevitably smacked of "trivialization": vehicles disgorging busloads of casually dressed people at sites whose significance they barely comprehended, to be surrounded by hawkers selling spent shells and helmets with bullet holes. Inevitably, however, as the war receded in time, the tourist/pilgrim distinction was blurred.[44]

One problem with preserving the battlefields as sacred sites for pilgrimages was that they reflected the mainly static nature of the war on the Western Front. They covered a wide swath of northern and eastern

France, from the Channel to the Swiss border, but the destruction itself was relatively localized. Only a few miles away from the band of bleak devastation, the pleasant countryside, often a joy to behold, was virtually untouched. The fact that one could get to the battlefields only by automobile or bus also contributed to dissipating the lugubrious aura, for motoring was still regarded as a distinctly pleasurable activity. A typical *Paris Herald* article describes a suggested trip to the devastated town of Soissons as "this day's delightful motor tour." One passed through charming towns and rolling fields that "give the appearance of big stretches of blue-green carpet" before encountering "our first views of the havoc of war."[45]

Once they passed into the "devastated areas," most visitors could not help reacting like typical tourists on sightseeing expeditions, for that is what they were. Florence Patton, a twenty-two-year-old Milwaukeean, had been quite upset by the devastation when she first saw the battlefields through the window of her Brussels-to-Paris train in September 1920. However, two months later, when she toured them with an American man and a chaperone in a chauffeured limousine from American Express, her reaction was much like any tourist visiting an unusual sight. She wrote her mother of passing through some "lovely, cultivated country" and then coming upon "ruined country, partly tilled, with stacks of barbed wire everywhere." That night in Reims, they walked along a ruined, deserted, moonlit street toward the cathedral, which seemed brightly lit inside, only to discover that it was a shell—the moon had provided the lighting. The next day, they visited the macabre "Trench of the Bayonets" near Verdun, where some 170 French soldiers, awaiting the order to attack with fixed bayonets, had been buried alive by a mine that exploded under them (a line of their bayonets still protruded through the earth) and other gruesome sights. Although she was clearly moved by all of this, in typical tourist fashion, she reported enjoying excellent meals and hotels and sent home a postcard of the ruined cathedral at Reims that read, "Am having a marvellous time."[46]

Of course, revisiting the battlefields was a different experience for the men who fought there. They were struck by how the battlefields had changed. Frank Smith, a veteran who returned in December 1920, wrote that the places where he had fought were practically unrecognizable.

> Everything is completely overgrown with weeds and underbrush, the trenches all caved in, and the dugouts appear to have been blown up. I

never saw such an absolutely deserted wilderness since I was born. Not a sound or sign of people anywhere. It certainly gave me the creeps.[47]

Smith had inadvertently put his finger on the Achilles' heel of the battlefield tourism industry: that the battlefields themselves were remarkably resilient. At first, it was said that the scars of war would be visible for generations to come. In late 1918, an American journalist said that although the towns might be rebuilt, the beauty and fertility of the countryside would not return for hundreds of years. A guidebook for Americans said that for "centuries to follow," the Argonne Forest, where American troops had fought, would bear "the sad imprint of an eternal despoliation."[48] That within six months of the Armistice, the treeless bogs, scarred by trenches, bunkers, and shell-holes, criss-crossed with barbed wire and strewn with the jetsam of millions of men, would be green—at first with weeds and then with farmers' crops—was practically inconceivable. Within a year, battlefield tourists were keeping one ear cocked for the sound of unexploded mines and shells being set off by peasants plowing them.

Officials tried to prevent the battlefields from merely disappearing under carpets of green. Coils of barbed wire were kept on the sides of the roads; impressive fortifications were protected from destruction; monuments were erected in places such as the Trench of the Bayonets, where a wealthy American paid for the marker. Nevertheless, as early as the summer of 1921 there was talk of tourists becoming "lost in the monotony of the battlefields."[49]

As the battlefields themselves disappeared, destroyed French towns became the major objectives. One-day trips from Paris to Reims were especially popular among Americans. They allowed time to lament the destruction of its cathedral (cited as an example of German barbarism, although in fact the Allies had destroyed it to prevent it from being used as an observation post) and yet be back in Paris for dinner.[50] The American Committee for Devastated France (ACDF) encouraged these and longer battlefield tours to gain support for its efforts to rebuild the towns, emphasizing how the brutish Germans had laid waste to them as they retreated in the summer of 1918.[51]

For Clara Laughlin, a Smith College graduate from Chicago who took the longer tour with five other women in the summer of 1921, the experience was, she wrote home, "one of the most impressive, awesome journeys—no! *the* most impressive awesome journey—that could be made, anywhere in the world." Emerging from the destroyed cathedral at Soissons, she and her companions "almost *burst* with furious indignation and hate" at the Germans, whom she called "the Beast." The next stops on the tour, to the even more devastated areas around Reims, Verdun, and the Argonne Forest, inspired even deeper rage. "One comes out of it all," she concluded, "with a sense . . . of the *sublimity* of human nature at its grandest and the bestiality-beyond-words of human nature at its worst." They returned from the tour, she said, filled with admiration for the heroism of the French people and "black, blinding *rage* against the barbarism of the bestial invaders. We came back feeling that there is but one *transcendent* virtue . . . *killing* Germans! Ridding the world of their noxious presence." She asked that her letters be circulated back home to gain support for the ACDF rebuilding effort.[52] Later, the ACDF turned the sixteenth-century chateau in which its women volunteers were headquartered into a lodge ("simply but daintily furnished with every essential comfort") for tourists visiting the ruined villages.[53]

Yet even this worthy effort was not immune to the trivialization endemic in the tourist experience. When the writer Malcolm Cowley returned home from France in August 1923, his French Line boat was crowded with three hundred "Good Will Girls." They were among the winners of contests, benefiting the ACDF, in which newspaper readers in three hundred American towns and cities paid ten cents a vote to choose a delegate to one of five "Good Will Missions" to France. During their last night at sea, they gathered on deck to give a sort of college yell:

> One, two, three, four,
> Who are we for?
>   America, America, America!
> Two, four, six, eight.
> Who do we appreciate?
>   France! France![54]

This kind of exuberance was hardly consonant with persistent efforts to preserve the pilgrimage aspect of the visit to the battlefields. In 1919, the remains of almost thirty thousand of the Americans who died in France were reburied in nine beautifully landscaped cemeteries that even today stir deep emotions. Monuments were erected at Bordeaux and Saint-Nazaire (later destroyed by the Nazis) to commemorate the Americans' arrival there, as well as at the sites of their major battles. Generals and politicians gave speeches invoking Lafayette and swearing that their sacrifices would never be forgotten.[55] (A visit to the massive monument at Belleau Wood today—practically deserted and forgotten, and incised with the names of long-forgotten battles—reminds one of the Shelley poem *Ozymandias,* about a traveler who encounters the remnants of a vast statue in the endless sands of the desert upon whose empty pedestal is inscribed: "My name is Ozymandias, King of Kings. Look upon my works, ye mighty, and despair!") Finally, as we shall see, in 1927, the American Legion held its convention in Paris, calling it "The Pilgrimage of the Army of Remembrance."[56] But by then the battlefields were low on the priority lists of most American tourists to France. Even Cook's, who dominated the enterprise, no longer promoted battlefield tours in the United State.[57] America, and its tourists, had changed too much.

⸺ ⸺

One group of soldiers was generally ignored by battlefield tourists: the many thousands of African Americans who had served in France. Yet the sojourn in France almost certainly affected them more than any other single group of troops. In America, they were subject to the harshest forms of segregation, disenfranchisement, and humiliation; in the South, where most of them were from, the mere accusation of accosting a white women in a suggestive manner could mean death at the hands of a lynch mob or sheriff. Now, in France, they had suddenly found themselves in a country where such things were quite unheard of.

As we saw in chapter 4, early-nineteenth-century Americans had often been struck by the apparent color-blindness of many of the French. After midcentury, the phenomenal success of the French translation of *Uncle Tom's Cabin,* Harriet Beecher Stowe's antislavery novel, spurred deep sympathy for the plight of African American slaves. (A well-meaning Paris hotel even called itself *"L'Hotel de l'Oncle Tom."*) French travelers' accounts supplemented this with depictions of the horrors of Southern slave markets.[58] A popular 1858 play presented a shocking portrayal of a Southern plantation owner as a brutish, foul-mouthed madman, wielding a whip and brandishing pistols, threatening and beating practically everyone in sight.[59] There were even vigorous condemnations of Northern discrimination against African American freemen—of color prejudice per se—a subject that even American abolitionists tended to avoid.[60]

This sympathy for African Americans persisted after the Civil War. In the 1860s and 1870s, French audiences flocked to the annual concert tours of the "Jubilee Singers," who sang Negro spirituals to raise money for Fisk University in Nashville.[61] The future prime minister, Georges Clemenceau, wrote articles from the United States denouncing the oppression of African Americans.[62] In the 1890s, the French press indignantly reported the wave of lynchings that swept the American South, as whites terrorized blacks into submission to white supremacy.[63] "Six more Negroes were lynched in Georgia," said an 1898 article in the major daily, *Le Temps*, describing how after one of the men accused of raping a white woman was hung, his body was pumped full of bullets, and then cut up in pieces and distributed among the crowd. It also criticized color prejudice in the North.[64] African American music became chic, as fashionable French society took to ragtime music and the "cake walk."[65]

Meanwhile, France's acquisition of a sub-Saharan empire helped stimulate interest in African religion and visual arts. The French government encouraged the sons of African elites to study in France. Once they mastered the French language and culture, they were to be treated as equals. Of course a condescending air surrounded what the French called their "civilizing mission," based as it was on the assumption that the natives' cultures were inferior to that of the French and should be replaced. But at least it assumed that the colored people were capable of becoming completely acculturated. This approach stood in stark contrast to that of Britain and the United States, where skin color relegated people to inferior status, no matter what their achievements. World War I sharpened these differences, as France was increasingly forced to rely on soldiers from Black Africa who were enticed, cajoled, and drafted into service. The French public was told that they had a particular aptitude for the mainstay of French infantry tactics, the bayonet charge, and were fighting heroically to defend their common mother country. The Senegalese were widely credited with having saved Paris in the second Battle of the Marne.

It was natural, then, that the good feelings toward Africans generated by this propaganda would spill over onto the African Americans who began arriving, in rigidly segregated units, in September 1917. The French applauded the black units warmly as they marched through the streets of the disembarkation ports.[66] Perhaps it was equally natural that the American authorities would do their best to suppress the social consequences of these good feelings. Like General Dwight Eisenhower in World War II, General Pershing wanted no black combat troops to be part of the AEF. However, he was happy enough to shunt them into labor battalions and have them unload ships, build roads, and bury the dead. When four regiments of black combat troops arrived, rather than have them fight under his command, Pershing had them assigned to the French army, supposedly on a temporary basis.[67]

The ten thousand men in these African American regiments were re-equipped with French uniforms and arms and served with the French army for the rest of the war. No significant problems were encountered on the racial front, although the same cannot be said with regard to the large majority of African American troops, mainly in labor battalions, who were under the direct control of the AEF. From the outset, the American authorities tried to prevent them from fraternizing with the French. The military police, whose brutality was already legendary among white troops, were ordered to treat talking with French women or entering a French home as serious offenses for black troops. Most cafés and other public places were declared off-limits to them. At one large supply depot, African American troops were confined to base for eight months.[68]

The unwillingness of the French military authorities to treat the African Americans under their command similarly became a sore spot in Franco-American relations. The Americans' expressions of shock that African Americans were allowed to frequent the same brothels as the white French troops were met with Gallic shrugs. A colonel on Pershing's staff circulated a document among the French officer corps, called "Secret Information Concerning Black American Troops," that tried to change this. If colored troops received equal treatment in France, it said, they might conclude they deserved the same in America. Yet white Americans thought that equality between the races would lead to mongrelization. They also thought blacks were deficient in intelligence, judgment, and morality—that they were a danger to society that had to be repressed. French officers should therefore avoid any intimacy with black American officers—they should not eat with them, shake hands with them, or speak to them except on military matters. French civilians should be told "not to spoil the Negroes." The memo ended with a warning that Americans were particularly outraged by any intimacy between white women and blacks.[69]

The French authorities ignored this advice. Instead, when the war ended, the document was leaked and read to an outraged Chamber of Deputies, which duly passed a resolution condemning racial prejudice and affirming France's commitment to equality.[70]

Meanwhile, as soon as the war ended, the restrictions on black American troops were tightened. In some towns, they were not allowed to venture off the main street, even to go to the post office. They were excluded from the huge Allied victory parade down the Champs-Élysées. M.P.'s tried to disabuse them of any ideas about socializing with French women by randomly beating defiant-looking ones into submission.[71] The French were shocked at the many incidents of mistreatment, especially when black Frenchmen were mistakenly on the receiving end. On 19 April 1919, after a group of them were beaten in Saint-Nazaire, two members of the Chamber of Deputies demanded the government take steps to stop "the harassment, attacks, and crimes perpetrated on colored French citizens and subjects" (one was from Martinique) by American soldiers and M.P.'s.[72]

Harsh as they were, the restrictions failed to prevent the French experience from giving African Americans ideas about their right to equality back home. Returning black doughboys' tales of a place where white men and women treated blacks as equals had an enormous ripple effect. The politically conservative African American newspaper, the *Chicago Defender* proudly headlined a September 1919 article entitled, "Why French Girls Adore Our Men." It quoted a Frenchman, responding to a letter to the *New York Evening Sun* denouncing "frog Janes," who wrote, "The good French girl loves a Negro." Returning white doughboys, the Frenchman wrote, were heaping calumny on French women because they refused to accede to American demands that they have nothing to do with the black American troops. "French women do not measure men according to the color of their skin," he said. "A white skin is not an essential attribute of French society or French citizenship."[73]

In the short run, the effects of the French experience on African American soldiers were visible in the bloody race riots and lynchings sparked by their return. In the "Red Summer" of 1919, race riots broke out in a number of American cities, particularly in the Midwest. Many returning African American doughboys paid with their lives, while still in uniform, for appearing to act as they did in France. In the longer run, it was also manifested in the pervasive idea among African Americans that France represented a refuge from racism at home. This, as we shall see, would add the race question to the tinderbox created by American tourism to France over the next decade.

Sixteen

"HOW'RE YOU GONNA KEEP 'EM DOWN ON THE FARM?"

> The Paris Americans of before the war were largely of a different class from those you see now. They used to be women of exceptional elegance, men of large affairs, with a goodly supply of lace-collared, flat-heeled schoolteachers doing a summer in Europe for five hundred dollars, without smiling. Now you see obsolete bump-toed shoes on men from goodness knows where: people, masses of them. Elegance has gone, people have come. Perhaps it's as it should be, but it isn't pretty.
>
> KATHLEEN HOWARD

The popular 1920s song, "How're You Gonna Keep 'Em Down on the Farm, After They've Seen Paree?" alluded to the doughboys who, after experiencing the "wine, women, and song" of France were unable to readjust to rural America. Indeed, some of them did not even return, and chose to be demobilized in France. Others returned to the United States and promptly caught a boat back to France, where they joined the flourishing American underground of ne'er-do-wells in Paris. (A number of them supported themselves by fleecing touring countrymen who, leery of sly Continentals, were easy prey to, say, a seemingly straight-talking fellow from Connecticut.[1]) But the song was also about an America torn between the traditional, puritanical values of rural and small-town America and the new hedonistic values associated with the rising consumer culture of the booming, heterogeneous cities. Representatives of the older America particularly resented the urban sophisticates who, in the words of a Ku Klux Klan leader, derided them as "hicks, hayseeds, and drivers of second-hand

Fords." This conflict lay at the root of many of the most controversial issues of 1920s America, including the Klan, Prohibition, immigration restriction, Protestant fundamentalism, and the status of women. It also spilled over into American tourists' views of France.[2]

The best-selling 1926 novel, *They Had to See Paris*, used the negative view of France propagated by the returning doughboys to exemplify the new urban values and reaffirm the older verities. It is the story of "Pike Peters," a decent, not very well-educated small-town car dealer from Oklahoma who strikes oil and becomes millionaire. His wife is satirized, in the prewar antifeminist manner, as a social climber with phony cultural aspirations. She decides they must visit Paris for a year, to see "the Louver" and to have their "children" (a boy in his early twenties, a girl of twenty-seven) "meet the right kind of people—we want to give them culture and refinement and travel."

When the family arrives in Paris, the wife becomes involved with the shallow expatriate community. The son decides to become an artist and moves into a studio with a pretty model. Dad manages to convince him that, since she poses nude, she is not marriage material. However, no sooner does Pike persuade his son to leave her than he himself falls victim to the wiles of an attractive demimondaine he encounters in an evening tour of Montmartre clubs. She stalks him outside the Ritz, where the family is staying, and lures him to her Left Bank apartment. However, just as he is about to succumb to her temptations, he realizes that he is falling into the very trap from which he just extricated his son and flees. Meanwhile, the daughter is being courted by a French "marquis" who seems overly impressed by the chateau they buy. A lawyer soon arrives at the castle with the nobleman's proposal of marriage, attached to which is a codicil promising to pay the groom two hundred thousand dollars. The Peters are told this is normal in the circumstances. The wife is all for it, but Pike refuses. The marquis offers to halve the amount, but Pike remains obdurate and the sleazy aristocrat disappears. The daughter then becomes attached to an American radio salesman in Paris who is moving back to the States, and they all end up returning to what will presumably be better lives back home.[3]

Variety described the 1929 movie version, which starred the folksy humorist Will Rogers in his first talking role, as a variation on the old "simple hick in a classy setting" story. It would be "a certain money-maker," said the entertainment weekly, "especially for the great southwest territory, where Rogers and fundamentalism and the *Saturday Evening Post* walk hand in hand."[4] But the book and movie also successfully tapped into the doughboys' persisting view of France as a country of cheats and connivers where sex was always on offer. At the very end of the book, an Oklahoma friend of Peter Pike asks him, "Did you parley-voo 'em?" (used in the book, as the doughboys did, to mean have sex with—as in the song, "Mademoiselle from Armentières, parlez-vous?") "'Sure!' said Pike and gave him a return poke. 'What do you think I went to Paris for?'"[5] Pike, readers knew, had not really "parlez-voo'd" anyone, but most doughboys' stories were almost certainly exaggerated, too. Nevertheless, the stories, articles, books, and movies such as Croy's, helped reinforce France's image as a destination for sex at the same as tourism to Europe was growing and changing.

Most of this upsurge came, not from denizens of rural and small-town America such as Pike and his friends, but from the middle class of America's cities. These urbanites also shared the doughboys' view of French sex and finagling but, unlike the ruralists, were on the front lines of the transition that was now in full swing from a culture based on hard work and production to one based on leisure and consumption. As the cultural historian Warren Susman noted, in this "new world of abundance-leisure-consumer-pleasure-orientation, more attention could be paid to the gratification of personal needs of all kinds."[6] Middle-class tourism to France naturally came to focus on personal pleasure—on "having a good time," or its close relative, "experiencing life."[7]

Yet puritanism was too strong a force in American culture to be shaken that easily. The weakening of the older basis of cultural tourism—the idea that visiting France meant engaging a superior, more sophisticated culture—meant that the old respect for French cultural achievements was replaced by increasingly patronizing allusions to French "gaiety" and joie de vivre. Inevitably, residual puritanism helped transform this into contempt for the natives' apparent lassitude and inefficiency, the symbol of which became the derisory weakness of their currency in the face of the dollar.

— —

As usual, changes in transportation helped lower the class barriers to tourism. In 1921, the United States passed legislation severely limiting immigration from Eastern and Southern Europe. In 1924, it virtually cut it off. This doomed the traditional market for steerage, which before the war had accounted for three-quarters of transatlantic passengers. Steamship lines then upgraded most of steerage to Tourist Third Class, ostentatiously declaring it off-limits to immigrants, who in fact had practically disappeared. "Students—Teachers—Tourists—Artists," said one company's circular, "No others need apply."[8]

At first, one writer said, Tourist Third Class merely meant "steerage prices without the accompanying odor of garlic," but competition quickly forced improved service, in the form of decent dining salons, lounges, and smoking rooms.[9] A Cornell student wrote home from the Cunard liner *Caronia* of "delicious meals" (five a day) and a "most comfortable" berth in a "remarkably large and roomy" stateroom he shared with three others. Cunard boasted that third-class passengers on that New York–Le Havre run included "lawyers, architects, educators, brokers, engineers, librarians and musicians."[10] In 1927, about 40 percent of the 322,000 Americans traveling to Europe in 1927 went "Tourist Third."[11] Companies also converted slower liners to one-class "cabin class" ships, offering the middle classes amenities almost approximating those of first class for considerably less than first-class fares.[12]

Meanwhile, first class lagged behind prewar levels, prompting some observers to comment that the upper classes were staying home in the summer to golf or sail near their country estates because the new wave of middle-class travelers was taking the luster out of the annual trip to Europe.[13] Yet the elite had not stopped going to Europe; they were just less visible. Some would sail to the Mediterranean in January and February, visit Italy and the Riviera, and then head north in their Rolls-Royces, with hired chauffeurs acting like the couriers of old. They would stop in the old spa towns and resorts, helping them regain much of their prewar glamour, and even introduced "King Jazz" to stuffy Biarritz.[14] After arriving in Paris at Easter, they would play prominent roles in the annual social season surrounding the May and June race meetings in Paris and Chantilly, where Vanderbilts, Drexels, Hearsts, and Appletons, as well as a new group of wealthy Californians, mingled self-confidently with each other and the steadily fading European aristocracy.[15]

As in prewar days, after the running of the Paris Grand Prix in June many would then head for the Channel resorts, particularly Dinard and exclusive Deauville, where they entertained in sumptuous villas purchased from the hard-pressed French elite. Indeed, the influx of new American money allowed upper-class social life to flourish there as never before. Half the people summering in Deauville were foreigners, mostly Americans.[16] It was American women who took the lead in reviving the prewar fashion of changing outfits six or seven times a day, making it unthinkable for a woman to go to Deauville for a week without at least two trunkfuls of clothes. (This was probably the equivalent of the prewar fourteen trunks, when one takes into account the flimsiness of 1920s women's fashions.)[17] American men were said to constitute a majority of the "plungers" at its glamorous gambling casinos, as well as those of other resorts.[18]

Wealthy American women also continued to be mainstays of the Paris fashion industry. In the early 1920s, they induced a panic among Paris's couturiers by buying the newly fashionable simple, straight-lined dresses from small dressmakers, but were soon brought back to the rue de la Paix by style changes that demanded the more intricate work at which the great houses excelled.[19] Their dollars fueled the rise of new fashion stars such as Lanvin and Coco Chanel, who pioneered the new girlish look in high fashion, and they were regulars at the seasonal showings of new collections that became popular in the 1920s.[20]

But the middle-class ascendancy could not be denied. In 1925, a French government agency estimated that a mere 2 percent of American visitors to France were "millionaires." Eighteen percent were only wealthy, while the large majority of the rest were middle-class businessmen, their wives, and students.[21] Middle-class preeminence was also reflected in the way the celebrities of middle-class mass culture—the movie and radio stars, sports heroes, and Broadway performers—stole the spotlight from the older upper class. On the luxury liners over, the captain, crew, and passengers fawned over these celebrities the way they used to kowtow to Vanderbilts and Astors.[22] Before the war, the English-language press in Paris was full of the activities of the visiting upper class. Now, they reported that movie stars Douglas Fairbanks and Mary Pickford stayed at the Crillon, while the singer Eddie Cantor preferred the Claridge, where Jack Dempsey had honeymooned. The prewar press had reported on which couturiers and milliners Anna Gould and Consuela Vanderbilt patronized. Now Americans were more interested in where cinema heroines such as Pickford, Gloria Swanson, Lilian Gish, and Dolores del Rio shopped.[23] The upper class tended to make news mainly when they were involved in particularly sensational murders, robberies, or divorces, such as the saga of the flight of the wife of the New York socialite Leonard "Kip" Rheinlander to Paris during his unsuccessful attempt to have their marriage annulled on the grounds that she had not told him that she "had Negro blood in her veins."[24]

Not all the middle class were simply Kathleen Howard's "men from goodness knows where." A reaction against America—disgust with its anti-intellectualism and political and social conservatism—had over-flowed across America from the prewar Bohemia in New York's Green-wich Village. Throughout the country, particularly in the Midwest, young college graduates who aspired to creative lives sought refuge from a civili-zation which placed businessmen on its highest pedestal. In 1920 and 1921, a number of the Francophilic college men who had served as volun-teers in France during the war returned to try to carve out careers as writers or artists. They were followed by another wave of younger men, who were somewhat less serious about art but more committed to rebelling against American puritanism.[25]

The new expatriates gravitated to the run-down area in Montparnasse bordering on the prewar American student quarter that was originally staked out by poor artists such as Amedeo Modigliani and Pablo Picasso. The dramatic rise in the value of the dollar against the franc from 1923 to 1927 allowed them to survive there on sums that would have hardly averted starvation in the States. About the only thing they had in common was a feeling that they were rejecting something about America.[26] Many of the advance guard of 1920 and 1921 had been well-versed in the French language and culture and tried to connect into French cultural currents.[27] This was rarely the case with the expatriates who followed. "Few Ameri-cans in Montparnasse could read French with any ease," a former denizen wrote in 1929, "and still fewer could speak more than enough to order their drinks." Any attempt to master the language or find out what was happening in France was regarded as "snobbish affectation." There was, he said, a "willful blindness to the culture and civilization of France."[28] Another recalled that "too many" associated only with each other, and "knew little more about the French, or France, or for that matter, Paris, than if they had remained at home in Greenwich Village."[29] For most of these visitors (they became expatriates only if they stayed more than two years) Paris's attraction lay in its cheap cost of living and its reputation for having replaced the Village as the capital of American Bohemianism.

The fact that the new expatriates clung together in an English-speaking island helped make them a tourist attraction in their own right. Like the San Francisco Hippies of 1967, exposure in the media back home turned them into a sight, to be peered at by passing busloads of middle-aged American tourists. It also prompted an invasion of their territory by visiting young sycophants. The idealized version of what they were up to was the usual one, harking back to Mürger's *La Vie de Bohème:* living in garrets, writing or painting, drinking wine all night, and consorting with *grisettes* and models. By then, this scenario had been the subject of so many novels, plays, films, operas, short stories, and guidebooks that it had become an integral part of American culture. In the 1920s, when pop-Freudianism popularized the idea that repressing sexuality made you neurotic, the carefree carousers could also be seen as satisfying important psychological needs.

Of course, the tour of Europe had long been a tradition among young college graduates, but the new generation was markedly different from its predecessors. Whereas the prewar ones were mainly well-established WASPs, many of the new cohort were the children or grandchildren of newer immigrants.[30] The Eastern seaboard had set the tone for previous travelers. Now, young people from other regions, particularly the Midwest, came to the fore, many of them ostentatiously fleeing puritanism and provincialism. The young writer Glenway Wescott said he came to Paris to overcome "my origins, my prejudices, my Wisconsin."[31]

Unlike Wescott, the agendas of most of the young tourists centered on pleasure, not creativity. The prospect of drinking in public, and to excess, became particularly attractive after Prohibition came into force on 16 January 1920.[32] The prospect of sex in its time-honored fantasized forms—with artists' models or genial prostitutes—continued to tantalize young men. The fact that most Paris artists no longer worked with nude models in their studios did little to weaken the myth of the willing models; nor did the sordid realities of streetwalking affect benign views of prostitutes. The most famous presumptive sites of these good times, the four Left Bank cafés near the intersection of Boulevards Montparnasse and Raspail—the Dôme, Coupole, Sélect, and La Rotonde—thus became major tourist attractions. The stories of the antics of drunken American writers and artists became legends; alluring artists' models were said to sit flashing come-hither looks at the tables, while prostitutes lingered over glasses of wine or slowly paced the adjacent sidewalks. "The thing to do" after graduating from college, recalled one participant, was "to go to the Café Dôme, study art, and practice sex."[33]

Yet by 1923, any models at the tables were far outnumbered by young American tourists looking for them. Within a few years there was hardly a French patron or a serious American writer or artist to be seen at the Dôme, or at the nearby American-style bars, such as the Closerie des Lilas, that probably served many more shots of whisky and cocktails than glasses of wine. Instead, there were throngs of boisterous, young drunken tourists.[34] "Booze has a very big B and Art a very small a on the Boulevard Montparnasse, today," wrote one observer in 1926.[35]

Still, young Americans continued to scour Montparnasse cafés searching for the elusive celebrities of the "artists colony." "On the Dôme terrace you will sooner or later see most of America's literary and artistic world, for there is probably no place on earth where so many Americans of distinction in the fine arts foregather as at the Café du Dôme," said a popular book about Paris in 1925.[36] Tour buses cruised by in ever-greater numbers, their guides intoning that they were seeing "some of the most famous artists and authors in the world."[37]

On the rare occasions when tourists actually discovered a serious artist or writer and tried to engage them in conversation, they were usually rebuffed. Hemingway shunned his early favorites, La Rotonde (Leon Trotsky's old café) and the Closerie des Lilas, as tourist-infested, and ended up moving to the Right Bank, where he patronized Harry's Bar. When the tourists caught up with him there, he took to holing up in the exclusive bar of the Ritz.[38] The Fitzgeralds, who regarded the tourists as "Neanderthals, with the human values of Pekineses, bivalves, cretins, goats," hid out in a remote part of Riviera for the summer.[39] Other serious writers and artists found less popular hangouts near the place de l'Odéon or moved to Paris suburbs. Some serious artists gravitated to Monet's old village, Giverny, which had been an American artist's colony since the 1890s. Others went further afield, to remote parts of Brittany. About the best-known writer to remain at the Dôme was Harold Stearns, whose *Civilization in the United States* was regarded as the second group of exiles' parting manifesto. He became a horse race tipster for the *Paris Tribune* and spent much of his time drunk on the café's terrace, ruing the annual summer invasion of "the earnest schoolteachers and flip flappers on a vacation that will not improve their minds."[40]

Yet the writers' work continued to encourage the invasion. Hemingway's 1926 novel *The Sun Also Rises,* one of the more important books romanticizing American life in Paris, begins with the hero picking up a prostitute and making the rounds of the Montparnasse cafés and bars. The writer Sinclair Lewis, widely regarded as the most trenchant critic of middle-class Middle America, made well-publicized visits to the Dôme and La Rotonde when he visited Paris.[41] Moreover, enough heavy-drinking putative writers and artists remained at the Big Four—many of them by cadging drinks from the tourists—to help maintain their reputation until the end of the decade. "Who goes to Paris and does not seek out the Dome?" said a *Literary Digest* article in January 1930. "There gather our literary and artistic expatriates—if they are not at the neighboring Coupole, The Select, or La Rotonde."[42]

— —

The *Literary Digest* was about as mainstream middle class as a magazine could get—it was a somewhat more challenging predecessor to the *Reader's Digest*. Yet this article, which made life in "the Mad Quarter of Paris" seem very attractive indeed, demonstrates how acceptable the culture of youthful rebellion had become among the very middle classes who were its main targets. The prewar tourists had also gawked at Bohemians, but sternly rejected their hedonism; now they found the Bohemians' arguments that their behavior reflected French respect for freedom and individualism and a willingness to let people enjoy themselves as they wished more persuasive.[43] What turn-of-the-century tourists had condemned as shocking self-indulgence was now "having fun," something that had become an important goal of middle-class American life. Indeed, "fun" now became an important word in marketing the trip to France. One steamship line called third class "Left Bank class," saying that it appealed to "fun-loving" people.[44]

Alcohol played a central role in this kind of fun. It began flowing as soon as the tourists boarded their ships and cracked open bottles of illegal liquor for their bon voyage parties. Once clear of restrictive American waters, the ships' bars would open and the drinking would begin in earnest. It would continue on the train from Cherbourg to Paris, which was often literally awash in alcohol. (Enterprising French thieves occasionally took advantage of Americans' willingness to drink anything offered them by slipping drugs into their drinks and robbing them.[45]) Upon arriving in Paris, fun-lovers would head for Harry's Bar, a knock-off of an American bar set up by an enterprising Scot in 1923, whose walls were hung with college pennants left by visiting Americans. Wealthier, older drinkers followed Hemingway to the Ritz, where two bars featured a dazzling array of American-style cocktails.[46] Paris waiters estimated that 85 to 90 percent of the Americans in restaurants now drank.[47] Drunken Americans regularly staggered onto the streets from the American-style bars and cafés of Montmartre and the Latin Quarter. As for Montparnasse, in 1927, a shocked Englishman wrote:

> Sustained, unblushing, public drunkenness among people of education can never before have attained such momentum as it has today in Mont-

parnasse among U.S. college youths and young and middle-aged American women. Not only do these drink almost without cessation potent "shots" for effect, but they virtually talk of nothing else but drink and the "drunks" they were on the night before, the "parties" they are going on to next. . . .[48]

It is difficult to tell whether middle-class tourists were more open to encounters with prostitutes than their prewar counterparts. We do know that there were more than enough prostitutes around—in the mid-1920s there were seventy thousand registered in Paris alone. We also know that "guides" and pornography vendors did a brisk trade where Americans congregated: on the rue de Rivoli ("America's street in Paris"), in the place de l'Opéra, and in nearby Harry's Bar.[49] Well-heeled tourists also had no trouble finding people to take them to opulent brothels, legal and discreet, or making arrangements with the women who sat by the bar at Maxim's day and night. What the French had called the "Grand Dukes' Tour" (of high-class brothels) before the war now became known as "*La Tournée des Américains.*"[50] On the Left Bank, cheaper prostitutes paced the sidewalks of Montparnasse and other tourist destinations, some of them charging as little as a quarter.[51]

However, much of the sexual titillation still involved the same kind of voyeurism as before the war. The development of the *charabanc,* a high open bus seating about thirty people, helped popularize tours of Paris "Night Life." They freed nighttime tourists from the clutches of cheating cab-drivers and allowed "respectable" men and women to patronize places that might normally be off limits to them. Many tourists got enough thrills without even emerging from the vehicles. Each evening, the blue busses would leave from near the place de l'Opéra on three-hour "Paris by Night" tours, crossing over the Seine to peruse the "artists" in the Montparnasse cafés, and then doubling back up to Montmartre, to gawk at the nightclubs, streetwalkers, and drunken foreigners.

Montmartre remained "the center of pleasure" for tourists, clinging to its reputation as an "artist's colony" even though high rents had long since driven out practically everyone with a claim to an artistic vocation.[52] The Folies Bergère, which before the war had been known for its dancing, became a standard stop on the way up to the hillside Gomorrah, its show now climaxing with a tableau of bare-breasted women. The Perroquet, also halfway to Montmartre, featured all-American shows of jazz bands and dancers. When tourists arrived in place Pigalle, at the bottom of the hill upon which Montmartre sits, some would head for the now-legendary Moulin Rouge, which featured the aging singer Mistinguette and the hoary cancan. (After a renovation in 1926, it tried a "New York–Montmartre" theme, importing half of its chorus line from New York, but the results were quite disastrous: the American and French dancers did not get along and the tourists wanted to see the famous old routines.) Others would venture into the bars and cabarets where obliging women sat at tables waiting to be asked to dance. The old days when one could order a cup of coffee were gone. Now, ordering a bottle of champagne was the universal price of admission. In some, waiters could be persuaded to slip revelers packets of cocaine along with the champagne. There were also conducted tours that took groups from place to place. Hired dancers, pretending to be denizens, would do the latest sexy dances. First it was the tango, then came the slinky "Apache" dance, said to be favored by the Paris underworld (to add to the frisson they would erupt into phony fights) and finally the Charleston, which swept Paris trendsetters in 1925.[53]

The Charleston craze was an outgrowth of perhaps the only authentically Parisian aspect of this nightlife—a postwar explosion of appreciation for African American music, particularly jazz. Although the origins of jazz in Paris are obscure, its popularity among the French seems connected with a general infatuation with Africa and *negritude*, at least among the "in crowd," which was fed by postwar disillusionment with the rational-industrialized world.[54] In 1921, Paris night spots began importing African American jazz musicians for the French patrons, parenthetically giving some Americans their first real exposure to that music form.[55] In Montmartre, American-style bars soon began converting themselves into jazz clubs. American tourists were happy to visit them, but many preferred that they be run on the same segregated basis as their counterparts in Harlem: the performers, waiters, bartenders, and even the beautiful manageress (such as the African American Florence Jones, who ran "Chez Florence" in Montmartre) could be black, but the clientele should be "lily-white."[56]

The hugely successful African American singer and dancer Josephine Baker, who exploded on the scene along with the Charleston in 1925, seemed to meld jazz and sex seamlessly, and her popularity reverberated up through Montmartre. By the mid-1920s, some of the Montmartre jazz bars had expanded into luxury cabarets with dance floors, decorated in tropical style, where a predominantly American clientele (the rest were mainly English), in evening clothes, would dance the tango and fox-trot to the music of African American bands. (At one place, where African

American singers sang spirituals and other Negro songs, homesick American tourists would insist that they also sing "My Old Kentucky Home" and "Suwanee River.")[57] After a successful one-year run with her own show at the Folies Bergère, Baker herself opened a cabaret in Montmartre.

Nightclubs catering mainly to Americans spread down around the place de l'Opéra and up the Champs-Élysées. The old Ambassadeurs, a cabaret catering to French white-collar workers that had featured Yvette Gilbert, the singer immortalized by Toulouse-Lautrec's posters, was turned into an American-style nightclub, with a floor show imported from the States. "Paris need no longer envy New York," said a Parisian wag. "New York can come to Paris without feeling uprooted." The foreigners "always make sure that the Paris that we show them is the one that they create in their own image."[58]

The more adventurous of the voyeuristic tourists were taken to see transvestites, either in bars or in performances such that of Barbette, a drag queen from Texas who did a high-wire act at the Cirque Medrano.[59] But there is little indication that France's greater tolerance of homosexuality played a role in encouraging American homosexuals to visit France. Glenway Wescott, the refugee from Wisconsin, and other Americans joined a homosexual circle in Villefranche, on the Riviera, that made a shrine of a Roman stela featuring a twelve-year-old boy and a Latin inscription indicating that he danced and "gave pleasure." However, the town was not yet the major destination for gay travelers it would become in the 1950s, when the U.S. Navy's Sixth Fleet was based there.[60] In any event, as we have seen, there were more than enough Americans pursuing other kinds of pleasure to help push cultural tourism far down on the tourist agenda. Not surprisingly, given the new values that were taking root among the middle class, many of them were women.

Seventeen

A FAREWELL TO

"CULTURE VULTURES"

During the 1920s the number of American women visiting France grew exponentially. In 1921, the *Paris Tribune* reported that more American women than men were coming to Paris.[1] By the middle of the decade they may have comprised over 60 percent of the summer tourists to Europe.[2] Yet both the auras of determinedly high-cultural tourism or mindless flirtatiousness that had often accompanied them through France rapidly disappeared.

France's growing reputation as a center of lesbianism played only a small role in this. Yes, the eccentric writer Gertrude Stein became well-known back home, her sexuality quite obvious by her looks and her ubiquitous partner, Alice B. Toklas. The American community in Paris buzzed with tales of the orgiastic parties staged by "the Amazon," Natalie Barney, at her large Left Bank home, where revelers worshipped at a backyard *temple à l'Amitié*. Sylvia Beach, patron of James Joyce and other literary greats (and daughter of the Reverend Beach, who was quoted in an earlier chapter defending the morals of young Americans in Paris) lived openly with her female French lover above her famous Left Bank bookstore, Shakespeare and Co. The prewar underground of lesbian hangouts expanded into an extensive, varied, and quite public nighttime world.[3] Yet there is no evidence that this had any significant effect on American tourism. The large majority of American women spending a week or so in Paris seem to have been unaware of this world or, if they encountered it, to have approached it only as curiosity seekers.

Yet the 1920s still brought distinct changes in what women did when they got to France. Now, most of them were from the new middle class— relatively complacent wives and daughters of newly prosperous businessmen or professionals—as opposed to the older upper-middle class, with their fierce quest for genteel "refinement." For the new middle class, culture was merely one of a number of things that one casually consumed, perhaps by perusing the *Literary Digest* or enrolling in the Book-of-the-Month Club.[4] It did not bring the rewards, in terms of status, that high culture had to the prewar genteel class. High culture therefore played an ever-diminishing role in their visits to Europe, particularly in France, where it received stiff competition from "having fun."

Clara Laughlin, an entrepreneurial Chicagoan, sensed the importance of this change quite early and carved out a successful career running a tourist agency, writing guidebooks, and hosting a radio program, all of which aimed at the new kind of middle-class women traveling to Europe. Her tourist agency, she said, planned European trips for women, not for cultural uplift, but "to give all the romance and charm desired by the woman hungry for foreign travel." She contrasted her tours with the "old-fashioned" ones, with their "tendency . . . to overrate the average avidity for art museums and cathedrals." Her popular guidebooks to Paris and France, known as "Bibles" for American women tourists, went into great detail, not on art and architecture, but on "human interest" stories, mainly soap-opera-esque tales of the lives and loves of the French ruling classes. The treatment of the Louvre in her guide to Paris is almost ridiculously short. "Many of my compatriots [regard] the Louvre and Luxembourg . . . almost resentfully as something that has '*got* to be done,'" she begins. "Now the truth is that few of us have the museum habit at home, even those who live in cities that own very good art collections." She therefore suggests brief forays to see a specific object such as the *Venus de Milo* or *Mona Lisa*. For those who were more serious, she suggested seeing the *Venus*, the *Winged Victory*, and the *Salle des Cariatides* (for the opulent decor), pausing along the way to look at anything else that caught one's eye.[5] The preface to her guide to France derides "the ill-prepared traveller trying to digest 'a dose of sights,' and comprehending nothing at all of the people he's living among." The best way to do the latter, she said, was to chat with the hotel manager, who probably spoke English.[6]

So, although Paris's artists continued to blaze new trails, few tourists took an interest in their work. Since most middle-class tourists were practically bereft of French language skills (in 1927, the French ambassador to Washington calculated that barely one in one hundred thousand Americans spoke or understood French), visits to French theater and bookstores were practically out of the question.[7] Each summer, when the tourist rush arrived, bookstore windows did feature copies of James Joyce's novel *Ulys-*

ses, which was published in Paris by Sylvia Beach, but this had little to do with literature and less to do with French culture. Most tourists purchased it because it had been banned from the United States for "obscenity" and hoped to find something titillating in its dense pages.[8]

Picasso had designed spectacular backdrops for Diaghilev's *Ballets Russes de Monte Carlo* and Igor Stravinsky wrote music for it, but there is no evidence of American tourists at the performances. In the early 1920s, French classical composers such as Maurice Ravel began to take jazz seriously, incorporating its sounds and rhythms into their music, but Americans only heard such music much later, after American composers such as George Gershwin returned from Paris inspired by them. Few middle-class tourists had ever attended an opera back home, so there was little reason to venture into one in Paris. They would merely admire the Opéra building itself and then stroll over to the luxurious shops on the nearby rue de la Paix, now called "the Main Street of American tourism," and walk down to the place Vendôme, in whose mansions some of the top couturiers had set up shop.

For most middle-class women, these elegant shops were mainly there for window-shopping. "Do you suppose there's enough money in all the world to buy the jewels in these windows?" said Clara Laughlin on a "radio tour" of Paris. "While as for the clothes—oh, dear! oh, dear!"[9] Their most pleasurable shopping was done elsewhere. The Galeries Lafayette and Au Printemps, not far from the place de l'Opéra and the American Express office, now became the favorite department stores, especially for ready-made women's clothes. Many liked to stretch clothes-shopping out, said the authors of *Paris Is a Woman's Town,* "to prolong the exquisite agony."[10] They would also scour the many smaller shops in the area, looking for bargains among the European goods that America's elevated tariffs made prohibitive at home.[11] When one tired, one could take a break in the Café de la Paix, on a corner at the place de l'Opéra, which had become an American Mecca during the war. There, watching the passing parade, Americans had a good chance of spotting someone from back home. "Every American in Paris settles [there] at some moment or other during his sojourn," said *Paris Is a Woman's Town.*[12]

In all of this, one senses a marked change from the shopping ventures of the prewar upper-middle class. Before the war, shopping had often been pretty serious business—an anxiety-ridden search for clothes to get through the social seasons back home, marked by second-thoughts, panic over packing, and the occasional moral qualm. Now, shopping abroad was a pleasurable leisure-time activity. It was, said an article in the *Saturday Evening Post*, "a definite part of the holiday mood which makes [Americans] enjoy travelling abroad." It quotes a tourist in France as saying that "over here [shopping] becomes part of the fun. . . . Even if I do have to buy an extra trunk or two and have to pay enormous duty when I get home and then sometimes give away half the things I've bought, I wouldn't miss the pleasure I've had buying them for anything."[13] Another article, calling shopping in Paris "great fun," concluded: "Shop for clothes, shop for thrills, shop for romance, shop for frills, shop for beauty, for education, for the comfort and joy of lovely things, but shop in Paris if you can."[14]

All of this—the abandonment of high culture as central to middle-class women's touring and the justification of shopping as "fun"—coincided with new attitudes making hedonism about as acceptable for middle-class women as for men. Their marriages were now expected to involve mutually-enjoyed sex, and women's expressions of sensuality were regarded as natural and healthy. The new ideal of "companionate marriage" meant that husbands and wives were also expected to be each other's best friends and share many leisure-time activities. A lot of these—such as drinking, dancing, dining, smoking, and popular music—involved sensual pleasures.

So, as women tourists' cultural pursuits declined, their sensual ones rose. "Of course we are all expected to start drinking as soon as the ship pulls out of New York harbor, and keep one happy mood of booze until we face the stern customs official on our return trip," Kathleen Howard wrote in 1922 in the normally stodgy *Saturday Evening Post*. (She also extolled the thrill of betting on the horses at Paris's racetracks!)[15] They now went to sexy places such as the Folies Bergère, Maxim's, and Montmartre clubs with men as their partners in fun, rather than to insulate them from shocking experiences. Howard's article recommends a visit to "the familiar Rat Mort," the famed Montmartre dive, for "entertainment of the usual cosmopolitan city type." It also suggests that at 3 A.M., "after a round of these night attractions," women go to one of the restaurants near Les Halles, the wholesale food market, for onion soup and beer.[16] The diary of Susan Ballow, a sixty-year-old University of Wisconsin professor, is blasé in the extreme about her visit with some younger friends to what she called the "worst places" in Montmartre in 1929. She recorded without comment that at the "Paradise" there were "girls naked except for combination suits in tableaux," but thought that the waiters looked "very stupid" in their angels' costumes. When the group moved on to Les Halles at 2 A.M., she seemed more interested in seeing how hard the workers in the food market worked than in the drinking, dancing, and onion soup that finished off the night.[17]

Nor were men any longer necessary to enjoy these things. A young Virginia woman who took a long tour of Europe with her mother in the summer of 1923 reported home that they "lunched and dined at all the attractive restaurants" near their Champs-Élysées hotel. In Monte Carlo, she gambled alone in the casino. When they stopped again in Paris, they did the rounds of risqué shows without male accompaniment. ("Have seen many shows," she wrote, "some of them amusing and others—well just French, and at first it takes my breath away. However, I'm told the Folies Bergère and the Casino de Paris are shows put on exclusively for Americans.") They also had tea at the elegant Château de Madrid in the Bois de Boulogne, which was noted for its lively dance floor, where respectable women might accept stranger men's invitations to dance.[18]

Not all such ventures ended happily. The Paris English-language papers were full of stories of single women tourists who were conned by scam artists or just simply robbed. A typical story told of the wealthy San Francisco divorcée Dora Kemp, who went alone to a tea dance at one of the smart dancing establishments in July 1923. There she was charmed by a Hungarian "baron" who, according to the police, was well-known there for his "stylish dress and polished manners." She invited him and his male "secretary" back to her hotel suite "for tea" and ended up drinking an American-style "bottoms up" toast with a glass of beer that they had drugged. As she weaved her way to bed, they gave a similar potion to her maid, in the other room, and proceeded to divest the comatose San Franciscan of seven thousand dollars worth of jewelry.[19]

The marked changes in women's roles were reflected very well in the 1929 guidebook, *Paris Is a Woman's Town*, written by two popular woman writers. The first hundred pages are devoted to shopping. These are followed by eighty pages of advice on where to stay, twelve of which discuss the relative merits of the foreign men who might try to pick one up there. Culture is relegated to two short chapters, a total of twenty-two pages, that include a discussion of cooking schools. Except for some information on art classes and mention of an American woman who led art and antique tours, they have little to do with high culture.

The final section—seventy pages under the rubric "If You Go to Paris to Have a Good Time"—is most revealing of the new attitudes. There was practically nowhere in Paris that they would not recommend for women alone. They did suggest that afternoon was the best time for the "rowdier" music halls, but the Folies Bergère was "something nobody but a minister's wife wants to miss in Paris." For dance halls, they recommended hiring *gigolos*—professional dance partners—either on a fee-for-dance basis or for a night out. Of course one had to make sure that these men had references, they said. There were too many stories of American women who had foolishly entrusted their jewelry and other valuables to some shady ones. However, they assured readers that "now gigoloing is a regular profession, recognized by the Paris Prefect of Police. Russians, recruited from the starving refugee groups, are especially high class. The Italians . . . are generally good dancers but often stupid and sometimes dishonest."

They also encouraged women to drink in bars and cafés and gave advice on wine selection. Women alone were advised to try all kinds of restaurants, and of course there was nary a hint of Victorian concern over unseemly feminine appetites for food. They praised the silken slabs of foie gras at one restaurant, the hearty *bœuf à la mode* at another, the stuffed snails at a third, and recommended "two Paris soups that are better than anything on land and sea—onion soup and *bouillabaisse*." The onion soup at Les Halles was especially good at 4 A.M., when one was wearing one's "smartest evening clothes," as a preface to a dawn walk along the Seine back to one's hotel.[20]

The changing nature of tourism was evident as well on the Riviera. Places where well-dressed upper-class *hivernants* had strolled the promenades in the cool light of the winter's day were transformed into flashy beach resorts for younger people spending a frenetic summer week or two of drinking and partying. The transition had been sparked, as it often was, by changes at the top. In 1922, the song writer Cole Porter rented a villa for the summer in Antibes and invited a slew of guests, including the well-off American expatriates, Gerald and Sara Murphy, to visit him. The Murphys liked it so much they came back each summer thereafter, building a villa and encouraging some of the local hotels and restaurants to stay open to cater to their guests, who included such notables as Pablo Picasso, Rudolph Valentino, and F. Scott and Zelda Fitzgerald. The Murphys' all-night drunken parties, immortalized by Scott Fitzgerald in *Tender Is the Night*, helped transform the image of the Riviera into that of a wealthy Montparnasse-by-the-Sea. Meanwhile, in 1923, Coco Chanel, the most celebrated of the new designers, not only decided that summer-holidaying there was chic, but strolled off a yacht "as brown as a cabin boy."[21] Soon, a tan was transformed from the mark of peasants, track-layers, and other poor folk forced to work in the sun, into something beautiful and sensual.

By American standards, the Riviera's minuscule beaches, many of which are not even sandy, were not much of an attraction. Yet by the mid-1920s, the memories of the Riviera Leave Zone and the area's growing reputation as a place where taboos were easily broken made it a standard stop for American tourists on their way from France to Italy. To the dismay of the area's luxury hotel owners, most of these tourists turned out to be decidedly downscale. They walked down Nice's Promenade des Anglais and its newly renamed extension, the Promenade des États-Unis, and peered into the gleaming white rococo Hôtel Negresco. Yet although they marveled at such ornate hotels, they stayed in and ate at modest little places such as those recommended by the new guru of affordable middle-class touring, Frank Schoonmaker, in his *Through Europe on Two Dollars a Day*.[22] The upper class henceforth avoided Nice, winter and summer, while writers and artists fled to more out-of-way places down the coast, such as Villefranche-sur-mer, which Rebecca West described as "the only place worth living in which British and American tourists haven't invaded."[23] Nevertheless, these decidedly déclassé new tourists shared one thing with their upper-class predecessors: to them, the Riviera represented sun and recreation. Cultural tourism was simply not on their agenda.

High culture was not completely marginalized in middle-class tourism. Some, particularly older upper-middle-class women who had the language skills and training to appreciate high culture, clung to the older values. As soon as Gertrude Slaughter, a writer from a prominent Milwaukee family, arrived in Paris, she headed for the Left Bank *bouquinistes* for reading material. She discussed the works of André Gide and Paul Valéry with French intellectuals, and spent almost every one of her eight evenings in Paris at the Opéra, Comédie-Française, Opéra Lyrique, or Théâtre de l'Odéon. But she read and spoke French with ease and had a number of French acquaintances. She was also of an age (fifty-seven) and background that slots her more with the prewar cultured upper-middle class than most other Milwaukeeans in Paris, whom she studiously avoided. Similarly, in 1921, Hannah Solomon of Chicago was fiercely determined to imbibe art, architecture, opera, and ballet in Paris. She even, in her words, "followed Grant Allen's program" in doing the art. But she and her husband were also exceptions: they were a late-middle-aged couple from a German-

Jewish-American subculture that placed a extraordinary value on high culture.[24]

However, American cultural tourism survived mainly because, as in the prewar era, it was shunted down to a lower level. College attendance soared during the 1920s, as postsecondary education became de rigueur for the offspring of the middle class. Liberal arts education, which experienced a particular boom, took a decided turn toward emphasizing the European cultural heritage.[25] Like their higher-class predecessors in the previous century, young middle-class men and women were now able to convince their parents that subsidizing trips to Europe would help them raise their cultural level and complete their education. The study of the Old World's art, architecture, and history now became the presumed objective of many thousands of touring college students. The women among them were thought to be particularly interested in cultural tourism because of the sophisticated aura it bestowed when one returned. A 1928 article that began, "Do you know a college woman under thirty whose book-shelf does not display the familiar red back of *A Guide to the Louvre?*" sounded remarkably like the 1840s view of the impact of the European tour on upper-class American men. It even echoed Ralph Waldo Emerson's view that it immensely benefited one's conversation (which he thought was the best way of exchanging ideas). "The trip abroad cannot be faked," it said. "The travelled manner gives final shine to that conversational front which is, after all, the beginning and the end of culture. . . . It is primarily for cultural reasons, therefore, that Innocence, during the last few years, has gone abroad *en masse.*"[26]

A host of organizations sprang to life to promote this kind of cultural touring in France. The Committee for Educational Travel in France organized summer courses in French provincial universities based on the French Civilization ones put on for soldiers at the end of the war, adding a final two-week "finishing course" in Paris to sweeten the package.[27] The venerable but cash-strapped Sorbonne (French students paid no tuition) climbed onto the bandwagon, putting on four-month courses in French Civilization for foreigners during its fall and spring terms. For six hundred francs (thirty-six dollars in 1924) students received a certificate of attendance, whether or not they had attended any of the lectures. Although there were no exams or assignments, this allowed them to say they had studied at the Sorbonne. For a mere two hundred francs, summer visitors could sign up for lectures entitled a "Special American Fortnight in Paris" and get similar bragging rights, but no certificate. Some Americans organized a music school for Americans in the Palace of Fontainebleau, offering students the chance to give concerts in the magnificent halls of the grand palace itself. They later added a fine arts section, which gave training in art appreciation and production.[28]

Dorothy Marsh, a Smith College graduate, left her job as manager of the American Women's Club in Paris to start a successful agency taking groups of college women around Europe's cultural high spots in motor coaches.[29] Another such agency featured organized discussions with European students at the major stops on its tours.[30] Cook's struck a deal with a professor who headed something called The American Institute of Educational Travel, offering a smorgasbord of tours under its rubric. One company had over a thousand agents drumming up business on college campuses across the country.[31]

By the mid-1920s, agencies such as these were bussing thousands of students through Europe on two-month summer tours of ten to twelve countries, at a cost of between $300 and $785 a person. Sometimes they booked whole ships for their charges. On 10 July 1926, the Cunarder *Andania* arrived in Cherbourg with six hundred students, who were then divided into fourteen groups and sent on separate tours. "Where gilded youth used to go by two and three with parents or tutor," said one observer, "youth today, gilded and ungilded, moves Europe-ward in mass formation, sometimes hundreds in a party, with all the enthusiasm of a college cheering section."[32] By 1928, first-class tours involving over two months ashore were costing over two thousand dollars. Their itineraries differed little from the nineteenth-century upper-class ones, except that they covered as much territory in eight weeks as the upper class would in a year, even after the introduction of the railroad. The tours normally began with a thrilling week in Paris, and then turned into an increasingly exhausting grind that took the women down through Marseille and Nice to Milan, Florence, Rome, and Naples, and then up to Venice, before wending their way through Switzerland, Germany, the Netherlands, and Belgium to end up, exhausted, with a week in London. The cheaper tours, which by then cost about six hundred dollars, involved third-class passage and no-frills travel and accommodation. They usually lasted but four weeks all told, which meant only two frenzied weeks ashore, anchored by five days of sightseeing in each of London and Paris.[33]

The role education and culture played in all of these experiences depended very much on the program, the students, and on one's definition of those things. Given the hedonistic student culture of the time, one can assume that, for many of these students and recent graduates (particularly the male ones), high culture took a backseat to "having a good time." Moreover, even for those interested in high culture, the pace at which most tours flashed by the high-cultural icons rivaled that of the legendary Cook's tours of the past, turning engagements with them into a blur. Trooping through miles of museums and seeing endless new sights often meant by the time they reached Florence, they were suffering from severe cases of sensory overload and developing a kind of immunity to new visual thrills. One observer said that it happened to many diligent young women tourists as early as their third day in Paris: they would spend the first two days in excited sightseeing, remarking upon how they knew of this incident from History 205 and recognized that building from Art 301. Then, she said, "Clara Laughlin's *So You're Going to Paris?* claims them, with its insidious suggestions for delightful places for lunch or tea as an antidote to sightseeing. Culture struggles briefly, then gives way to cuisine." Sightseeing would then be increasingly interspersed with shopping, and the second day's vow to revisit the Louvre would never be fulfilled.[34]

One could also argue that, given the age and social milieu of the young tourists, personal relationships with the others on the tour would normally have become their paramount interest early in the tour. The conversation at the stupendous sights would as often as not be of the "and-he-said-to-me-and-I-said-to-her" variety, rather than what one normally associates with cultural tourism. Nevertheless, since the tours were structured around sightseeing, rather than recreation, and visits to places of high-cultural interest were usually central to them, they did constitute cultural, rather than recreational tourism.

Students were by no means the only customers for conducted tours. Cook's continued to offer a wide variety of tours for adults, joined, belatedly by American Express. Many of these tours were tailored to specific groups, such as Cook's 1927 Catholic "Pittsburgh Pilgrimage to Lourdes" (a destination whose popularity surged in the 1920s) or the Methodist Epworth League's 1924 tour "to see the far-flung lines of Methodist achievement."[35] Others were postconvention trips for organizations, such as the Rotary and Lions Clubs, that began holding international conventions in Europe.[36] These fast-paced tours visited the usual suspects—the Champs-Élysées, Eiffel Tower, Notre Dame, and so on—allowing tourists to say little more than that they had actually seen these wonders. Few of these returning tourists would claim that they had returned more "cultured," yet neither would they say they had taken them to have a good time.

Indeed, what they were indulging in was travel "out of curiosity," which is a form of cultural tourism. If one listened hard, one might even have heard echoes of the old nineteenth-century idea that seeing these famous products of Old World civilization somehow made one a better person.

Although these tours at least kept the flames of cultural tourism flickering in France, the most important carry-over from the earlier era remained the idea that France was a sensual pleasure ground. The most significant aspect of this, though, was that whereas the middle classes of previous years had feared that indulging in these pleasures would change them for the worse, those of the 1920s thought that doing so would improve them.

The rise of the new consumer society had contributed to the erosion of many of the old values upon which fear of pleasure had been based. Now, not only was one defined by such things as what car one drove and how one dressed, one was also judged on how one spent one's leisure time. In this context, the trip to Europe became yet another consumer product. In one sense, this was a sign that the phenomenon that Veblen had seen among the turn-of-the-century rich—that one was defined by what one consumed, rather than what one produced—had now triumphed among the middle class. But Veblen had thought that it was only the quest for social status that motivated this kind of consumption. Many of the middle-class tourists of the 1920s hoped that experiencing the pleasures of a trip to France would bring benefits, not so much in terms of social status, as in terms of personal psychological development.

This was because the reigning kind of consumerism played on middle-class insecurity by tantalizing people with the dream that what they consumed could change their identities—that it would lead to some kind of positive personality change.[37] Inevitably, some tourists hoped that experiencing what France was now most noted for, its joie de vivre, would improve their personalities, and consequently their lives. Visiting Paris should change one's view of life, said Clara Laughlin. "It always hurts me deeply," she said, "when I hear of people who have spent the money and taken the time and effort to go to Paris, and come away without having *felt* it, and loved it, and got that new point of view on life which Paris gives us—if we let it."[38] Paris's beauty, its romance, and above all its gaiety, it was thought, should bring out aspects of oneself that had been repressed. "France had done something to [my husband]," said a 1927 article in the *Ladies' Home Journal.* "Now he wanted to 'step out' all the time. . . . And the thing you'll remember when you get back home is not the tallest church tower in France, but the lonely foreign gentleman, with the war decorations on his chest, who followed you with his eyes, as you walked into the room."[39] "Paris is beyond words. To my mind it is the most alluring, romantic and fascinating city I ever dreamed of and I could stay here forever," wrote the Virginian woman who visited it with her mother. "The way of anything French is perfection to me."[40] True, she had seen some raunchy shows, but this was part of the experience. It helped make her a more sophisticated, worldly person. Clearly, she felt that she was returning from Paris a better person than when she arrived.

It all amounted to a rather striking turnabout. One hundred years earlier, Americans had come to France mainly as cultural tourists, expecting that self-improvement would come from the "taste" and sophistication they acquired by exposing themselves to the treasures of Old World civilization. The current notion was that recreational tourism—having a good time, having fun—would do the same trick.

Those still troubled by lingering puritanism, with its strictures against abandoning work for play, could now fall back on the Cornelius Vanderbilt defense: that the trip was a well-deserved break from the pressures of hard work in an advanced, competitive society. In his 1927 guidebook, Frank Schoonmaker, explaining why more Americans went to France than all other European countries put together, said, "The French live their lives as they drink their wine, slowly, enjoying it all. And to the American, harassed and hurried, France offers the great boon of leisure."[41] Early-nineteenth-century Americans, other than Vanderbilt, had commonly salved their puritan consciences by justifying the trip as an exercise in self-improvement through exposing oneself to France's more advanced culture and civilization. Now, the situation was reversed. The cultural justification was being replaced by a recreational one that emphasized France as a place for escaping the pressures of a more advanced society. So, in the minds of many touring Americans, one of the world's great centers of high culture had been transformed into just another venue for leisure-time activities. It was like a rather quaint, less-developed country where one could let one's hair down and have an enjoyable holiday. This was bound to have an impact on the increasingly sensitive French.

Eighteen

UNHAPPY HOSTS,

UNWELCOME VISITORS

On the evening of 26 July 1926, a mob of Frenchmen shouting anti-American epithets suddenly attacked American tourists boarding large charabancs for "Paris by Night" tours. American tourists in other parts of France were subjected to similar abuse. Yet President Calvin Coolidge responded by placing much of the blame on the tourists themselves. Why? Even within the myopic Coolidge Administration the realization had dawned that the rise of the new kind of middle-class tourism was combining with a marked transformation of French attitudes toward America to seriously threaten American relations with France. There seemed to be implications for the rest of Europe as well. What would later be called "the Ugly American" phenomenon had reared its head.[1]

As we have seen, the French began to sour on Americans visitors in 1919, when the doughboys appeared to have overstayed their welcome. However, some French "modernizers" still admired America's restless energy.[2] They clung to the dream that closer ties between the two cultures would bring a happy fusion of the American practicality and eye for the future and French sophistication and respect for the past. "On the one side," said one, "practical sense, love of enterprise, and the habit of prompt decisions; on the other side, refinement of taste, logical and clear thinking, and the precious art of *nuances*."[3]

These hopes were embodied in one of the most talked-about plays of 1919, *Les Américains chez nous* (The Americans among Us), by the distinguished Academician Eugène Brieux. Staged at the prestigious Théatre de l'Odéon (and produced on Broadway in 1920), it is about a middle-aged AEF officer, "George Smith," who falls in love with France and stays on in a town in Burgundy after the war. He buys part of the ancestral estate of a well-bred but down-at-the-heels country lawyer and sets about developing the land in the efficient, American way: chopping down ancient fruit trees, stringing telegraph wire on unsightly poles, and building ugly sheds for a small factory. He then falls in love with the man's daughter, a middle-aged spinster who has devoted herself to her father and younger brother, a physician. She is upset that her brother wants to marry a domineering American Red Cross nurse and move to Chicago, where she will work with the poor in settlement houses. The climax comes with a labor revolt against the dehumanizing American production methods in Smith's new factory. The son's ability to quell it by getting both sides to understand each other gains the respect of his American fiancée. Newly submissive, she decides to remain in France after her marriage and become a Frenchwoman. Smith and the daughter are then betrothed and all come to recognize that American pragmatism and efficiency must be tempered by French respect for family, tradition, and the emotions. At the end, the nurse symbolizes how she is being transformed into a French woman when, for the first time in her life, she cries.[4]

A benign version of the prewar American millionaire stereotype also persisted in popular French theater, cinema, and literature. The stupendously rich *"oncle d'Amérique"* became the very wealthy businessman—a sensible, generous man who often solved the heroine's problems by marrying her. The pretty young American woman and the handsome, athletic, young American man, whose naiveté lent him a certain charm, were also popular characters. Franco-American marriages were portrayed, as in Brieux, as happy combinations of Old World civilization and New World wealth and good looks.[5]

However, more powerful influences were countering this Americanophilia. The first postwar tourists hinted at what was to come when they made clear their displeasure with France's arcane business methods. "In what pertains to 'business' Paris has much to learn from us," said a 1920 article on touring Paris. "Every small transaction is a vexation. . . . After an interminable meal in a chain restaurant the diner presents his check. In New York he would be out of the door in ten seconds; in Paris, there is a painful adding up . . . and five, ten minutes are wasted."[6] The invasion of American business and production methods that followed seemed to bring with them the twin nightmares of the new American industrial system, "Taylorism" and "Fordism." The first, named after the American engineer Frederick Winslow Taylor, was the system of breaking down complex skilled jobs into simple, repetitive steps demanding no skill. (It was against this system that Smith's Burgundy workers rebelled.) The second was the fiendish twist the automaker Henry Ford seemed to have added to Taylorism by linking it to a relentless moving assembly line. These seemed to epitomize all that was wrong with America. To the political Left, it was in the forefront of enslaving the working class. To conservative defenders of traditional France, it was a culture that subordinated creativity, intelligence, and individual expression to production. It was dominated by men like George Babbit, the fictional shallow, materialistic businessman whose creator, Sinclair Lewis, was much admired in Europe.[7]

These fears were exacerbated by a postwar influx of American businessmen setting up shop in Paris and the spread of their advertising methods.[8] The smug confidence of American business leaders that their system represented the future of the world made things worse, provoking dire warnings against following their lead. A biting book by the popular author Georges Duhamel on his trip to America bore the ironic title *Scènes de la vie future* [Scenes of Life in the Future]. The difference between the two cultures, he said, was epitomized by the contrast between the smiling prostitutes who would welcome him into a whorehouse in France and those he encountered in Manhattan. There he found "ten wenches sitting in front of little doorless stalls," who greeted him "with fixed stares and a strangely preoccupied air." "They looked at me," he wrote, "with faces colored by the same kind of dulled indifference that one notices in the crowds at the cinemas, restaurants, and pleasure palaces." American food also reflected this: "Nothing looks healthy, natural. Even the fruit, even the eggs, seem affected by machines. The most basic foods leave an after-taste of industrial waste." He contrasted the large impersonal American cafeteria with the friendly French bistro. In the former, people sat in long rows of individual chairs with one paddle-shaped arm, looking at the backs of other diners' necks and "chewing melancholically." In the convivial bistro, people were squeezed together, enjoying hearty food.[9]

Prohibition seemed to provide more than ample proof of American barbarism. "Yankee civilization" is a contradiction in terms," wrote one French intellectual. "I call people who drink wine civilized. . . . A people who, on the pretext of morality, deprives itself of wine and, under the cover of this pretext, makes money and commits acts of banditry . . . is nothing but a barbarous people."[10] The propensity of American tourists in France to get drunk provided ample evidence for this. In the 1930 novel *Babel d'amour,* an ambitious young gold digger asks the heroine, "What about Americans? In short, the dollar?" The heroine replies that Americans who are generous with presents exist only in America.

> From the moment an American male steps off the boat in Europe, he wraps his lips around the neck of a bottle and doesn't get up from under the table until he's ready to leave. To them, France is like molasses for a honey bee. . . . They suck up those prohibited drinks. They get drunk on the divine liquor at 8.00 in the evening and don't revive until six the next day.[11]

The Scopes trial—the 1926 prosecution, in Dayton, Tennessee, of a biology teacher for contravening the state's law against teaching Darwinian evolution—provided further proof of America's repression of liberty. "The freedom of the Yankees has long since become a fairy tale," said a well-known writer. "Nowadays they spend all their time making tyrannical laws. . . . It is crime to kiss a girl in public, a crime to spread evolutionary doctrines, a crime to impugn the truth of the Bible." Another writer said, "What is grotesque about the Dayton affair is that the whole of America participated in it. . . . We observe with regret that America has no elite." The Paris press reported a Milwaukee preacher's proposal that the Statue of Liberty be demolished and replaced by a statue of Christ as if it were a popular suggestion.[12]

America's popular culture seemed to exemplify its superficiality. Jazz, the Charleston, "flapper" outfits, American movie heros and heroines— all were attacked as mindless diversions. Americans hoping to prove they were not descended from monkeys were going to have a tough time, said one writer.

> Their jazz bands are certainly monkey orchestras; their attitude toward women, and their materialistic conception of life are not above the level of quadrupeds. Only one thing distinguished them from monkeys before, and they have given it up: it was the ingestion of alcoholic drinks.

The author of an "Anthology of Imbecility" awarded the world championship to the United States. French imbecility was "insignificant" compared to the American kind, he said, "despite the democratic stultification and the Americanization of French life."[13]

American popular culture was also charged with corrupting French youth. One writer, bemoaning the closing of an old cabaret, blamed the disappearance of "la vie Parisienne" on foreign tourism and on America's influence on the young. "A young Parisian of today," he said, "seems nearer to an American of his own age than to a compatriot of the prewar period."[14] The French youth further infuriated the critics by paying little heed to these warnings. They were "absolutely indifferent" to the older generation's attacks on American culture, said the writer Paul Morand, who sympathized with the young.[15] An attempt to have French youths in the Latin Quarter boycott American movies, cigarettes, clothing, and alcoholic drinks fizzled.[16]

The movie industry seemed to raise the spectre of Americanization at its worst.[17] Although movies were invented in France, it was in America that, after about 1912, they were transformed from short one-reelers, shown in raucous nickelodeons, into expensive, multi-reel productions exhibited in large, sedate theaters. After the war, few production companies in the devastated economies of Europe could compete with the Americans when it came to financing these lavish productions and theaters. The French movie industry—without a language barrier to protect it in an age of silent films—virtually collapsed. By the mid-1920s, about 80 percent of the tickets sold in French cinemas were for American movies. American chains now owned over half of France's movie houses.[18]

French politicians and intellectuals accused the American moviemakers of appealing to the lowest common denominator with mindless romances, violence, and gangsters. Some conservatives condemned them for promoting women's equality, something one commentator called the worst thing about American culture. He charged that the short skirts, bobbed hair, and curt exchanges of "let's go for a drive" made a mockery of the old ways of courtship, which involved long love letters and promises to take care of a woman for the rest of her life. Nowadays, he said, audiences laughed hysterically at prewar French films showing traditional courtship, yet nowhere was family life more threatened than in America, where divorce was on the rise.[19]

American movies were also accused of disparaging France and its achievements. Films implying that the Americans had won the war (one showed only American troops marching in the 1919 victory parade down the Champs-Élysées) were said to insult the graves of the French who had actually done so. *Beau Geste* was banned for defaming the French Foreign Legion. The Will Rogers movie, *They Had to See Paris*, was condemned for portraying Paris as full of "*cocottes, grisettes,* and *demi-mondaines.*"[20]

In this context, American tourism was naturally regarded as another agent of Americanization. Men-about-town complained that Americans had displaced them in Paris's night spots. "In the Paris of the dollar," wrote one, "we Parisians must be content with the worst seat near the kitchen . . . or in the passageway to the cloakroom. The proprietor will not even honor us with a look, and the doorman scarcely thanks us for our tip."[21] The magazine *L'Illustration* complained that the "rustic visitors, confident of the omnipotence of a full wallet," had no compunctions about going to the most luxurious restaurants in casual clothes. "To them, the mysteries of our eating and social customs are distressing enigmas. . . . Three hundred Parisians dining create a discreet murmur: fifty foreigners at table unleash an infernal brouhaha."[22] "What business have we natives with our paper francs in Paris, the fairgrounds for Americans," says a character in Paul Morand's *l'Europe galante* (1925). "In France I feel as if I were living in a conquered land."[23]

The apparent American takeover of the heart of fashionable Paris aroused particular resentment. A distinguished French scholar tried to explain French sensibilities on this account to Americans:

> The triangle marked by the [Hotel] Crillon, the Opéra, and the hotel Régina—that is to say, as vast a section as forty blocks along Fifth and Madison Avenues—is entirely American, and practically as forbidden to the French as the Concession Quarter in Shanghai is forbidden to the Chinese, because they can afford there neither a room, nor a meal, nor a jewel there.[24]

Merchants in this area came under fire for the "English spoken" signs in their windows. Some Parisians suggested that, since English was the majority language there, perhaps "*On parle français*" signs would be of more use.[25] An American wrote, "Really, when you see the insolence with which foreigners . . . take possession of Paris, it justifies the worst xenophobia. . . . You are confronted everywhere by signs in the two languages."[26]

There was more than enough xenophobia to go around. "The enemy is the master of the city!" said a contributor to the newspaper *Paris-Midi*. "The barbarians have brought to Paris their vices, their morbid germs, their ferments of destruction! They are degenerate and rotten, physically, intellectually, and morally. They offend our eyes, our ears, our nostrils."[27] "Most of these strangers have little education," said a more restrained paper. "They behave in a displeasing manner and their barbarity gets worse after they have drunk."[28]

American tourists were also blamed for high prices.[29] "The American invasion of France has resulted in only thing for us: increased cost of living," said one columnist. "France is becoming an Anglo-Saxon colony. There are too many of these parasites here, eating our food, drinking our wine, going untaxed, and paying ridiculously little for everything they consume, thanks to the exchange."[30] *Paris-Midi* called American tourists "destructive grasshoppers" and demanded that they be made to pay for their purchases in gold, rather than paper francs. In 1918, it said, the invaders "were in khaki, now they have returned in tourist garb. They have traded gun for fork, but still continue to live on this country."[31] The Communists charged that department stores excluded French shoppers when they raised their prices 30 to 60 percent, yet foreigners continued to grab everything in sight.[32] A more genteel writer complained that porters in railway stations turned their backs on French-speakers in favor of Americans.[33] There were persistent demands for a tax on tourists, which mainly meant American ones.[34]

White American racism added another dimension to this reaction against American tourism. In French eyes, racism was yet another baleful aspect of American culture that tourists were importing to France. "America is a country in which it is a crime to drink, make love, or be a Negro," said the poet and theatrical producer Rodolphe Darzens.[35]

The contrast between French and white American treatment of African American doughboys as well as the French government's denunciations of American racism in 1919 helped make France a magnet for African Americans in the 1920s. Black publications such as the National Association for the Advancement of Colored People's (NAACP's) magazine, *The Crisis,* contrasted the equal treatment African Americans received in France with their ill-treatment back home.[36] The *Chicago Defender* regularly reported on the warm welcome the French gave to black intellectuals, entertainers, and athletes. In August 1923, it ran a large front-page photo of French troops in the Ruhr, with a white soldier flanked by two tall black ones. The caption read: "This friendly intermingling is characteristic of the French, who have formed a lasting hatred of American whites because of their color prejudice."[37]

African American writers and artists such as Countee Cullen, Langston Hughes, Claude McKay, Paul Robeson, and other leaders of the 1920s "Harlem Renaissance" felt they had found a refuge from racism in France.[38] Well-off African Americans, with hardly a first-class hotel in the United States that would welcome them, discovered the relatively discrimination-free pleasures of touring France. They would sometimes stop at the Left Bank studio of black sculptor Augusta Savage to have busts of themselves made. Well-off black honeymooners began choosing Paris over Niagara Falls, where they had to cross over to the Canadian side for hotels that would accommodate them.[39] By the summer of 1926, there were enough African Americans in Paris to support sales of the *Defender* there. "The whites have begun to notice the keen line of distinction the French draw between them and dark-skinned Americans," the *Defender* reported that August. "A black face is always preferable in resorts, cafés, hotels and other public places catering to foreign trade."[40]

The black tourists appreciated such things as eating in places where the seats next to them did not remain vacant all through their meals.[41] Yet, while they enjoyed their easy acceptance by the French, they could not ignore the hostility they sparked among white American tourists, many of whom refused to patronize the restaurants, cafés, and other public places that admitted blacks on an equal basis. Incidents such as that which befell Walter White, a light-skinned African American who became head of the NAACP, were common. When he sat down to dinner at a Paris restaurant with a dark-skinned friend, a white American at another table became apoplectic. He exclaimed, "The idea of a white man lowering himself to eat with a nigger!" and demanded that the black man be ejected, an order that the proprietor refused.[42] There were frequent scuffles between black Americans and white Americans trying to eject them from Montmartre bars.[43] American men caused nasty incidents almost nightly at the Moulin Rouge, where it was common for French women to dance with dark-skinned men.[44]

In 1923, a major dance hall, the Bal Tabarin, caved in to the American pressure and advertised that whites only would be admitted. A Paris tourist agency announced that it would segregate the colors on tours, confining blacks to separate busses and train compartments. Another acceded to the demands of American tourists and refused to take four black French officer cadets on one of its Paris bus tours. A black French doctor who was a war veteran was refused service in a Boulevard Montparnasse bar that, in deference to its American patrons, adopted a policy of not serving blacks. In another widely reported incident, Americans about to set out on a battlefields tour in a charabanc objected to the presence of a black French surgeon, who had served in the army for four and a half years during the war. Their protests were ignored, and the vehicle set off. A few miles outside of Paris, however, they again demanded his removal. A heated argument ensued, in which the Americans, insisting they would not ride with a "nigger," threw him off the bus and forced the driver to continue on.[45]

That black Frenchmen were on the receiving end of this treatment, and that some French people kowtowed to the dollar and went along with it, outraged much of the French press. Racism was an American import, they said, that should be resisted.[46] Protests were made in the National Assembly. The French foreign office condemned tourists who, "forgetting that they should respect our laws and customs, have on several occasions violently demonstrated their disapproval of colored people from the French colonies sitting beside them in public places and, using abusive language, have demanded their ejection." If such incidents were repeated, it said, "sanctions will be taken."[47] Premier Poincaré issued a declaration that it was "inadmissable that our compatriots from Africa, who showed their devotion to their adopted land during the war, should be insulted and ridiculed in their own land."[48]

Hard on the heels of this, though, a group of white Americans drinking in a Montmartre bar demanded that two black men who walked in be ejected. When the blacks protested, the Americans, with the help of some waiters, pounced on them and threw them out on the sidewalk, breaking one of their eyeglasses. As it turned out, they had fallen upon Kojo Tovalou Houenon, a Dahomean "prince." He was not only the most prominent leader of the Pan-African movement in Paris, he was also an advocate of the view that France was not a racist country. Indeed, in February 1919 he had told delegates to the Pan-African Congress in Paris that they should look upon that city as the promised land for "the race of Cham," that "the great black family make Paris its spiritual home." Paris, he said, would become the Babel of the black race, because "not only is there no race prejudice in France, it is also fighting for its disappearance [in the rest of the world.]"[49]

The French press erupted in outrage against the Americans. *Le Temps* pointed out that Kojo Tovalou was the respected author of a brilliant linguistic analysis of French and a philosophical inquiry into nature of liberty. Another paper said that white Americans, who themselves were not "thinkers or refined intellectuals," called Negroes inferior beings who could not understand the complexities of civilized life. Yet they had caused the barman to throw out "a veritable colored Pascal."[50] President Poincaré issued another statement expressing his shock and ordered the bar closed. The prefecture of police announced that the race issue was now one of the government's foremost preoccupations and warned that any other establishment that tried to bar Negroes would also be closed.[51] Poincaré followed this up by banning D. W. Griffith's epic movie *Birth of a Nation*, which demonized blacks as credulous rapists and glorified the Ku Klux Klan. The French government had only recently approved a severely censored version of the controversial 1915 film, and it had been shown for only two days.[52]

The government action reinforced France's favorable image among African Americans. The *Chicago Defender* ran a cartoon of an axe, labeled "Premier Poincaré's Ultimatum," about to chop off the head of a serpent, "Color Prejudice," slithering onto France's shores from America. "'KEEP COLOR LINE AT HOME' SAYS FRANCE," read one of its headlines. "WE TALK, FRANCE ACTS," was the headline of an article saying France did not "foster or tolerate institutions or practices that play up or perpetuate the pompous pride of one race at the expense of another."[53] One of its reports from Paris said the controversy over *Birth of a Nation* had "increased the hatred for" white Americans. "The native shrugs his shoulders and says, 'Let them stay at home; we have no color line over here. We fight side by side, we eat side by side, we die side by side.'"[54]

The American press, even in the South, almost unanimously condemned the offensive tourists, but this went unreported in the French press. It had larger fish to fry.[55] A *Defender* report from Paris hinted at this when it said the French press supported the blacks against the Americans because "it is now a known fact that American white tourists are not wanted over here. There is an outward attitude against them by all class of Frenchmen."[56] Indeed, the condemnations of American racial practices, like the opposition to Americanization, were part of a larger, nastier turn against America that was provoked by a deepening financial crisis for which the United States was held responsible.

Disillusionment with Woodrow Wilson and the American refusal to sign the Treaty of Versailles had been followed by a growing feeling that the United States did not back French demands that Germany be forced to pay the enormous reparations for the costs of the war that the treaty assessed. Yet not only had the United States refused France's pleas for loans to help its postwar reconstruction, it insisted that France pay every nickel of the wartime debt it had run up buying food and equipment from America—with interest. With Germany unable to maintain reparations payments, France found it practically impossible to repay these loans. "They fought the war *with* us; they made the peace *against* us," became a common sentiment in France.[57]

Differing views of the Great War exacerbated the problem. Americans believed that their intervention had pulled the Allies's chestnuts from the fire. The French looked upon America's contribution as mainly economic. Even after the Americans declared war, it was now said, they had dithered, subjecting their army to over a year of training before finally committing it to battle just as the war was ending. American losses (49,000 dead) paled in comparison to the 1,385,000 lost by France, which began the war with less than half the United States's population.[58]

Soon after the war ended, French veterans' organizations began pleading with their American counterparts to forgive the loans, and the French government entered into what would turn out to be years of futile negotiations toward that end.[59] By the summer of 1923, when French indignation over American racism peaked, France's wartime allies were also being labeled "Shylocks." At a soccer match in the 1924 Olympics, held in Paris that year, the French crowd jeered the American flag and beat up some American fans when the U.S. team scored an upset victory over the French side.[60]

The franc continued to fall, inflation soared, and the French economy stagnated. Yet Americans who invoked Lafayette and proposed that France be let off the hook could not budge their government. A new, revisionist view of the Great War blamed its outbreak mainly on France and Russia. France's record of "persistent aggression and militarism" made it a doubtful candidate to lead Europe into peace, said one of its leading proponents.[61] Worse, the American government insisted that the principle that debts must be repaid was the bedrock of civilization.[62] In Paris, drunken American tourists would provoke bar-room brawls by asking the French, "Why don't you pay your debts?"[63]

The French grew increasingly bitter. Veterans said the loans had paid for the blood they spilled during the fifteen months between the American declaration of war and their arrival on the battlefield.[64] A veterans' newspaper in Nice said, "It was we who held the line until you came. . . . America gave her dollars. Blood and gold fought together, or so we thought. But apparently we were wrong. Now Uncle Sam presents his bill."[65] Rumors spread that, with France unable to pay the debt, the United States was going to demand its West Indian colonies in recompense.[66]

In May 1926, the French government agreed to a plan to stretch out the debt payments over sixty-five years, but doubts arose as to whether the National Assembly would risk approving it. As a result, the franc fell into a tailspin. In 1919, the French had grumbled about it being worth only nineteen cents; by June 1926, it was four cents, and heading for its mid-July low of two cents.[67] The French press and politicians blamed the crisis on the American insistence on debt repayment. "Our allies of 1918 have declared financial war on us," said a provincial newspaper, as French people in the provinces as well as Paris began harassing passing American tourists.[68]

On July 11, twenty thousand French veterans staged a silent march through Paris to protest the debt agreement. Led by a platoon of legless and armless men in wheelchairs and tricycles, followed by another of blinded men, and then one of horribly scarred men with no faces, they laid a huge wreath stuck with little American flags at the monument to George Washington in place des États-Unis. An accompanying plaque asked the American people to "reconsider" the proposed settlement, which would "lead to the ruin of France and the loss of her independence." The five thousand veterans who paraded in Nice were not so polite. American tourists there were greeted by handbills and posters violently denouncing the accords, saying that the French had become slaves to American financial interests.[69] Although the Paris march was widely reported in the American press, the veterans were generally dismissed as dupes of demagogic French politicians. The consensus in the United States remained that the debts must be paid.[70]

The massive influx of American tourists in the summer of 1926 made for an explosive mixture. By July, an estimated two hundred thousand of them were in France, most of them from the fun-loving middle class.[71] Yet the edge was taken off their fun by the old conviction, stoked by the returning doughboys, that the French cheated them at every turn. Now they were concerned that they were not receiving the full benefits of the devaluation of the franc. The persistent belief that there were different prices for Americans and natives ("I want the Frenchman's price, not the American one," was a common refrain) led to numerous arguments with exasperated shopkeepers.[72] In a September 1926 interview in Paris, the novelist Theodore Dreiser, back in Paris for the first time since 1912, berated the French for overcharging Americans. "The wrong kind of restaurant" charged him four dollars for two cups of chocolate, he said, because he was dressed like an American (in flannels and a soft-collared shirt). America and France were following opposite trajectories, he concluded. "You have passed from idealism to materialism. We are passing from materialism to idealism."[73] The prominent New York anticorruption lawyer, Samuel Untermeyer, complained of "the prodigal waste and expenditure of American tourists" and the "delight" people in certain countries took in "robbing Americans."[74]

Yet, to the French, these Americans seemed like incredible misers. "Most of these visitors are full of sordid avarice," said a Paris newspaper. "In most restaurants they eat so many hors d'ouevres that they cannot hold anything afterward."[75] Americans vigorously protested cab fares, leading to fistfights with drivers who were insulted by being tipped a few *sous*— less than a penny. One athlete gained notoriety by knocking down a driver who charged him the official three-franc supplement for taking him past the city limits.[76] A delegation of Americans even lodged a protest with their ambassador against Paris retail stores for closing from noon to 2 P.M., presumably as some kind of anti-American plot.[77]

To make matters even worse, as francs plummeted in value, some tourists took to plastering them on the walls of railway compartments and onto their luggage, like hotel and steamship labels, or throwing them on the streets and chuckling as French passers-by scurried after them. The naive American habit of asking foreign waiters and salespeople, "How much is that in real money?" became especially offensive.[78] Not surprisingly, then, in mid-July, individuals and small groups of Frenchmen began attacking American tourists in the Left Bank and Montmartre. On at least one occasion a policeman who came to the tourists' aid was forced to fire shots in the air. Parisians routinely swore at the uncomprehending Americans in sightseeing busses, and crowds began to jeer and deliberately impede the passage of the "Paris by Night" ones.[79]

The latter vehicles now became a symbol of all that irked the French. On the evening of 23 July 1926, several hundred well-dressed Frenchmen gathered around five such busses near the Boulevard des Italiens as they prepared to leave to view Paris's nighttime jollity. Shouting "Vive la France!" they attacked three of the busses, breaking their windows and forcing them to leave empty. They then pushed their way onto the two other busses, swinging canes at the terrified tourists and sending them fleeing. By the time the police arrived, the crowd had swelled to over two thousand, roaming the area, insulting and occasionally attacking Americans.[80]

The Americans instinctively blamed the Communists. However, the Communist paper, *L'Humanité*, roundly condemned the outburst as "an explosion of chauvinist stupidity." It too was against paying the debt, it said, "but that doesn't mean manhandling an American drunk who, just like his bourgeois French counterpart, wants to make merry in Montmartre. IF OUR COMRADES SEE ANY SUCH INCIDENTS THEY SHOULD SET THEMSELVES TO STOPPING THEM."[81] Followers of the Far Right seemed likelier culprits, and one of its main organs, *Action Française,* was evasive about responsibility. It blamed the tourists for "throwing bundles of money around," and raised the spectre of more attacks if they did not stop parading around Paris "as if the French had no rights in their own home" and acting "as if Paris did not exist except as a spectacle for foreigners."[82]

Irate U.S. senators called on tourists to boycott France; Americans staying on the French side of Lake Geneva packed up and moved to the Swiss side after being met with shouts of "Shylocks" and "usurers" on the streets. Many of those in the resorts of southwestern France crossed the border into Spain.[83] Tourists arriving on the liners at Cherbourg grew apprehensive about debarking. The American embassy in Paris was bombarded by cables asking if it were safe for Americans to come to France.[84]

Apprised of these events, the White House feared that the crisis would torpedo the shaky debt agreement. President Coolidge, a taciturn man who normally made few pronouncements, called a press conference to assure the French that he did not think the anti-American demonstrators represented French opinion. *Exactly* what he said, though, is not clear. In those days reporters were forbidden to quote presidents directly. In addition, up to this point he had built a successful political career by avoiding straight talking, and on this occasion he did not disappoint. He seems to have said that, after being briefed on the Paris situation, he could not hold the tourists themselves blameless. He thought there were two kinds of America tourists abroad. First, there were the "bumptuous" ones [*sic*] who, once they learned that foreigners were entitled to consideration and respect, would improve their behavior. The second group were a greater problem: they constantly criticized the way things were done in Europe and provoked animosities and demonstrations such as those that had just occurred. If they did not like what they found abroad, he said, they should return home.[85]

The French press reported Coolidge's message with little comment. However, the French government ordered the police to prevent future demonstrations. The police, assuring tourists that they would be protected, stationed patrolmen every fifty yards along the boulevards. The level of "boulevard-baiting" consequently declined, and there were no further mob-scenes, but ugly incidents, particularly ones involving tour busses, continued, on-and-off, for the rest of the summer.[86] "A bunch of American tourists were hissed and stoned yesterday in France," Will Rogers said in early August, "but not until they had finished buying."[87] A few days before, a Russian immigrant protesting the debt accords took a sledgehammer to the stone monument in the place des États-Unis commemorating the American volunteers who served in the French forces during the war. It depicted the poet Alan Seeger, who was killed fighting in the French army, reaching out to aid a *poilu*. Whether by design or not, by chopping off Seeger's arm and leg, the Russian managed to change it to one of a maimed American reaching out for help from the *poilu*.[88] The *Chicago Defender* reported that one of the ways the French were demonstrating their "dislike" of white American tourists was that "French girls are going out of their way to do those things which will most irritate [them]. French girls everywhere are lionizing dark skinned Americans and they can be seen any day clinging to the arms of their dark escorts, visiting the cafés and restaurants where white Americans eat."[89]

At the end of the summer, many tourists were still swearing they would never return to France.[90] However, the end of the peak tourist season and the steady recovery of the franc against the dollar—it was up to four francs by December—took some of the edge off the anti-Americanism. An informal modus vivendi on the debt, whereby the French began making payments on it without actually ratifying the agreement to do so, also seemed to improve matters.[91] Nevertheless, both French resentments and invidious American stereotypes of the French continued to fester. In April 1927, Samuel Untermeyer returned from Paris and complained: "Envy, hatred, and contempt for American tourists is boldly paraded, [yet] the more they insult us the faster we continue to come and the more of our money we pour into their coffers." Servants in the hotels and restaurants, and even in private homes in France, he said, jeered at and sometimes refused to wait upon Americans.[92] An excellent opportunity for conflict to resurface seemed due just five months later, when the very doughboys who had contributed so much to the negative views on both sides were to return, as the American Legion, to hold their convention in Paris.

To the Legion leadership, the idea of holding their annual convention in Paris, where it had been founded, on the tenth anniversary of American intervention into the war, had originally made good sense. It could be billed as a pilgrimage, where veterans could visit the hallowed grounds where comrades had died. This would remind people of its members' sacrifices at a time when disillusionment with the war was spreading and reinforce the organization's claims to represent true "Americanism" in the current struggle against Bolshevism and other subversive dangers. At the same time, since the annual conventions had become fun-loving affairs, it would also satisfy the veterans' touristic impulse to see Paris—a place that had been off-limits to most of them during the war.

The events of the summer of 1926 cast doubts on the wisdom of having over twenty thousand of them, plus many of their wives, descend on Paris.[93] However, in May 1927, the prospects brightened when Charles Lindbergh guided his single-engine plane through the clouds and landed at Le Bourget airport, just outside of Paris, completing the first solo flight across the Atlantic. Not only did the feat cause a sensation in America, it also caught the imagination of many thousands of Frenchmen. About one hundred thousand of them rushed to the airport to give him a tumultuous hero's welcome. The tall, shy, good-looking Midwesterner combined the image of the American as a handsome, courageous risk-taker with his country's reputation for technological prowess. Even the Communists could not resist. *L'Humanité* saluted him as "A MAN, one of the best calibre," and pointed out that the "modest young guy who managed the marvellous feat" was no "flying madman" with "miraculous luck." Rather, his success was due the technical quality of his plane and equipment as well as his courage.[94] Still, in the longer run, Lindbergh's feat did little to lessen French resentment over the supposed American betrayals of the postwar decade.[95] Nor did it do much to change the darkening French view of American tourists.

The situation took a further ominous turn in late August 1927, less than four weeks before the convention was to begin, when the state of Massachusetts sent the two Italian-American anarchists Nicola Sacco and Bartolomeo Vanzetti to the electric chair. Their death sentences for the murder of an armored car guard in 1921 had become a symbol of American xenophobia and antiradical hysteria. The campaign to save them had drawn a rising chorus of protest from leftists around the world. Now, when news arrived in France that the sentence had actually been carried out, violent riots broke out, as an estimated fifty thousand people marched on the U.S. embassy and the offices of American newspapers in Paris.

Once again, American tourists became targets. Attacks were mounted on the tourist attractions of what *L'Humanité* called "the Montmartre of the Americans, symbol of the dollar at play." Barricades were erected, windows were broken, cars overturned, and tourist bars and nightclubs were ransacked. The Moulin Rouge, a prime symbol of American tourism, was a particular target. Policemen firing shots in the air managed to prevent the mob from wrecking its main *salle,* but failed to save the rest of it from serious damage. Two-hundred-and-eleven demonstrators were arrested, eighteen of whom were quickly sentenced to several months in prison.[96] The weeks that followed saw attacks on Americans in the Riviera. A bomb was thrown at the American consulate in Nice and another one exploded in a dance hall frequented by Americans, killing one client and injuring six others.[97]

As the Legion's arrival date neared, the Left, with considerable justification, accused it of having encouraged the executions. The Communists said the Legionnaires represented "rationalization, the Ku Klux Klan, Fordism, the electric chair, a dry regime, getting plastered, and *'Mademoiselle combien?'*"[98] But mainstream French politicians hoped to use the visit to make some political hay. Hard-liners saw it as an opportunity to dust off their old uniforms and rekindle wartime emotions to gain support for their program of keeping Germany prostrate while rearming France. Others hoped it would soothe the hard feelings of the previous year's debt crisis.[99] When the vanguard of 350 leaders arrived in Cherbourg in mid-August, the progovernment paper *Le Matin* reported that they shouted "Vive la France" when they stepped ashore. The goal of this "pilgrimage," it said, was to revisit the battlefields and the cemeteries of the front.[100]

Yet in fact the convention took place almost entirely in Paris, and the government therefore took careful control of events in that potentially explosive place. It ordered that no Legionnaires were to be jailed, but also told nightclubs to close at midnight. It brought out the revered old war hero Marshal Foch for a solemn ceremony in memory of the two nations' war dead, but held it at a small cemetery in Suresnes, outside of Paris, that was practically inaccessible to demonstrators. It declared the day of the Legionnaires' five-hour parade down the Champs-Élysées a national holiday, but stationed ten thousand soldiers with fixed bayonets along its route to protect them. It also interspersed French veterans carrying French flags among the marchers, making it difficult for spectators to taunt or attack them. A group of construction workers who jeered the Americans from a work site were quickly arrested. Some days later, three Communists caught putting up anti-Legion posters were sentenced to two months in prison. Another, whose steel belt was deemed to be a prohibited weapon, was given three months.[101]

Thanks in part to this heavy government hand, the convention week passed without major incident. Yet the pilgrimage aspect remained for the most part obscure, despite some visits to the battlefields, and the dedication of a large monument to the American dead at Saint-Mihiel, site of one of their major battles.[102] The Socialist paper, *L'Œuvre,* was pretty much on target when, before the convention began, it said expectations of what the "pious pilgrimage" would bring were symbolized by a souvenir ashtray with a picture of a drunken American soldier, balancing a champagne glass in one hand, kissing a naked Frenchwoman. On one side it said "Allez-up," on the other, "American Legion, 1927."[103]

In fact, for most participants, the criterion of the convention's success was that of the middle-class recreational tourist: whether a good time was had by all. How this was defined was already apparent on the special trains carrying the Legionnaires from Cherbourg to Paris. The French had provided free mineral water for the veterans. The vets used it as "mix" for cognac in the nonstop parties that ensued. The American newspapers in Paris, profiting from a bonanza in extra sales, told of how much fun the veterans were having in Paris, and how amusing the Parisians found them. Although they also told of how much the wives enjoyed visiting Montmartre, the Vermont delegation's theme song became the convention favorite:

> Oh, we've got no wives with us,
> We've got no wives with us,
> There may be wives with some other guys,
> But we've got no wives with us.[104]

Even the Legion's leadership ended up downplaying the pilgrimage aspect of the convention. They said the main event, the five-hour parade, had "won a victory of personality over the hearts of the French nation."[105] In it, middle-aged men in outlandish uniforms, such as the Floridians' band, clad from head to toe in bright orange (to resemble the state's fruit) paraded down the streets, playing lively, light-hearted music, led by baton-twirling drum majors. Although the official version had it that the Parisians gave the parade an enthusiastic reception, unofficial reports said they were at best unresponsive, at worst, sullen.[106] Some said the French onlookers found the absence of any sense of pilgrimage especially offensive. They thought the gay, carnival mood mocked their view of the war as a sacred sacrifice—that it was "America's big laugh at Europe." The only cheers came from Americans.[107]

As might have been predicted, what the Legionnaires' thought of as one of the endearing aspects of their behavior—drunken pranks in public—made them a particular target for their French critics. *L'Humanité* said that every ten meters on the main streets of Paris there were two or three Legionnaires, fat, red-faced, and "drunk as skunks," propositioning women. "From Montparnasse to Montmartre," it said, "they were staggering around, bellowing, drinking and vomiting."[108] The poet William Carlos Williams, who was visiting Paris at the time, recalled that "the feeling against the Americans . . . was running high. We were in a fair way to being hated. I could feel it everywhere."[109]

When the convention ended, some disgruntled Frenchmen added an unhappy coda to the proceedings by trying to derail a special train carrying a delegation of 150 Legion leaders as it sped toward Nice. The Legionnaires then proceeded to dissipate any sympathy this might have gained them by getting drunk at the welcoming dinner at the Nice Casino. They paraded around, chanting, singing, and accosting women, as the French dignitaries struggled through their welcoming addresses.[110]

Although it was the rowdy Legionnaires who caught the eye of the French, the changed nature of American tourism was really symbolized by the considerable number of Legionnaires and their wives who could be seen each day of the convention lining up to buy American-style ham sandwiches, doughnuts, and coffee at the Legion "hospitality tent."[111] The interesting thing is that, despite their apparent misgivings about French food and suspicion of French merchants, there was general agreement among these very middling people from Middle America that they were having a very good time. Indeed, in Legion lore, the convention would be a legend in this regard for many years to come.

And after all, was that not what France was supposed to be all about? It was largely because of the persistence of this idea—that one could have a good time there—that, despite its reputation for anti-Americanism, France remained by far and away the most popular European destination for Americans. Each summer from 1926 to 1929, well over a quarter of a million Americans came to Paris. In the last years of the decade, fully 90 percent of all American tourists to Europe visited France. In April 1929, on the eve of what would be the last great summer touring season for decades, the writer T. R. Ybarra said, "No matter where an American visitor does not go on his European tour, he almost certainly goes to Paris. . . . It's the center of the American tourist's universe."[112]

Nineteen

EPILOGUE

Three years after the Legion convention, there began a pilgrimage that did touch some hearts. In March 1929, Congress authorized the government to pay for a "Pilgrimage of Gold Star Mothers and Widows" to visit the graves of their sons and husbands in France. In May 1930, the first of the six thousand women who accepted the invitation began to arrive. A group of 136 spent three nights in Paris, where they laid a wreath at the grave of the Unknown Soldier, met French women who had also lost sons and husbands, and took some sightseeing tours, including a sanitized, one-and-a-half-hour "Paris by Night" one. They then spent seven days visiting the battlefields, seeking out the graves where their children and husbands were buried, before returning for two more days in Paris and then home.[1]

Aside from the greater degree of decorum, another thing distinguished the Gold Star Mothers from the Legionnaires: a small group of African American mothers and wives were invited to participate, albeit on the same segregated basis as their sons and husbands had fought and died. They traveled as one group, were billeted separately on the ship over, and were shunted into separate trains and hotels once they arrived in France.[2]

The French tourist industry was more than happy to welcome the Gold Star mothers because the onset of the Great Depression dealt a body blow to American tourism to France. Ironically, this struck just as the government was finally facing how important foreign tourism had become to the economy. Its enthusiasm for encouraging American visits to the battlefields had petered out rather quickly after the 1920 fiasco. The shipping companies had lobbied it to encourage American tourism in the early 1920s, when they panicked over the loss of steerage passengers, but the response (a minor government office to promote foreign tourism was set up) was hardly overwhelming.[3] When Americans expressed concerns over price-gouging, the government blamed German propaganda.[4] For much of the decade, Americans cited statistics on the importance of American tourist spending to warn that French anti-Americanism would kill the goose that laid the golden egg. However, the belated French steps to protect American tourists and welcome the Legion had more to do with politics than economics. Only in the late 1920s did the government begin to recognize that tourism had changed, in the words of one official report, from "the egotistical art of traveling" to a "national industry of hosting: [that it had] moved completely from the domain of individual or collective pleasure to that of the general economy."[5]

The French set about trying to deal with tourists' complaints about overcharging by forcing hotels to publish their rates. But this was too little, and too late to counter the economic changes that were hammering tourism.[6] The steady rise in the franc after 1927 helped persuade many of the Left Bank habitués who had themselves become tourist attractions that the time had come to return home. The 1929 stock market crash and the Depression that followed finished off the process by cutting off checks from home. By 1930, the Left Bank "scene" had moved back to Greenwich Village, or Chicago, or Connecticut.[7] Few tourists now came to the Montparnasse cafés hoping to catch glimpses of the great and the near-great. Indeed, there were now relatively few Americans tourists anywhere in Europe.

Ironically, by cutting the ground from under middle-class tourism to Europe, the Great Depression helped inaugurate another Golden Age of Tourism. With the hoi polloi out of the way, upper-class tourism again took center stage. Magnificent ocean liners such as the *Normandie,* probably the most beautiful liner ever built, slid down the ways. Shipping lines again concentrated on satisfying the luxurious tastes of the upper class. The rich and the celebrated could swoop into the Ritz, Crillon, Meurice, and George V hotels in Paris and join in the "seasons" at Deauville, Trouville, and Cannes without having to make their way through crowds of Rotarians from Newark cluttering up the sidewalks.

This high-class image of European travel was revived for a while after World War II, when the fast luxury liners were converted back from troopship duty and new ones joined them on the transatlantic run. But the writing was on the wall, not so much in the scheduled airplanes that were now flying in greater numbers across the Atlantic, as in the increasing tendency of both air and shipping lines to again cater to the middle class. The glamorous couples in jewels and formal dress sipping champagne and dancing their way across the Atlantic on the *Normandie* and its postwar replacement, the *France,* turned out to be an aberration—the stuff of little more than Woody Allen–esque reveries. By the mid-1960s some shipping lines, harking back to the 1920s, were even converting vessels into student-only ships.

By then as well, the French were reacting to these American visitors in much the same way as they had reacted to their predecessors in the 1920s. As in the 1920s, French resentment combined opposition to American foreign policy with a more generalized indictment of American culture, whose most visible representatives were, at first, American troops, and then American tourists. Some of the French again took pride in their country being a haven for African Americans. As in the 1920s, it gave them a moral platform from which to condemn American racism. Yet, also as in the 1920s, France's reputation for anti-Americanism did little to discourage American tourism, which continued to swell during the 1960s and 1970s.

These two decades marked the high point of the era of modern mass tourism in the strict sense of the terms "modern" and "mass." After World War II, the number of white middle-class families had expanded exponentially, and they migrated in great numbers to the suburbs. They provided a huge mass market for the consumer goods industries and a mass audience for the three virtually identical networks that dominated television, their major source of entertainment and information. Industry after industry tried to mass produce products for what was assumed to be this homogeneous class of white, middle-class, and suburban families. Those involved in foreign tourism tried to sell them experiences that were as predictable and reassuring as their food. In the case of France, this meant a kind of cultural tourism, involving packaged sightseeing tours, that insulated them as much as possible from the natives, who were regarded as potentially hostile.

However, in the 1970s, the never-really-homogeneous middle-class mass market began to fragment. Cable television ate away at the audience for the three networks. Food and other producers were forced to cater to every-more-diverse tastes. The tourist industry diversified its product mix as well. Cultural critics call the abandonment of the modern "one style fits all" idea in art, literature, and architecture "post-modernism." People who make more money than them call it market segmentation. Whatever it was, by the late twentieth century it seemed that everyone was scrambling to satisfy what had previously been dismissed as minority tastes. Virtually all classes and racial and ethnic groups were now regarded as a potential overseas tourists. The middle class among them were being offered a dazzling array of seaside sojourns, Alpine holidays, "pleasure cruises," spa cures, "gourmet" dining trips, guided tours to exotic places, and other ventures that, like gambling holidays, had previously been restricted to the upper class. France, its luster as the capital of American cultural tourism long dimmed, became just another venue for these multifold activities.

Behind this diversity and all of these changes, though, there lay what may be one of the immutable laws of modern tourism—that its pleasures (and pains) pass relentlessly down the class ladder. As we have seen, the whole process of overseas tourism had begun with an upper-class quest for culture. Enmeshed as this was with social status, it soon opened the Pandora's Box of snobbery. In the course of differentiating their kind of tourism from those in the classes below, the upper class moved toward a kind of tourism revolving around incestuous socializing and conspicuous leisure. The class below, reflecting the rise of women as major players in determining the cultural agenda, altered the goal of cultural tourism somewhat, to emphasize moral development more than sophisticated "taste." Yet they still remained wedded to the older ideal of cultural tourism until the early 1900s, when they began to follow the upper class's lead into "recreational" tourism. However, unable to emulate the upper class in terms of holidays comprising long stretches of status-affirming indolence and socializing, they made something more amorphous—pleasure—the goal of their trips, particularly after World War I.

Of course pleasure, including those of the flesh, had not by any means been absent from previous generations' touring agenda. Indeed, the newer tourists could plug into an ample heritage of stereotypes and expectations about French "gaiety." However, the consumer culture of the 1920s gave tourism for pleasure a tremendous boost. It made overseas travel a commodity that middle-class people could purchase to make their lives more pleasurable. One now bought a trip to France for the reasons one bought a Dodge convertible: "to have a good time." Better still, in a reversal of the older ideal of cultural tourism, which saw moral improvement as coming from putting in the hard work of learning a foreign country's language and studying its cultural icons, the new middle class took to the idea that just enjoying oneself could lead to self-improvement. Indeed, experiencing French joie de vivre might bring about a personality transformation just as profound as that which Harriet Beecher Stowe thought she experienced in the Louvre.

Although it would seem that, for many, France had become what the armed forces newspaper had warned against in 1917 (a mere "pleasure ground"), the Puritan work ethic had by no means disappeared from middle-class America. Holiday pleasure-seekers therefore also called their trips, as did Commodore Vanderbilt, a well-deserved break from the daily routine of hard work. As French economist Pierre Py has observed, the growth of the very industrial system that allowed for the rise of mass tourism also created the demand for it, in the form of the relentless pressures of work and daily life that millions of people now sought to escape.[8]

It is no accident if this sounds not much different from what takes place in much of the holidaying world today. That American tourists in 1920s France often acted as their descendants do as they lie on a tropical beach, asking an adult "boy" to bring them another drink, should come as no surprise. Although it may take on other undertones where white people visit lands inhabited by duskier ones, it seems to be inherent in the dynamic of mass tourism for pleasure. After all, recreational tourists usually want to visit a place, not its people. They naturally judge the locals mainly in terms of how they contribute to or detract from the pleasure of their holiday.

Much the same can be said about modern sightseeing. The older nineteenth-century ideal of cultural tourism still echoed among many of the middle-class tourists of the 1920s, mainly as the feeling that actually seeing France's famous sights was somehow uplifting. Yet since the late eighteenth century, sightseeing had increasingly taken place from within the confines of moving vehicles—boats, diligences, trains, private automobiles and finally, busses. This normally valorizes inanimate objects rather than the people who created or live among them. Indeed, often they just get in the way of actually seeing the sights. Until the 1920s, the condescension toward the natives that this kind of sightseeing can breed was countered by the American tourists' belief that there were aspects of French culture that were superior to their own. Moreover, unlike places such as Egypt, Peru, Yucatan, or even Italy, where sightseers hardly associated the monumental sights produced by past civilizations with the people who now lived there, the French were clearly to be credited with having produced what the tourists were admiring.

However, the rising middle class of the twentieth century were much less educated in France's language, history, and culture. These patriotic inhabitants of what had become the world's leading industrial nation were increasingly confident of their own cultural superiority, at least in what really counted, and that was business and industry. Moreover, beneath their praise of French gaiety and joie de vivre there lurked the Protestant suspicion that these in fact made the French unfit to compete in the modern world. By the 1920s, this had developed into a full-blown attitude of superiority to the backward natives, whose taxicabs were now rattle-traps and plumbing seemed medieval. At the same time, the common belief that the French were out to cheat American tourists added an antagonistic note. These feelings persisted into the end of the century, when they were exemplified by the common tourist dictum that, "France would be a wonderful place, were it not for the French."

Yet the old ideal of the nineteenth-century cultural tourist—that seeing the sights and "tramping through the Louver" was uplifting—also persisted. It too lingers today, among at least some of the people who stand patiently in the lines that snake back from glass pyramid that is now the entrance to the Louvre, who survive the crush of chattering tour groups to take in the magnificence of Notre-Dame cathedral, who marvel at the Sainte-Chapelle, and ride the escalator to catch the superb view from the top of the Pompidou Center. Like Harriet Beecher Stowe and countless middle-class tourists who followed her, they believe that, somehow, experiencing beauty brings self-improvement—that even if one is not an expert in it, allowing it to strike one's inner being makes one a better person. This is, after all, the essence of cultural tourism, and there are probably few among us who have not felt it.

The flame of the kind of high-cultural tourism represented by Thomas Jefferson, sitting on the parapet admiring the new Hôtel de Salm, also still flickers, albeit in different colors. The torch passed through people like Thomas Appleton, Philip Hone, Jane Addams, and the wartime volunteers who were ready to die for France to intellectuals such as the poet Perry Cornell, who was so infatuated with French culture that, after his first visit there in the late 1920s he changed his name to Pierre François Cornell-Dechert.[9] After World War II, it was picked up by a new generation of writers, intellectuals, artists, and jazz musicians, who found a spiritual home on the Left Bank in Paris despite (or perhaps because of) the contempt that many of their French counterparts expressed for their country. As in the 1920s, they spurred a generation of young college graduates to visit France, but this time it was not just to get drunk. The new generation avoided fixed itineraries, stayed in cheap hotels or hostels, and (unaffected by the lipophobia of later generations) lived on bread, cheese, and paté. They made devout pilgrimages to cultural shrines such as the cafés de Flore and Deux-Magots, where the Existentialists had held forth, and the spot on the rue de l'Odéon where Sylvia Beach's bookstore had stood. They peered at the masterpieces in the now-dingy Louvre, marveled at the Impressionist collection at the Musée du Jeu de Paume and sought out the Rodin and other smaller museums. They took second and third-class trains to the marvelous cathedral at Chartres and, unknowingly following in Jefferson's footsteps, down through Burgundy to Orange, Avignon, and Nîmes. Later, they would return to do similar things in more comfortable circumstances. They are still there today, although they are practically invisible amidst the over fifty million tourists who annually visit France, whose population barely surpasses that. But one would not want to call too much attention to them, lest they start demanding to be called travelers, rather than tourists. This might just stoke the embers of traveling snobbery and reignite yet another fruitless debate on the difference between the two terms.

Notes

Frequently cited sources are identified by the abbreviations listed below.

AAA	Archives of American Art, Smithsonian Institution, Washington, D.C.
AN	Archives Nationales, Paris
CATG	*Cook's American Traveler's Gazette*
CD	*Chicago Defender*
CE	*Cook's Excursionist and Tourist Advertiser*
CE-AM	*Cook's American Excursionist and Tourist Advertiser*
CHS	Chicago Historical Society, Chicago, Illinois
CUL	Rare Books and Manuscripts Division, Cornell University Libraries, Ithaca, New York
EJ	*The Journals and Miscellaneous Notebooks of Ralph Waldo Emerson*, 16 vols. (Cambridge: Harvard University Press, 1960–1982)
HL	Houghton Library, Harvard University
JP	*Papers of Thomas Jefferson*, 19 vols., ed. Julian Boyd et al. (Princeton: Princeton University Press, 1950–1974)
LC	Manuscripts Division, Library of Congress, Washington, D.C.
LD	*Literary Digest*
LHJ	*Ladies' Home Journal*
MHS	Massachusetts Historical Society, Boston
NYPL	Manuscripts Division, New York Public Library, New York
NYT	*New York Times*
NYTM	*New York Times Magazine*
PH	*New York Herald—Paris Edition*
PT	*Paris Tribune*
SDP	U.S. Department of State, Papers, National Archives, Washington, D.C.
SEP	*Saturday Evening Post*
SHSW	Archives and Manuscripts Division, State Historical Society of Wisconsin, Madison
SL	*Memoir and Letters of Charles Sumner*, ed. Edward L. Pierce, vol. 1 (London: Sampson, Low, 1878)
SSC	Sophia Smith Collection, Smith College Library, Northampton, Massachusetts
UNC-CHL	Research Collections, University of North Carolina–Chapel Hill Library

UVaL   Special Collections, University of Virginia Library, Charlottesville
VaHS   Virginia Historical Society, Richmond

PREFACE

1. Daniel Boorstin, *The Image: A Guide to Pseudo-Events in America* (New York: Harper and Row, 1987), 77–117; Dean McCannell, *The Tourist: A New Theory of the Leisure Class* (New York: Shocken, 1976); Paul Fussell, *Abroad: British Literary Travelling between the Wars* (New York: Oxford University Press, 1980), 37–49.

2. *Toronto Globe and Mail,* 1 Jan. 1997. A recent collection of studies of European communities' reactions to tourism is much more nuanced. Jeremy Boissevain, *Coping with Tourists: European Reactions to Mass Tourism* (Providence and Oxford: Berghahn Books, 1996).

3. See Malcolm Crick, "Representations of International Tourism in the Social Sciences: Sun, Sex, Sights, Savings and Servility," *Annual Review of Anthropology* 18 (1989): 307–44, for an excellent review of the literature.

4. Boorstin, *The Image,* 85.

5. Fussell, *Abroad,* 41–42. Most, however, disagree, and urging people to travel as travelers and not tourists has become an industry in its own right. A typical exhortation reads: "The genuine traveler will pride himself on not being mistaken for a tourist, will eschew the packaged tour, make an effort to see places off the beaten track, actually attempt to communicate with the natives, or residents, and will refuse to swallow the old bromides developed to describe or characterize every country, city, or monument. Instead, the real traveler will seek personal discoveries in every unfamiliar place or custom. . . ." Harold Darling, *Bon Voyage: Souvenirs from the Golden Age of Travel* (New York: Abbeville Press, 1990), n.p.

6. John Gagnon and Cathy Greenblat, quoted in Newsline, "Tourists—Strangers in a Strange Land," *Psychology Today* 10 (Dec. 1976): 26.

7. I would be loath to go as far as the semiotician Jonathan Culler, who accuses Fussell of "hysterical smugness" and ascribes his "ferocious denigration of tourists" to the possibility that, as an American professor of English, he was probably enraged at being mistaken for a tourist in England. However, he does go on to make the good point that, "Ferocious denigration of tourists is in part an attempt to convince oneself that one is not a tourist. The desire to distinguish between tourists and travelers is a part of tourism—integral to it rather than outside it or beyond it." Jonathan Culler, "The Semiotics of Tourism," in Culler, *Framing the Sign: Criticism and Its Institutions* (Norman: University of Oklahoma Press, 1989), 156.

8. Gagnon and Greenblat, in "Tourists—Strangers," 26.

9. René Duchet, *Le Tourisme à travers les âges, sa place dans la vie moderne* (Paris, 1949), 14.

10. John Urry, *The Tourist Gaze: Leisure and Travel in Contemporary Societies* (London: Sage, 1990), 96.

CHAPTER ONE

1. John Rutledge Jr., the son of a wealthy South Carolina planter, and Thomas Lee Shippen, scion of a prominent Philadelphia family.

2. He had previously called this the "pleasantest" kind of travel he had even undertaken. Jefferson to William Short, 21 May 1787, in *JP,* 11:371.

3. Jefferson to John Rutledge, Jr., 19 June 1788, *JP,* 13:262–77.

4. Jefferson to Charles Bellini, 30 Sept. 1785, *JP,* 8:568. In 1787, he wrote his friend Madame Tott, "Have you been, Madame, to see the superb picture now exhibiting chez Mme. Drouay? All Paris is running to see it." The picture, of Marius about to be assassinated, "fixed me like a statue for a quarter of an hour, or half an hour, I do not know which, for I lost all ideas of time, 'even the consciousness of my existence.'" Jefferson to Madame de Tott, 28 Feb. 1787, *JP,* 8:187–88.

5. Jefferson to Madame de Tott, 28 Feb. 1727, *JP,* 8:187–88.

6. Josiah Tucker, *Instructions for Travellers* (1757), 3, in Barbara Carson, "Early American Tourists and their Commercialization of Leisure," in Gary Carson et al., eds., *Consuming Interests: The Style of Life in the Eighteenth Century* (Charlottesville: University of Virginia Press, 1994), 401.

7. William E. Mead, *The Grand Tour in the Eighteenth Century* (Boston: Houghton Mifflin, 1914), 207–45.

8. Alain Corbin, *The Lure of the Sea: The Discovery of the Seaside in the Western World, 1750–1840* (Oxford: Polity, 1994), 43–50.

9. James Boswell, *Boswell's Life of Johnson* (Oxford: Oxford University Press, 1965), 724.

10. Piers Brendon, *Thomas Cook: 150 Years of Popular Tourism* (London: Seeker and Warburg, 1991), 9.

11. Ibid.

12. Jefferson thought the royal courts of Europe were particularly dangerous for Grand Tourists and in his letter to the two young Americans warned that they should be "seen as you would the Tower of London or Menagerie of Versailles, with their lions, tigers, hyenas and other beasts of prey, standing in the same relation to their fellows." Jefferson to John Rutledge, Jr., 19 June 1788, *JP,* 13:262–77. Ironically, among the ribald young Grand Tourists was Simon Bolívar, the immensely wealthy son of a Venezuelan landowner, whose experience in the particularly debauched court of Spain is often said to have turned him into a revolutionary.

13. Mead, *The Grand Tour in the Eighteenth Century,* 104.

14. *Virginia Magazine,* 42:317, cited in Marie Kimball, *Jefferson: The Scene of Europe, 1784–1789* (New York: Coward McCann, 1950), 256.

15. Jefferson to Bellini, *JP,* 8:568.

16. Merrill Petersen, *Thomas Jefferson and the New Nation* (New York: Oxford University Press, 1970), 385.

17. Tobias Smollett, *Travels through France and Italy,* ed. Frank Felsenstein (Oxford: Oxford University Press, 1979), 59.

18. Ibid., 43.

19. Cited in Elizabeth B. White, *American Opinion of France from Lafayette to Poincaré* (New York: Knopf, 1927), xii.

20. The peace treaty between the two countries signed in 1763 brought a great upsurge in British travel to France. Mead, *Grand Tour,* 105.

21. Almost a hundred years later, Dessin's, the hotel in Calais about which Sterne

wrote this was still dining out, as it were, on the fame the book brought it. When Boston literary lights James and Annie Fields stayed there in 1859 they were delighted to find a large copy of Sterne's work, opened to the flattering section, prominently displayed, and to be shown the room where he stayed. Annie Fields diary, 11 Aug. 1859, Annie Adams Fields Papers, MHS.

22. Indeed, the last lines in the book, when the narrator discovers a chambermaid in his darkened room at night and appears to persuade her to join him in bed, is one of the classic scenes in literature—a reflection of countless male travelers' erotic fantasies through the ages. Laurence Sterne, *A Sentimental Journey through France and Italy, by Mr. Yorick,* ed. Ian Jack (London: Oxford University Press, 1968). Italy figured in the title, in imitation of Smollett's book, but Sterne's traveler never got there. The book ends in Lyon.

23. Thomas Jefferson to Madame de Tott, 28 Feb. 1787, *JP,* 8:187–88; James Gabler, *Passions: The Wines and Travels of Thomas Jefferson* (Baltimore: Bacchus Press, 1995).

24. He still had hopes that France's absolute monarchy, whose support had been crucial to American success in the war for independence from Britain, would transform itself into what we now call a constitutional monarchy, with two houses of parliament. Jefferson to Abigail Adams, 21 June 1785, *JP,* 8:239. Later, he would write: "A more benevolent people, I have never known, nor greater warmth and devotedness in their select friendships. Their kindness and accommodation to strangers is unparalleled, and the hospitality of Paris is beyond anything I had conceived to be practicable in a large city." Thomas Jefferson, *The Autobiography of Thomas Jefferson* (New York: Putnam's, 1914), 157.

25. Mr. Yorick, Sterne's narrator, traveled with six shirts and a pair of black breeches, while Jefferson prided himself in having only one trunk with him on his tour through the South of France.

26. "They only serve to insulate me from the people among whom I am," he said.

27. Jefferson to Madame de Tessé, 20 Mar. 1787, *JP,* 11:226. It is now the Palace of the Legion of Honor. In Paris, the Left Bank is the south bank of the Seine.

28. Jefferson to William Short, 15 Mar. 1787, *JP,* 11:214.

29. When he was forced to stop over at an inn which "present[ed] in the first moment nothing but noise, dirt, and disorder," he wrote, "A traveler, says I, retired to his night to a chamber in an Inn, all his effects contained in a single trunk, all his cares circumscribed by the walls of his apartment, . . . writes, reads, thinks, sleeps, just in the moments when nature and the movements of his body and mind require. . . . He finds how few are our real wants, how cheap a thing is happiness, how expensive a one pride." Jefferson to Madame de Tott, 5 Apr. 1787, *JP,* 11:270.

30. Gordon S. Wood, *The Radicalism of the American Revolution* (New York: Knopf, 1992), 99–103. Were he to send her news, he wrote Madame de Tessé from Nimes, "I should tell you stories a thousand years old. I should detail to you the intrigues of the courts of the Caesars, how they affect us here, the oppressions of their Praetors, Praefects etc. I am immersed in antiquities from morning to night. For me the city of Rome is actually existing in all the splendor of its empire." Jefferson to Madame de Tessé, 20 Mar. 1787, *JP,* 11:226.

31. Jefferson to Tessé, 20 Mar. 1787, *JP,* 11:226.

32. "I am now in the land of corn, wine, oil, and sunshine," he wrote William

Short, his secretary back in Paris. "What more can man ask of heaven? If I should happen to die in Paris I will beg of you to send me here, and have me exposed to the sun. I am sure it will bring me to life again." Jefferson to William Short, 27 Mar. 1787, *JP,* 11:246. Jefferson used the term corn as the English did, to mean the staple crop, in this case wheat.

33. Jefferson to James Madison, 20 Sept. 1785, *JP,* 8:535.

34. Jefferson to Tessé, 20 Mar. 1787. It was on the trip down to Nîmes that Jefferson was able to make a wine-lover's pilgrimage to the renowned vineyards of Burgundy. At a shipper's establishment in Beaune he sampled the 1782 vintage of Montrachet, then as now the greatest of French white wines. Alas, after caressing the wine he gulped at its price. Failing to negotiate a lower price, he took the road without having placed an order. However, five days of journeying could not rid his memory of that ambrosaic wine. As soon as he arrived in Lyon he rushed off a letter to the tonnelier in Beaune asking to have it bottled and sent to his Paris address. He inquired as well about the prices of some fine Burgundy reds, but struck a note familiar to many who have also blanched at high French wine prices: He asked the tonnelier if he had understood him as saying that there were other wines, from vineyards adjacent to Montrachet, which were just as good but much cheaper. Jefferson to Parent, 13 Mar. 1787, *JP,* 11:211–12. Later, in Bordeaux, he stocked up on more wine, ordering six dozen bottles of its finest to be sent to his home in Virginia and 250 bottles of Sauterne for his table in Paris. Petersen, *Thomas Jefferson,* 335.

35. Albert Babeau, *Paris en 1789,* Paris, Firmin-Didot, n.d. [1900?], 28–37.

36. Of course none of these were really completed at the time. The Madeleine was not well enough along to be consecrated before the Revolution, and remained in flux for many years. Ste-Geneviève was a functioning church, but was then much-changed during its conversion to the Panthéon and after. One of St.-Sulpice's belfries is still unfinished.

37. Katherine Amory, *The Journal of Mrs. John Amory* (Boston: n.p., 1923), 26–33.

38. About the only Parisian diversion she admitted to enjoying was going with Jefferson to watch balloon ascents. Lynne Withey, *Dearest Friend: A Life of Abigail Adams* (New York: The Free Press, 1981), 164–65; David Scheoenbrun, *Triumph in Paris: The Exploits of Benjamin Franklin* (New York: Harper and Row, 1976), 164–66.

39. Abigail Adams to Mrs. Cranch, 20 Feb. 1785, in Philip Rahv, *Discovery of Europe: The Story of the American Experience in the Old World* (Garden City, N.J.: Doubleday, 1960), 42–44.

40. Withey, *Dearest Friend,* 196–98.

41. Ibid., 164–66.

42. *The Diary and Letters of Gouverneur Morris,* ed. Anne Cary Morris (1888; New York: DiCappo, 1970), 1:54, 68–89, 85–87.

43. Shackelford, *Thomas Jefferson's Travels,* 25.

CHAPTER TWO

1. The winter was out because of its fierce storms, as were "the equinoxes," the weeks straddling March 21 and September 21 when the trade winds shifted and ships were often plagued either by storms or long periods of being becalmed.

2. Thomas Jefferson to Francis Eppes, 30 Aug. 1785, *JP,* 8:451.

3. William Lee, *A Yankee Jeffersonian: Selections from the Diary and Letters of William Lee of Massachusetts,* ed. Mary Lee Mann (Cambridge: Harvard University Press, 1958), 2–8.

4. William Berrian, *Travels in France and Italy in 1817 and 1818* (New York: Swords, 1821), 12–15.

5. France, Ministère de l'Intérieur, Police Générale (hereafter MI-PG), "Étrangers entrés en France ou qui ne sont pas sortis, 1816–1817," Archives Nationales, Paris, F/7/9889/b.

6. John Malcolm Brinnin, *The Sway of the Grand Saloon: A Social History of the North Atlantic* (New York: Delacorte, 1971), 4–5; Zacharia Allen, *The Practical Tourist, or Sketches of the Useful Arts, and of Society, Scenery, etc., etc., in Great-Britain, France, and Holland* (Providence: Beckwith, 1832), 1:2–14.

7. France, MI-PG, "États numériques des passagers qui se sont embarqués pour l'Amérique en 1837, 1838, 1839, et 1840" [May 1840], F/7/12337.

8. Brinnin, *Sway,* 10–11.

9. Ibid., 16.

10. Abigail De Hart Mayo, *An American Lady in Paris, 1828–1829: The Diary of Mrs. John Mayo,* ed. Mary Mayo Crenshaw (Boston: Houghton Mifflin, 1927), 3. The ship carrying John Carter Brown, thirty-year-old scion of the Rhode Island family that founded the university of that name, was not so lucky, but Brown seems to have been little affected by the experience. The diary of his trip to France begins quite matter-of-factly: "Since my shipwreck on the coast of France and my long confinement on the Downs I have kept no journal of my proceedings," with no further reference to the wreck. John Carter Brown diary, 27 Mar. 1823, John Carter Brown Library, Brown University, Providence.

11. Margaret Fuller, *The Letters of Margaret Fuller,* ed. Robert H. Hudspeth (Ithaca: Cornell University Press, 1983–), 4:12–14.

12. Brinnin, *Sway,* 20; Berrian, *Travels,* 31.

13. John L. Gardner diary, 23 May 1823, in Gardner Family Papers, Series II, MHS.

14. Ibid., 25 May 1823.

15. Thomas Appleton, *Life and Letters of Thomas Gold Appleton,* ed. Susan Hale (New York: Appleton, 1885), 92.

16. Brinnin, *Sway,* 16.

17. Seasickness was listed as a cause of death on at least one occasion, when a consumptive woman died on Francis Parkman's crossing in 1845. Francis Parkman to John E. Parkman, 29 Aug. 1845, Francis Parkman Papers, Series III, MHS (hereafter Parkman Papers III).

18. John L. Gardner diary, 23 May 1823.

19. Allen, *Practical Tourist,* 1:16–17.

20. L. J. Frazee, *The Medical Student in Europe: Or, Notes on France, England, Italy, etc.* (Cincinnati: Applegate, 1852), 30.

21. *EJ,* 4:110–11.

22. Léonce Peillard, *Sur les chemins de l'océan: Paquebots, 1830–1972* (Paris: Hachette, 1972), 60–61; Brinnin, *Sway,* 56–72; *The Diary of Philip Hone,* ed. Allan Nevins (New York: Dodd, Mead, 1927), 1:316.

23. Amos Adams Lawrence diaries, Nov. 1839, in Amos Adams Lawrence Diaries and Account Books, box 1, vol. 2A, MHS.

24. Ibid., 30.

25. James F. Clarke to Anna Clarke, 16 July 1849, in James F. Clarke Papers, MHS.

26. John Doyle diary, 26–27 Nov. 1840, Doyle Family Papers, VaHS.

27. Saunders diary, [July 1828], 2–3.

28. Doyle diary, 25 Nov. 1840.

29. John L. Gardner diary, 23 May 1823.

30. *EJ*, 4:111.

31. John H. Gould, "Ocean Passenger Travel," *Scribner's Magazine* 9 (Apr. 1891): 400.

32. Doyle diary, 8–9 Dec. 1840.

33. Saunders diary, [July 1828], 20.

34. John Gardner, on the packet *Amethyst* in 1823, recorded pulling up alongside a brig of the same name, four weeks out of London and bound for Quebec. "We begged her," he wrote, "to report us, which probably will be in the Quebec papers, but it is uncertain if it will reach the eyes of our friends in Boston." John Gardner diary, 5 May 1823.

35. Francis Parkman to John E. Parkman, 8 Aug. 1845, Parkman Papers III.

36. Saunders diary, [July 1828], 25–27.

37. When Thomas Jefferson found out that Abigail Adams had booked passage for herself and her daughter on the voyage to join her husband, John, in Europe in 1784, he was so disturbed by the idea of them sailing without a male escort that he rushed to Boston the day before they left and tried to prevail upon them to cancel and sail to France with him. Lynee Withey, *Dearest Friend: A Life of Abigail Adams* (New York: Free Press, 1981), 153.

38. George Shackelford, *Thomas Jefferson's Travels in Europe, 1784–1789* (Baltimore: Johns Hopkins University Press, 1995), 8.

39. When Emerson sailed in 1832 he took the same mattress his brother had used for his European trip. Gay Wilson Allen, *Waldo Emerson: A Biography* (New York: Viking, 1981), 196.

40. Brinnin, *Sway*, 4–18.

41. Amos A. Lawrence diary, Nov. 1839 entries, Amos A. Lawrence Diaries, box 1, vol. 2A.

42. Francis Parkman to John E. Parkman, 29 Aug. 1845, Parkman Papers III.

43. Gould, "Ocean Passenger Travel," 405.

44. *EJ*, 10:332.

45. John Jay, and his wife Cornelia took a sailing ship, the *Henry Hill*, to Marseille in 1863, planning to board it again when it proceeded to Sicily. However, after spending five bilious weeks in a storm-tossed crossing followed by two weeks either becalmed or bucking strong headwinds in the Mediterranean, Cornelia refused to reboard in Marseille and insisted on returning on a steamer from Southampton, England. *The Diary of Cornelia Jay* (Rye, N.Y.: n.p., 1928), 92–120.

46. "The Grand Tour Diary of Robert C. Johnson, 1792–1793," ed. Vernon Snow, *Proceedings of the American Philosophical Society* 102 (1958): 84.

47. Paul Gerbod, "Les Touristes étrangers à Paris dans la première moitié du xixe siècle," *Bulletin de la Société de l'Histoire de Paris et de l'Île de France,* 1983, 245.

48. France, MI-PG, "Américains," F/7/2236.

49. They did not learn it was over until 11 Februrary 1815.

50. France, MI-PG, "Étrangers entrés en France ou qui ne sont pas sortis, 1816–1817," F/7/9889/2–4; Gerbod, "Les Touristes étrangers," 243.

51. Statistics are sketchy, but few Americans are recorded as sailing from Calais in 1820. France, MI-PG, "Américains," F/7/2236; "État des voyageurs embarqués a Calais, 1820," F/7/3048.

52. Brown diary, 27 Mar. 1823.

53. Gerbod, "Les Touristes étrangers," 243.

54. France, MI-PG, F/7/3870.

55. Gerbod, "Les Touristes étrangers," 246.

56. Ibid., 243.

57. France, MI-PG, F/7/12183/A, F/7/12180; Gerbod, "Les Touristes étrangers," 245. Guillaume de Bertier de Sauvigny, relying mainly on some of the same, very raw data on entries to seaports, came up with lower estimates—an average of one thousand American arrivals per year from 1816 to 1848. However, port arrivals, which often just recorded the name of a head of a family, and ignored servants, were not complete and did not include those arriving overland. Guillaume de Bertier de Sauvigny, *La France et les Français vus par le voyageurs américains, 1814–1848* (Paris: Flammarion, 1982), 17–19.

58. *The Diary of Philip Hone,* ed. Bayard Tuckerman (New York: Dodd, Mead, 1889) 1:144.

59. Out of about eighty or so who arrived each day in April and May and one hundred a day in June, the number of Americans among them increased from five a day in April to eight in mid-May and ten to twelve in mid-May and June. France, MI-PG, F/7/12183/A.

60. The first was those touristically congenial years of the Bourbon Restoration, from 1815 to 1830. Gerbod, "Les Touristes étrangers," 243.

CHAPTER THREE

1. Barbara Carson, "Early American Tourists and the Commercialization of Leisure," in *Of Consuming Interests: The Style of Life in the Eighteenth Century,* ed. Cary Carson et al. (Charlottesville: University of Virginia Press, 1994), 390–98.

2. *Letters/Washington Irving,* ed. Ralph M. Aderman et al. (Boston: Twayne, 1978), 1:xxiv–xxv.

3. John A. Clark, preface to *Glimpses of the Old World* (Philadelphia: Marshall, 1840).

4. Berrian, *Travels,* 2.

5. Topliff to Mr. Dorr, 18 Mar. 1829, in Samuel Topliff, *Topliff's Travels: Letters from Abroad in the Years 1828 and 1829,* ed. Edith S. Bolton (Boston: Boston Athenaeum, 1906), 184.

6. Abigail De Hart Mayo, *An American Lady in Paris, 1828–1829: The Diary of Mrs. John Mayo,* ed. Mary Mayo Crenshaw (Boston: Houghton Mifflin, 1927), 118–21.

7. Emma Willard, *Journal and Letters from France and Great Britain* (Troy, N.Y.: Tuttle, 1833), 9–10, 14.

8. Stuart Blumin, *The Emergence of a Middle Class: Social Experience in the American City, 1760–1900* (Cambridge: Cambridge University Press, 1989), 207.

9. George Sellers, *The Market Revolution, 1815–1846* (New York: Oxford University Press, 1991), 364–95; Gordon Wood, *The Radicalism of the American Revolution* (New York: Knopf, 1992), 277, 285.

10. Frederic C. Jaher, *The Urban Establishment: Upper Strata in Boston, New York, Charleston, Chicago and Los Angeles* (Urbana: University of Illinois Press, 1982), 235–36.

11. Ronald Story, *The Forging of an Aristocracy: Harvard and the Boston Upper Class, 1800–1870* (Middletown: Wesleyan University Press, 1980), 13–19; Jaher, *Urban Establishment*, 235–38; Blumin, *Emergence of a Middle Class*, 206–11.

12. France, MI-PG, F/7/2236.

13. Washington Irving to William Irving, Jr., 14 Aug. 1804, *Letters/Washington Irving*, 1:54. Before Irving's brother Peter left New York for France in 1807 he arranged to travel with a stranger who, despite being an "invalid" traveling for health reasons, assured Irving he would be "a brisk traveler." When this proved not to be the case, and he fell ill when they arrived in France, Irving abandoned him and traveled alone for the next nine months. Peter Irving to Richard Dodge, 7 Jan. 1807, in "Peter Irving's Journals," *NY Public Library Bulletin* 44 (1940): 5.

14. John P. Geortuer diary, 28 May 1827, UNC-CHL.

15. Jaher, *Urban Establishment*, 60.

16. Gay Wilson Allen, *Waldo Emerson: A Biography* (New York: Viking, 1981), 208–9.

17. Paris was the most advanced center of medical studies in the 1830s and 1840s, and attracted several hundred American students during that time.

18. Thomas Gold Appleton, *Life and Letters of Thomas Gold Appleton*, ed. Susan Hale (New York: Appleton, 1885), 9, 125; Edwin Hoyt, *The Improper Bostonian: Dr. Oliver Wendell Holmes* (New York: Morrow, 1979), 52–53.

19. George S. Emerson diary, George B. Emerson Papers, box 14, MHS.

20. Drew Gilpin Faust, *John Henry Hammond and the Old South* (Baton Rouge: Louisiana State University Press, 1982), 186–203.

21. *James Colles, 1788–1883: Life and Letters*, ed. Emily Johnston De Forest (New York: n.p., 1926), 76–77.

22. Bayard Tuckerman, introduction to *The Diary of Philip Hone*, ed. Bayard Tuckerman (New York: Dodd, Mead, 1889), 2:iii.

23. Henry B. Humphrey diary, 29 Apr. 1839, MHS.

24. Because of the relative rarity of women traveling overseas in those days, and their importance among the reading public, they published a disproportionate number of travel accounts. The proportion of women quoted here is therefore by no means representative of their presence among the tourists.

25. Alpheus Hardy diary, 1845–46, 1:1–6, MHS.

26. Theodore Lyman [to wife], Oct. 30, 1848, Theodore Lyman III Papers, box 9, MHS.

27. Tuckerman, ed., *Diary of Philip Hone*, 1:99.

28. Barbara Welter, "The Cult of True Womanhood," *American Quarterly* 18 (summer 1966): 151–74. S. G. Goodrich, a fifty-year-old from New York, arrived in Havre in 1846 with his wife and five small children. Some days later a James Bulloch, age fifty-two, arrived with his two daughters and two female companions for them. France, MI-PG, "État des passeports de voyageurs arrivés de l'étranger au Havre, 1846," F/7/12344.

29. Eight of the women were maids and six were teenaged daughters accompanying parents. Four of the adult women were not with husbands, but only one was single—an eighteen-year-old girl obviously out to meet family. The three others were listed as "Madame," and two of them, accompanied by children, were from New Orleans, where many families still maintained ties to France. Although it is impossible to say what proportion of the visitors were tourists, the fact that arrivals peaked in May, June, and July, the favorite months for tourism, and tailed off after that would indicate that a significant number were tourists. France, MI-PG, "État des passeports de voyageurs arrivés de l'étranger au Havre, 1846," F/7/12344.

30. One ambitious twenty-two-year-old from Mobile, Alabama had himself classified as "*voyageur.*" Ibid.

31. Topliff to Dorr, 6 May 1829, in Topliff, *Topliff's Travels*, 226.

32. Ibid., 3–4.

33. Among the many examples of this genre are: William Berrian, *Travels in France and Italy in 1817 and 1818* (New York: Sword, 1821); Orville Dewey, *The Old World and the New*, 2 vols. (New York: Harper, 1836); and John Mitchell, *Notes from Over Sea* (New York: Gates and Stedman, 1845).

34. Few women would have purchased the diary that John Carter Brown used while touring France in 1823. Published in London in 1819, *The Tourist's Pocket Journal* promised to "save the Traveller much trouble in his tour, and enable him to give, in connected form, a clear and concise account of every circumstance that may occur in the course of the journey." It featured two facing pages for each day. One page, blank, was for "Observations." The facing one, labeled "Expences," was subdivided into "Posting, Diligence, Fiacres, etc.; Carriage, Horses; Turnpikes; Breakfast; Dinner (private); Table d'hôte, or Ordinary; Tea and Coffee; Théâtre and Exhibitions; Supper; Lodging, Apartments; Wearing Apparel; Washing; Guide and Interpreter; Servants; and Sundries." *The Tourist's Pocket Journal* (London: Samuel Leigh, 1819). The English feminist Mary Wollstonecraft noted these differences in 1796. Catherine Barnes Stevenson, *Victorian Women Travel Writers in Africa* (New York: Twayne, 1982), 9–10.

35. William Raser, "Notes on Paris," 1817–18; diary, 1817–18, NYPL.

36. James Clarke to Anna Clarke, 16 July 1849, James Freeman Clarke Papers, MHS.

37. Berrian, *Travels*, 11–12.

38. E. g., *Galignani's Traveller's Guide through France*, 10th ed. (Paris: Galignani, 1831), xxxii–xxxv; *Galignani's New Paris Guide* (Paris: Galignani, 1848), ii.

39. Daniel Boorstin, *The Image: A Guide to Pseudo-Events in America* (New York: Harper and Row, 1987), 77–117; Paul Fussell, *Abroad: British Literary Travelling between the Wars* (New York: Oxford University Press, 1980), 37–49; Dean McCannell, *The Tourist: A New Theory of the Leisure Class* (New York: Shocken, 1976), 94–96.

40. These, he said, seemed "to impose upon others the necessity of paying me some attention, for in these larger places oftentimes no notice is taken of all such letters, and if there is, nine times out of ten only by formal, ceremonious dinner—and there ends your acquaintance, except perhaps a passing call, or a card left at your door." John Carter Brown diary, 27 Mar. 1823, John Carter Brown Papers, John Carter Brown Library, Brown University, Providence, R.I.

41. Topliff to Dorr, 18 Mar. 1829, in Topfliff, *Topliff's Travels*, 186.

42. "Between the various urban stops, tourists relaxed their attention, displaying a sort of blindness as they crossed the countryside. In the carriage, they would reread the appropriate authors in order better to savor the richness of the next stop. . . ." Corbin, *Lure of the Sea*, 45.

43. Elizabeth McKinsey, *Niagara Falls: Icon of the American Sublime* (Cambridge: Cambridge University Press, 1985), 58.

44. Louis Lutens, *Itinéraire des routes les plus fréquentées, ou Journal de plusieurs voyages aux villes principales de l'Europe, depuis 1768 jusqu'en 1783* 6 ed'n. (London: Faden, 1793); *Journal of Travels Made through the Principal Cities of Europe* (London: J. Wallis, 1782); Jefferson to John Rutledge Jr., 19 June 1788, *JP,* 13:268.

45. The company that published the travel journal that John Carter Brown used offered thirteen different guidebooks for continental travel, including *Planta's New Picture of Paris, Planta's Gazetteer for France, Reichard's Itinerary of France and Belgium,* and *A Descriptive Catalogue of the Pictures in the Louvre. Tourist's Pocket Journal,* passim.

46. Stevenson, "Victorian Women Travel Writers," 9–10; James Buzard, *The Beaten Tack: European Tourism Literature and the Ways of Culture, 1800–1918* (Oxford: Oxford University Press, 1992), 68–70; *Galignani's Traveller's Guide through France; Galignani's New Paris Guide.*

47. George Putnam, *The Tourist in Europe* (New York: Wiley and Putnam, 1838).

48. Henry [?] to John Lowell, 2 Feb. 1850, in George B. Emerson Papers, box 7, MHS.

49. Anne T. J. Bullard, *Sights and Scenes in Europe* (St. Louis: Chambers and Knapp, 1852), 189–90.

50. Thomas Philbrick, introduction to *Gleanings in Europe: France,* by James Fenimore Cooper (Albany: State University of New York Press, 1983), xxxii–xxx.

51. Appleton, *Life and Letters,* 93.

52. Buzard, *Going Abroad.*

53. It became less common after that, but Henry James still made the courier a central character in his 1878 novel of Americans traveling in Europe, *Daisy Miller.*

54. Caroline M. Kirkland, *Holiday Abroad, or Europe from the West* (New York: Baker and Scribner, 1849), 119–22.

55. Ambrose Carlton to James Gardner, 28 June 1854, Carlton Family Papers, VaHS.

56. Anne Catherine Jones diary, 29 June 1851, UNC-CHL.

57. Margaret Quincy Greene diary, 9, 10, 14 Nov. 1838, MHS.

58. Henry B. Humphrey diary, 11 Sept. 1839, MHS.

59. *Tour du Monde: Nouveau Journal de Voyages* No. 1 (premier semestre, 1860), 1.

60. Mark Twain, *The Innocents Abroad,* in *The Complete Travel Books of Mark Twain: The Early Works,* ed. Charles Neider (Garden City: Doubleday, 1966), 136–37.

CHAPTER FOUR

1. Caroline Kirkland, *Holidays Abroad: or Europe from the West* (New York: Baker and Scribner, 1849), 120.

2. In 1845, Francis Parkman, writing from France, told his three daughters in the States. "Pray learn, every one of you," he wrote, "to speak as well as write French, if you ever hope to come to Europe." Francis Parkman to Mary B. and Elira Parkman, 18 June 1845, Parkman Papers, box 4, MHS.

3. Thomas Philbrick, preface to *Gleanings from Europe: France*, by James Fenimore Cooper (Albany: State University Press of New York, 1983), xv.

4. When his wife began to lose heart, Colles warned her: "It is necessary that you learn to speak; how would it be to be in France and not speak much French?" James Colles to Mrs. Colles, 21 Mar. 1841, in *James Colles, 1788–1883: Life and Letters*, ed. Emily Johnston De Forest (New York: n. p., 1926), 122.

5. Ibid., 78. They were also pleased to discover that it was indeed the international language, and used it to get along in Italy and other countries they visited. Mrs. Colles to James Colles, Jr., 16 Dec. 1842, ibid., 159.

6. Henry [?] to John Lowell, 3 Apr. 1850, George B. Emerson Papers, box 7, MHS.

7. Sumner to George Hillard, 6 Jan. 1838, in *SL*, 228; Sumner diary, 18 Jan. 1838, *SL*, 240.

8. After six months there, he proudly noted in his diary that he had been able to understand the risqué humor in a satirical revue. "The piece was full of rather broad wit which would have been disgusting in English," he wrote, "but there is a lightness about French which carries one over many a dirty bog when an Englishman would sink deep." George S. Emerson diary, 17 Jan. 1848, George B. Emerson Papers, box 14, MHS.

9. Margaret Fuller to Caroline Sturgis, 28 Nov. 1846, *The Letters of Margaret Fuller*, ed. Robert Hudspeth (Ithaca: Cornell University Press, 1983–1994), 4:250.

10. *Galignani's Traveller's Guide through France* (Paris: Galignani, 1831), xlvii.

11. Washington Irving to William Irving, Jr., 14 Aug. 1804, in *Letters/Washington Irving*, ed. Ralph Aderman et al. (Boston: Twayne, 1978), 1:56.

12. James Clarke to Anna Clarke, 28 Aug. 1849, James F. Clarke Papers, MHS.

13. Ibid.

14. Elizabeth Cady Stanton, *Eighty Years and More* (London: Unwin, 1898), 94.

15. William Lee to Susan Lee, 29 Nov. 1809, in *A Yankee Jeffersonian: Selections from the Diary and Letters of William Lee of Massachusetts*, ed. Mary Lee Mann (Cambridge: Belknap Press, 1958), 84.

16. Isaac Carow, journal, 12 June 1827, in *American Backlogs: The Story of Gertrude Tyler and Her Family*, ed. Edith Kermit Roosevelt and Kermit Roosevelt (New York: Scribner's, 1928), 213. Amos Lawrence, anticipating that they would search his luggage but not his person, stuffed all his cigars into the pockets of the clothes he wore on the Dover-Boulogne ferry in 1839. His diary then records the denouement familiar to most such sweaty-palmed smuggling tourists: "Officers on quay. Through the customs house. Am not examined. Carry my cigars to hotel and empty them in drawers." Amos Lawrence diary, 8 Dec. 1839, Amos Amos Adams Lawrence Diaries and Account Books, box 1, MHS.

17. Anne Catherine (Boykin) Jones diary, 16 June 1851, UNC-CHL.

18. John Sanderson, *Sketches of Paris, or The American in Paris* (Philadelphia: Carey and Hart, 1838), 1:15. Although the book was published in 1838, the letters upon which it was based were written in 1835.

19. Frazee, *Medical Student*, 91. He must have used milk tongue-in-cheek. At that time American alcohol consumption had reached an all-time high, led by whiskey, which was consumed in enormous quantities in western states such as Kentucky.

20. Jefferson to Charles Bellini, 30 Sept. 1785, *JP*, 8:568.

21. James Fenimore Cooper, *Gleanings from Europe*, ed. Thomas Philbrick and Constance A. Denne (Albany: State University Press of New York, 1983), 90–91.

22. Topliff to Mr. Dorr and Family, 30 Mar. 1829, in Topliff, *Topliff's Travels*, 199. Charles Sumner was pleasantly surprised to be served wine with his breakfast on his first two days in France, and said he was "not disinclined to adopt the usage." The time at which one breakfasted was still very flexible. His first one, at noon, was very late, he noted, even for France. His second, of mutton chop, wine, and coffee, was at 9 A.M. Sumner diary, 29 Dec. 1837, *SL*, 219.

23. Willard, *Journal and Letters*, 20.

24. Arthur M. Schlesinger, *Paths to the Present* (Boston: Houghton Mifflin, 1964), 226.

25. The down side, he thought, was "because this was at the *table d'hôte* and there was no menu to choose from, I never knew how much of an article to eat, as I did not know what would next be introduced." Frazee, *Medical Student*, 34–35.

26. Amos Lawrence diary, 30 Dec. 1839.

27. William Raser diary, n.d., 1818, NYPL.

28. Amos Lawrence diary, 21 Dec. 1839.

29. Amos Lawrence diary, 23 Dec. 1839. George Putnam was horrified to find that his diligence had left without him after making a brief stop at 11 P.M. However, "after a *hot* chase of two miles," he was able to overtake it on foot. George Putnam, *The Tourist in Europe* (New York: Wiley and Putnam, 1837), 203.

30. Thomas Cole diary, 4 May 1831, Thomas Cole Sketchbooks, Detroit Institute of Art, Archives of American Art Microfilm D39.

31. *Galignani's New Paris Guide* (Paris: Galignani, 1848), 1–3.

32. James Clarke to Anna Clarke, 9 Feb. 1849, James Clarke Papers. George Hillard had a similar experience at the other end of the country. He took a diligence from Marseille to the terminus of the railway from Avignon, where an engine hoisted it, passengers, and baggage onto a flat car. They rode like that to Avignon, had dinner, and then rode all night on the diligence's wheels to Lyon. George Hillard diary, 24 Apr. 1848, in George Hillard Journals, vol. 2, MHS.

33. Smollett was just about as moved by his first sight of the Maison Carrée in Nimes as Jefferson. The amphitheater, he said, was "counted the finest monument of its kind" and the Maison Carrée was a "beautiful edifice" that "enchants you with the most exquisite beauties of architecture and sculpture." Smollett, *Travels through France*, 84–85.

34. Corbin, *Lure of the Sea*, 45–46, 140–44. In the English-speaking world, the poet Alexander Pope played a leading role in cultivating this ideal. Admiration for the paintings of Claude (his real name was de Gelée, but he was called Lorrain, or Lora-

inne, after his birthplace) helped inspire a revolution in English landscape gardening, with the construction of idyllic gardens with half-hidden classical "follies," such as that still evident in the extraordinary garden at Stourhead. This, in turn, was reflected back in France, where, just before the Revolution, architects such as Pierre Contant replaced formal Italian-style gardens such that at Chamarande, outside of Paris, with an English-style ones, or created new ones, such the one at the Bagatelle, in Paris's Bois de Boulogne.

35. James Buzard, *The Beaten Track: European Tourism, Literature, and the Ways of Culture, 1800–1918* (Oxford: Oxford University Press, 1992), 10; "The picturesque is found anywhere the ground is uneven," said the French sociologist Roland Barthes many years later. Roland Barthes, *Mythologies* (London: Cape, 1972), 74.

36. Patricia Jasen, "Romanticism, Modernity, and the Evolution of Tourism on the Niagara Frontier," *Canadian Historical Review* 72 (1991): 288.

37. Irving to Alexander Beebe, 8 Aug. 1804, *Letters/Washington Irving*, 1:63.

38. Putnam, *Tourist in Europe*, 203.

39. Katherine Bigelow Lowell Lawrence diary, 12 Dec. 1850, Lamb Family Papers, MHS.

40. Edmund Burke, *A Philosophical Inquiry into the Origin of Our Ideas of the Sublime and Beautiful* (London: Rivington, 1812), 95–96.

41. Ibid., 96.

42. K. Lawrence diary, 16 Dec. 1850.

43. Francis Parkman diary, 14 June 1845, Francis Parkman Papers III, box 4, MHS.

44. Putnam, *Tourist in Europe*, 205, 238.

45. Ibid., 238.

46. Patrick McGreevy, "Vision at the Brink: Imagination and the Geography of Niagara Falls" (Ph.D. diss., University of Minnesota, 1984), 6–7; Christopher Mulvey, *Anglo-American Landscapes: A Study of Nineteenth-Century Anglo-American Travel Literature* (Cambridge: Cambridge University Press, 1983), 187–208.

47. George Mead, *The Grand Tour in the Eighteenth Century* (Boston: Houghton Mifflin, 1914), 247–48; Robert C. Smith, "Eighteenth-Century Americans on the Grand Tour," *Antiques* 68 (Oct. 1955): 344–47; Malcolm Andrews, *The Search for the Picturesque: Landscape Aesthetics and Tourism in Britain, 1760–1800* (Aldershot: Scholar Press, 1989), 45–47; McGreevy, "Visions at the Brink," 7–39.

48. Pierre-Marie Auzas, *Eugène Viollet Le Duc, 1814–1879* (Paris: Caisse Nationale des Monuments Historiques, 1979), 25–51.

49. *Letters/Washington Irving*, 1:47.

50. Others would push on to northern Germany, the Netherlands and Belgium, returning to England from Antwerp.

51. Putnam, *Tourist in Europe*, 203.

52. Amos Lawrence diary, 23 Dec. 1839.

53. Henry Humphrey diary, 5 Sept. 1839, MHS.

54. Topliff, *Topliff's Travels*, 126.

55. Willard, *Journal*, 27.

56. Louis A. Cazenove to Mother, n.d. [1824], Louis A. Cazenove Papers, Library

of Congress; Henry Wadsworth Longfellow, *Outre-Mer: A Pilgrimage beyond the Sea* (Boston: Ticknor, 1848), 24; Emma Willard, *Journal and Letters from France and Great Britain* (Troy, N.Y.: Tuttle, 1833), 27.

57. Sumner to George Hillard, 13 Jan. 1838, *SL,* 234.

58. The tale of her tragic death tapped into the same kind of emotion that Harriet Beecher Stowe later exploited with her heart-rending description of the prolonged death of the angelic child Eva in *Uncle Tom's Cabin.* Ann Douglas, *The Feminization of American Culture* (New York: Doubleday, 1988), 4–5.

59. Clarke to Anna Clarke, 8 Aug. 1849, Clarke Papers.

60. Recalling his local guide's patter on this score, E. J. Frazee wrote that "although the end to be accomplished did not justify the means employed—a pretence that she was inspired—yet we cannot but feel a deep sympathy for this unfortunate person, and regard her as less at fault in heart, than erring in judgement." Frazee, *Medical Student,* 36.

61. Irving to William Irving Jr., 17 Aug. 1804, *Letters/Washington Irving,* 1:59.

62. Elizabeth B. White, *American Opinion of France* (New York: Knopf, 1927), 9.

63. Ibid., 42. Hostility to the Bourbons increased in the 1820s, as they helped restore conservative monarchies in Europe and threatened to snuff out the newly independent governments in Latin America.

64. Charles Geortuer diary, 19, 23, and 28 May 1827, UNC-CH; Willard, *Journal and Letters,* 23–24; Caroline W. Cushing, *Letters Descriptive of Public Monuments, Scenery, and Manners in France and Spain* (Newburyport, Mass.: Allen, 1832), 1:146–155; Henry McLellan, *Journal of a Residence in Scotland and Tour through England, France, Germany, Switzerland and Italy,* ed. I. McLellan Jr. (Boston: Allen and Ticknor, 1834), 255–62; Topliff, *Topliff's Travels,* 137–42; Abigail De Hart Mayo, *An American Lady in Paris, 1828–1829: The Diary of Mrs. John Mayo,* ed. Mary Mayo Crenshaw (Boston: Houghton Mifflin, 1927), 58–64; George Bancroft diary, 30 May and 4 July 1821, in *Life and Letters of George Bancroft,* ed. Mark Anthony de Wolfe Howe (New York: Scribner's, 1908), 1:105–6, 109.

65. White, *American Opinion,* 94.

66. Ibid., 94–95.

67. Nevins, ed., *Diary of Philip Hone,* 1:30–31.

68. Curiously, one of those with a climatalogical explanation was Henry McLellan, a man from Massachusetts, where extreme weather conditions were hardly unknown. Henry B. McLellan, *Journal of a Residence in Scotland, and a Tour through England, France, Germany, Switzerland, and Italy* (Boston: Allan and Ticknor, 1834), 250–51.

69. White, *American Opinion,* 124.

70. *EJ,* 7:249; White, *American Opinion,* 119–31.

71. William Lee diary, 24 May 1796, in Lee, *A Yankee Jeffersonian,* 26–27.

72. Phillip Rahv, *The Discovery of Europe* (Garden City: Doubleday, 1960), 65–66. Alexis de Tocqueville, America's most famous liberal admirer, was not so sure. Much of his insight into America derived from analyzing the unique conditions of social equality that made political equality possible in America, conditions that, being absent in France, precluded this kind of political democracy there.

73. Putnam, *Tourist in Europe,* 6.

74. "In England, there is an aristocracy of manners, in France there is a democracy of manners," he wrote. Samuel Topliff to Mr. Dorr, 30 Mar. 1829, in Topliff, *Topliff's Travels*, 197.

75. Bancroft to President Kirkland, 21 Aug. 1821, in *Life and Letters of George Bancroft*, 116.

76. This was in part, he thought, because "territory is accorded with great equality among her citizens," and "the Church is comparatively no burden on the State and Equality is proclaimed by nature from the cradle to the grave." Theodore Sedgwick III diary, 23–31 Aug. 1836, Sedgwick Papers, Miscellaneous, MHS.

77. John Doyle diary, 2 Mar. 1840, Doyle Family Papers, VaHS.

78. George Emerson diary, 8 Jan. 1848. Fifteen years earlier, his cousin Ralph Waldo also observed that people mingled on the streets without social distinction. Gay Wilson Allen, *Waldo Emerson: A Biography* (New York: Viking, 1981), 514.

79. Frazee, *Medical Student*, 126.

80. Sumner diary, 19 Jan. 1838, *SL*, 241.

81. Quoted in *Memoir and Letters of Charles Sumner*, ed. Edward L. Pierce (Boston: Roberts Brothers, 1877), 1:297.

82. It probably owed something to the popularity, in the 1820s and 1830s, of James Fenimore Cooper's tales of vanishing Indians, even though the Indians were generally portrayed as a rather sorry lot, and the 1827 trip to France of a group of Osage Indians paying homage to Lafayette. Around that time, French sympathy for the plight of the Indians increased. In the 1840s, the artist George Catlin made a big splash in Paris by showing off another band of Indians. King Louis-Philippe commissioned a large number of portraits of these "noble savages" but was overthrown before the pictures, now considered masterpieces of that genre, could be delivered to the museum at the palace of Versailles. Catlin spent the next years unsuccessfully trying to get the United States government to buy them. Thomas Philbrick, introduction to Cooper, *Gleanings from Europe: France*, xxi; René Rémond, *Les États-Unis devant l'opinion française, 1815–1852* (Paris: Armand Colin, 1962), 2:730–33; George Catlin, *Catlin's Notes of Eight Years' Travels and Residence in Europe, with His North American Indian Collection* (New York: Burgess, Stringer, 1848).

83. *The Diaries of Andrew D. White*, ed. Robert M. Ogden (Ithaca: Cornell University Press, 1959), 30. In 1864, William Brawley, an ex-Confederate soldier, was nonplused to find that his landlady "could not realize for a long time that all the inhabitants of America were not black. . . . She still eyes me curiously as if expecting some transformation." William Brawley diary, n.d. [1864], 90.

84. "Dr. Spencer, I was told, had great difficulty in convincing an Interne at the Hotel Dieu [hospital] that he was an American, simply because he was white." Frazee, *Medical Student*, 126.

85. Drew Gilpin Faust, *James Henry Hammond and the Old South* (Baton Rouge: Louisiana State University Press, 1982), 203.

86. Catherine Anne (Boykin) Jones diary, 16 June 1851, UNC-CHL.

87. Putnam, *Tourist in Europe*, 281–82.

88. She told of a young American, just arrived at Havre, who told their landlady, a Lafayette liberal who admired the American political system, "that her admiration was altogether misplaced—that ours was mere government of the mob, which fortunately

however was not going to last long." Willard said she failed to change his views, but some days later, when she arrived in Paris, a note from him awaited her saying, "Tell Mrs. Willard that I am already twenty per cent more of an American than when I landed in France." Willard, *Journal and Letters*, 21–22.

89. Sumner to Simon Greenleaf, 7 Dec. 1837, *SL*, 209–10; Sumner to George Hillard, 30 Jan. 1838, *SL*, 245; Sumner to Judge Story, 21 Apr. 1838, *SL*, 288.

90. Drew Gilpin Faust, *John Henry Hammond and the Old South* (Baton Rouge: Louisiana State University Press, 1982), 201–2.

91. Colles to James Colles, Jr., Jan. 30, 1842, in *Colles Letters*, 142.

CHAPTER FIVE

1. Lawrence Levine, in *Highbrow/Lowbrow* (Cambridge: Harvard University Press, 1988), has argued that the distinction between high and low culture did not really take hold in America until later in the nineteenth century. His case seems to be strongest with regard to Shakespeare and symphonic music, neither of which were important in American tourism to France. For most tourists, art, architecture, opera, ballet, and theater were the main cultural draws, and most of these in forms which were popular among the upper and bourgeois classes, not the hoi polloi. This is not to say that more popular forms of culture, such as music halls, circuses, and vaudeville, did not draw them too. As we shall see, this was particularly true after the mid-nineteenth century.

2. Guillaume de Bertier de Sauvigny, *La France et les Français vus par les voyaguers américains, 1814–1848* (Paris: Flammarion, 1982), 189–204.

3. Sumner to George Hillard, 12 Jan. 1838, *SL*, 234.

4. Fuller to Caroline Sturgis, 28 Nov. 1846, in *The Letters of Margaret Fuller*, ed. Robert N. Hudspeth (Ithaca: Cornell University Press, 1983), 4:250.

5. Topliff to Mr. Dorr and Family, 30 Mar. 1829, in Samuel Topliff, *Topliff's Travels: Letters from Abroad in the Years 1828 and 1829*, ed. Edith Stanwood Bolton (Boston: Boston Athenaeum, 1906), 199.

6. *The Diary of Philip Hone*, ed. Bayard Tuckerman (New York: Dodd Mead, 1889), 1:227.

7. The American doctor who accompanied him seems not to have been as impressed. Reacting to being squeezed in with the multitude crowding the hall, he supposedly said, "She's quite a *spry* little thing, but I guess it ain't worth while to be squeezed to death for the sake for the sake of seeing a gal hop and skip ever so well." George Putnam, *The Tourist in Europe* (New York: Wiley and Putnam, 1838), 196.

8. Instrumental music was not nearly as popular among tourists, even though it made no demands on language skills. Young Samuel Ward saw Paganini and Liszt perform, but he had musical ambitions of his own. Maude Howe Elliot, *Uncle Sam Ward and His Circle* (New York: Macmillan, 1938), 64–67. Even though performers and composers such as these, and Chopin, Wagner, and Berlioz, were regularly in Paris in the 1830s and 1840s, few other tourists went to purely instrumental performances. This was in part because there were no regular concert series in public auditoriums—concerts were still arranged individually—but instrumental music concerts never became popular among tourists to Paris, perhaps because France always seemed to lag behind Austria and Germany in this regard. Indeed, by the late nineteenth

century, this was one field in which New York and Boston could probably compete with Paris.

9. Handwritten notes, three pages, John L. Gardner Papers, MHS. Fifteen years later, Sedgwick and his father did practically the same thing. Theodore Sedgwick diary, 21–31 Aug. 1836, Sedgwick Papers, Miscellaneous, MHS.

10. Ralph Waldo Emerson diary, 15 July 1833, *EJ,* 1:202.

11. Cooper, *Gleanings: Switzerland* (fall 1828), 2:237–38.

12. Robert Hughes, *Culture of Complaint* (New York: Oxford University Press, 1993), 173.

13. Sumner diary, 28 Dec. 1837, *SL,* 218; Sumner to Francis Lieber, 9 Mar. 1838, *SL,* 264.

14. Cooper to Richard Cooper, July 1826, in James Fenimore Cooper, *Gleanings in Europe: France,* ed. Thomas Philbrick (Albany: State University Press of New York, 1983), 76–77.

15. Sumner diary, 20 Dec. 1837, *SL,* 221.

16. Emma Willard, *Journals and Letters from France and England* (Troy, N.Y.: Tuttle, 1833), 26–27.

17. Ibid.

18. Henry Ward Beecher, *Star Papers: Experiences of Art and Nature* (New York: J. C. Derby, 1857), 48.

19. Norval White, *New York: A Physical History* (New York: Atheneum, 1987), 88–89.

20. James Fenimore Cooper, *A Residence in France,* 88–89, quoted in Neil Harris, *The Artist in American Society* (New York: Braziller, 1966), 164.

21. Louis Cazenove to Mother, [indecipherable date] 1824, Louis Albert Cazenove Papers, LC.

22. William Raser, "Notes on Paris," 1817–18, William Raser Papers, NYPL.

23. Donald J. Olsen, *The City as a Work of Art: London, Paris, Vienna* (New Haven: Yale University Press, 1986), 35–36.

24. Putnam, *Tourist in Europe,* 183.

25. Willard, *Journals and Letters,* 30. Curiously, three years later, Emerson's first impression was of "a loud modern New York of a place," yet most of it was hardly modern. *EJ,* 4:197.

26. Cushing, *Letters,* 17.

27. French women would hike their dresses up to calves or knees when walking down these streets, but modesty prevented American women from following suit, resulting in dresses soaked in filthy water. Mrs. Caleb [Caroline] Cushing, *Letters, Descriptive . . . France* (Newburyport, Mass.: Allen, 1832), 17.

28. The pensions and apartments tourists moved to for longer stays were usually within a short stroll of the boulevards, for most new housing construction in the years from 1820 to about 1850 took place within an easy walk of them. Olsen, *City as Work of Art,* 42.

29. Raser, "Notes on Paris," 1817–18.

30. Putnam, *Tourist in Europe,* 183.

31. Albert Babeau, *Paris en 1789* (Paris: Firmin-Didot, n.d. [c. 1900]), 90.

32. The project, which involved cutting down some lines of fine old trees, was met by intense opposition by neighbors and others crying "vandalism"—an early example of an unsuccessful neighborhood movement to limit development. Ibid., 90.

33. Babeau, *Paris en 1789,* 89–105. It is not known how many foreigners were there on 13 July 1789, when Camille Desmoulins leaped onto one of the café tables and shouted "Enough talk . . . Let's arm ourselves," beginning the violent phase of French Revolution.

34. In this book I use the American numeration of floors, with the ground floor the first floor, rather than the European one.

35. Putnam, *Tourist in Europe,* 190.

36. In the mid-1840s, when the Reverend Clarke visited it, the prostitutes and outside streetwalkers had been banned from aggressively soliciting patrons in the interior courtyard (they had to use the sidewalks outside) so he was able, in good conscience, to write of how he "enjoyed walking through the Palais-Royal by gaslight, admiring its splendid shops," and returned a few nights later to dine in one of its fine restaurants. Clarke to Anna Clarke, 22, 28 Aug. 1849, James F. Clarke Papers, MHS.

37. Babeau, *Paris en 1789,* 110–17. Katherine Amory noted in her 1776 diary that they "are very delightful with rows of trees on each side. It was fill'd with the best Company in the Coaches." Katherine Amory diary, 22 Apr. 1776, in *The Journal of Mrs. John Amory, 1775–1777* (Boston: n.p., 1923), 28.

38. Clarke to Anna Clarke, 28 Aug. 1839, Clarke Papers.

39. Putnam, *Tourist in Europe,* 185. The Champs-Élysées, which he also gushed over, was too broad to be considered a street.

40. Mrs. Amory found the Tuileries gardens "finely laid out and ornamented with noble statues, some of them of a prodigious size." Amory diary, 17 Apr. 1776, in *Amory Journal,* 27.

41. Appleton, *Life and Letters of Thomas Gold Appleton,* ed. Susan Hale (New York: Appleton, 1885), 124.

42. Clarke to Anna Clarke, 28 Aug. 1839, Clarke Papers.

43. Francis Parkman diary, 1 May 1844, Francis Parkman Papers II, vol. 6B, MHS.

44. Thomas Cole diary, 4 May 1831, in Thomas Cole, "Sketchbooks," Detroit Institute of Art, AAA microfilm D39.

45. John Sanderson, *Sketches of Paris, or The American in Paris* (Philadelphia: Carey and Hart, 1838), 1:193.

46. John Vanderlyn to Peter Vanderlyn, n.d. [1796], John Vanderlyn Papers, State Historical Site, Kingston, N.Y. AAA microfilm 1040.

47. Lucy Bakewell Audubon to Fanny Anderson, 11 June 1831, James Audubon Papers, J. P. Morgan Library, New York, N.Y., AAA microfilm N68–12.

48. Frazee, *Medical Student,* 127–29.

49. Andrew McClellan, *Inventing the Louvre: Art, Politics and the Origins of the Modern Museum in Eighteenth-Century Paris* (Cambridge: Cambridge University Press, 1994), 3–48; Katherine Amory diary, 24 Apr. 1776, in *Amory Journal,* 28.

50. In her 1776 diary, Katherine Amory, who had no special knowledge of art, mentions its "many fine paintings," especially the Rubens series. Katherine Amory diary, 24 Apr. 1776, in *Amory Journal,* 28.

51. It had remained the seat of the Royal Academy of Painting and Sculpture, but the only display there was a collection of models of France's fortified towns, used for military planning and therefore off-limits for foreigners.

52. McClellan, *Inventing*, 95.

53. John Vanderlyn to Peter Vanderlyn, n.d. [1796], Vanderlyn Papers.

54. The museum was still regarded as primarily a teaching institution. It was open to the public three days out of ten, he noted, with the other days reserved for artists copying the works. John Vanderlyn to Peter Vanderlyn, 10 Mar. 1798, Vanderlyn Papers.

55. McClellan, *Inventing*, 198.

56. *Galignani's New Paris Guide* (Paris: Galignani, 1848), 196. While this too was a principle which museums would follow down to today, the way they were hung—in tiers of three or even four, covering practically every inch of wall space, persisted for only about three-quarters of a century.

57. Beecher, *Star Papers*, 72–73.

58. Sanderson, *Sketches of Paris*, 1:111.

59. Eighty-seven percent of the paintings in New York's Metropolitan Museum by American artists born before 1780 are portraits. Harold E. Dickson, *Arts of the Young Republic: The Age of William Dunlap* (Chapel Hill: University of North Carolina Press, 1968), 41.

60. Appleton, *Life and Letters*, 132.

61. Sumner to George Hillard, 13 Jan. 1838, *SL*, 234.

62. Joan Rubin, *The Making of Middlebrow Culture* (Chapel Hill: University of North Caroline Press, 1992), 1–5; Harris, *Artist*, 43–45.

63. Vernon Snow, ed., "The Grand Tour Diary of Robert C. Johnson, 1792–1793," *Proceedings of the American Philosophical Society* 102 (1958): 85–86.

64. *The Diary of Philip Hone*, ed. Allan Nevins (New York: Dodd, Mead, 1927), 1:93.

65. Tuckerman, ed., *The Diary of Philip Hone*, 1:222.

66. Dickson, *Arts in the Young Republic*, 47; Harris, *Artist*, 98–99; Jaher, *Urban Establishment*, 235–36.

67. Nancy Cott, *The Bonds of Womanhood: "Women's Sphere" in New England, 1780–1835* (New Haven: Yale University Press, 1979), 63–100.

68. The paintings in the Luxembourg Palace were inferior to those in the Louvre, she wrote, because they were "works of artists of the French School, which are not thought by connoisseurs to be equal to those of Italy." *An American Lady in Paris, 1828–1829: The Diary of Mrs. John Mayo*, ed. Mary Mayo Crenshaw (Boston: Houghton Mifflin, 1927), 65–66.

69. Sometimes, when galleries refused to do so, the works were defaced. Harris, *Artist*, 132–33.

70. Willard, *Journal and Letters*, 62.

71. Cooper, *Gleanings: France*, 217–18.

72. Caroline Kirkland, *Holidays Abroad; or Europe from the West* (New York: Baker and Scribner, 1849), 123.

73. Willard, *Journal and Letters*, 211–12.

74. John Griscom, *A Year in Europe* (New York: 1823), 1:251, cited in Harris, *Artist*, 133.

75. Willard to Mr. A. H. Lincoln, 18 Dec. 1830, in Willard, *Journals and Letters*, 134–36. Caroline Cushing simply avoided the problem of assessing all this material. In her otherwise highly opinionated travel memoir of the 1820s, she gave a detailed description of the building, but said nothing of the individual paintings. Cushing, *Letters*, 28–29.

76. The Philadelphian John Sanderson wrote of taking a "modest Yankee" ("please excuse the tautology," he added) there who took one look at a naked Venus getting out of her bath and said, "let us go out, I don't think this is a decent place." But Sanderson used this probably exaggerated tale to make himself look like a a sophisticate, and later says this kind of provincial prudery is not seen among men from south of New England. Sanderson, *Sketches of Paris*, 1:71–72.

77. Sumner diary, 13 Feb. 1838, *SL*, 250.

78. William W. Stowe, *Going Abroad: European Travel in Nineteenth-Century American Culture* (Princeton: Princeton University Press, 1994), 82. He said there were "certainly some first rate pictures. Leonardo da Vinci has more pictures here than in any other gallery and I like them well despite the identity of the features which peep out of men and women. I have seen the same face in his pictures I think six or seven times. Murillo I see almost for the first time with great pleasure." *EJ*, 4:197.

79. Appleton, *Life and Letters*, 130–33.

80. Elinor M. Tilton, *Amiable Autocrat: A Biography of Oliver Wendell Holmes* (New York: Schuman, 1947), 91–92.

81. Frazee, *Medical Student*, 52.

82. Amos Lawrence diary, 10 Dec. 1839, in Amos. A. Lawrence Diaries, box 1, MHS. Lawrence's love of art was apparent in Italy, which he visited before France. His diary from there is full of references to his love for Poussin and Derlain, as well as the Rennaissance masters, especially Titian, Veronese, and Tintoretto. Much of his time in Rome was spent shopping for paintings, two of which he finally bought. Ibid., 3 Mar.–3 Apr. 1839.

83. Sumner to Hillard, 13 Jan. 1838, *SL*, 234.

84. Tilton, *Amiable Autocrat*, 91–92, 114.

85. When King Louis-Philippe was overthrown in 1848 and the furnishings of the Tuileries palace were auctioned off, Colles was the successful bidder for an immense, monogrammed dinner service from the royal manufactory at Sèvres and an antique gilded clock. *Life and Letters of James Colles*, ed. Emily Johnston De Forest (New York: n.p., 1926), 128–30, 192–93, 207–8.

86. Putnam, *Tourist in Europe*, 184.

87. Sanderson, *Sketches of Paris*, 1:193, 200.

88. George W. Curtis, *The Potiphar Papers* (New York: Putnam, 1853), 18.

89. "In the Luxembourg," he added, "I was again disappointed in not finding the pictures of the Old Masters on walls, but in their place those same wretched French productions." Thomas Cole diary, 4 May 1821, in Thomas Cole Sketchbooks, Detroit Institute of Art, AAA Microfilm D39.

CHAPTER SIX

1. Rev. Andrews Norton to Sumner, 6 Nov. 1837, *SL,* 201.

2. Peter Irving to Richard Dodge, 7 Jan. 1807, in "Peter Irving's Journals," *NY Public Library Bulletin* 44 (1940): 5.

3. Irving to William Irving, Jr., 22 July 1804, in *Letters/Washington Irving,* ed. Ralph M. Aderman et al. (Boston: Twayne, 1978), 1:39.

4. Irving to Peter Irving, 5 Sept. 1804, ibid., 1:73.

5. Gay Wilson Allen, *Waldo Emerson: A Biography* (New York: Viking, 1981), 209.

6. George W. Curtis, *The Potiphar Papers* (New York: Putnam, 1854), 224.

7. James Fenimore Cooper, *Gleanings in Europe: France* (Albany: State University of New York Press, 1983), 183.

8. William Lee diary, 18 Feb. 1796, in *A Yankee Jeffersonian: Selections from the Diary and Letters of William Lee of Massachusetts,* ed. Mary Lee Mann (Cambridge: Belknap Press, 1958), 13.

9. Washington Irving to [?] Beebee, 22 July 1804, in *Letters/Washington Irving,* ed. Ralph M. Aderman et al. (Boston: Twayne, 1978), 1:77–78.

10. John Sanderson, *Sketches of Paris, or The American in Paris* (Philadelphia: Carey and Hart, 1838), 1:29.

11. John Vanderlyn to Peter Vanderlyn, n.d. [1796], John Vanderlyn Papers, Senate House State Historical Site, Kingston, N.Y., AAA microfilm roll 1040.

12. Topliff to Mr. Dorr and Family, 30 Mar. 1829, in Samuel Topliff, *Topliff's Travels: Letters from Abroad in the Years 1828 and 1829,* ed. Edith Stanwood Bolton (Boston: Boston Athenaeum, 1906), 194–96.

13. Washington Irving to [?] Beebee, 22 July 1804, in *Letters/Washington Irving,* 1:77–78.

14. "Do not speak of this in America," she added. Fuller to Caroline Sturgis, 28 Nov. 1846, in *The Letters of Margaret Fuller,* ed. Robert N. Hudspeth (Ithaca: Cornell University Press, 1983–), 4:251–52.

15. Dickens replied that if his own son were that chaste "he would be alarmed on his account, as if he could not be in good health." *EJ,* n.d. [1848], 10:333.

16. Gay Wilson Allen, *Waldo Emerson: A Biography* (New York: Viking, 1981), 209; *EJ,* n.d. [1848], 10:330.

17. Emma Willard, *Journals and Letters from France and Britain* (Troy, N.Y.: Tuttle, 1833), 233; Lois Banner, *American Beauty* (Chicago: University of Chicago Press, 1983), 44–65.

18. William Raser, "Notes on Paris," 1817–18, William Raser Papers, NYPL.

19. Willard, *Journals,* 233–34.

20. After telling his brother that French women could "set fire to the head and set fire to the tail," Washington Irving added, "but as to the *heart* I must be a little better acquainted with the language . . . before I will suffer *that* to be affected." However, in fact his letters indicate that the French women were too occupied with the intricate intrigues of their own society to bother with transient American men. Washington Irving to William Irving, Jr., 22 July 1804, in *Letters/Washington Irving,* 1:39.

21. Albert Babeau, *Paris en 1789* (Paris: Firmin-Didot, n.d. [c. 1900]), 90.

22. Jill Harsin devotes much of her book to trying to explain the subtleties of prostitution's legal status in France. Selling one's sexual favors itself was never illegal, but

it was deemed an offense against a number of laws, going back to the seventeenth and eighteenth centuries. Neither, on the other hand, was it ever legal. It was just "tolerated." Jill Harsin, *Policing Prostitution in Nineteenth-Century Paris* (Princeton: Princeton University Press, 1985), 56–94. The result was the creation of a number of terms to describe the various kinds of prostitutes and institutions which, the translator of Alain Corbin's *Les Filles de noce: Misère sexuelle et prostitution aux 19e et 20e siècles* (Paris: Aubier Montaigne, 1978) correctly points out, cannot be translated into English. Alan Sheridan, introduction to Alain Corbin, *Women for Hire: Prostitution and Sexuality in France after 1850,* trans. Alan Sheridan (Cambridge: Harvard University Press, 1990), xviii.

23. These were mainly on the rues Vivienne and Richelieu. France, Ministère de l'Intérieur, Police Générale [MI-PG], "Étrangers de passage à Paris, An X-1814, et 1819" AN F/7/2236, F/7/2237.

24. Stephen Longstreet, *We All Went to Paris: Americans in the City of Light, 1776–1971* (New York: Macmillan, 1972), 82.

25. Laure Adler, *La Vie quotidienne dans les maisons closes, 1830–1930* (Paris: Hachette, 1990), 161; Harsin, *Policing,* 70–71; Topliff to Mr. Dorr and Family, 29 Mar. 1829, in Topliff, *Topliff's Travels,* 199.

26. Augustus K. Gardener, *Old Wine in New Bottles* (New York: Francis, 1848), 110–12.

27. John L. Gardner diary, 20 Oct. 1823, Gardner Family Papers II, MHS.

28. Paper in "Visit to Europe, J.L.G 1823" volume, ibid.

29. Adler, *La Vie quotidienne,* 10–11; Paul Gerbod, "Les Touristes étrangers à Paris dans la première moitié du xixe siècle," *Bulletin de la Société de l'Histoire de Paris et de l'Île de France,* 1983, 249.

30. Florentine made a previous entry in his diary during his earlier stay. She wrote *"Je vous aime toujours, et vous ne m'aimez plus"* but he scratched it out, apparently after they were reconciled and he began giving her money again. Maude H. Elliot, *Uncle Sam Ward and His Circle* (New York: Macmillan, 1938), 69–70, 79–80.

31. Edwin Hoyt, *The Improper Bostonian: Dr. Oliver Wendell Holmes* (New York: Morrow, 1979), 290; *Life and Letters of Thomas Gold Appleton,* ed. Susan Hale (New York: Appleton, 1885), 125; Elinore M. Tilton, *Amiable Autocrat: A Biography of Dr. Oliver Wendell Holmes* (New York: Henry Schuman, 1947), 92.

32. Amos Lawrence diary, 14 Dec. 1839, Amos Adams Lawrence Diaries, box 1, MHS.

33. Ibid., 21 Dec. 1839.

34. Ibid., 27 Dec. 1839; Harsin, *Policing Prostitution,* 47. One of the et ceteras may well have been oral sex. Later in the century, when the practice became popular in New York City bawdy houses, it was called "the French treatment" or "French Love" and was said to have been imported from France. Timothy J. Gilfoyle, *City of Eros: New York City, Prostitution, and the Commercialization of Sex, 1790–1920* (New York: Norton, 1992), 177.

35. One result of their higher status was that they were able to avoid compulsory ᵣ ᵉdical inspection, thereby exposing their higher-class patrons to more danger than thcᵣe who patronized the *maisons de tolerance.* Adler, *La Vie quotidienne,* 23–35.

36. Amos Lawrence diary, 19 Dec. 1839.

37. Gerbod, "Les Touristes étrangers," 249–50.

38. George W. Curtis, *The Potiphar Papers* (New York: Putnam, 1853), 229.

39. By 1870, well over half of Paris's working women, fully sixty thousand of them, earned derisory incomes from needlework. Otto Friedrich, *Olympia: Paris in the Age of Manet* (New York: Simon and Schuster, 1992), 222.

40. Sanderson, *Sketches of Paris*, 1:142.

41. Theodore B. Witmer, *Wild Oats Sown Abroad* (Philadephia: Peterson, 1853), 66.

42. George S. Emerson diary, 9 Jan. 1848, in George B. Emerson Papers, box 14, MHS.

43. Wideawake [pseud.], *Paris after Dark* (Paris: Pache, 1868), 22.

44. Ibid., 34–37.

45. J. C. D. Clark, *English Society, 1688–1832* (Cambridge: Cambridge University Press, 1985), 95–100.

46. Notes in John L. Gardner diary, 15–19 Oct. 1823, in "Visit to Europe, J.L.G 1823" volume, Gardner Family Papers II, MHS.

47. France, MI-PG, "États Journaliers, Paris," 1816–1817, 1832, F/7/9898/B-C, F/7/12180.

48. Sumner diary, 31 Dec. 1837, *SL*, 225.

49. Curtis, *Potiphar Papers*, 229.

50. Clarke to Anna Clarke, 22, 28 Aug. 1849, Clarke Papers.

51. Alfred Devau, *Les Plaisirs de Paris* (1867; reprint, Paris: Seesam, 1991), 154. By the 1880s it was so well known in America that a famous New York City concert saloon, where performers and waitresses doubled as prostitutes, called itself the Bal Mabille. Gilfoyle, *City of Eros*, 228–29.

52. George Putnam, *The Tourist in Europe* (New York: Wiley and Putnam, 1837), 190.

53. The latter, he noted approvingly, had "more good nature, more cheerfulness, and greater equanimity of temper," and unlike the French, did not "kindle in a moment, and burst out in such uncontrollable transports of passion." William Berrian, *Travels in France and Italy in 1817 and 1818* (New York: Swords, 1821), 369.

54. Gilfoyle, *City of Eros*, 17–18.

55. Henry McLellan, *Journal of a Residence in Scotland and Tour through England, France, Germany, Switzerland and Italy*, ed. I. McLellan, Jr. (Boston: Allen and Ticknor 1834), 239.

56. Henry B. Humphrey diary, 13 Sept. 1839, Henry B. Humphrey Diaries, MHS.

57. Abigail De Hart Mayo, *An American Lady in Paris, 1828–1829: The Diary of Mrs. John Mayo*, ed. Mary Mayo Crenshaw (Boston: Houghton Mifflin, 1927), 52.

58. Alpheus Hardy diary, 13 Dec. 1845, Alpheus Hardy Diaries, MHS.

59. George S. Emerson diary, 24 June 1847.

60. Ibid., 5 Jan. 1848.

61. Ibid., 27 Jan. 1847.

62. Ibid., 29 Jan. 1847.

63. In Italy, he had become convinced that he had made a mistake in leaving France, which he loved, particularly since he felt on the verge of mastering the language. In his diary from Italy, which he abandoned before he returned, he complains

of dark moods that he cannot overcome. After returning to Boston he continued to despair over finding a calling in life (he had already flirted with the ministry and law). On occasion, he seemed to pull out of his depression but finally succumbed to it. Ironically, his father took some satisfaction in the fact that he died a virgin. George S. Emerson diary, vols. 1 and 2; correspondence in George B. Emerson Papers, box 5, MHS.

64. Amos Lawrence diary, 12 Dec. 1839.

65. Jean-Paul Aron, *Le Mangeur du XIXe siecle* (Paris: Robert Laffont, 1973), 13–55.

66. In 1829, Philip Hone mourned the death of "Simon, the celebrated cook, . . . a respectable colored man, who has for many years been the most fashionable cook in New York." *The Diary of Philip Hone,* ed. Allan Nevins (New York: Dodd, Mead, 1927), 1:11.

67. See Harvey Levenstein, "Two Hundred Years of French Food in America," *Journal of Gastronomy* 5 (spring 1969): 67–69. It was three years before the patrician Philip Hone, who heard that "it was on the Parisian plan and very good," got around to trying it. "It satisfied our curiosity but not our appetites," he wrote in his diary. Nevins, ed., *Diary of Philip Hone,* 1:33.

68. William Raser diary, n.d. [1817], William Raser Papers, NYPL.

69. Topliff to Dorr and Family, 30 Mar. 1829, in Topliff, *Topliff's Travels,* 200–201.

70. Mayo, *American Lady in Paris,* 16–17.

71. Francis Parkman diary, [1834], 238–39, Parkman Papers, Series III, MHS.

72. Hoyt, *Improper Bostonian,* 50; Aron, *Le Mangeur,* 64–65.

73. Hale, ed., *Life and Letters of Appleton,* 125–33.

74. *The Diary of Philip Hone,* ed. Bayard Tuckerman (New York: Dodd, Mead, 1889), 1:261.

75. As if to show that he had not succumbed only to refined food, he also praised French economy in food. "Nothing is wasted here, while in New York enough is thrown away to feed a hundred thousand Parisians. Many of their most delicate . . . dishes are made of things we reject as garbage." He was particular impressed by the delicacy and variety of their soups. He arrived with a typically American fear of camouflaged meat. "Now," he said, "I eat whatever is set before me, taking care to smother all that *looks* like a horse steak, cat stew, or rat pie in tomatoes." Thurlow Weed, Letters, 23 Sept. 1843, in Thurlow Weed, *Letters from Europe and the West Indies* (Albany: Weed, Parsons: 1866), 288–89; ibid., 14 Jan. 1852, 459–60.

76. Curtis, *Potiphar Papers,* 38.

77. Anne Catherine Jones diary, 16 June 1851, UNC-CHL. She seems to have been exposed to American imitations during summer vacations in mountain resorts in New England.

78. Henry [?] to John Lowell, 2 Apr. 1850, George B. Emerson Papers, box 7, MHS.

79. Aron, *Le Mangeur,* 59–60.

80. Ibid., 78–90.

CHAPTER SEVEN

1. Harriet Beecher Stowe, *Sunny Memories of Foreign Lands* (Boston: Phillips, Sampson & Co., 1854), 2:410–18.

2. The narrator, an equally ignorant woman, continues, "Wasn't it affable in such a great monarch towards a mere republican? I wonder how people can slander him so, and tell such stories about him." George W. Curtis, *The Potiphar Papers* (New York: Putnam, 1853), 233.

3. The occasion was her publication, in 1869, of a defense of Lady Byron, the poet Lord Byron's wife, whom she had befriended in 1857, against the dead poet's mistress's charge that he had been driven to infidelity by his frigid wife. Stowe's article saying that Lady Byron had confided in her, before her death, that it was his incestuous affair with his half-sister that had ruined the marriage, sparked outraged protests that she was being taken in by Lady Byron, who exploited her well-known weakness for aristocratic connections. By then, Stowe had a reputation as a major-league name-dropper. Edwin Hoyt, *The Improper Bostonian: Dr. Oliver Wendell Holmes* (New York: Morrow, 1979), 227–28.

4. David Van Zanten, *Building Paris: Architectural Institutions and the Transformation of the French Capital, 1830–1870* (Cambridge: Cambridge University Press, 1994), 6–73; Donald J. Olsen, *The City as a Work of Art* (New Haven and London: Yale University Press, 1986), 142–45.

5. Van Zanten, *Building Paris,* 6–45, 198–255; Witold Rybczynski, *City Life: Urban Expectations in a New World* (New York: Harper Collins, 1995), 149–51; Otto Friedrich, *Olympia: Paris in the Age of Manet* (New York: Simon and Schuster, 1992), 130–43.

6. This system was more successful in the western part of the city than in the northern quarter or on Left Bank, something that was fortunate for the erstwhile Emperor, for it was in the west of the city that he had secretly speculated in land. Olsen, *City,* 144–45.

7. John Munn diary, 22 Dec. 1866, John Munn Volumes, vol. 32, CHS.

8. Olsen, *City,* 145.

9. Andrew Longacre to James Longacre, 14 Feb. 1861, Longacre Family Papers, AAA microfilm 1046.

10. Eliza Endicott Peabody Gardner diary, 5 June 1859, Gardner Family Papers II, MHS.

11. Munn diary, 22 Nov. 1866.

12. W. Pembroke Fetridge, *Harper's Hand-book for Travellers in Europe and the East* (New York: Harper's, 1867), 97.

13. Mark Twain, *The Innocents Abroad,* in *The Complete Travel Books of Mark Twain: The Early Works,* ed. Charles Neider (Garden City: Doubleday, 1966), 88.

14. Grace Greenwood [Sara Lippincott], *Stories and Sights of France and Italy* (1867; New York: Alden, 1886), 26–27.

15. In fact, this continued a process that had begun some years earlier, when some Americans who admired the architectural and artistic achievements of France under Louis XIV and Napoleon lamented the inability of their seemingly anti-aesthetic countrymen to produce or appreciate such works. Neil Harris, *The Artist in American Society* (New York: George Braziller, 149–51).

16. Annie Fields to Sarah [?], 12 Oct. 1859, Annie Adams Fields Papers, MHS.

17. Brawley, *Journal,* 59.

18. Ibid., 66.

19. Greenwood, *Stories and Sights,* 76–77, 88–89.

20. Brawley, *Journal,* 54.

21. *CE,* 1 Feb. 1867, 3.

22. Friedrich, *Olympia,* 140–45.

23. Elizabeth Butt White, *American Opinion of France* (New York: Knopf, 1927), 173.

24. "Think of it," he wrote. "Rome has more majesty, Trèves has more antiquity, Venice is more beautiful, Naples has more grace, London has more wealth. What then has Paris? The Revolution. Paris is the pivot around which, on a given day, history turned." The guidebook section was also not your typical one. It pointed out where heretics and books had been burned, monks were attacked, mobs were dispersed, great minds were born and great works were performed. "Oh France," he concluded, "You will be Humanity. . . . In the same way as Athens became Greece and Rome became Christianity, you, France, are becoming the world." Victor Hugo, introduction to *Paris-Guide, 1867,* reprinted as Victor Hugo, *Paris, Paris* (Paris: n.p., 1895), 13–43.

25. *PH,* Aug. 28, 1937.

26. *CE,* 1 Feb. 1867, 5.

27. New York *Daily Tribune,* 14 June 1867; Adolph Joanne, *Le Guide Parisien* (Paris: Hachette, 1863), 15–17; Paul Gerbod, *Voyages au pays des mangeurs de grenouilles: La France vue par les Britanniques du XVIIe siècle à nos jours* (Paris: Albin Michel, 1991), 112.

28. *Paris-Promeneur, Paris-Touriste* (Paris, 1863), 4.

29. Mary Babcock diary, 21 Feb. 1866, in Emily W. Alward Papers, CUL.

30. Ibid., 1866.

31. Munn diary, 28, 30 Nov. 1866.

32. Twain, *Innocents Abroad,* 100.

33. *Galignani's New Paris Guide for 1855* (Paris: Galignani, 1855), iii.

34. Rybczynski, *City Life,* 149–51.

CHAPTER EIGHT

1. Mrs. A. T. J. Bullard, *Sights and Scenes in Europe: A Series of Letters* (St. Louis: Chambers & Knapp, 1852), 23–27, 32. Harvard University instructors were paid an average of about $2,000 in 1850, when one could live "very nicely" in a "comfortable" house with two servants on $1,500. Ronald Story, *The Forging of an Aristocracy* (Middletown: Wesleyan University Press, 1980), 83. The famed Brooklyn preacher Henry Ward Beecher was paid $3,500 a year. James Clarke, *Eleven Weeks in Europe; and What May Be See in That Time* (Boston: Ticknor, Reed, and Fields, 1852), x.

2. In 1851, after the *Arctic* completed a voyage with a particularly distinguished passenger list, the Americans among them decided to counter criticism of the government subsidies by issuing a statement praising the ship's comfort, speed, and safety. John O. Choules, *Young Americans Abroad* (Boston: Gould and Lincoln, 1852), 28.

3. John H. Gould, "Ocean Passenger Travel," *Scribner's* 9 (Apr. 1891): 406–7; John Malcolm Brinnin, *The Sway of the Grand Saloon* (New York: Delacorte, 1971), 117–93.

4. There was also a Canadian line, leaving from Montreal, that offered the advantage, later exploited by the famed Canadian Pacific liners, of spending the first seven hundred

miles of the voyage in the sheltered Saint Lawrence River and Gulf of Saint Lawrence. Six other lines also competed in American ports, including two well-regarded German ones, which stopped at Southampton on their way to Bremen and Hamburg. Gould, "Ocean Passenger Travel," 407; New York *Daily Tribune*, 14 June 1867.

5. Paul Gerbod, *Le Tourisme français en Europe* (Aix-en-Provence: Centre des Hautes Études Touristiques, 1993), 22.

6. Paul Gerbod, *Voyages au pays des mangeurs de grenouilles: La France vue par les Britanniques du XVIIIe siècle à nos jours* (Paris: Albin Michel, 1991), 111–12; Mary Blume, *Côte d'Azur: Inventing the French Riviera* (London: Thames and Hudson, 1992), 37.

7. Annie Fields diary, 30 Oct. 1859, Annie Adams Fields Papers, MHS. In 1827, it took three and a half days of nonstop travel by diligence. Journal of Isaac Carow, 4, 9 Apr. 1827, in *American Backlogs: The Story of Gertrude Tyler and Her Family*, ed. Edith Kermit Roosevelt and Kermit Roosevelt (New York: Scribner's, 1928), 219.

8. *Paris-Promeneur, Paris-Touriste* (Paris, 1863), 3.

9. "Going Abroad," *Putnam's Magazine*, n.s. 1 (1868): 530–31, quoted in William Stowe, *Going Abroad: European Travel in Nineteenth-Century American Culture* (Princeton: Princeton University Press, 1994), 8.

10. Henry Ward Beecher, *Star Papers: Experiences of Art and Nature* (New York: Derby, 1857), 9–91.

11. Adolph Joanne, *Le Guide Parisien* (Paris: Hachette, 1863), 39–41; *Paris-Promeneur*, 5.

12. Couriers still specialized in negotiating one through customs and smoothing the way for intercity travel. Katherine Bigelow Lawrence diary, 20 July 1850, Lamb Family Papers, MHS.

13. Mark Twain, *The Innocents Abroad*, in *The Complete Travel Books of Mark Twain: The Early Works*, ed. Charles Neider (Garden City: Doubleday, 1966), 80–85.

14. Ibid., 85; Piers Brendon, *Thomas Cook* (London: Seeker and Warburg: 1991), 247.

15. *CE*, 1 Feb. 1867, 3; Brendon, *Cook*, 74–78.

16. *CE*, 6 Aug. 1863.

17. Some of the fifty ladies and gentlemen who accompanied the elder Cook were disappointed by their accommodations in what had been touted as a "palace" in Rome. This, said the philosophical Cook, "gave rise to manifestations of discomfort which marred to some extent the remainder of the trip. They are not all happy that live in palaces." *CE*, Feb. 1, 1867, 3, 5–7.

18. *CE*, 1 Feb. 1867, 3, 5–7. As they would for the rest of the century, Cook's took pains to make their dollar-wise American clientele feel superior to their more profligate countrymen. "The ambitious Americans who crowd the Grand Hotel and the [Grand Hôtel du] Louvre are injuring others by the profuseness with which they sport their money in Paris," he wrote. "As a rule, they are the most lavish on extraordinary occasions, and the Parisian hotel-keepers know them too well not to take advantage of their liberality." Ibid., 15 Mar. 1867, 7.

19. *CE*, 1 Feb. 1867, 5–7; Brendon, *Cook*, 74–78.

20. John Choules, *The Cruise of the Steam Yacht North Star* (Boston: Gould and Lincoln, 1854), 18.

21. Ibid., 25–26.

22. Ibid., 26–29.

23. Ibid., 19.

24. Ibid., 169.

25. He could not have gone for his mail, for he had done that late the previous day, when he first arrived, and mail from America only arrived about once a week.

26. George Hillard diary, 25–28 Apr. and 5, 8 May 1848, George Hillard Journals, MHS.

27. Even so, it was money, rather than class, that was the major barrier to meeting other Americans. They were reputable enough to be greeted by the ambassador and invited to an embassy ball, but could not attend because they did not have the proper dress. Bayard Taylor, *Views A-Foot, or Europe Seen with Knapsack and Staff,* rev. ed. (New York: Putnam's, 1884), 380.

28. A raft of British "families abroad" novels and stories featured mendacious social-climbing mothers traveling to the Continent to try to foist off their daughters on their unsuspecting betters. James Buzard, *The Beaten Track: European Tourism Literature and the Ways of Culture* (Oxford: Oxford University Press, 1992), 142–44.

29. "Going Abroad," *Putnam's Magazine,* n. s. I (1868): 530–38, cited in Stowe, *Going Abroad,* 6–7.

30. Warren Susman, "Pilgrimage to Paris: Backgrounds of American Expatriation, 1920–1934" (Ph.D. diss., University of Wisconsin, 1957), 59.

31. Mrs. A. T. J. Bullard, *Sights and Scenes in Europe: A Series of Letters* (St. Louis: Chambers & Knapp, 1852), 214.

32. Elizabeth Eppes diary, 1854–1855, VaHS.

33. Ibid.; Ann Gordon diary, 22 July, 21 Aug., and 20 Sept. 1857, VaHS.

34. Eliza Gardner diary, 5 June 1859, Gardner Family Papers II, MHS.

35. John C. Jay, Jr., diary, 18 Nov.–14 Dec. 1867, NYPL.

36. Amos A. Lawrence diary, 17, 25–28 June 1870, Amos A. Lawrence Diaries, box 1, MHS. When tourists and expatriates did meet in public places, they were usually off the beaten tourist track. Annie Fields had already spent almost two months socializing in Paris when she and her husband were invited to accompany an expatriate to the magnificent mass celebrated on 22 November, the saint's day of Saint Cecilia, patron saint of musicians, with a huge orchestra and chorus at the church of Saint-Eustache. Just as she seated herself, prepared to be swept away by Mozart's glorious music, "American friends surrounded us, cutting off with their chatty ways the little hopes we might have cherished of an hour's reflexion in the consecrated place." Annie Fields diary, 23 Nov. 1859.

37. John Doyle diary, 15 Mar. 1840, Doyle Family Papers, VaHS.

38. "Sister Lissie" [Elizabeth Lowell] to John Lowell, 1 Apr. 1851, George B. Emerson Papers, box 7, MHS.

39. George S. Emerson diary, 7 Feb. 1848, George B. Emerson Papers, box 14, MHS.

40. Annie Fields diary, 3 Dec. 1859; Annie Fields to Sarah, 30 Nov. 1859, Fields Papers.

41. Annie Fields to Boylston, 22 Dec. 1859, Fields Papers.

42. Annie Fields to Sarah, 12 Oct. 1859, Fields Papers.

43. Ann Gordon diary, 20 Sept. 1857.

44. Mary Potter Babcock diary, 15 Jan. to 4 Apr 1865, Emily W. Alward Papers, CUL.

45. Eliza Gardner diary, 6, 15, 16 June 1859.

46. The former figure would also have included Southerners, at least for the first four months. U.S. Bureau of the Census, *Historical Statistics of the United States* (Washington, D.C., 1976), 1:402.

47. Older people and females were exempt from the draft and wealthy men could pay substitutes to take their places.

48. Mary Eliot Parkman to Edward Twisleton, 8 Sept. 1862, Dwight Family Papers, HL.

49. *The Journal of William H. Brawley, 1864–1865,* ed. Francis Brawley (Charlottesville: n.p., 1970), vi–vii, 261, 115.

50. *CE,* 1 Feb. 1867, 5. The novelist Jules Verne was one of the passengers on the voyage taking the first such group from New York to Brest. Léonce Paillard, *Sur les chemins de l'ocean: Paquebots, 1830–1972* (Paris: Hachhette, 1972), 99.

51. John D. Stahl, "Mark Twain's Images of Europe" (Ph.D. diss., University of Connecticut, 1982), 17.

52. U.S. Bureau of the Census, *Historical Statistics* (1976), 1:402.

53. An 1875 guidebook by William Hemstreet was entitled *The Economical Tourist: A Journalist Three Months Abroad for $430* (New York: S. W. Green, 1875).

54. New York *Daily Tribune,* 14 June 1867.

55. Harriet Hanford to Mother, 17 Oct. 1869, Harriet (Hanford) Kimball Papers, CHS.

56. Caroline Barrett White diary, 9 Sept. 1855, American Antiquarian Society (microfilm in: *American Women's Diaries: New England Women*).

57. John Munn diary, 13 Nov., 7 Dec. 1865, John Munn Volumes, CHS.

58. Katherine Bigelow Lawrence diary, 6 Dec. 1850, Lamb Family Papers, MHS.

59. Ibid., Nov.–Dec. 1865.

60. He, his wife, son and daughter moved into two rooms—males in one, females in another.

61. Munn diary, 11 Nov. 1866.

62. Lorenza Beribineau diary, 15–16 Oct. 1851, Francis Cabot Lowell II Papers, MHS.

CHAPTER NINE

1. James Fields, ms. poem dated 15 Nov. 1859, Annie Adams Fields Papers, MHS.

2. Eliza Gardner diary, 4 June 1859, Gardner Family Papers II, MHS.

3. Ibid., 5 June 1839. George's account books for the years just before his marriage in 1854, which have numerous entries for entertaining men friends at his club, provide a glimpse of the kind of sex-segregated social life men of his class led. George A. Gardner, Account Books, ibid.

4. Amos A. Lawrence diary, 18 Apr. 1870, in Amos Adams Lawrence Diaries and Account Books, box 1, MHS.

5. Despite the age difference, she did not outlive the energetic older man. Within ten years it was she who was dead. Ellen Twisleton to Lucy Emerson, 25 Sept. 1852,

George B. Emerson Papers, MHS; Mary Eliot Parkman to Edward Twisleton, various dates, Dec. 1862–Dec. 1863, Dwight Family Papers, HL.

6. When, in 1853, the parents of twenty-year-old Gertrude Tyler decided it was time for her to return to America from Paris, her older brother was sent over specifically to accompany her back. D. Tyler to Gertrude Tyler, 26 Dec. 1853, in Edith Kermit Roosevelt and Kermit Roosevelt eds., *American Backlogs: The Story of Gertrude Tyler and Her Family* (New York: Scribner's, 1928), 184. The title of Adele Trafton's book about her 1869 European tour, *American Girl Abroad*, implies that she traveled alone, but that was just for titillation. In fact she was with a married woman, probably an aunt. Adele Trafton, *An American Girl Abroad* (Boston: Lee and Shepard, 1872). Some ships had separate saloons and female cabin stewards for women, but these were used mainly by widows and other women heading for family reunions. Mary Potter Babcock diary, 14–27 Oct. 1866, CUL.

7. Males such as Mark Twain and Henry James writing about travel felt constrained to adopt a variety of literary stratagems to affirm their masculinity. William W. Stowe, *Going Abroad: European Travel in Nineteenth-Century American Culture* (Princeton: Princeton University Press, 1994), 55–73, 125–193.

8. Anne Catherine Jones diary, 23 June 1851, UNC-CHL.

9. Katherine Baetjer, "Extracts from the Paris Journal of John Taylor Johnston," *Apollo* 114 (Dec. 1981): 414.

10. Grace Greenwood [Sara Lippincott], *Stories and Sights of France and Italy* (Boston: Ticknor and Fields, 1867), 40.

11. John Doyle diary, 15 Mar. 1840, Doyle Family Papers, VaHS.

12. Eliza Gardner diary, 20 June 1859. Gardner also visited the Jewish cemetery, where she "wondered what was the significance of the baskets of stones and piles of cards placed on an altar" in the tomb of the actress Rachel. Ibid.

13. Katherine Bigelow Lowell Lawrence diary, 24 Nov. 1850, Lamb Family Papers, MHS.

14. Even the tomb of Abélard and Héloïse "was nothing extraordinary—only I thought they were resting more peacefully than they deserved." Jones diary, 23 June 1851.

15. Sumner to Judge Story, 14 May 1838, *SL*, 294.

16. Amos A. Lawrence had headed straight for it on his second day in Paris in 1839, but reported "No bodies there" in his diary. Amos Lawrence diary, 13 Dec. 1839, Amos Lawrence Diaries and Account Books, box 1, MHS.

17. Baetjer, "Extracts from Journal of Johnston," 413.

18. The poem was by Thomas Hood. Edwin Van Cise diary, n.d. [1870–71], Edwin Van Cise Papers, box 2, LC.

19. Jones diary, 16, 29 June 1851.

20. Joan Shelley Rubin, *The Making of Middlebrow Culture* (Chapel Hill: University of North Carolina Press, 1992), 4.

21. Clifford Edward Clark, Jr., *The American Family Home* (Chapel Hill: University of North Carolina Press, 1986), 67.

22. Mrs. A. T. J. Bullard, *Sights and Scenes in Europe: A Series of Letters from England, France, Germany, Switzerland and Italy* (St. Louis: Chambers and Knapp, 1852), 198–99.

23. Peter C. Marzio, *The Art Crusade: An Analysis of American Drawing Manuals* (Washington, D.C., 1976), cited in Lawrence W. Levine, *Highbrow/Lowbrow: The Emergence of Cultural Hierarchy in America* (Cambridge: Harvard University Press, 1988), 155.

24. Caroline M. Kirkland, *Holidays Abroad; or Europe from the West* (New York: Baker and Scribner, 1849), vi.

25. Ann Douglas, *The Feminization of American Culture* (New York: Doubleday, 1977), 1–13. She also says travel writing was popular among these women, and male authors of the same sensibility, as a way of making respectable what might otherwise be suspected to be a leisurely pursuit. Ibid., 137.

26. Bullard, *Sights and Scenes*, 198.

27. Ibid., 63.

28. Henry Ward Beecher, *Star Papers; or Experiences in Art and Nature* (New York: Derby, 1857), 57 (emphasis added).

29. Beecher would kiss his close friend Theodore Tilton, editor of the *Independent*, when they met and parted, and was not at all nonplused to be found sitting on his lap, reciting the Sermon from the Mount, one day when Tilton's wife walked in on them. Donald Yacovone, "Abolitionists and the 'Language of Fraternal Love,'" in *Meanings for Manhood: Constructions of Masculinity in Victorian America*, ed. Mark. C. Carnes and Clyde Griffen (Chicago: University of Chicago Press, 1990), 85–94. As if to confirm his heterosexuality, he later had an affair with Mrs. Tilton that scandalized the nation.

30. Harriet Beecher Stowe, *Sunny Memories of Foreign Lands* (Boston: Phillips, Sampson & Co., 1854), 2:156–57. Vernet was also his brother Henry Ward Beecher's favorite. Beecher, *Star Papers*, 68. That same year, Theodore Witmer's rather rakish memoir extolled this "I may not be a connoisseur but I know what I like" approach to the art of the Louvre and other great galleries. He advised ignoring the cant of guidebooks and guides and allowing one's own eye and emotions to be the guide. Theodore Witmer, *Wild Oats Sown Abroad* (Philadelphia: Peterson, 1853), 59–134.

31. Stowe, *Sunny Memories*, 2:149. (Stowe's brother Charles's journal alternates with Stowe's letters in this book, which was nevertheless published only under her name.) Harriet Beecher Stowe's biographer, Joan Hedrick, puts a somewhat different spin on Stowe's advocacy of sentimentality as a tool for appreciating art. She sees it as a reaction against the kind of cultural divide that was opening up between high culture and popular entertainment which would soon see highbrow critics relegate her works to the inferior realm of "melodrama." Joan D. Hedrick, *Harriet Beecher Stowe: A Life* (New York: Oxford University Press, 1994), 268–69.

32. Having seven children and two miscarriages in eleven years seems to have done much to cool the poor woman's ardor. Mary Kelley, *Private Woman, Public Stage* (New York: Oxford University Press, 1984), 250–84; Clark, *American Family Home*, 66–67.

33. Emma Willard, *Journal and Letters from France and Great Britain* (Troy, N.Y.: Tuttle, 1833), 137–38.

34. She called it the *Venus de Milon*. Stowe, *Sunny Memories*, 169. If anything, her preacher brother Henry Ward Beecher seems to have been more discomfited by nudity than she. "I am heartily tired of French nakedness," he wrote. "I am willing always to see the human form sculptured or painted when it seems to subserve a good pur-

pose. . . . But, so to paint women that . . . you admire beauty instead of following the sentiment . . . is too bad. I am sick of naked harems. . . ." Beecher, *Star Papers*, 69.

35. The older galleries were updated and a magnificent new wing was constructed. Part of it contained lavish royal apartments, and another part was devoted to more gallery space.

36. The parents of seventeen-year-old Gertrude Tyler, of Norwich, Connecticut, forced her through this kind of regimen when they shipped her to Paris in 1852, clearly attempting to make her more marketable in the marriage bazaar. She vowed she would not marry until she was at least twenty-five ("I want to enjoy myself first," she said) but dutifully submitted. The visual arts, however, are mentioned only once, in a reference to a quick trip to the Louvre taken shortly after her arrival. Gertrude Tyler to Mother, 24 Apr. 1852, in Roosevelt and Roosevelt, eds., *American Backlogs*, 139.

37. Clara Crowninshield diary, 3–11 Sept. 1836, in *The Diary of Clara Crowninshield: A European Tour with Longfellow, 1835–1836*, ed. Andrew Hilen (Seattle: University of Washington Press, 1956), 293–95.

38. Katherine Lawrence diary, 23–30 Nov. 1850.

39. Annie Fields diary, 15 Oct. 1859–2 Jan. 1860. Annie Fields to Boylston [?], 27 Nov. 1859; Fields to Mother, 26 Dec. 1859, Fields Papers.

40. Harriet Hanford to Mother [Celia Ann Hanford], 27 Mar. 1870, in Harriet Hanford Kimball Papers, CHS.

41. Eliza Gardner diary, 10, 18 June 1859.

42. Adele Grafton, *An American Girl Abroad* (New York: Lee and Shepard, 1872), 80; Hawthorne diary, 8 Jan. 1858, in Nathaniel Hawthorne, *The French and Italian Notebooks*, ed. Thomas Woodson (Columbus: Ohio State University Press, 1980), 15.

43. *The Diaries of Andrew White*, ed. Robert Morris Ogden (Ithaca: Cornell University Press, 1959), 15–36.

44. John C. Jay, Jr. diary, 8 Nov.–3 Dec. 1866, NYPL.

45. Nathaniel Hawthorne diary, 8, 10 Jan. 1858, in Hawthorne, *French and Italian Notebooks*, 15. A full day at the Louvre, it might be noted, was not quite the grind it is today. The museum was only open from 10 to 4, which means that the guards would have started clearing the place out at about 3:30. *Galignani's New Paris Guide for 1855* (Paris: Galignani, 1855), preface.

46. Mark Twain, *The Innocents Abroad*, in *The Complete Travel Books of Mark Twain: The Early Works*, ed. Charles Neider (Garden City: Doubleday, 1966), 93.

47. James Colles to James Ombrosi, Apr. [n.d.], 1843, in *James Colles, 1788–1883, Life and Letters*, ed. Emily Johnston De Forest (New York: n.p., 1926), 167–68; 206–8.

48. Annie Fields diary, 29 Nov. 1859.

49. Mary Eliot Parkman wanted to commission Jean-August Ingres to copy a painting in the Louvre that she wanted to give to her sister, but she had her brother-in-law actually try to make the deal with the great painter. Mary Eliot Parkman to Edward Twisleton, 26 Oct. 1862, Dwight Family Papers, HL.

50. Katherine Betjer, ed., "Extracts from the Paris Journal of John Taylor Johnston, First President of the Metropolitan Museum," *Apollo*, Dec. 1981, 410–16. Although he donated ten thousand dollars to the new Met in 1870 and remained president until

1889, his railroad went bankrupt in the aftermath of the Panic of 1873 and he was forced to auction off his collection, at a loss. Ibid., 411.

51. Even the serious poet Henry Wadsworth Longfellow was impressed. Crowninshield diary, 6 Sept. 1836, in *Crowninshield Diary*, 294.

52. George Putnam, *The Tourist in Europe* (New York: Wiley and Putnam, 1837), 200.

53. Annie Fields to Lissie [?], 20 Oct. 1859, Fields Papers.

54. "The immense variety of material, the treasures of art, the opulence, the ingenuity, the inexhaustible fertility of manufacture displayed" in the shops of London and Paris, he wrote, "is an evidence of civilization and refinement as high as even the Museums, Theatres, Picture Galleries and Parks. And then the Cheapness! Everybody can look—gratis." *The Journal of William H. Brawley*, ed. Francis Poe Brawley (Charlottesville: n.p., 1976), 50.

55. Ibid.

56. Crowninshield diary, 6 Sept. 1836, in *Crowninshield Diary*, 294.

57. In 1845, the Reverend Francis Parkman dutifully sent back a trunkful of fashionable fabrics, along with news that stripes were "in vogue" and "entirely plain silks are quite out of vogue." Francis Parkman to Mrs. Francis Parkman, 4 June 1845, Parkman Papers III, box 4, MHS.

58. Grafton, *American Girl Abroad*, 244–45.

59. Lorenza Stephens Berbineau diary, 13–15 Nov. 1851, Francis Cabot Lowell II Papers, MHS.

60. Amos Lawrence diary, 25 June 1870, in Amos Adams Lawrence Diaries and Account Books, box 1, MHS. A week earlier, when the goods were being ordered, his diary reads: "Appt. with dressmakers and milliners as usual." Ibid., 17 June 1870.

61. Catherine Jones diary, 29 June 1851.

62. Caroline White diary, 5 Sept. 1855.

63. John Munn diary, 11 Nov. 1866, John Munn Volumes, CHS.

64. W. Pembroke Fetridge, *Harper's Hand-Book for Travelers in Europe and the East* (New York: Fetridge, 1867), 150.

65. "The world goes there," the Reverend Parkman told his wife, "and are waited on by some hundred polite apprentices, female as well as male, and some speak English, much to my satisfaction." Francis Parkman to Mrs. Francis Parkman, 4 June 1845, Parkman Papers III, box 4.

66. Fields to Sarah, 12 Oct. 1859; Fields to Lissie, 20 Oct. 1859; Fields to Mother, 8 Nov. 1859, Fields Papers.

67. Fields to Mother and Louisa, 19 Sept. 1869, Fields Papers.

CHAPTER TEN

1. John H. Gould, "Ocean Passenger Travel," *Scribner's Magazine* 9 (Apr. 1891): 407–8; John Malcolm Brinnin, *The Sway of the Grand Saloon: A Social History of the North Atlantic* (New York: Delacorte, 1971), 242–43.

2. *America Abroad: A Handbook for the American Traveller* (London, 1895), 10.

3. In 1877, Thomas Cook and Sons complained that this made the number of sailings unresponsive to passenger demand. Although passenger demand had in-

creased in the past few years, depressed economies had meant less cargo and fewer sailings. *CE*, Nov. 1877, 3.

4. It carried 908 first-class passengers, 592 in second, and 1,772 in steerage. The eagle jutted out so far forward of the bow in order to make it world's longest passenger ship. Brinnin, *Sway*, 387.

5. Ibid., 389.

6. Alain Corbin, *L'Avènement des loisirs, 1850–1960* (Paris: Aubier, 1995), 68.

7. Undated clipping [1875], William Buehler diary, vol. 1, MHS.

8. Mary Cable, *Top Drawer* (New York: Atheneum, 1984), 115.

9. Brinnin, *Sway*, 377.

10. Corbin, *L'Avènement*, 77.

11. Mary Lawrence diary, 14, 19 Feb. 1901; "A resumé of the glorious year of 1901," ibid., 1902, 1–3, Marian Lawrence Peabody Papers, MHS.

12. Mary Lawrence Peabody diary, 15 Nov., 1 Dec. 1910, ibid.

13. One ship's manifest, in 1892, lists Mrs. August Belmont, wife of the fabulously wealthy banker, as traveling with both a maid and manservant. On the other hand, Mr. and Mrs. Isidore Straus, from a rival banking family, traveled with no servants at all. Passenger list, MS *Fulda*, Feb., 1892, in Laura J. Libbey diary [1892], vol. 1, p. 2, NYPL. On the *Titanic*, there was one servant, nurse, or governess for every family unit of four or five people registered in first class. Brinnin, *Sway*, 377.

14. Jacqueline Tozier, *The Travelers' Handbook: A Manual for Transatlantic Tourists*, rev. ed. (New York: Funk and Wagnalls, 1907), 27–28.

15. In 1885, Dana and Jennie Bense allowed their teenaged niece, Eva, to take her pet dog "Little Dainty" along on their European tour. When they ascended the Arc de Triomphe in Paris they left the dog with one of the arch's custodians and returned to find it had escaped. Three days later, after they had the police placard the city with lost dog notices, a woman showed up with the animal, much to the relief of the distraught Eva. Jennifer A. Bense diary, 20, 23 Nov. 1885, Bense Family Papers, NYPL.

16. *PH*, Oct. 4, 1887.

17. *PH*, 27 Jan. 1897.

18. Tozier, *Handbook*, 22–27; Women's Rest Tour Association, *A Summer in England with a Continental Supplement: A Handbook for the Use of American Women* (Boston: Ochs, 1900), 13.

19. These parties also provided excellent cover for thieves to board ships and scavenge among the valuables in the state rooms. So common did these robberies become that in 1890 that the Red Star line issued its tickets in an envelope with a large "CAUTION" on it, warning passengers not to leave valuables in their state rooms and to entrust their baggage only to "the company's servants." Alfred S. Roe diary [1890–94], 1, NYPL.

20. Amy Waters diary, 9 June 1907, NYPL; Polly [?] to Mary Lawrence, 13 Feb. 1901, in Mary Lawrence diary, 1900; Mary Lawrence diary, 13 Feb. 1901, Mary Lawrence Peabody diary, 19 Aug. 1910.

21. Women's Rest Tour Association, *Summer*, 12.

22. Amy Rosenthal diary, 25 May 1902, NYPL.

23. To Robert Louis Stevenson, who crossed in second class in 1879, the main advantage over steerage, from which it was separated by only a thin wall, was a dining room and crockery for the miserable food. Brinnin, *Sway,* 260–61.

24. *CE,* Mar. 1878, 13.

25. Passengers were allowed only a small handbag or two, to be hung on hooks, and one valise or twelve-inch-high "steamer trunk," to be slid under a bunk. Libbey diary, 1892; Waters diary, 9 June 1907.

26. U.S. Bureau of the Census, *Historical Statistics of the United States from Colonial Times to 1976* (Washington, D.C., 1976), 1:402; *PH,* 2 July 1892; "The Swelling Tide of Foreign Travel," *NYTM,* 6 May 1928, 6.

27. The Hamburg-America line tried leasing out the first-class dining room of the *Amerika* to a leading continental *restaurateur,* who charged à la carte prices. Tozier, *Handbook,* 27.

28. A. J. Burkhart and S. Medlik, *Tourism* (London: Heinemann, 1974), 14.

29. Marthe-Paul Adam, "Passagère!" *Femina,* 1 Feb. 1904, 103.

30. William Pembroke Fetridge, *Hand-books for Travellers in Europe and the East* (New York: Fetridge, 1887) 1:xxiv.

31. For example, they set a fare of $100 as the minimum for passage during the summer season of 1897. William F. Dix, "Foreign Travel," *Outlook,* 62 (3 June 1899): 296.

32. J. Perry Worden, "Touring in Europe on Next to Nothing," *Review of Reviews* 10 (Jan. 1894): 91; Tozier, *Handbook,* 28–29. The agreement included the American Line, the so-called French Line (the Compagnie Générale Transatlantique), the Holland-America Line, and the British White Star Line. Its main achievement was to develop a system whereby the tickets issued by any of the eight lines who were members of the Morgan "Combination" would be honored by the other. Ibid., 30–31.

33. Henry Seaver diary, postscript [1898], MHS.

34. In 1907, return passages on the Cunard or White Star Lines could be had for $75 for second class and $100 for first. *America Abroad,* 1907, 13.

35. *Roe* diary [1890], 1–5.

36. Gould, "Ocean Passenger Travel," 408.

37. They "generally manage to have a fairly good time," the *Times* reported. "They don't have any concerts, nor do they eat their dinner to music, but what they get in the line of food is substantial, and they have comfortable berths in which they can sleep as well as any saloon passenger." *NYT,* 2 Sept. 1910.

38. *America Abroad,* 1907, 12.

39. *Paris-Promeneur, Paris-Touriste* (Paris, 1863), 20.

40. Goujon, *Cent ans de tourisme en France* (Paris: Cherche Midi, 1989), 25–28; André Rauch, *Vacances en France de 1830 à nos jours* (Paris: Hachette, 1996), 15–20.

41. Alain Corbin, *The Lure of the Sea: The Discovery of the Seaside in the Western World, 1750–1840,* trans. Jocelyn Phelps (Oxford: Polity, 1994), 271–77.

42. *Paris-Promeneur,* 11, 20.

43. Paul Gerbod, *Voyages au pays des mangeurs de grenouilles: La France vue par les Britanniques du XVIIe siècle à nos jours* (Paris: Alben Michel, 1991), 89–90. The upper-class folks who considered themselves the real *hivérnants,* as opposed to the *nouveaux* who began to flood the place in the late 1880s, stayed for six months, perhaps because

one can never be sure when winter is over in England. Robert S. Rudney, "From Luxury to Popular Tourism: The Transformation of the Resort City of Nice" (Ph.D. diss., University of Michigan, 1979), 61.

44. Goujon, *Cent ans,* 32.

45. Mrs. Henry Field, *Home Sketches in France* (New York, 1875), 65.

46. Rudney, "From Luxury," 39, 65.

47. Mary Blume, *Côte d'Azur: Inventing the French Riviera* (London: Thames and Hudson, 1992), 37.

48. Société de Statistique de Paris, "Procès-verbal de la séance du 22 mai 1912," *Journal de la Société de Statistique de Paris,* June 1912, 265.

49. Annie Fields diary, 2 Jan. 1860, Annie Adams Fields Papers, MHS.

50. Miss Mercer, who spoke French, soon cottoned on to the ruse and forced the woman to give her back the seat. John Munn diary, 24 Oct. 1865, John Munn Volumes, CHS.

51. Henriette Greenebaum Frank diary, 24 Sept. 1908, Greenebaum Sisters Travel Journals, CHS. Part of the problem might have been her husband's demeanor. Some days later, she wrote, when they boarded on the train to Cherbourg, he "had some words with the other occupants" of the compartment, apparently over the placement of the luggage, "so we did not talk to them, which made our 6 hrs. trip very restful." Ibid., 30 Sept. 1908.

52. Grace Matthews [Ashmore] diary, 15 June 1901, NYPL.

53. Poultney Bigelow, "From London to Lourdes in a Steam Carriage," *The Independent* 52 (7 June 1900): 1368–73.

54. Cable, *Top Drawer,* 168.

55. *Express Guide to Paris and Environs* (Paris: Frédéric Maya, 1907), 139.

56. *Paris en Voiture, guide en trois langues* (Paris, 1904), 6.

57. Charles C. Crane, "An Automobile Trip through France," *The Independent* 58 (15 June 1905): 1351.

58. Booth Tarkington, "Some Americans Abroad," *Everybody's Magazine* (Aug. 1907): 174.

59. Edith Wharton, "A Motor Flight through France," *Atlantic Monthly* 98 (Dec. 1906): 733 (emphasis added).

60. Charles F. Speares, "Toll of the Tourist," *American Review of Reviews* 36 (July–August 1907), 724.

61. Mildred Cox diary, 23 May 1908, Mildred Cox Howes Papers, MHS.

62. *PH,* 4 July 1907.

63. Ibid., 23 July 1907.

64. Ibid., 15, 16 Aug. 1902.

65. Ibid., 16, 17 July 1912.

66. There is no mention of the fate of the bicyclist. Ibid., 10 Aug. 1912.

67. Walter Hale, *The Ideal Motor Tour in France* (New York: Dodd, Mead, 1914), 1–12.

68. *PH,* 11 Aug. 1912.

69. Robert M. Coyle, *Fenceless France: The Story of an Automobile Ride* (Philadelphia: George Buchanan 1908), 13.

70. Hale, *Ideal Motor Tour,* xii.

CHAPTER ELEVEN

1. Thorstein Veblen, *A Theory of the Leisure Class: An Economic Study of Institutions* (New York: Macmillan), 1902.

2. Paul Gerbod, *Voyages au pays des mangeurs de grenouilles: La France vue par les Britanniques du XVIIIe siècle à nos jours* (Paris: Albin Michel, 1991), 137.

3. *Appleton's European Guide Book*, 20th ed. (New York: Appleton, 1883), 286–87; Otto Friedrich, *Olympia: Paris in the Age of Monet* (New York: Simon and Schuster, 1992), 229–30.

4. *CE*, 1 Aug. 1870, 5.

5. Georges Girard, "Les Bons touristes," *L'Opinion*, 7 Aug. 1920, 151.

6. Edward Van Cise diary, "France," 1870–71, Edward Van Cise Papers, box 2, LC.

7. Annie J. Bradley diary, n.d. ("Monday") [Aug. 1872], NYPL.

8. Mary Eliot (Dwight) Parkman to Sophia, 29 Sept. 1872, Dwight Family Papers, HL.

9. The shell of the Tuileries palace was not pulled down until 1883.

10. Aimee Rotch Sargent diary, 5 Dec. 1874, Lamb Family Papers, box 25, MHS.

11. William Buehler diary, 25 Aug. 1875, MHS; Roger Woolcott to father, n.d. [1874], Woolcott Family Papers, box 2, MHS.

12. W. Pembroke Fetridge, *Rise and Fall of the Paris Commune* (New York: Harper, 1871); Laura Libbey diary [1892], 3:389, NYPL.

13. Mary M. George, *A Little Journey to France* (Chicago: Flanagan, 1902), 34.

14. Georges Dupeux, *French Society, 1789–1970*, trans. Peter Wait (London: Metheun, 1976), 151–82.

15. Gerbod, *Voyages*, 135–39.

16. American socialites were not the only ones to rely on it. Each day, two hundred copies were sent to the court of the Czar of Russia. Al Laney, *Paris Herald: The Incredible Newspaper* (New York: Appleton-Century, 1947), 13–20.

17. Richard Harding Davis, *About Paris* (New York: Harper, 1895), 197.

18. Henry James wrote that Americans living in Paris were "outsiders" because they came from "an exclusively commercial" country which was a "pure democracy." Also, Europeans could not imagine that they would really forfeit the privileges of high social position at home to live in a foreign country. Henry James, "Americans Abroad," *Nation* 27 (3 Oct. 1887): 208–9.

19. Mary Cable, *Top Drawer: American High Society from the Gilded Age to the Roaring Twenties* (New York: Atheneum, 1984), 120.

20. Urban Gohier, *Le Peuple du XXe siècle aux États-Unis* (Paris: Charpentier, 1907), 266.

21. Madame [Julietta] Adam, "Society in Paris," *North American Review* 150 (Apr. 1890): 490–504.

22. Theodore Child, *The Praise of Paris* (New York: Harper and Brothers, 1893), 62–63.

23. Stephen Birmingham, *Our Crowd: The Great Jewish Families of New York* (New York: Harper and Row, 1967), 142–47; Horace Sutton, *Travelers: The American Tourists from Stagecoach to Space Shuttle* (New York: Morrow, 1980), 68–69. The Mrs. Bernstein injured in the car accident while en route to Étretat in 1912 that was described in chapter 10 was Seligman's daughter.

24. In 1899, prominent Chicago Jews felt they were enough of a presence in France, and important enough to its economy, to threaten a boycott of Paris if Dreyfus was not exonerated. *NYT,* 3 Sept. 1899.

25. Rowland Strong, "Americans in Paris," *Harper's Weekly* 54 (2 Apr. 1910): 14.

26. Virginia Rosenthal diary, 7–17 June 1902, NYPL; Henriette Greenebaum Frank diary, 28, 29 Apr. 1910, 3, 4 Sept. 1910, in Greenebaum Sisters' Travel Journals, CHS. Three years earlier, when they encountered some other Americans at Kenilworth Castle in England, Frank's husband swore he overheard one say to another: "Only Americans and meshuggene goyim come here." Frank diary, 1 July 1907.

27. Theodore Child, *Summer Holidays* (New York: Harper, 1889), 248–51.

28. *Le Tourisme,* 10 (3 June 1877), n.p.; ibid., 14 (10 June 1877), n.p.; Child, *Praise of Paris,* 79–80.

29. "There is quite a little American colony here," one tourist wrote of Dinard in August 1875, at the height of its season. Edith Rotch diary, 23 Aug. 1875, MHS.

30. *PH,* 8 July 1892.

31. Isabel Shaw to Mother, 24 Dec. 1899, 3 Jan. 1900, in George Russell Shaw Papers, 1899–1904, MHS. The French "season" in Pau, which has now reverted to obscurity, centered on a horse racing meeting. Charles Rearick, *Pleasures of the Belle Époque: Entertainment and Festivities in Turn-of-the-Century France* (New Haven: Yale University Press, 1985), 158.

32. Hebe Dorsey, *The Age of Opulence: The Belle Époque in the Paris Herald, 1890–1914* (New York: Abrams, 1987), 124; *PH,* 7 July 1901.

33. Jennifer A. Bense diary, 13 Apr. 1889, Bense Family Diaries, NYPL.

34. Gerbod, *Voyages,* 138–39. In the mid-1990s, some French friends were surprised to hear that it had ever been a stylish resort.

35. *American Society in Europe* 1 (May, 1891): 6; ibid., 2 (Jan. 1892): 139; Mary Blume, *Côte d'Azur: Inventing the French Riviera* (London: Thames and Hudson, 1992), 42–43; *PH,* 15 Mar. 1896.

36. Mrs. Henry Fields, *Home Sketches in France* (New York, 1875), 65.

37. Frances Haxall to Rosalie (Haxall) Thompson, 21 Apr. 1875, Haxall Family Papers, VaHS. They may well have been buried in the large section of Menton's cemetery with the graves of foreigners which is now, ironically, a tourist attraction.

38. *Paris-Promeneur, Paris-Touriste* (Paris, 1863), 18.

39. John Polson, *Monaco and its Gaming Tables* (London: Eliot Stock, 1881), 15–18; Blume, *Côte d'Azur,* 39–41.

40. Robert S. Rudney, "From Luxury to Popular Tourism: The Transformation of the Resort City of Nice" (Ph.D. diss., University of Michigan, 1979), 56–60.

41. Sunbathing was not yet among those amusements, for the last thing the pre-World War I leisured class wanted was to be bronzed like peasants, track-layers, and others who worked outdoors. When the luxurious Negresco Hotel opened in 1903 on the Promenade des Anglais (the sun-drenched boulevard that runs along Nice's beachfront), its main entrance was not on the boulevard but on the shady side, to protect guests from the sun's rays. Ibid., "Luxury," 52–62.

42. *American Society in Europe* 2 (Oct. 1891): 104.

43. James Buzard, *The Beaten Track: European Tourism, Literature and the Ways of Culture, 1800–1918* (Oxford: Oxford University Press, 1992), 225–26.

44. Rémy Saisselin, *The Bourgeois and the Bibelot* (New Brunswick: Rutgers University Press, 1984), 84.

45. Frederic Jaher, *The Urban Establishment: Upper Strata in Boston, New York, Charleston, Chicago and Los Angeles* (Urbana: University of Illinois Press, 1982), 269–72.

46. Saesslin, *Bourgeois,* 81.

47. He protected himself by buying only on the condition that the objects might be returned within a year for a full refund. Lazare Weiller, "J. Pierpont Morgan," *France-Amérique* 4 (May 1913): 281–82.

48. *NYT,* 24 Apr. 1910; Neil Harris, *Cultural Excursions* (Chicago: University of Chicago Press, 1990), 262.

49. Harris, *Cultural Excursions,* 259.

50. Charles L. Robertson, "Left Bank–Right Bank: Americans in Paris before World War II," unpublished ms. of talk at Reid Hall Centennial, Paris, June, 1993.

51. Cable, *Top Drawer,* 175.

52. Harris, *Cultural Excursions,* 262.

53. In the 1880s, Paris also displaced Italy as the place for the upper classes to preserve their images for posterity. With times still hard, well-known French artists were willing to set aside their allegories of half-naked Ancients and tortured Christian martyrs to pick up some cash by portraying American society women decked out in the silk, jewels, and finery they had acquired in Paris. James Gordon Bennett recommended Alexandre Cabanel, who was best known for his paintings of early Christian martyrs, to readers of the *Paris Herald* as someone who "knows how to be courteous to his visitors." *PH,* 7 Oct. 1887.

54. Theodore Child, "Along the Parisian Boulevards," *Harper's New Monthly Magazine* 85 (Nov. 1892): 870.

55. Marian Adams to Pater, 21, 28 Sept. 1879, in Marian Adams, *The Letters of Mrs. Henry Adams,* ed. Ward Thoron (Boston: Little, Brown, 1936), 179–83.

56. *PH,* 7 Oct. 1887.

57. Ada Cone, "The Woman's Paris," *Scribner's* 24 (Nov. 1898): 555–57.

58. Ibid., 554.

59. Dorsey, *Age of Opulence,* 46.

60. Cable, *Top Drawer,* 116.

61. Amy Waters diary, 31 July–12 Sept. 1907, NYPL.

62. Mary Lawrence diary, 3, 6, 10 Apr. 1901, Marian Peabody Lawrence Papers, MHS.

63. Grace Matthews (Ashmore) diary, 31 May 1901, NYPL; Stuart Blumin, *The Emergence of the Middle Class: Social Experience in the American City* (Cambridge: Cambridge University Press, 1989), 291–92.

64. Jennie McGraw to Judge [McGraw], 15 Oct. 1878, Jennie McGraw Fiske diary, McGraw Family Papers, CUL.

65. Mary Cadwalader Jones, *European Travel for Women* (New York: Macmillan, 1900), 158.

66. She hoped to return to Paris in the spring, "but it will all be so terribly expensive that I am rather doubtful." Annie [?] to Mary Lawrence, 14 Nov. 1899, inserted in Mary Lawrence diary, 1899.

67. Mrs. Charles Hunt diary, 31 Jan. 1882, Charles H. Hunt Papers, CHS.

68. Stephen Mennell, *All Manners of Food: Eating and Taste in England and France from the Middle Ages to the Present* (Oxford: Basil Blackwell, 1985), 157–61.

69. Jefferson Williamson, *The American Hotel* (New York: Knopf, 1930), 215.

70. *Le Monde,* 18 Oct. 1876.

71. Harvey Levenstein, *Revolution at the Table: The Transformation of the American Diet* (New York: Oxford University Press, 1988), 10–22; "Two Hundred Years of French Food in America," *Journal of Gastronomy* 5 (spring 1989): 67–89; Julian Street, "Paris à la Carte," *Everybody's Magazine* 25 (July 1911): 23–26.

72. "We can tell you the merits of half the restaurants in Paris," she wrote her father. Clover Adams to Pater, 21 Apr. 1873, 28 Sept., 5, 12 Oct. 1879, in *Letters of Mrs. Henry Adams,* 98, 180–89. Henry had become enamored with the top French restaurants much earlier, during his visit in 1860. Henry Adams, *The Education of Henry Adams* (Boston: Houghton Mifflin, 1961), 96.

73. Gherardi Davis diary, 17–20 July, 14–18 Aug. 1908, in "The Story of My Life," ms. in Gherardi Davis Papers, NYPL. *Henri,* as it was properly called, was regarded by many as Paris's finest restaurant. *Express Guide to Paris* (Paris: Frédéric Maya, 1911), 163.

74. Julian Street, *Paris à la Carte* (New York: John Lane, 1911), 21.

75. Grace Matthews [Ashford] diary, 30 May 1901, NYPL.

76. Adams to Elizabeth Cameron, 25 Sept. 1895, in Adams, *Letters,* 332.

77. Street, *Paris à la Carte,* 73–75.

78. Jennie Reekie, *The London Ritz Book of Customs and Manners* (London: Ebury Press), 1991.

79. When the famous actress Lillian Russell dined there in the 1890s, it was in one of its private rooms, where she was able to conceal her ability to out-eat her friend, the legendary gourmand "Diamond Jim" Brady. Levenstein, *Revolution,* 12.

80. *American Society in Europe* 2 (Jan. 1892): 160.

81. *NYT,* 7 Aug. 1898.

82. Reekie, *Ritz,* 22.

83. Mildred Cox diary, 22, 24 May 1908, Mildred Cox Howes Papers, MHS.

84. Street, *Paris à la Carte,* 13–14.

85. Edmond Benjamin and Paul Desachy, *Le Boulevard, croquis parisiens* (Paris: Marpon et Flammarion, 1893), 18, quoted in Rearick, *Pleasures,* 160.

CHAPTER TWELVE

1. Laura Libbey diary, 1890, 1, NYPL.

2. Mary Lawrence Peabody diary, 19 Aug. 1910, Marian Lawrence Peabody Papers, MHS.

3. Alfred Roe, the ex–high school teacher from Worcester, Massachusetts, was met in Paris by the art student from Emporia, Kansas, with whom he shared a cabin, and given a tour of the city. Alfred Roe diary, [1890], NYPL.

4. Mary Cadawalder Jones, *European Travel for Women* (New York: Macmillan, 1900), 55; Josephine Tozier, *The Traveler's Handbook: A Manual for Transatlantic Tourists,* rev. ed. (New York: Funk and Wagnall's, 1907), 36–39. Men and women would get so tired of wearing the same basic outfit they would not wear it again until the

return voyage. Women's Rest Tour Association, *A Summer in England with a Continental Supplement: A Handbook for the Use of American Women* (Boston: Ochs, 1900), 10–12.

5. "Another of those men . . . who expects to come play with Alice, whom he has quite a crush on," she wrote to her parents. Elizabeth Telling to Family, 15 Feb. 1914, Telling Papers, box 5, SSC.

6. She purchased a first-class ticket from Lyon to Paris only because the train, the fastest in Europe, was all first class. Jane Addams to Sarah Haldeman, 22 June 1884, Jane Addams Memorial Collection, University of Illinois at Chicago Circle, microfilm copy in LC.

7. Elizabeth Pennel, "Travelling in Provincial France," *The Chautauquan* 13 (Aug. 1891): 637.

8. Women's Rest Tour Association, *Summer*, 73.

9. *CE*, Dec. 1877, 5.

10. Mastering its mass of detailed information was so difficult that one Englishman facetiously suggested that Oxford add a class in Bradshaw to its mathematics curriculum. Josephine Tozier, an American who cited this quip, suggested that if the mathematician in the touring party began studying Bradshaw in early March, the fares and schedules would be deciphered by the first of June. Tozier, *Travelers' Handbook*, xi–xii.

11. Laura Libbey was particularly satisfied with them. Only once did she get an undesirable hotel room, she said. If she was put in a room on the third floor in a hotel without an elevator she would sit on the first floor steps until her demand for a room on a lower floor was granted. Laura Libbey diary, [1903], vol. 1, NYPL.

12. Mark Twain, *Europe and Elsewhere* (1927), 214–16, cited in Piers Brendon, *Thomas Cook* (London: Seeker and Warburg, 1991), 247.

13. Brendon, *Cook*, 247.

14. *CE*, Dec. 1887, 5.

15. These were, Cook's boasted, the largest "personally conducted tours" ever to leave America. *CE*, Nov. 1877, 4; ibid., Mar. 1878, 8, 10; ibid., 1 May 1878, 5.

16. Ibid., Mar. 1878, 4.

17. Ibid., 1 May 1878, 5.

18. One of the tasks of Miss Gostrey, the character in Henry James's *The Ambassadors* who shepherds parvenu Americans around Europe, is to wean them from the tradition of "the matutinal beefsteak." A craving for it is one of the things that makes being in Europe an "ordeal" for the hero's businessman friend, Waymarsh. Henry James, *The Ambassadors* (New York: Norton, 1964), 30–36.

19. *CE*, Mar. 1878, 4.

20. *CE-AM*, June 1891, 7.

21. *CE*, Mar. 1878, 8.

22. In 1883 the company announced that "over two thousand ladies and gentlemen, representing every state in the Union," had taken its "Annual Education Vacation Parties" in the five previous years. *CE-AM*, Feb. 1883, 17.

23. Ibid., Jan. 1883, 4.

24. Ibid., Feb. 1889, 9.

25. Ibid., May 1893, 15–16; July 1895, 13; Nov. 1899, 12–14.

26. It included second cabin ocean passage, third-class return rail tickets from Glasgow or Liverpool to Paris, accommodation and meals in London and Paris, two tickets to the fair, a trip to Versailles, and all fees for transfers and porters. It could even be paid for over time, at $6 a month. The next year a longer tour with better accommodations was only $175. Ibid., Nov. 1889, 14; ibid., Mar. 1901, 8.

27. *NYT,* 6 Sept. 1900. On that occasion, a number of travel agents went under, leaving travelers stranded all over France and Italy.

28. Ralph Reed, *American Express, Its Origin and Growth* (New York: Newcomen Society, 1952), 20.

29. William A. Coffut, untitled article from *Washington Chronicle*, n.d., in *CE-AM,* May 1891, 12.

30. *CE,* Dec. 1877, 4.

31. *CE,* Nov. 1877, 5; ibid., Mar. 1878, 8.

32. She and her friend did not want to travel "at the cost of health and strength." Ibid., Dec. 1877, 5. Needless to say, Cook's was reassuring on that score, as was Coffut, the Washington newspaperman cited above, who wrote in 1891, "that our pace and performance were not wholly exhausting is proved by the fact that six of the party were women." Coffut, op. cit.

33. *CE-AM,* Apr. 1883, 3; Coffut, op. cit. Mary Cadawalder Jones's *European Travel for Women* (1900), which placed great store in the cultural benefits of a European tour, recommended Cook's highly for advance purchase of tickets for steamers, trains, and hotels, but did not recommend its tours, even for those who wished to do the highlights of Europe rapidly. Jones, *European Travel,* 22.

34. *NYT,* 22 Apr. 1899. In 1873, Marian Adams struck a similar note about the Louvre: "Every time one comes back to the good pictures they seem better," she wrote her father. Marian Adams to Pater, 14 Sept. 1873, in Marian Adams, *The Letters of Mrs. Henry Adams,* ed. Ward Thoron (Boston: Little, Brown, 1936), 178.

35. She was also concerned that her twenty-year-old daughter, who accompanied them with a friend, was making little progress in French and music. Caroline Barrett White diary, Nov.–Dec. 1882, microfilm in American Antiquarian Society, *American Women's Diaries: New England Women* (New Canaan, Conn.: Readex, 1984).

36. Raymond Williams. *Culture and Society* (Harmondsworth: Penguin, 1961), 124–25; Lawrence Levine, *Highbrow/Lowbrow: The Emergence of Cultural Hierarchy in America* (Cambridge: Harvard University Press, 1988), 223–24.

37. Alan Trachtenberg, *The Incorporation of America: Culture and Society in the Gilded Age* (New York: Hill and Wang, 1992), 143–45.

38. Alan Holder, *Three Voyagers in Search of Europe: A Study of Henry James, Ezra Pound, and T. S. Eliot* (Philadelphia: University of Pennsylvania Press, 1968), 28.

39. Levine, *Highbrow/Lowbrow,* 215.

40. Henry James, *The Bostonians* (Harmondsworth: Penguin, 1966), 290.

41. Saisselin, *Bourgeois,* 91–102. They conveniently ignored, of course, Ruskin's socialist sympathies.

42. Rémy Saisselin, *The Bourgeois and the Bibelot* (New Brunswick: Rutgers University Press, 1984), 96–98; Levine, *Highbrow/Lowbrow,* 215.

43. The Los Angeles County Museum of Art originated in 1888 as the Ruskin

Club, founded to promote the serious study of art. Frederick Jaher, *The Urban Establishment: Upper Strata in Boston, New York, Charleston, Chicago, and Los Angeles* (Urbana: University of Illinois Press), 646–47.

44. Carl Vrooman, *The Lure and Lore of Travel* (Boston: Sherman, French and Co., 1914), 49.

45. Levine, *Highbrow/Lowbrow*, 215; Henry James, *Hawthorne* (1879; New York: St. Martin's Press, 1967), 34–35.

46. Henry James, *The Pension Beauregard*, cited in Van Wyck Brooks, *New England: Indian Summer, 1865–1915* (New York: Dutton, 1940), 284.

47. Anne Bense diary, 21 Nov. 1885, Bense Family Papers, NYPL.

48. Emily Morgan Rotch diary, 21 Nov. 1881, Lamb Family Papers, MHS.

49. Sanford Cutler diary, 19–21 Aug. 1885, Cutler Family Papers, MHS.

50. Elizabeth Telling to Dearest Family, 14 Feb. 1913, Telling Papers, box 5, SSC.

51. She did add, almost defiantly, "I only know that I am pleased with the Murillos" and others. Caroline White diary, 10 July 1888.

52. Harris, *Cultural Excursions*, 262–64.

53. Even Cook's, whose tours were derided by the genteel class, tried to hitch a ride on this notion. "There is not a lady or gentleman in America with a desire for or love of culture who is not constantly thinking of Europe," said *Cook's Excursionist* in 1883. *CE-AM*, Feb. 1883, 17.

54. Düsseldorf enjoyed a brief co-habitation with Paris as *the* center for artists' training in the late 1870s and 1880s, but was soon elbowed from the scene. Brooks, *New England: Indian Summer*, 151–55.

55. *NYT*, 12, 18, 28 May 1890.

56. "He knows that every color in nature is itself full of varied tones and colors. On this account he runs himself to ground . . . and his green tree becomes, with every crude paint dabbed into it, more red than green, his sun more blue than yellow." Robert A. Boit diary, 9, 10, 16 Nov. 1890, in Robert A. Boit Papers, MHS.

57. Warren Susman, "Pilgrimage to Paris: The Backgrounds of American Expatriation, 1920–1934," (Ph.D. diss., University of Wisconsin, 1957), 78–90.

58. Henry James, "A Little Tour in France," *Atlantic Monthly* 41 (Jan. 1878): 67–76.

59. For reasons that are not clear, a French abbé is hired to give French lessons to the two teenaged girls but not to the teenaged boy, who was expected to work on the language on his own. Perhaps this was because he was freer to talk with strangers. Edward Everett Hale and Susan Hale, *Young Americans Abroad: Being a Family Flight by Four Young People and their Parents through France and Germany* (Boston: Lathrop, 1898), 41–65, 81–85.

60. Ibid., 81–84.

61. Ibid., 97–98.

62. Ibid., 126.

63. Ibid., 126–30.

64. Trachtenberg, *Incorporation*, 140–42.

65. Chautauqua Literary and Scientific Circle, *A Reading Journey through France* (Cleveland, Chautauqua Assembly, 1900), 14.

66. Ibid., 65.

67. Nevertheless, he then proceeded to outline just such a quick trip. Grant Allen, *The European Tour* (New York: Dodd, Mead, 1899), 1, 16, 35, 88–89, 96.

68. Ibid., 90.

69. Harvey Levenstein, *Revolution at the Table: The Transformation of the American Diet* (New York: Oxford University Press, 1988), 10–22, 60–71.

70. The other guests drank wine with the meal, but he drank tea. "Between meals," he wrote, "the men and many women are all in the boulevards under trees and awnings, drinking biere, café, absinthe. Such a life! No wonder Germany, with her armies of students and scholars, marched down and overthrew her!" Van Cise diary [1870], 121, Edwin Van Cise Papers, box 2, LC.

71. Mark Twain, *A Tramp Abroad* (New York: Harper, 1905), 2:258–59, 312.

72. Alfred Roe diary, n.d. [Sept.–Nov. 1890], NYPL.

73. White diary, 6 Dec. 1882.

74. A fine meal with wine at Voisin or another of the top restaurants could be had for only 20 francs, or $3.86. *Express Guide to Paris and Environs* (Paris: Frédéric Maya, 1911), 163.

75. White diary, Dec. 1882; July 1888.

76. "They eat only two meals a day," he wrote of the French, "but have very rich cooking to lose their appetites." Van Cise diary [1870], 121.

77. *America Abroad: A Handbook for the American Traveller* (London, 1891), 62.

78. Ibid., 1893, 95.

79. Ibid., 1895, 92.

80. Ibid., 91.

81. *Express Guide*, xxiii.

82. *America Abroad*, 1895, 92.

83. The brasserie meal, for example, was a selection from the hors d'oeuvres cart, poulet with cêpes, and strawberries and cream. Jane Cowl diary, 18–27 July 1907.

84. Willie Allen to Mrs. G. W. Allen, 1 Sept. 1895, in George W. Allen Papers, UNC-CHL.

85. Elizabeth Telling to Dearest Family, 15 Feb. 1914, Telling Papers, box 5.

86. White diary, July 1888.

87. *NYT*, 21 July 1895.

88. Henry M. Seaver diary, 21 July 1898, MHS.

89. S. D., "The Cooks of Paris," *Nation* 98 (25 June 1914): 747–48.

90. The closing of the Café de Paris, in 1910, was thought to symbolize the end of the Belle Époque. Hebe Dorsey, *The Age of Opulence: The Belle Époque in the Paris Herald, 1890–1914* (New York: Abrams, 1987), 88.

91. Chautauqua did note, with a notable lack of enthusiasm, that "Paris will always be the aribiter of fashion." Chautauqua, *A Reading Tour*, 22.

92. Emphasis added. Marian M. George, *A Little Journey to France* (Chicago: Flanagan, 1902), 18.

93. Laura Comer diary, 2, 4, 6, 7 Aug. 1872, UNC-CHL.

94. Gunther Barth, *City People: The Rise of Modern City Culture in Nineteenth-Century America* (New York: Oxford University Press, 1980), 113–16.

95. Mary Mayo [Ingle] diary, 22 July 1885, VaHS.

96. Josephine Eppes diary, 1 Sept. 1890.

97. *NYT,* 8 Dec. 1895.

98. Ibid.

99. W. Pembroke Fetridge, *Harper's Hand-Book for Travelers in Europe and the East* (New York, Fetridge, 1887), 1:350.

100. Cowl diary, 19 July 1907.

101. Willie Allen to Mrs. G. W. Allen, 1 Sept. 1895, in George W. Allen Papers, UNC-CHL; Jones, *European Travel,* 156.

102. Dreiser, *Traveler at Forty,* 288–89.

103. It had actually been spawned by officials in rival Nice, which did not yet allow gambling, who charged that an average of three losers a week did themselves in. One Nice official put the number for January 1880 alone at 24. Monte Carlo defenders said that not more than one in one hundred thousand visitors killed themselves, which would have been a little over three a year in 1880. John Polson, *Monaco and Its Gaming Tables* (London: Elliot Stock, 1881), 59–61.

104. Laura Libbey cut out a newspaper drawing of "Suicide Cemetery" with playing cards scattered in the foreground for her diary. Laura Libbey diary, 1892, 27, NYPL.

105. Anne Bense diary, 29 Nov., 10 Dec. 1885, NYPL.

106. Mary Lawrence diary, 1 Apr. 1901, Marian Lawrence Peabody Papers, MHS.

107. Libbey diary, 1892, 27. On the other hand, the diary of the Chicagoan Virginia Rosenthal, from a Jewish-American subculture that approved of gambling, tells of spending two nights in Monte Carlo 1902 during which she, her husband, and another Jewish couple all tried their luck. "Lost $25" [a not inconsiderable sum], she recorded laconically. Virginia Rosenthal diary, 19 June 1902, NYPL.

108. White diary, 28 Jan. 1883.

CHAPTER THIRTEEN

1. Margaret Fuller, "Letter from Paris," in Philip Rahv, *The Discovery of Europe: The Story of the American Experience in the Old World* (Garden City: Doubleday, 1960), 101–2.

2. Van Wyck Brooks, *New England: Indian Summer, 1865–1915* (New York: Dutton, 1940), 284.

3. George William Curtis, *The Potiphar Papers* (New York: Putnam, 1853), 28–30, 183–229.

4. The latter made himself "a thing that is neither male nor female, neither fish, flesh, nor fowl—a poor, miserable, hermaphrodite Frenchman." Mark Twain, *The Innocents Abroad,* in *The Complete Travel Books of Mark Twain,* ed. Charles Neider (Garden City: Doubleday, 1966), 1:59, 239–40.

5. Mark Twain and Charles Dudley Warner, *The Gilded Age: A Tale of Today* (New York: Trident, 1964), chap. 33. Harriet Beecher Stowe used almost the same phrases to describe the reverse scenario—a family of parvenus arriving in Washington trying to dine out on their success in breaking into Napoleon III's parvenu court.

6. Henry James, "Americans Abroad," *Nation* 27 (3 Oct. 1878): 208–9. One can already see here support for Van Wyck Brooks's observation that "what seemed to James really important was not morals but manners." Brooks, *New England: Indian Summer,* 294.

7. "I.M.," "Americans Abroad," *Nation* 27 (17 Oct. 1878): 239.

8. Henry Adams to Elizabeth Cameron, 29 Aug. 1895, in Marian Adams, *The Letters of Mrs. Henry Adams*, ed. Ward Thoron (Boston: Little, Brown, 1936), 311.

9. Edith Wharton, "A Second Motor-Flight through France, II," *Atlantic Monthly* 101 (Feb. 1908): 170–1; id., "A Second Motor-Flight through France, III," *Atlantic Monthly* 101 (Mar. 1908): 346; id., "A Motor Flight through France," *Atlantic Monthly* 98 (Dec. 1906): 739.

10. Charles Battle Loomis, "Some Americans Abroad. I. 'There's Only One Noo York,'" *Century* 61 (Jan. 1901): 449–72.

11. Charles Battle Loomis, "Some Americans Abroad. II. The Man from Ochre Point, New Jersey," *Century* 61 (Feb. 1901): 507–10.

12. Charles Battle Loomis, "Some Americans Abroad. IV. Little Miss Flutterly's Dissertation on War," *Century* 61 (Apr. 1901): 904–5; id., "Some Americans Abroad. V. The Cosmopolitanism of Mr. Powers," *Century* 62 (May 1901): 134–38.

13. Anon., "The Contributors' Club," *Atlantic Monthly* 96 (Aug. 1905): 287–88.

14. Anne Warner, "Seeing France with Uncle John," *Century* 72 (June 1906): 289–301; ibid. (July 1906): 459–72; ibid. (Aug. 1906): 549–58.

15. Loomis, "Some Americans. I.," 472.

16. John Kendrick Bangs, "Boggs Visits the French Capital," *Harper's Weekly* 55 (3 June 1911): 13.

17. William Frederick Dix, "Foreign Travel," *Outlook* 62 (3 June 1899): 294.

18. Anglo-American, "About Paris," *Harper's Weekly* 49 (9 Sept. 1905): 1311.

19. Mary Lawrence Peabody diary, 23 Aug. 1910, Marian Lawrence Peabody Papers, MHS.

20. Henriette Greenebaum [Frank] diary, [1907], 34–35, Greenebaum Sisters Travel Journals, CHS.

21. Tarkington, "Some Americans," 169.

22. *CE*, Dec. 1877, 4.

23. Minnie B. Goodman, "Americans on the Eiffel Tower," *Harper's Weekly* 34 (1 Nov. 1890): 851.

24. Loomis, "Americans Abroad. V.," 138; id., "Americans Abroad. II.," 510.

25. Chauncey M. Depew, "Benefits of a Vacation in Europe," *The Independent* 58 (June 1905): 1248.

26. Brendon, *Cook*, 251.

27. Tarkington, "Some Americans," 173.

28. Ibid., 173–74.

29. James, "Americans Abroad," 209.

30. Rahv, *Discovery*, 368.

31. Adams to Elizabeth Cameron, 25 Sept. 1895, in *The Letters of Henry Adams*, ed. J. C. Levenson et al. (Cambridge: Harvard University Press, 1988), 4:330.

32. James De Mille, *The Dodge Club; or Italy in 1859* (New York: Harper and Row, 1869), 88, cited in William Stowe, *Going Abroad: European Travel in Nineteenth-Century American Culture* (Princeton: Princeton University Press, 1994), 143–46.

33. Stowe, *Going Abroad*, has an excellent analysis of how this was done.

34. Alan Trachtenberg, *The Incorporation of America* (New York: Hill and Wang, 1982), 145.

35. Aimée Rotch Sargent diary, 10 Dec. 1874, MHS; Mary Stoughton diary, 28 May–11 June 1879, NYPL; Mary Mayo [Ingle] diary, 24 July 1885, VaHS.

36. Emily Morgan Rotch diary, Nov.–Dec. 1889, MHS.

37. See Olivia Cushing diary, vol. 1, 1882–85, H. C. Andersen Papers, box 19, LC.

38. Mildred Cox diary, 9–22 Apr. 1909, Mildred Cox Howed Papers, MHS.

39. Jennie McGraw to Judge [?], 6, 15 Oct. 1878, Jennie McGraw Fiske Estate Papers, CUL; McGraw to Judge [?], 11 Dec. 1878, in Jenny McGraw Fiske, diaries, McGraw Family Papers, CUL.

40. L. C. Davidson, *Hints to Lady Travellers at Home and Abroad* (London: Illife and Son, 1889), 63.

41. Laura Libbey diary, [1892], 22, NYPL.

42. Women's Rest Tour Association, *A Summer in England with a Continental Supplement: A Handbook for the Use of American Women* (Boston: Ochs, 1900), 14; Mary Cadwalader Jones, *European Travel for Women* (New York: Macmillan, 1900), 3, 134.

43. Lizzie W. Champney, *Three Vassar Girls Abroad* (Boston; Estes and Lauriat, 1883), 16; Women's Rest Tour, *Summer*, 13.

44. Willie Allen's groups ranged from four to seven, depending on where they were. Willie Allen, letters, 1895, 1902, George W. Allen Papers, UNC-CHL.

45. The young women pelted each other enthusiastically with confetti during the carnival parade and flocked to hotel dances in the evening, but primly disappeared from public view for all of Sunday. John F. Tarbell, Travel Journal, 1876–77, LC.

46. Based on registrants in Paris's better hotels whose gender was identifiable in *The American and Colonial Gazette* of 15 and 30 June 1888, 14 and 28 July 1888, and 11 Aug. 1888. The proportions are from the list for 30 June 1888. There were 103 women unaccompanied by men, 53 with husbands, 57 men without women, and 38 whose gender was not given. About sixty percent of the considerably smaller number of arriving Americans who registered in the Anglo-American bank in Paris in September 1891 were women. *American Society in Europe* 2 (Sept. 1891): 78.

47. "Editor's Easy Chair," *Harper's Magazine* 115 (Oct. 1907): 803.

48. Dix, "Foreign Travel," 294.

49. N. A., "Edith and I in Paris," *LHJ* 17 (Jan. 1900): 5.

50. The history books dealt mainly with Renaissance and Baroque culture and architecture. Jones, *European Travel for Women*, 8, 19–20.

51. Champney, *Three Vassar Girls*, 19–29.

52. Laura Libbey diary, n.d. [1903], 468, NYPL.

53. Jane Addams to Sarah Addams Haldeman, 22 June 1884, Jane Addams Papers, University of Illinois-Chicago Circle; Addams to Ellen Starr, 22 June 1884, ibid.; Addams to Mrs. James Goddard, 23 June 1884, ibid.; Allen F. Davis, *American Heroine: The Life and Legend of Jane Addams* (New York: Oxford University Press, 1973), 36.

54. Henrietta Schroeder diary, 1 Dec. 1889, MHS.

55. Ibid.

56. Davis, *American Heroine*, 36.

57. Ibid., 36.

58. J. Anne Bense diary, 3, 7 Dec. 1885, and Evangeline Bense diary, 6 Dec. 1885, both in Bense Family Diaries, NYPL. Other American women were held spellbound

by a French Protestant preacher who said he was working to rid the South of France of what one of them, Caroline White, called "the miserable priestcraft of the country," which she blamed for its poverty. Caroline White diary, 18 Dec. 1882, microfilm in American Antiquarian Society, *American Women's Diaries: New England* (New Canaan, Conn.: Readex, 1984).

59. Quoted in Thorstein Veblen, *The Theory of the Leisure Class* (Boston: Houghton Mifflin, 1973), 232.

60. Esther Matson, "The Lure of Travel," *New England Magazine* 36 (July 1907): 632.

61. Gail Bederman, *Manliness and Civilization: A Cultural History of Gender and Race in the United States, 1880–1917* (Chicago: University of Chicago Press, 1995), 16–19.

62. Cited in Brooks, *New England: Indian Summer,* 289.

63. Booth Tarkington, "Some Americans Abroad," *Everybody's Magazine* 17 (Aug. 1907): 169.

64. Addams to Sarah Addams Haldeman, 12 Dec. 1887, Jane Addams Papers, University of Illinois-Chicago Circle.

65. Jones, *European Travel,* 155.

66. *NYT,* 21 July 1895; *NYT,* 18 Mar. 1900; "Edith and I in Paris," *LHJ* 17 (Jan. 1900): 5.

67. Margaret Chapin Bageley to Mary Lawrence, 26 Jan. 1900, in Mary Lawrence diary, 1900, Marian Lawrence Peabody Papers, MHS.

68. See Richard Fox and T. J. Jackson Lears, *The Culture of Consumption: Critical Essays in American History, 1880–1980* (New York: Pantheon, 1983); David E. Shi, *The Simple Life: Plain Living and High Thinking in American Culture* (New York: Oxford University Press, 1985); William Leach, *Land of Desire: Merchants, Power, and the Rise of a New American Culture* (New York: Random House, 1993).

69. What with the accompanying corsets and crinolines, one evening dress would take up most of a handbag. Elizabeth Pennel, "Travelling in Provincial France," *Chautauquan* 13 (Aug. 1891): 633–39.

70. Jane Addams to Sarah A. Addams Haldeman, 6 June 1884, Addams Papers.

71. Willie Allen to Hattie Allen, Aug. 25, 1895; Willie Allen to Ruth Allen, 4 Aug. 1906, George Allen Papers, UNC-CHL.

72. D.A.M. [Mrs. Warren] Tufts diary, 1907, n. p., MHS.

73. "Edith and I in Paris," *LHJ* 17 (Jan. 1900): 5; *NYT,* 18 Mar. 1900.

74. She argued that American women's relaxed behavior among men was often misinterpreted as flirtatiousness in Paris where (upper class, of course) young girls were brought up apart from young boys. As a result, young French women were not as comfortable as Americans in the presence of males and French men were not as understanding and solicitous towards women as American men. Lucy Hooper, *Under the Tricolor, or the American Colony in Paris* (Philadelphia: Lippincott, 1880), 153–58.

75. She continues, "and never heard the proverb—'There are two kinds of girls, girls who flirt and girls who go to Vassar College.'" Champney, *Three Vassar Girls,* 40.

76. Thomas Beer, *The Mauve Decade* (1926; reprinted, with an introduction by Frank Freidel, New York: Vintage 1961), 35; M.E.W. [Mrs. John] Sherwood, "American Girls in Europe," *North American* 150 (June 1890): 681–83.

77. Ruth Cranston, "The European Idea of the American Girl," *Independent* 67 (9 Sept. 1909): 596.

78. Van Wyck Brooks, *New England: Indian Summer,* 284–85.

79. Richard Harding Davis, *About Paris* (New York: Harper, 1895), 198.

80. Cranston, "European Idea," 593–94.

81. By 1915, a total of 454 American women had married titled or prominent foreigners. A. E. Hartzell, *Titled Americans* (n.p., 1951), 357, cited in Frederick Jaher, *The Urban Establishment: Upper Strata in Boston, New York, Charleston, Chicago and Los Angeles* (Urbana: University of Illinois Press, 1982), 650.

82. Mary Cable, *Top Drawer: American High Society from the Gilded Age to the Roaring Twenties* (New York: Atheneum, 1984), 127.

83. Isabel Shaw to Mother, 27 Oct. 1899, George Russsell Shaw Papers, MHS.

84. "She dresses beautifully," she wrote, "has the most piquant face and is the slenderest person I ever saw. . . . Her waist can't be sixteen inches round." Mary Lawrence diary, 7 Apr. 1901.

85. Charles Dana Gibson, *The Education of Mr. Pipp* (New York: Russell, 1900.) To our eyes, the daughters are (literally) incredibly beautiful, but at the time they were thought to represent a realizable ideal. Indeed, the idea that American women were the prettiest in the world was reflected in much of the popular thought about American women touring Europe.

86. Rémy Saisselin, *The Bourgeois and the Bibelot* (New Brunswick: Rutgers University Press, 1984), 77–80, 105–15; Beer, *Mauve Decade,* 24–35.

87. Simon Jeune, *De T. Graindorge à A. O. Barnabooth: Les types Américains dans le roman et le théâtre français* (Paris: Marcel Didier, 1963), 249–64; André Tardieu, *Notes sur les États-Unis* (Paris: Calmann-Levy, 1908), 53–54.

88. Madame [Juliette] Adam, "Those American Girls in Europe," *North American Review* 151 (Oct. 1890): 402.

89. *Femina,* 15 Feb. 1904, 45; André Chaignon, "Le Garden-Party de *Femina* au Cercle Saint-James," ibid., 15 July 1904, 233–35; André Chaignon, "La Vie mondaine Dinard," ibid., 15 Aug. 1904, 285–87.

90. Tardieu, *Notes,* 55.

91. Léo d'Hampol, "American Girls in Paris," *Femina,* 15 June 1904, 197–98.

CHAPTER FOURTEEN

1. William Acton, *The Functions and Disorders of the Reproductive Organs* (1857), cited in Peter Filene, *Him/Her/Self: Sex Roles in Modern America* (New York: Harcourt Brace, 1975), 101–2.

2. Gail Bederman, *Manliness and Civilization: A Cultural History of Gender and Race in the United States, 1880–1917* (Chicago: University of Chicago Press, 1995), 16–20.

3. The Reverend Howard Gill told the congregation in Paris's American Church February, 1888, that there were only two kinds of Americans tourists to Europe. Some "sought out the art of the Old World and they found it. Others sought out the disappointing pleasures of man's lowest nature, and they found them, and them only, with all their bitter and harsh after flavor." *PH,* 6 Feb. 1888.

4. Samuel P. Orth, "Paris," *Atlantic Monthly* 112 (Sept. 1913): 387.

5. Theodore Dreiser, "Paris," *Century Magazine* 86 (Oct. 1913): 907.

6. "Unhappy France is now swept from the face of the earth," she concluded rather optimistically. Julia Ward Howe diary, 20 Jan. 1871, in Laura E. Richards and Maude Howe Eliot, *Julia Ward Howe* (Boston, 1916), cited in Elizabeth White, *American Opinion of France from Lafayette to Poincaré* (New York: Knopf, 1927), 240.

7. Andrew White, *Autobiography* (1880), 1:506, cited in White, *Opinion*, 248.

8. George M. Harper, *Masters of French Literature* (New York, 1901), 31; *Nation*, 26 Sept. 1907, cited in White, *Opinion*, 240.

9. Missing from these entries is Twain's wit, perhaps because he thought that, "To be witty in France is very simple—one merely needs to be dirty." Mark Twain, *Mark Twain's Notebooks and Journals*, ed. Frederick Anderson, Lin Salamo, and Bernard L. Stein (Berkeley and Los Angeles: University of California Press, 1975), 2:322–23.

10. *Le Temps*, 14 Nov. 1894; Stanley Weintraub, *Whistler: A Biography* (New York: Weybright and Talley, 1974), 37–44, 385–94.

11. Edward S. Martin, "This Busy World," *Harper's Weekly* 39 (18 May 1895), 473.

12. *NYT Saturday Review of Books*, 2 Oct. 1897.

13. Frank B. Smith, *The Real Latin Quarter* (New York: Funk and Wagnalls, 1901), 103–4.

14. Ibid., 69–83.

15. Bill Blackbeard, introduction, Richard F. Outcault, *The Yellow Kid: A Centennial Celebration of the Kid Who Started the Comics* (Northampton: Kitchen Sink Press, 1995), 76–79; *New York World*, 21, 28 Feb. 1897, in ibid., n.p.

16. "European Rest Cure," Appendix B in David Levy, "Sentimental Journeys of the Big-Eyed Sightseer: Tourism and the Early Cinema," unpublished ms [1992], 24.

17. Smith, *Real Latin Quarter*, 82–102.

18. "The Latin Quarter of Today," *Harper's Weekly* 46 (11 Jan. 1902): 42–43.

19. *NYT Saturday Review of Books*, 2 Oct. 1897; Julian Street, "Paris à la Carte," *Everybody's* 25 (July 1911): 28. Another American wrote: "The young girls of the past took care of and toiled for their student loves. . . . The element of self-sacrifice that lifted their lives from the common rut of immorality is entirely absent from their successors of today. . . . They insist on wearing showy dresses, and they must have money." John T. Conway, *Footprints of Famous Americans in Paris* (London and New York: John Lane, 1912), 233–34.

20. Fédéric Moret, "Images de Paris dans les guides touristiques vers 1900," *Le Mouvement Social*, 160 (July–Sept. 1992): 94.

21. Ralph Blumenfeld, "The Streets of Paris," *Outlook* 87 (26 Oct. 1907): 401.

22. Charles Rearick, *Pleasures of the Belle Époque: Entertainment and Festivity in Turn-of-the-Century France* (New Haven: Yale University Press, 1985), 61–74.

23. Blumenfeld, "Streets of Paris," 403.

24. [N.A.,] *Guide des plaisirs à Paris* (Paris: n. p., [1905?]), 71–73.

25. Richard Harding Davis, "The Show-Places of Paris," *Harper's Magazine* 90 (Oct. 1894): 91–92.

26. Rearick, *Pleasures*, 84; Theodore Dreiser, "Paris," *Century Magazine*, 86 (Oct. 1913): 906.

27. *Guide des Plaisirs*, 118.

28. Theodore Dreiser, *A Traveler at Forty* (New York: Century, 1913), 250.

29. Julian Street, *Paris à la Carte* (New York: John Lane, 1911), 35.

30. *Guide des plaisirs,* 122.

31. Dreiser, *Traveler,* 242–43.

32. Rearick, *Pleasures,* 74.

33. George Chauncey, *Gay New York: Gender, Urban Culture, and the Making of the Gay Male World, 1890–1940* (New York: Basic Books, 1994).

34. Shari Benstock, *Women of the Left Bank: Paris, 1900–1940* (Austin: University of Texas Press, 1986), 46–60; Stephen Longstreet, *We All Went to Paris: Americans in the City of Light* (New York: Macmillan, 1972), 330–49.

35. Women like Jane Addams, it has been argued, instead chose to play adrogynous roles as "public mothers." Caroll Smith-Rosenberg, *Disorderly Conduct: Visions of Gender in Victorian America* (New York: Knopf, 1985), 245–67.

36. T. J. Jackson Lears, "From Salvation to Self-Realization: The Therapeutic Roots of the Consumer Culture," in *The Culture of Consumption,* ed. Richard Wightman Fox and T. J. Jackson Lears (New York: Pantheon, 1983), 9–10.

37. Theodore Child, "Along the Parisian Boulevards," *Harper's Magazine* 85 (Nov. 1892): 860.

38. Francisque Sarcey, "The Boulevards of Paris," *Scribner's Magazine* 9 (June 1891): 678.

39. Davis, "Show-Places of Paris," 125–39.

40. Willie Allen to George Allen, 21 Aug. 1895, Allen Papers, UNC-CHL.

41. Francis Shaw to Mother, 11 Oct. 1899, George Shaw Papers, MHS.

42. "Edith and I in Paris," *LHJ* 17 (Jan. 1900): 6.

43. *NYT,* 8 June 1896; Simon Newcomb, "France as a Field for American Students," *Forum* 23 (May 1897): 320–26.

44. Smith, *Real Latin Quarter,* 167–70.

45. "The Latin Quarter of Today," *Harper's Weekly,* 46 (11 Jan. 1902): 43.

46. Sylvester W. Beach, "The American Student in Paris," *Independent* 54 (25 Sept. 1902): 207.

47. *NYT,* 30 Apr. 1894; "The American Educational Art Institute," *Critic,* 26 (29 June 1895): 485.

48. *PH,* 13, 22 July 1912.

49. Randolph Bourne, letter from Paris, 13 Dec. 1913, in Philip Rahv, *The Discovery of Europe: The Story of the American Experience in the Old World* (Garden City: Doubleday, 1960), 455.

50. Mildred Stapley, "Is Paris Wise for the Average American Girl?" *LHJ* 23 (Apr. 1906): 16, 54.

51. "Defending the American Girl Student Abroad," *LD* 48 (7 Feb. 1914): 259. The author of that allegation was not identified.

52. Moreover (she fibbed), since the young women usually chose pensions "in the nicer quarters of Paris, in Passy, Auteuil, etc." (Right Bank districts where the expat American colony resided), they always had expats to help and entertain them. Ibid., 260.

53. Ibid., 261.

54. Adams to William H. Phillips, 10 Sept. 1895, in *The Letters of Henry Adams,* ed. J. C. Levenson et al. (Cambridge: Harvard University Press, 1988), 4:323.

55. George Carpenter, "My Impressions of France," [1888?], ms. in George Carpenter Papers, Rare Book and Manuscript Library, Columbia University Libraries, New York, N.Y.

56. Stanley Weintraub, *Whistler: A Biography* (New York: Weybright and Talley, 1974), 380–1. Upon learning of the first outburst, Henry James recorded it and made the aging American who forgoes the life in Paris for a reluctant return home the central character of his novel *The Ambassadors.* Ibid.

57. Guy Carryl, "The Playground of Paris," *Harper's Magazine* 108 (Dec. 1903): 35.

58. Anthony Rotundo sees it as a feminizing influence on American masculinity. E. Anthony Rotundo, *American Manhood: Transformations in Masculinity from the Revolution to the Modern Era* (New York: Basic Books, 1993), 262–64.

59. "Editor's Easy Chair," *Harper's Magazine* 115 (Oct. 1907): 803.

60. René Rémond, *Les États-Unis devant l'opinion française, 1815–1852* (Paris: Armand Colin, 1962), 2:570–72.

61. Paul Gerbod, *Voyages au pays des mangeurs de grenouilles: La France vue par les Britanniques du XVIIIe siècle à nos jours* (Paris: Albin Michel, 1991), 85–99; "Les Touristes étrangers à Paris dans la première moitié du XIXeme siècle," *Bulletin de la Société de l'histoire de Paris et d'Île de France,* 1983, 251.

62. William Berrian, *Travels in France and Italy in 1817 and 1818* (New York: Swords, 1821), 51. The maladroit English tourist, a ridiculously dressed "Milord" flush with money, was a stock object of French satire. Gerbod, *Voyages,* 86–87.

63. Abigail de Hart Mayo, *An American Lady in Paris, 1828–1829: The Diary of Mrs. John Mayo,* ed. Mary Mayo Crenshaw (Boston: Houghton Mifflin, 1927), 13.

64. Edwin Hoyt, *The Improper Bostonian: Dr. Oliver Wendell Holmes* (New York: Morrow, 1979), 49. Even in 1891, an American woman reported from the provinces, "It is always an advantage to tell a French peasant that you are not English, but American." Elizabeth Robins Pennell, "Traveling in Provincial France," *Chautauquan* 13 (Aug. 1891): 636.

65. Sumner diary, 11 Mar. 1838, *SL,* 267.

66. René Rémond, *Les États-Unis devant l'opinion française, 1815–1852* (Paris: Armand Colin, 1962), 2:732–41.

67. Bertrand Lemoine, *La Statue de la Liberté* (Brussels: Mardaga), 1986; Oscar Handlin, *The Statue of Liberty* (New York: Newsweek, 1976), 22–59.

68. Simon Jeune, *De Graindorge à Barnabooth* (Paris: Marcel Didier, 1963), 152–60; Jean-Baptiste Duroselle, *France and the United States,* Chicago: University of Chicago Press, 1978), 76–77.

69. Bellesort, "L'Américanisme en France," *Revue Hebdomadaire* 37 (Apr. 1928): 260–63.

70. A 1910 article in the magazine of the new *Comité France-Amérique,* an elite organization formed to promote fruitful interchange between France and the New World, said Americans excelled in business and the practical arts. Some day, they might even approach France in the arts and culture. After all, had not Venice also begun as society of merchants? Paul Adam, *Vues d'Amérique* (Paris: Allendorf, 1906); Gabriel Hanotaux, "L'Œuvre du Comité France-Amérique," *France-Amérique* 1 (Jan. 1910): 2–15; "Pourquoi le Comité France-Amérique a été fondé: le devoir de la

France," ibid. 4 (Apr. 1913): 201–4; "S.G.," "L'activité du Comité France-Amérique de 1910–1913," ibid., 302–7; Firmin Roz, "Remarques sur la pensée et l'art aux États-Unis," ibid. 1 (Feb. 1910): 74–79.

71. *NYT,* 17 Dec. 1904. Theodore Roosevelt's popularity in France might seem unusual, given the intensity of French opposition to the Spanish-American War in 1898, with which he was closely identified. There was an anti-American demonstration and, for the first time, Americans were taunted and treated rudely in public places. However, the opposition seems to have been rooted in the kind of right-wing, super-patriotic circles that were antithetical to liberal "modernizers" as well. *Le Temps,* 7 Mar. 1898; *NYT,* 4 June 1898.

72. Alexander H. Ford, "The Americanization of Paris," *Independent* 59 (6 July 1905): 23–30.

73. *Le Temps,* 16 Sept. 1899.

74. Rowland Strong, "Americans in Paris," *Harper's Weekly* 54 (2 Apr. 1910): 13.

75. Léo d'Hampol, "American Girls in Paris," *Femina,* 15 June 1904, 197–98.

76. Robert M. Coyle, *Fenceless France: The Story of an Automobile Ride* (Philadelphia: George Buchanan, 1908), 15.

CHAPTER FIFTEEN

1. Raymond Weeks, "An American in Paris—Declaration of War—Starting for the Front," *Nation* 99 (27 Aug. 1914): 245–46; "The Magic Change of Paris," *LD* 49 (22 Aug. 1914): 307; "Tourist Stories from Europe's Metamorphisis," ibid., 49 (12 Sept. 1914): 472–81; "An American Woman Flees from Paris," *Outlook* 108 (2 Sept. 1914): 34–36.

2. H. O. Loderhouse, "History of Morgan, Harjes & Cie.," in J. P. Morgan Jr., Papers, Morgan Library, New York, box 116; Morgan, Harjes to Jack Morgan, 2 Aug. 1914, in ibid., box 33. My colleague Martin Horn brought these to my attention.

3. Piers Brendon, *Thomas Cook* (London: Seeker and Warburg, 1991), 255.

4. Paul Goujon, *Cent ans de tourisme en France* (Paris: Cherche Midi, 1989), 47, 53.

5. Warren Susman, "Pilgrimage to Paris: The Backgrounds of American Expatriation, 1920–1934" (Ph.D. diss., University of Wisconsin, 1958), 103–10.

6. David Kennedy, *Over Here: The First World War and American Society* (New York: Oxford University Press, 1980), 205. They spent much of their time in training camps, waiting for reinforcements and learning to use French equipment. Only in the summer of 1918, about four months before war's end, were the bulk of the forces committed to battle.

7. The latter results reflected the idiocy of the tests more than that of the subjects. Ibid., 187–88.

8. Elizabeth White, *American Opinion of France from Lafayette to Poincaré* (New York: Knopf, 1927), 285; Frank Freidel, *Over There: The Story of America's Great Overseas Crusade,* rev. ed. (New York: McGraw-Hill, 1990), 46–55. See also the doughboys' comments in "My Impressions of France and the Army," 2 vols. [1919], in W. D. Pennypacker Papers, SHSW.

9. Peter G. Filene, *Him/Her/Self: Sex Roles in Modern America* (New York, Harcourt Brace, 1974), 115; Kennedy, *Over Here,* 186.

10. "My Impressions," vol. 1.

11. Edward Coffman, *The War to End All Wars: The American Military Experience in World War I* (New York: Oxford University Press, 1968), 133.

12. Yves-Henri Nouailhat, *Les Américains à Nantes et Saint-Nazaire: 1917–1919* (Paris: Belles Lettres, 1972), 128–29. Sales of pornographic books, some translated into English, and "dirty" postcards also boomed. Ibid., 130.

13. The French, unable to decipher "doughboy," called them "Sammies" to distinguish them from the British "Tommies."

14. These often involved young women hoping that life in America would offer them freedom from the stifling restrictions of small-town France. Nouailhat, *Les Américains*, 214–16.

15. W. W. Baldwin to Calvin Coolidge, 23 Oct. 1926, Calvin Coolidge Papers, PPF 203a, LC.

16. In May 1918, Edith Holliday, a Red Cross volunteer, wrote home from Paris that "there are so many Americans here it does not seem quite like Paris." They were practically all civilians. Edith Holliday to Bunny, 17 May 1918, in Edith Holliday Papers, MHS.

17. Henry G. Dodge, "Why Paris Smiles," *Harper's Weekly* 61 (11 Dec. 1915), 560. Some air raids eventually led to nightly blackouts, though, making the streets look rather "weird," said an American Red Cross worker. Edith Holliday to Bunny, May 17, 1918, Edith Holliday Papers, MHS.

18. Herbert A. Gibbons, "How We Can Help France," *Century Magazine* 44 (Aug. 1917), 527–32; Elizabeth Sergeant, "America Meets France," *New Republic* 13 (29 Dec. 1917): 240–43.

19. *Stars and Stripes*, 22 Feb. 1918, cited in Kennedy, *Over Here*, 206.

20. [Howard V. O'Brien], *Wine, Women and War: A Diary of Disillusionment* (New York: J. H. Sears, 1926), 18, 25; 161–213.

21. Frank Smith diary, 28 Nov. 1918, MHS.

22. *Le Matin*, 27 Jan. 1919.

23. *PT,* 1 Aug. 1921.

24. [O'Brien], *Wine, Women and War*, 300.

25. Nouaihlat, *Les Américains*, 193–216; Charles Hoyt, quoted in Freidel, *Over There*, 226.

26. "Rapports sur des crimes et des délits commis sur la territoire française par des militaires de l'Armée Américain," 24 Feb. 1919; "Méfaits causés par les Américains en France," 30 May 1919; "Méfaits commis par les Américains en France," n.d. [1919]; "Rapport du capitaine Sapin sur des attaques à main armeè par des militaires Américains," 16 Sept. 1919, in France, Ministère de l'Intérieur, "Cooperation des polices Française et américaine pour répression des délits de droit commun dans lesquels sont impliqués des militaires américans, 1918–1919," Archives Nationales de France, F7 14700.

27. Le Sous-Secrétaire d'Etat de la Justice Miliraire à M. le Géneral Commandant en Chef des Forces Expéditionnaires Américaines, 21 May 1919; Pichon à [Ambassador] Campbell Wallace, 3 May 1919, ibid.

28. Rapport du Chef du Brigade Renaud à IIe Légion de Gendarmerie, 25 Sept. 1919, ibid.

29. The male-female ratio of 50 to 1 left something to be desired, necessitating "tag-dances." Freidel, *Over There*, 195–97.

30. Katherine Fife to Mamma, 20 Dec. 1918, and Fife to Jamie, 20 Dec. 1918, in Ella K. Fife Papers, box 1, UVaL.

31. Most of the hotels had been requisitioned by the French government during the war, and the U.S. army had begun to send wounded there to recuperate. The Americans also helped to blaze a new tourist frontier by being the first to take to its beaches in large numbers during the warmer months. Robert Rodney, "From Luxury to Popular Tourism: The Transformation of the Resort City of Nice" (Ph.D. diss., University of Michigan, 1979), 110.

32. Paul Bolton entry, 5 July 1919, "My Impressions," vol. 1.

33. Jean-Baptiste Duroselle, *La France et les États-Unis: des origines à nos jours* (Paris: Seuil, 1976), 114.

34. *Le Matin*, 15 Jan. 1919. Cook's also anticipated a huge influx. It reprinted a March 1919 *New York Tribune* piece that said many of the million people trying to book passage to Europe were "anxious to visit the battlefields of France." Oline Howe, "A Million Waiting to 'See Where It Happened,'" *New York Tribune*, 16 Mar. 1919, in *CATG*, Apr. 1919, 7.

35. Michelin & Cie., *Americans in the Great War*, 3 vols. (Cleremont-Ferand: Michelin, 1919).

36. David Lloyd, "Pilgrimage and Remembrance in British Travel Writing before the War," unpublished ms. [1994,] Cambridge University, U.K., 10–11.

37. *CATG*, Jan. 1920, 1; *CATG*, Mar. 1920, 3; *CATG*, Apr. 1920, 7.

38. "French Preparations for the American Tourist Trade," *LD* 63 (Dec. 20, 1919): 84.

39. Girard, "Les bons touristes," *L'Opinion*, 7 Aug. 1920, 151.

40. *NYT*, 12 Feb. 1920; *NYT*, 2 May 1920; and *NYT*, 8 June 1920; "French Preparations," 84.

41. *NYT*, 23 May 1920; *NYT*, 9 June 1920; *NYT*, 27 May 1921; *NYT*, 4 June 1921; "The Doubtful Pleasures of European Travel Up to Date," *LD* 65 (20 May 1920): 72–78.

42. U.S. Bureau of the Census, *Historical Statistics of the United States, from Colonial Times to 1970* (Washington, D.C., 1976), 1:405. Many were not tourists, but immigrants to America visiting the homelands that had been cut off during the war.

43. Michelin, *Americans*, 1:49.

44. George Mosse, *Fallen Soldiers: Reshaping the Memory of the World Wars* (New York: Oxford University Press, 1990), 152–56; G. Curt Piehler, *Remembering War the American Way* (Washington, D.C.: Smithsonian Press, 1995), 93–103.

45. *PH*, 2 July 1921.

46. Florence Patton to Mother and Dad, 23 Sept. 1920 and 27 Nov. 1920, and Florence Patton to L. Patton (postcard), 25 Nov. 1920, Florence Patton Fitzgerald Papers, SHSW. Cook's rail-and-auto tours from Paris also did Reims, and, like the American Express tours, implied that the cathedral had been destroyed by the Germans. (In fact it was destroyed by the Allies, to prevent its being used as an observation post by the Germans.) However, Cook's tours centered on the northern area, around Arras and Amiens, where the fighting was done by British, French, Canadians, and

Australians. For some reason, its guides said that the bloody battle of Vimy Ridge, later the site of a huge Canadian monument, had been won by the French. Hannah Greenebaum Solomon diary, 23 July 1921, Greenebaum Sisters Travel Journals, CHS.

47. Frank Smith to Dick [Alfred Barksdale?], 11 Dec. 1920, Alfred Barksdale Papers, UVaL.

48. John-Henry Nivart-Chatelain, *Guide Book to France for Americans* (Liège, Paris, n.p.: 1921), 144.

49. *PT,* 16 July 1921.

50. Hannah G. Solomon diary, 6 July 1921, in Greenebaum Sisters Travel Journals, CHS.

51. "France's Devastated Areas, Yesterday and Today," *LD* 72 (11 Feb. 1922): 38–39.

52. "The hillsides are *thick* with crosses," she continued, "marking the places where hundreds of thousands of brave men lie, who died for *us,* that the Beast might not defile us." Clara Laughlin to Buddy, 31 July 1921, Clara Laughlin Papers, box 1, SSC.

53. *PH,* 8 July 1922.

54. Their visits to the depressing battlefields were only part of their prize, which included visits to the Riviera and the mountains of Savoie, culminating with a week in Paris. *PH,* 10 Sept. 1923; Malcolm Cowley, *Exile's Return* (New York: Viking, 1931; Compass Books ed., 1956), 171–72.

55. "Ties That Bind France and the United States," *LD* 72 (11 Feb. 1922): 40. At the dedication of the monument at Belleau Wood, the U.S. Navy admiral's speech rather inappropriately recalled that the only time before battle at that spot that the Marines and Army had fought together had been in helping to repress the Boxer Rebellion in China. *PH,* 23 July 1923.

56. Chet Shafer, *The Second A.E.F.: The Pilgrimage of the Army of Remembrance* (New York: Doty, 1927).

57. Thomas Cook and Sons, *How to See France* (London: Cook, 1921–1925).

58. Mme. Élysée Reclus, "Fragment d'un voyage a la Nouvelle-Orléans (1855)," *Le Tour du Monde* (1860): 177–92.

59. Simon Jeune, *De Graindorge à Barnabooth* (Paris: Marcel Didier, 1963), 24.

60. René Rémond, *Les États-Unis devant l'opinion française, 1815–1852* (Paris: Armand Colin, 1962), 2:733–41.

61. Shelby T. McCloy, *The Negro in France* (Lexington: University of Kentucky Press, 1961), 231.

62. Jean-Baptiste Duroselle, *France and the United States: From the Beginnings to the Present* (Chicago: University of Chicago Press, 1978), 77.

63. E.g., *Le Temps,* 28 and 30 Dec. 1890, 13 Apr. 1891, 26 Mar. 1892, 21 May 1895, and 7 Apr. 1896.

64. Ibid., 27 July 1898; 8 Aug. 1890.

65. In 1904, African American dancers demonstrating the "cake-walk," the "transatlantic," the "Boston-Ball," and other dances were the major attraction at the French women's fashion magazine *Femina*'s annual garden party. "Le Garden-Party de *Femina* au Cercle Saint-James," *Femina,* 15 July 1904, 233–35.

66. Nouahilhat, "Les Américains," 208.

67. André Kaspi, *Le Temps des Américains* (Paris: Sorbonne, 1976), 181–86; Arthur E. Barbeau and Florette Henri, *The Unknown Soldiers: Black American Troops in World War I* (Philadelphia: Temple University Press, 1974), 17–19, 89–163.

68. Ibid., 114–15; Freidel, *Over There,* 63.

69. Ibid., 114–15.

70. Ibid., 115.

71. Ibid., 115, 167.

72. Nouailhat, "Les Américains," 209.

73. *CD,* 27 Sept. 1919.

C H A P T E R   S I X T E E N

1. *PT,* 7 July 1921.

2. Of course these worldviews were not confined to either sphere geographically. There were also many "ruralists" in the cities.

3. Homer Croy, *They Had to See Paris* (New York: Harper, 1926; Grosset and Dunlap, 1929).

4. *Variety,* 16 Oct. 1929.

5. Croy, *They Had to See Paris,* 302.

6. Warren Susman, *Culture as History* (New York: Pantheon, 1984), 112.

7. [E.M.M.], "Prodigal Tourist Returns," *NYTM,* 15 Nov. 1925, 14.

8. Another company said third cabin was "exclusively reserved for students and tourists and that no immigrants or other third-class passengers will be on board." "Young America to Invade Old Europe," *NYTM,* 5 Apr. 1925, 6.

9. *CATG,* Mar. 1926, 9–11; Frank Schoonmaker, *Through Europe on Two Dollars a Day* (New York: McBride, 1927), 7.

10. M. S. Rukeyser, "American Returns from Europe," *World's Work* 55 (Nov., 1927): 83–84; Perry Cornell to parents, 20 July 1929, in Selma Marian Pratt Papers, CUL; *PH,* 26 July 1926.

11. "The Swelling Tide of Foreign Travel, *NYTM,* 6 May 1928, 6.

12. By 1925, fully half of the transatlantic liners were in this category. Ibid.

13. Only about one-quarter of tourists went first class by mid-decade. Ibid.; Robert F. Wilson, *Paris on Parade* (New York: Robert McBride, 1925), 344; Rukeyser, "America Returns," 83. Some lines eliminated first class completely on their slower boats. Alexis Gregory, *The Golden Age of Travel, 1880–1939* (New York: Rizzoli, 1991), 204.

14. Wilson, *Paris on Parade,* 346–48; Paul Goujon, *Cent ans de tourisme en France* (Paris: Cherche Midi, 1989), 54.

15. *PT,* Aug. 1921; *PH,* 23 July, 7 Aug. 1923; *NYT,* 12 Aug. 1928; Helen Josephy and Mary Margaret McBride, *Paris Is a Woman's Town* (New York: Coward McCann, 1929), 272–75.

16. *PT,* 29 Aug. 1926; Gabriel Desert, *La vie quotidienne sur les plages normandes du second Empire aux années folles* (Paris: Hachette, 1983), 133–34.

17. *PT,* 21 Aug. 1921.

18. Basil Woon, *The Paris That's Not in the Guide Books* (New York: Robert McBride, 1926, 1931), 110–11.

19. Woon, *Paris,* 58.

20. Clara Laughlin, "Radio Talk," 2 Feb. 1926, Laughlin Papers, SSC; Kathleen Howard, "How Paris Sets the Styles," *LHJ* 37 (Nov. 1920): 17, 74–76; Howard, "Paris Shops," *SEP* 195 (2 Dec. 1922): 38; Fashionable American stores had begun buying outfits from Paris couturiers before the war, but no lady of fashion would consider buying a dress that was available back home. Wilson, *Paris on Parade*, 78.

21. *NYT,* 12 Mar. 1926.

22. Alain Corbin, *L'Avènement des loisirs, 1850–1960* (Paris: Aubier, 1995), 70.

23. Josephy and McBride, *Paris Is a Woman's Town*, 26–29.

24. *PT,* 18 July 1926; *CD,* 24 July 1926. Of course the activities of the upper class continued to be reported, but mainly on the "social pages." C. Wright Mills originally made the point about the rise of celebrities as a distinct part of the establishment in *The Power Elite* (New York: Oxford University Press, 1956).

25. Warren Susman, "Pilgrimage to Paris: The Backgrounds of American Expatriation, 1920–1934" (Ph.D. diss., University of Wisconsin, 1968), 103–10.

26. In his thorough study of them, Warren Susman was unable to find much that the new expats had in common, except that their expatriation was an expression of criticism of civilization in the United States. Ibid.

27. Malcolm Cowley, *Exile's Return* (New York: Viking, 1931).

28. Alex Small, "No Inhibitions, and No Work," *PT,* 7 Apr. 1929.

29. Samuel Putnam, *Paris Was Our Mistress: Memoirs of a Lost and Found Generation* (New York: Viking, 1947), 53.

30. When one of the traditional Saturday sailing days from New York fell on the Jewish holiday, Yom Kippur, there was a noticeable fall in the number of passengers on the seven departing liners. *PH,* 19 Sept. 1926.

31. Susman, 320–28. Susman analyzed the Midwesterners' shift from searching for civilization in Chicago to New York and then Paris in a chapter aptly entitled "Eastward the Flight of Culture." Susman, "Pilgrimage," 135–46.

32. Mercifully, absinthe, whose wormwood base had killed thousands, was now illegal—otherwise it would likely have taken a frightful toll among Americans.

33. Meyer Levin, *In Search* (New York, 1950), 30, quoted in Susman, "Pilgrimage," 252.

34. *NYT,* 16 Dec. 1928; Putnam, *Paris Was Our Mistress,* 68–71; Josephy and McBride, *Paris,* 249.

35. Woon, *Paris,* 264.

36. Wilson, *Paris on Parade,* 215.

37. Ibid., 28.

38. Catherine Reynolds, "Hemingway's Haunts," *Gourmet,* Apr. 1992, 73; Stephen Longstreet, *We All Went to Paris* (New York: Macmillan, 1972), 318.

39. Brendon, *Cook,* 263.

40. *PT,* 1 June 1926.

41. Woon, *Paris,* 269.

42. "The Mad Quarter of Paris," *LD* 104 (4 Jan. 1930): 18.

43. Susman, "Pilgrimage," 296–97.

44. Gregory, *Golden Age,* 204.

45. *Paris Herald,* 28 Aug. 1926.

46. Al Laney, *Paris Herald: The Incredible Newspaper* (New York: Appleton-

Century, 1947), 118; Longstreet, *We All Went to Paris*, 318; Steven Watts, *The Ritz of Paris* (New York: Norton, 1964), 144.

47. *NYT*, 20 Aug. 1922.

48. Ferdinand Touhy, London *Graphic* [1927], in "American Blight in Artistic Montparnasse," *LD* 95 (22 Oct. 1927): 28–29.

49. Wilson, *Paris on Parade*, 276; Woon, *Paris*, 259–60; Horace Sutton, *Travelers: The American Tourist from Stagecoach to Space Shuttle* (New York: Morrow, 1980), 138.

50. Woon, *Paris*, 237.

51. Tony Allan, *Americans in Paris* (Chicago: Contemporary Books, 1977), 13–14; Laney, *Paris Herald*, 5.

52. "Paris Is Ready to Welcome the American Tourist and His Money," *LD* 69 (23 Apr. 1921): 50; *Paris-Guide* (Paris: Comité France-Amérique, 1925), 61.

53. Robert de Beauplan, "Au Paris du Dollar," *L'Illustration*, 23 Oct. 1926, 46–50; Diana Bourbon, "Paris by Night Is a Tourist Myth," *NYTM*, 20 June 1926, 4; *PH*, 30 July 1927; *NYT*, 9 Dec. 1928; Woon, *Paris*, 244–45, 261–62.

54. Some date it to the popularity the African American 369th Regiment's band, but its music was quite remote from what was later called jazz (and many of its musicians were Puerto Rican.) Others credit a group of white doughboys, the "White Lyres," who stayed on after the war. Woon, *Paris*, 230–31.

55. Significantly, the Chicagoan Hannah Solomon described an evening at the foremost of those clubs, Les Acacias, as "a typical Parisian evening." Hannah Solomon diary, 22 June 1921, Greenebaum Sisters Travel Journals, CHS.

56. *Paris-Guide*, 65.

57. "American Nights in Paris," *NYTM*, 6 May 1928, 7.

58. De Beauplan, "Au Paris du dollar," 50.

59. Allan, *Americans in Paris*, 59.

60. Mary Blume, *Côte d'Azur: Inventing the French Riviera* (London: Thames and Hudson, 1992), 32. My evidence on the Sixth Fleet is necessarily anecdotal.

CHAPTER SEVENTEEN

1. *PT*, 18 July 1921.

2. *NYT*, 19 June 1927; "The Swelling Tide of Foreign Travel, *NYTM*, 6 May 1928, 6.

3. William Wiser, *The Crazy Years: Paris in the Twenties* (London: Thames and Hudson, 1983), 111–23; Hari Benstock, *Women of the Left Bank, 1900–1940* (Austin: University of Texas Press, 1986), 93, 113–15, 173–77.

4. Warren Susman, *Culture as History* (New York: Pantheon, 1984), 112. Joan Rubin analyses the rise of this "Middlebrow Culture" in *The Making of Middlebrow Culture* (Chapel Hill: University of North Carolina Press, 1992).

5. "Miss Clara Laughlin's Chicago Service," *The Cunarder*, n.d., 28, clipping in Laughlin Papers, box 1, SSC; Clara Laughlin, *So You're Going to France!* (Boston: Houghton Mifflin, 1927), vii; Clara Laughlin, *So You're Going to Paris!* (Boston: Houghton Mifflin, 1924), 74–78.

6. Laughlin, *So You're Going to France!* xi–xii.

7. Henry Bérenger, "Franco-American Relations," reprint from *Les Echos*, June 1927, in Calvin Coolidge Papers, PPF, 203a, LC.

8. It sold for ten times the price of a comparable French-language book. Robert F. Wilson, *Paris on Parade* (New York: Robert McBride, 1925), 240–41.

9. Kathleen Howard, "How Paris Sets the Styles," *LHJ* 37 (Nov. 1920): 17, 74–76; Handwritten radio script, n.d., Laughlin Papers, box 1.

10. Helen Josephy and Mary Margaret McBride, *Paris Is a Woman's Town* (New York: Coward-McCann, 1929), 26.

11. Kathleen Howard, "Paris Shops," *SEP* 195 (2 Dec. 1922): 36.

12. Josephy and McBride, *Paris Is a Woman's Town*, 248.

13. Maude Parker Child, "How Much for That? The American Bargain Hunter Abroad," *SEP* 198 (11 July 1925): 14.

14. Kathleen Howard, "Paris Shops," *SEP* 195 (2 Dec. 1922): 36, 40.

15. Kathleen Howard, "Paris Magic," *SEP* 195 (21 Sept. 1922): 21, 144.

16. "Such places are innumerable," she continues, and your friends will tell you of a new one nightly." Howard, "Paris Magic," 146.

17. Susan Ballow diary, 25 May 1929, Susan Ballow Papers, SHSW.

18. Ethel [?] to Alfred Barksdale, 15 July, 29 Aug., 12 Sept., and 3 Oct. 1923, Alfred Barksdale Papers, UVaL. As if to atone for this, they planned to go to the opera. Her relationship to Alfred is unclear.

19. *PH*, 26 July, 11 Aug. 1923.

20. Josephy and McBride, *Paris*, 101, 243, 258–70. This is the only time I have seen bouillabaisse, the lusty fish soup so closely identified with Marseille and the Mediterranean, called a "Paris soup." In any event, neither it, nor the onion soup, which was served with a thick cheese crust, could ever be considered a "dainty" dish of the kind thought appropriate for prewar genteel women.

21. Mary Blume, *Côte d'Azur: Inventing the French Riviera* (London: Thames and Hudson, 1992), 70–85.

22. Frank Schoonmaker, *Through Europe on Two Dollars a Day* (New York: McBride, 1927); Robert S. Rudney, "From Luxury to Popular Tourism: The Transformation of the Resort City of Nice" (Ph.D. diss., University of Michigan, 1979), 122–24.

23. Dorothy B. Gilliam, *Paul Robeson, All-American* (Washington, D.C.: New Republic Book Co., 1976), 47.

24. Gertrude Slaughter diary, 5–18 Feb. 1927, Gertrude Slaughter Papers, SHSW. Hannah Greenebaum Solomon diary, 14 June–9 July 1921, in Greenebaum Sisters Travel Journals, CHS.

25. Warren Susman, "Pilgrimage to Paris: The Backgrounds of American Expatriation, 1920–1939" (Ph.D. diss., University of Wisconsin, 1958), 253–55.

26. Frances Warfield, "Innocence Abroad," *Scribner's Magazine* 84 (Oct. 1918), 457.

27. *NYT*, 29 Mar. 1925; *NYT*, 16 May 1926; *PH*, 21 July 1927; Nivart-Chatelain, *Guide Book*, 273; "The Newest Innocents Abroad," *New Republic* 51 (29 June 1929): 138–39; Josephy and McBride, *Paris*, 196–97.

28. Raymond Waters, "Vacation Courses for Foreigners in French Universities," *School and Society* 20 (23 Aug. 1924): 247–48; M. V. Vernier, *How to Enjoy and Get the Very Best of Paris* (Bonn, Paris, [n.p.], 1921, 1923), 39; Josephy and McBride, *Paris*, 223–25.

29. Marsh Tours pamphlets, in Marsh Family Papers, SSC, box 4.

30. "The Newest Innocents Abroad," *New Republic* 51 (29 June 1929).

31. *CATG*, Apr. 1926, 18.

32. *Paris Herald,* 9 July 1926; "Swelling Tide," 6.

33. Warfield, "Innocence," 458–64.

34. Ibid., 459.

35. *CATG*, June 1927, 1. The latter's first stop was Epworth, England, birthplace of Methodist founder John Wesley. Wilson, *Paris on Parade*, 354–55.

36. *CATG*, Jan. 1927, 18.

37. Jonathan Friedman, *Consumption and Identity* (Chur, Switzerland: Harwood Academic Publishers, 1994), 21–22; Colin Campbell, *The Romantic Ethic and the Spirit of Modern Consumerism* (Oxford: Basil Blackwell, 1987), pt. 2.

38. "The Story of an Idea," typescript in Laughlin Papers, box 1.

39. Hortense King, "Don't Let Them Tell You But Do as I Say When You Go to Europe This Summer," *LHJ* 44 (May, 1927): 199.

40. Ethel [?] to Alfred Barksdale, July 15, 1923 Barksdale Papers, box 2, UVaL.

41. Schoonmaker, *Europe on Two Dollars a Day*, 44.

CHAPTER EIGHTEEN

1. The term, popularized in the 1960s and 1970s, was a misnomer on two levels. As used in the William Lederer novel of that name, it was a term of endearment applied by grateful Filipinos to a benign CIA agent who understood them and helped them repel the Communist threat. However, it soon became a pejorative for overbearing, insensitive Americans abroad who were quite the opposite of the original prototype.

2. André Chaumeix, "Images de l'Amérique," *Revue des Deux Mondes* 57 (May 1930): 928–38.

3. Abbé Felix Klein, "How the Real France Feels," *The Review* 1 (27 Sept. 1919): 429. Edith Wharton, by then a long-time resident of Paris, shared this postwar hope. See Edith Wharton, *French Ways and Their Meaning* (New York: Appleton, 1919.)

4. Eugène Brieux, *Les Américains chez nous*, in *La Petite Illustration*, 1 Feb. 1920, 2–30; Robert de Flers, "M. Brieux's Americans," *Living Age*, 304 (28 Feb. 1920): 542–44; T. M. Parrott, "Brieux's Latest Play—Americans in France," *Weekly Review* 3 (28 July 1920): 95–96; O. W. Firkins, "The Americans in France," ibid. 3 (8 Sept. 1920): 215–16. "'Les Américains Chez Nous'—A Dramatic Tribute from Eugène Brieux," *Current Opinion* 68 (Apr. 1920): 488–94.

5. Ralph Schor, *L'Opinion française et les étrangers en France, 1919–1939* (Paris: Sorbonne, 1985), 162–64.

6. [T.D.P.], "The Traveler's Paris of Today," *American Review of Reviews* 61 (June 1920): 625.

7. It is no surprise that in 1930 he became the first American to win the Nobel Prize for literature.

8. Wesley Frost [Consul], "Monthly Political Review, Marseille, June, 1926," 851.00/803, SDP.

9. Georges Duhamel, *Scènes de la vie future* (1929; Paris: Mercure de France, 1951), 162.

10. Jean Cassou, in *Dialogue entre deux mondes,* ed. Gérard de Catalogne (Paris, 1931), 92.

11. Pierre Zenda, *Babel d'amour* (Paris: A. Michel, 1930), 32.

12. T. S. Wauchope,"What the French Think of Us," *American Mercury* 3 (Dec. 1925): 482–84.

13. Ibid., 485.

14. *NYT,* 21 Apr. 1929.

15. Morand in *Dialogue entre deux mondes,* 168. Morand himself did not share these concerns.

16. *NYT,* 8 Dec. 1929.

17. David Strauss, *Menace in the West: The Rise of French Anti-Americanism in Modern Times* (Westport: Greenwood, 1977), 141–47.

18. René Jeanne, "L'Invasion cinématographique américaine," *Revue des Deux Mondes* 55 (15 Feb. 1930): 865–77; The advent of sound movies, and a weak quota system, helped reduce this to about half in 1930, but the Germans made up much of the shortfall. Jacques Portes, "Hollywood et la France, 1896–1930," *Revue Française d'Études Américains,* no. 59 (Feb. 1994): 32–33.

19. Curiously, he compares contemporary American mores unfavorably with those in Edith Wharton's *Age of Innocence,* the story of how polite society crushed true romantic love. André Bellesort, "L'Américanisme en France," *La Revue Hebdomadaire* 37 (Apr. 1928): 270–79.

20. Jeanne, "L'Invasion," 879–82.

21. Robert De Beauplan, "Au Paris du dollar," *L'Illustration,* 23 Oct. 1926, 50.

22. "Le Semainier," *L'Illustration,* 28 Aug. 1926, in Schor, *L'Opinion française,* 470.

23. Whauchope, "What the French Think of Us," 485.

24. Ernest Dimnet, "Are Americans Hated in Paris?" *Outlook* 142 (3 Mar. 1926): 331.

25. F. Duquesnel, "Les Étrangers à Paris," 561. In 1928, the Paris press applauded a Montmartre café owner for doing just that. *NYT,* 26 Aug. 1928.

26. Sullivan, "Yankee in Paris," 161.

27. Wauchope, "What the French Think of Us," 486.

28. *L'Ere Nouvelle,* quoted in *NYT,* 25 July 1926.

29. F. Duquesnel, "Les Étrangers à Paris," 561; Vincent O'Sullivan, "The Yankee in Paris," *American Mercury* 3 (Oct. 1924): 161.

30. Wauchope, "What the French Think of Us," 485.

31. *NYT,* 18 Apr. 1926.

32. *L'Humanité,* 23 July 1926.

33. G. De Villemus, "Tourists Welcome and Unwelcome," *Living Age,* 330 (Sept. 11, 1926): 586, from *L'Echo de Paris,* 6, 10 Aug. 1926.

34. *NYT,* 1 June 1924; De Villemus, "Tourists," 588.

35. Wauchope, "What the French Think of Us," 482.

36. "Main Street, Paris," *Crisis* 25 (Oct. 23): 272; "France and the Color Line," *Crisis* 27 (Dec. 1923): 78–79. In October 1923, it ran a poem by Colonel Charles Young. A West Point graduate, he had been the highest ranking African American officer in 1917, but when the AEF was sent over he was denied promotion to brigadier general and the command of the black combat regiments that would have gone with

it by forcibly retiring him on specious medical grounds. Entitled a "Negro-Mother's Cradle Song," the poem evoked the memory of the black men who had died fighting for freedom in France, hoping that it would help bring it to America. Charles Young, "A Negro-Mother's Cradle-Song," *Crisis* 25 (Oct. 1923): 272.

37. *CD*, 22 Sept. 1923; *CD*, 13 Oct. 1923; *CD*, 17 Nov. 1923; *CD*, 21 Aug. 1926; *CD*, 4 Aug. 1923.

38. Blanche Ferguson, *Countee Cullen and the Negro Renaissance* (New York: Dodd, Mead, 1966), 68–70, 106; Martin Duberman, *Paul Robeson* (New York: Knopf, 1988), 91–95; Dorothy B. Gilliam, *Paul Robeson, All-American* (Washington, D.C.: New Republic Book Co., 1976), 47–49; Anthony Platt, *E. Franklin Frazier Reconsidered* (New Brunswick: Rutgers University Press, 1991), 56–59.

39. Blanche Ferguson, *Countee Cullen and the Negro Renaissance* (New York: Dodd, Mead, 1966), 68–70, 106, 123; *CD*, 1 Aug. 1923. In 1923, the Great Northern Steamship Company, an ephemeral company set up by "progressive businessmen" to provide inexpensive travel to Europe, tried to cash in on transatlantic black tourism with a full-page ad for shareholders and passengers in the *Crisis*. It assured the fearful that "Lives of passengers will be protected by EVER-WARM SAFETY SUITS which prevent drowning." *Crisis* 26 (July 1923): 138.

40. *CD*, 7, 21 Aug. 1926.

41. Ferguson, *Countee Cullen*, 104.

42. Walter White, "The Color Line in Europe," *Annals of the American Academy of Political and Social Science* 140 (Nov. 1928): 333.

43. *CD*, 23 Aug. 1923.

44. *CD*, 11 Aug. 1923.

45. Ibid.; "Colored Frenchmen and American 'Meteques,'" *LD* 78 (1 Sept. 1923): 40–44.

46. "Colored Frenchmen," *LD* 78 (1 Sept. 1923): 40–44.

47. *Le Temps*, 2 Aug. 1923; *PH*, 1 Aug. 1923.

48. *Le Temps*, 10 Aug. 1923.

49. Philippe Dewitte, "Le Paris noir de l'entre-deux-guerres," in Kaspi, *Le Paris des étrangers: depuis un siècle* (Paris: Impremerie Nationale, 1989), 162.

50. *Le Temps*, 22 Aug. 1923.

51. *Le Temps*, 19 Aug. 1923; *PH*, 10 Aug. 1923.

52. *PH*, 20 Aug. 1923; *CD*, 25 Aug. 1923. American film distributors were not hurt—a French distribution company had just paid half a million francs for the exclusive rights to show it in France.

53. *CD*, 27 Oct. 1923.

54. *CD*, 25 Aug. 1923.

55. "Colored Frenchmen," 42–43.

56. *CD*, 25 Aug. 1923.

57. André Tardieu, "What France Thinks of Her War-time Allies," *Harper's Magazine* 152 (May 1926): 670.

58. André Kaspi, *Le Temps des Américains, 1917–1918* (Paris: Sorbonne, 1976), 341–42.

59. *NYT*, 5 June 1920; Jacques Duroselle, *La France et les États-Unis: des origines à nos jours* (Paris: Seuil, 1976), 114–37; Henry Blumenthal, *Illusion and Reality in*

Franco-American Diplomacy, 1914–1945 (Baton Rouge: Lousiana State University Press, 1986), 122–51.

60. O'Sullivan, "Yankee," 160.

61. Harry Elmer Barnes, *The Genesis of the World War* (New York: Knopf, 1929), 699–700.

62. Oswald Chew, *France: Courageous and Indomitable* (Boston, 1925).

63. Sam Putnam, *Paris Was Our Mistress*, 54.

64. Damon Woods, "French Opinion of the Washington Debt Agreement," 21 May 1926, RG84, Records of Foreign Service Posts, vol. 859, no. 870, SDP.

65. *PT,* 12 July 1926.

66. Strothers to State, 13 Feb. 1925, 711.51/32; Consulate in Marseille to State, 17 Mar. 1925, 711.51/33, SDP.

67. Melvyn P. Leffler, *The Elusive Quest: America's Pursuit of European Stability and French Security, 1919–1933* (Chapel Hill: University of North Carolina Press, 1979), 138–47.

68. *Le Loire Republicaine,* 16 May 1926; Lester Maynard, [Consul, Le Havre] "Local Ill-Feeling toward the United States," 11 June 1926, 711.51/38, SDP.

69. *Le Matin,* 12 July 1926; *PH,* 12 July 1926; *PT,* 12 July 1926.

70. "French Wounds and American Dollars," *LD* 90 (24 July 1926): 7–8.

71. *NYT,* 24 July 1926.

72. Schor, *L'Opinion française,* 469; *NYT,* 29 July 1926.

73. *PT,* 23 Sept. 1926.

74. *NYT,* 25 Apr. 1927.

75. *L'Ere Nouvelle,* quoted in *NYT,* 25 July 1926.

76. "American Tourist and European Immigrant," *New Republic* 48 (Sept. 8, 1926): 59.

77. Diment, "Are Americans Hated?" 234; *NYT,* 29–30 July 1926.

78. Maynard, "Local Ill-Feeling," 11 June 1926, SDP; *NYT,* 24, 31 July 1926; *NYT,* 24 Aug. 1926; Dimnet, "Are Americans Hated?" 334; "Our Tourists' Troubles in France, " *LD* 90 (14 Aug. 1926): 12.

79. *L'Humanité,* 21 July 1926; *PT,* 21, 22 July 1926; *NYT,* 20, 21, 23, and 24 July 1926.

80. *Le Matin,* 24 July 1926; *NYT,* 24 July 1926.

81. *L'Humanité,* 25 July 1926.

82. *Action Française,* 23, 26 July 1926.

83. *NYT,* 25, 26, 30 July 1926; *NYT,* 1 Aug. 1926.

84. *NYT,* 27 July 1926.

85. The convoluted *New York Times* report, which was the fullest one, did not make understanding him any easier. *NYT,* 28 July 1926. There is no record of the conference in the State Department's archives. His notes and transcript of it probably went up in flames with the rest of his papers, which his wife, perhaps wisely, ordered destroyed when he died.

86. Schor, *L'Opinion française,* 473–76; *PT,* 28 July 1926; *NYT,* 29 July 1926; *NYT,* 7, 15 Aug. 1926.

87. *NYT,* 3 Aug. 1926.

88. *PH,* 28 July 1926.

89. *CD*, 7 Aug. 1926.

90. *NYT*, 28 Aug. 1926.

91. Schor, *L'Opinion française*, 475; C. Benedek, "The Paris of the Rising Franc," *Living Age* 332 (1 Mar. 1927): 389–91; Leffler, *Elusive Quest*, 133–34.

92. *NYT*, 25 Apr. 1927.

93. *NYT*, 16 Sept. 1926.

94. *L'Humanité*, 22–24 May 1927.

95. Arthur Bullard, "Lindbergh vs. Uncle Shylock," *Outlook* 147 (12 Oct. 1927): 171–73.

96. *Le Matin*, 24, 25 Aug. 1927; *L'Humanité*, 24–26 Aug. 1927.

97. *L'Humanité*, 24, 25, 29 Aug. 1927; Al Laney, *Paris Herald: The Incredible Newspaper* (New York: Appleton-Century, 1947), 242; Schor, *L'Opinion française*, 480–81. Typically, the leftists staged competing demonstrations. The Communists called the anarcho-syndicalist protest at the American embassy a "pseudo-demonstration," even thought the two martyrs were part of that movement. *L'Humanité*, 24 Aug. 1927.

98. *L'Humanité*, 25, 29, 31 Aug. 1927, 20 Sept. 1927.

99. Bullard, "Lindbergh vs. Uncle Shylock," 171–73.

100. *Le Matin*, 17 Aug. 1927.

101. H. G. Moody, *"Meet the King": The Story of the Second A.E.F.'s Pilgrimage after Hitting the Paris Trail* (New York: Winwick, 1931), 11–13; Laney, *Paris Herald*, 243–44; *Le Matin*, 20 Sept. 1927.

102. *Le Matin*, 16–25 Sept. 1927.

103. *L'Œuvre*, 24 Aug. 1927.

104. Laney, *Paris Herald*, 242–44; *PH*, 22 Aug. 1927; Chet Shafer, *The Second A.E.F.: The Pilgrimage of the Army of Remembrance* (New York: Doty, 1927), 19.

105. Shafer, *Second A.E.F.*, 21.

106. Ibid., 14–21; Laney, *Paris Herald*, 244. *Le Matin* reported that "Paris, joyous and enthusiastic, acclaimed the great parade." *Le Matin*, 22 Sept. 1927.

107. *LD* 95 (15 Oct. 1927): 38; Moody, *"Meet the King,"* 12–13.

108. *L'Humanité*, 18, 21 Sept. 1927.

109. When he ordered a bottle of expensive Meursault in a restaurant, two young French men beside him, thinking that he could not possibly appreciate it, said to each other: "Look at them. There it is again. *Dégoutant*—disgusting." William Carlos Williams, *The Autobiography of William Carlos Williams* (New York: Random House, 1951), 252–53.

110. Moody, *"Meet the King,"* 19–20.

111. Ibid., 14.

112. *NYT*, 28 Mar. 1927; *NYT*, 26 Aug. 1928; Schoonmaker, *Through Europe*, 44; Y. T. Ybarra, "Turistus Americanus," *Outlook* 151 (24 Apr. 1929), 647.

CHAPTER NINETEEN

1. Alvaretta Taylor, "My Trip to France," May 23, 1930; American Pilgrimage Gold Star Mothers and Widows, "General Information for Pilgrims," May 30, 1930, in Frank Taylor Papers, Eastern Washington State Historical Society, Spokane, Washington.

2. David Kennedy, *Over Here: The First World War and American Society* (New York: Oxford University Press, 1980), 367–68.

3. Robert Lanquar and Robert Hollier, *Le Marketing touristique* (Paris: Presses Universitaires de France, 1981), 4.

4. *NYT,* 4 June 1921; *NYT,* 13 May 1922.

5. Robert Lanquar, *Sociologie du tourisme et des voyages* (Paris: Presses Universitaires de France, 1985), 6.

6. France, Commissariat National du Tourisme, *Les Prix des hôtels en France* (Paris: 1929–).

7. See Malcolm Cowley's *Exile's Return* (1934; New York: Viking, 1951), for a description of this process.

8. Pierre Py, *Le Tourisme: Un phénomène économique* (Paris: La Documentation Française, 1992), 9.

9. Perry Cornell to Mummy and Daddy, 20 July 1929, in Selma Marian Pratt Papers, CUL.

Index

A. and W. Galignani: bookstore, 32–33, 38, 92, 99; guidebook, 32–33, 38, 304n. 56

abattoir, visits to, 110

Abélard, tomb of, 109–10, 315n. 14

About Paris (Davis), 192

absinthe, 343n. 32

Les Acacias (club), 344n. 55

accommodations: advertisements for, 91; and anti-Americanism, 271; bars in, 171; at battlefields, 225, 228; brothels near, 71, 75; at Channel ports, 39; choices of, 181–82; dining at, 79, 169–70; for middle class, 159; near expositions, 159; pensions as, 184–85, 189, 205; regulations for, 278; servants in, 106; for students, 206–8; surroundings of, 56–57, 87, 91, 302n. 28; for upper class, 99–101; for women tourists, 184–85; for working class, 96. *See also names of specific hotels*

ACDF (American Committee for Devastated France), 227–28

Action Française (periodical), 270

Adams, Abigail, 9–10, 68, 291n. 37

Adams, Henry: on American culture, 163; on American tourists, ix, 179, 183, 188; and dining, 153; on French people, 208

Adams, John, 6, 11

Adams, Julietta, 143

Adams, Marian, 150, 327n. 34

Addams, Jane, 158, 186–87, 189, 190, 336n. 35

adultery, attitudes toward, 10, 69–70, 199

AEF (American Expeditionary Force), 218

Africa, French colonialism in, 230

African Americans: as caterers, 79; dance of, 230, 243; and foreign travel, xi–xii, 263–66, 271; Gold Star Mothers and Widows, 277; music of, 229–30, 236, 243–44; as soldiers, 229–32, 263. *See also* race; slavery

airplanes: and middle-class travel, 278; slogan of, 13; transatlantic flight of, 272

Aix-en-Provence, 8

Aix-les-Bains, 130, 144

alcohol: American attitudes toward, 39–40, 239–40, 297n. 19; and American Legion convention, 274–75; and drunkenness, 203, 239–40, 259–60, 267; and foreign travel, 239; and post-WWI lifestyle, 239, 241–42, 248, 259–60; at restaurants, 153; and soldiers, 221–22. *See also* beer; clubs; wine

Alcott, Louisa May, 184, 191

Aldegani's (restaurant), 171

Allen, Grant, 169, 251

Allen, Willie, 172, 174, 190, 205, 332n. 44

Allen, Zacharia, 17, 22

Alps (French and Swiss), 43, 45

Ambassadeurs (club), 244

The Ambassadors (James), 326n. 18, 337n. 56

America Abroad (periodical), 130, 170–72

Les Américains chez nous (Brieux), 257–58

American Chapel, 100–101, 105, 193

American Committee for Devastated France (ACDF), 227–28

cal schools of, 165, 168; nudes in,
62–64; portraits, 61, 324n. 53. *See
also* art appreciation
Palace of the Legion of Honor, 288n. 27
Palace of the Popes (Avignon), 45
Palais-Royal: description of, 56–57, 77;
gambling in, 76; gardens of, 9;
plans for, 212; prostitution in, 71,
72–73, 78; restaurants in, 79, 81;
shops in, 118, 190
Palestine. *See* Holy Land
Palmer, Mrs. Potter, 149
Pan-African Congress, 265
Panthéon, 162
Paquin (couturier), 150, 152
Parc Monceau, 86
Paris: boulevards in, 57–58, 86; changing attitudes in, 65–66; characteristics of, 9–10, 55–57; gambling in,
76; layout of, 55; medical studies
in, 28, 293n. 17; as model, 86–87;
political upheaval in, 140–44; prostitution in, 71–76; sewers of, 109;
social season in, 236; tourist circuit
in, 144–45, 240, 242, 257, 269,
277; 1850s transformation of, 86–
92, 114, 310n. 6; wartime blackouts
in, 220. *See also names of specific sections, sites, and streets*
Paris after Dark (Wideawake, pseud.),
75
Paris at Night (guidebook), 201
"Paris by Night" tours, 242, 257, 269,
277
Paris Exposition (1867). *See* expositions;
Universal Exposition (1867)
Paris Herald (newspaper), 135, 142,
324n. 53
Paris Is a Woman's Town (guidebook),
247, 249–50
Paris-Midi (newspaper), 262–63
Paris-Promeneur, Paris-Touriste (publica-
tion), 91, 95, 131
Paris Tribune (newspaper), 245
Parkman, Rev. Francis: on department
store, 318n. 65; on fashion, 318n.

57; on language, 296n. 2; on Paris,
58, 67; on restaurants, 80; on scenery, 43; on transatlantic crossing,
20, 21, 290n. 17
Parkman, Mary Eliot, 103, 141, 317n.
49
parks: constructed in Paris, 86; Sunday
in, 9. *See also* gardens
patriotism, heightened by foreign travel,
50–51
Patton, Florence, 226
Pau, on tourist circuit, 144–46
Peabody, Harold, 181
Peabody, Mary, 157–58, 181
The Pension Beauregard (James), 164
pensions: as accommodations, 184, 205;
dining at, 189; popularity of, 185.
See also accommodations
Père Lachaise cemetery: Communards
killed in, 140; visits to, 109–10
Perroquet, shows at, 242
Pershing, Gen. John, 219, 230–31
Petit Palais, construction of, 92
Phelps, Sheffield, 133–34
Philadelphia Academy of Fine Arts, 27
photographs, function of, 34–35
Picasso, Pablo, 149, 238, 247, 250
Pickford, Mary, 237
picturesque, definition of, 42–43
pilgrimages: to battlefields, 225–29, 273;
convention as, 271–74; definition
of, 225; of mothers and widows,
277
place de la Révolution, 58
place de l'Odéon, 240
place de l'Opéra, 91, 221, 242, 244, 247.
See also Opéra
place Pigalle, 242–43
place Vendôme, 58, 63, 151, 247
Planta's Gazetteer for France (guidebook),
295n. 45
Planta's New Picture of Paris (guidebook), 295n. 45
Plaza Athénée (hotel), 153
Plymouth Rock (ship), 18–19
Poincaré, Raymond, 265–66